Frommer's®

London with Kids

1st Edition

by Rhonda Carrier

Here's what the critics say about Frommer's:

"Amazingly easy to use. Very portable, very complete."

—*Booklist*

"Detailed, accurate, and easy-to-read information for all price ranges."
—*Glamour Magazine*

"Hotel information is close to encyclopedic."

—*Des Moines Sunday Register*

"Frommer's Guides have a way of giving you a real feel for a place."
—*Knight Ridder Newspapers*

WILEY

Wiley Publishing, Inc.

About the Author

Rhonda Carrier was born in the Midlands but spent much of her teens wandering, and lived in Hong Kong and Vienna before studying languages and literature at Cambridge and the Sorbonne in Paris. She finally settled in London in the mid 1990s, where she worked as a writer and editor for local guides and listings magazines, as well as publishing some award-winning short fiction. Since meeting her husband, the writer Conrad Williams, she has divided her time between their flat in Marylebone and a crumbling old cognac farm in France, accompanied by their sons Ethan and Ripley.

Published by:

Wiley Publishing, Inc.

111 River St.
Hoboken, NJ 07030-5774

ISBN-13: 978-0-7645-4993-9
ISBN-10: 0-7645-4993-6

Editor: Jennifer Reilly
Production Editor: Ian Skinnari
Cartographer: Tim Lohnes
Photo Editor: Richard Fox
Production by Wiley Indianapolis Composition Services

Front cover photo: Young girl holding British flag on Westminster Bridge
Front and back cover top photo: Illuminated House of Parliament panorama

For information on our other products and services or to obtain technical support, please contact our Customer Care Department within the U.S. at 800/762-2974, outside the U.S. at 317/572-3993 or fax 317/572-4002.

Wiley also publishes its books in a variety of electronic formats. Some content that appears in print may not be available in electronic formats.

Manufactured in the United States of America

5 4 3 2 1

Contents

6 Exploring London With Your Kids   139

7 Neighborhood Strolls   193

8 For the Active Family   200

9 Shopping   219

10 Entertainment for the Whole Family   242

List of Maps

For my sons Ethan and Ripley Williams: It's been an adventure and a privilege to rediscover London with you.

Acknowledgments

A huge debt of love, gratitude, and admiration to Conrad, who has done the hardest work of bringing up the kids for the best part of three years. Extra special thanks also to Holly and Jarvis McGrath, for accompanying us on some of our more eccentric and far-flung odysseys (all of them worth it), and for generally being there.

I'd also like to express my fond gratitude to the following for their support, companionship, input, and feedback:

Judy and Joe Reynolds; Adi and Charlotte Welch; Sophie, Stef, and Johanna Bureau; Kasha and Lola Harmer; Nick, Kate, Charlie, and Bella Royle; Shelley Flacks and Mia Michalski; Paula Grainger and Michael and Nate Marshall Smith; Ayesha, Viv, and Rohan Luthra; Esme Major and brood; Gemma Hirst; Jonty Spibey and Jason, Perdy, and Tabitha Hirst; Liz Wyse; Christi Daugherty; Pete Fiennes and Sarah Guy; Diana Tyler; Heather Brice and crew; and Yve White.

Thanks too to our parents David, Mary, Leo, and Grenville, and to my brother David and stepfather Tim, for support and faith over the years.

Additional thanks to my patient and industrious editor Jen Reilly, and to the innumerable individuals at London attractions, hotels, restaurants, stores, entertainment venues, and PR companies who helped fill in the blanks.

—Rhonda Carrier

An Invitation to the Reader

In researching this book, we discovered many wonderful places—hotels, restaurants, shops, and more. We're sure you'll find others. Please tell us about them, so we can share the information with your fellow travelers in upcoming editions. If you were disappointed with a recommendation, we'd love to know that, too. Please write to:

Frommer's London with Kids, 1st Edition
Wiley Publishing, Inc. • 111 River St. • Hoboken, NJ 07030-5774

An Additional Note

Please be advised that travel information is subject to change at any time—and this is especially true of prices. We therefore suggest that you write or call ahead for confirmation when making your travel plans. The authors, editors, and publisher cannot be held responsible for the experiences of readers while traveling. Your safety is important to us, however, so we encourage you to stay alert and be aware of your surroundings. Keep a close eye on cameras, purses, and wallets, all favorite targets of thieves and pickpockets.

Other Great Guides for Your Trip:

Frommer's Irreverent London
Frommer's London
Frommer's Memorable Walks in London
London For Dummies
Suzy Gershman's Born to Shop London
The Unofficial Guide to London

Frommer's Star Ratings, Icons & Abbreviations

Every hotel, restaurant, and attraction listing in this guide has been ranked for quality, value, service, amenities, and special features using a **star-rating system.** In country, state, and regional guides, we also rate towns and regions to help you narrow down your choices and budget your time accordingly. Hotels and restaurants are rated on a scale of zero (recommended) to three stars (exceptional). Attractions, shopping, nightlife, towns, and regions are rated according to the following scale: zero stars (recommended), one star (highly recommended), two stars (very highly recommended), and three stars (must-see).

In addition to the star-rating system, we also use **six feature icons** that point you to the great deals, in-the-know advice, and unique experiences that separate travelers from tourists. Throughout the book, look for:

Finds	Special finds—those places only insiders know about
Fun Fact	Fun facts—details that make travelers more informed and their trips more fun
Moments	Special moments—those experiences that memories are made of
Overrated	Places or experiences not worth your time or money
Tips	Insider tips—great ways to save time and money
Value	Great values—where to get the best deals

The following **abbreviations** are used for credit cards:

AE	American Express	DISC	Discover	V	Visa
DC	Diners Club	MC	MasterCard		

Frommers.com

Now that you have the guidebook to a great trip, visit our website at **www.frommers.com** for travel information on more than 3,000 destinations. With features updated regularly, we give you instant access to the most current tripplanning information available. At Frommers.com, you'll also find the best prices on airfares, accommodations, and car rentals—and you can even book travel online through our travel booking partners. At Frommers.com, you'll also find the following:

- Online updates to our most popular guidebooks
- Vacation sweepstakes and contest giveaways
- Newsletter highlighting the hottest travel trends
- Online travel message boards with featured travel discussions

1

How to Feel
Like a London Family

London is at the forefront of almost anything you care to mention: fashion, art, music, food, architecture, politics, finance, and so much more. If it's happening, you can bet that Britain's capital is involved somewhere along the line. Its great selling points are its vast size and extraordinary diversity—more than 300 languages are spoken here, and by 2015 it is estimated that 40% of Londoners will be from ethnic minorities. Very few places on Earth can rival London's cultural depth and rich heritage—combined, they create a city that proves endlessly fascinating to both its inhabitants and visitors.

Yet London inspires and maddens in equal measure. Ask any Londoner how they feel about the city, and they will roll their eyes and unleash a litany of complaints about the traffic, the crowds, and the prices. These caveats prove doubly annoying when you have kids. In fact, many people up and leave the capital when they start a family. Their reasons are no doubt valid, but I would argue that they should stay put, since London is actually one of the world's *greatest* cities for children.

When I started this book, circumstances had just brought my husband and me back to the city we love after the best part of a year in a ramshackle French farmhouse. My second son, Ripley, was just a few months old and quite happy to explore any patch of floor on which we placed him, but his brother, Ethan, was a 2-year-old bundle of energy who needed a constant flow of stimulation and entertainment. How, I wondered, would we cope in our tiny Marylebone flat? Was it fair to bring kids up in London?

I was wrong to worry. My husband and I thought we knew this city to its core, having regularly written and edited for local guides and listings publications. It had been part of our job to keep up, as best anyone can, with its lightning-speed changes, including the latest restaurant, shop, and hotel openings. But rediscovering London from a new point of view—that of our children—has been a revelation. I have been, quite literally, astounded by the range and variety of activities that are on offer here for kids of all ages. In fact, what you read between these pages is only a small sampler—the crème de la crème—of all there is to experience here as a parent or a child.

Perhaps the biggest revelation of all has been just how much fun you can have in this expensive city for free or for very little money. Sure, there are high-priced premium attractions to be had, but for each of them you'll find a wealth of wonderful parks and urban farms, one-off museums and galleries with great free workshops, and neighborhood cafes welcoming hungry families on a budget. Which brings me to two main pieces of advice. The first is not to underestimate the power of the simple or everyday: When I first visited London on day trips with my intrepid grandmother Molly, riding the Tube truly awed me. How, I wondered, did anyone ever manage to navigate its tangle of colored lines? (Don't worry; it's actually a breeze.) Keep in mind that a simple bus ride on a classic red double-decker might be all it takes to set Junior's heart aflutter. The second is to accept the appeal of the tacky where kids are concerned: as a kid, I adored all the rampantly tourist stuff that now riles me, such as Madame Tussaud's.

Much of the skill of being a parent is about learning to stop being a control freak and to go with the flow. If that means occasional trips to a wax museum instead of an art museum, or burgers and fries in a loud themed restaurant over authentic Asian dishes in a Vietnamese canteen, so be it—there'll be other times to soak in art, and other dinners. Family holidays are about pleasing everyone, while recognizing that not everyone can be pleased at the same time. Luckily, London caters to all tastes, moods, and whims, so it's easy to get the balance just right.

1 Frommer's Favorite London Family Experiences

- **Seeing the Sights from the Top of a Double-Decker Bus:** Get an overview of some of London's top sights from one of its red public buses, and you'll score one of the city's best bargains. The iconic open-backed Routemaster model is being phased out, but the newer buses are more spacious and comfortable, and bus travel has the advantage of giving you a feel for where places are in relation to one another, unlike the Tube. Armed with a Family Travelcard, you can jump off if something takes your fancy, and resume your tour when you are ready.

  One of the City's best routes is the **no. 15** between Paddington and the East End via Piccadilly Circus, Trafalgar Square, and Fleet Street. Attractions you will see include Selfridges department store, the National Gallery, The Savoy Hotel, St. Paul's Cathedral, the Monument, and the Tower of London. Traffic is the only downer when you travel by bus, but special lanes on many streets mean you never get snagged in the worst jams, and if you're not in a hurry you can sit back and let the sights, smells, and sounds of the City wash over you. Sit on a front seat on the top deck for prime views. See p. 53.

- **Kite-Flying on Parliament Hill:** The 98m (320-ft.) summit of Hampstead Heath, with its views of St. Paul's Cathedral and farther afield, is the city's top spot for flying kites; on windy weekends it's full of kids and parents flying one-liners. (For more ambitious stunts with fancier kites, you're better off going down to the open area near the Lido.) Be sure to stop by the **Kite Store** in Covent Garden for supplies. See p. 240.

- **Going to the Dogs:** An afternoon or evening at **Walthamstow Stadium** is a real East End institution, where you'll encounter genuine characters, as well as exciting greyhound racing. Continue the Cockney theme with pie and mash (beef pie and mashed potatoes), or even jellied eels, at **Manze's** (76 Walthamstow High St., E7; ✆ **020/8520-2855**), one of London's oldest traditional pie and mash shops, with an original tiled interior. See p. 258 and 136.

- **Munching the Morning Away at Borough Market:** Encourage kids' interest in real food by taking them on a snacking trip around this historic market under the railroad arches, now a gourmet food market on Friday and Saturday. Up to 70 stalls offer free tasting samples of delicious cheeses, breads, cakes, jams, and other goodies, many of them organic and all produced with love. Don't miss the candy at the Burnt Sugar Sweet Company, the pastries at Pudding Lane, or the chorizo rolls at Spanish specialist Brindisa. See p. 233.

- **Tackling the Sights and Delights of Kensington:** There's no avoiding this neighborhood west of the center, with its trio of world-class and wonderfully child-friendly museums (the Victoria and Albert Museum, Natural History Museum, and Science Museum) and its green spaces—Kensington Gardens, containing the Diana Memorial Playground; and Hyde Park, where you can horseback-ride, in-line skate, row on winding Serpentine lake, and much, much more. Don't even contemplate trying to squeeze it into a single day—you might do it justice in about a week. See chapters 6 and 8.

- **Talking to the Animals in Battersea Park:** If there was ever a zoo to win the hearts of kids, the newly refurbished **Battersea Park Children's Zoo** is it, with its Mouse House, Farm Yard Encounter, and Butterfly Banquets areas; its cafe with outdoor tables where you can listen to exotic bird song as you eat; and its playground, indoor toddlers' toys, and wildlife gift shop. After touring the zoo, your family can explore the rest of Thameside Park with its ducks and herons, boating lake, fountains, peace pagoda, play parks, toddlers' club, art gallery, and more. Nearby, Battersea Rise and Northcote Road make up a little haven of child-friendly eateries such as Boiled Egg & Soldiers and Le Bouchon Bordelais. See chapters 6 and 8.

- **Enjoying a Traditional Afternoon Tea:** Most swank hotels in the city serve this highly civilized and very English ritual at premium prices (typically, about £20/$38 a head). The Ritz, Claridge's, and the Dorchester all welcome kids and provide highchairs. Another great spot is the new cafe-restaurant **The Wolseley** (160 Piccadilly; ⓒ **020/7499-6996**), which, despite its deeply grand interior—complete with Japanese lacquer screens—has crayons and pictures to keep little ones amused as they wait for their finger sandwiches and fruit scones with homemade jams and clotted cream. Note that smart dress is generally required for these venues. See p. 96.

- **Ambling by the River:** Inhale the salty tang of the tidal Thames on a walk along the cultural hotbed of the South Bank eastward from Westminster Bridge. As well as close encounters with bridges both historic and modern, and fabulous views of St. Paul's Cathedral and the Tower of London, you can break your walk at a stunning array of attractions, including the British Airways London Eye, the Tate Modern, and Shakespeare's Globe Theater. You can also shop at the crafts outlets of Gabriel's Wharf or Oxo Tower, or even "beachcomb" when the tide is low. Finish up at Shad Thames, an atmospheric quarter of converted old spice warehouses. See p. 198.

- **Riding in a London Taxi:** This isn't a cheap way of getting around town, but even if you make public transport your mainstay, be sure to try at least one trip in a traditional black cab—though not at rush hour, when you'll notch up a heavy bill for the luxury of sitting in a queue of traffic. Once ensconced, you're more than likely to strike up a conversation with your "cabbie"—many like nothing better than the chance to share their worldviews with passengers. And before

Greater London Area

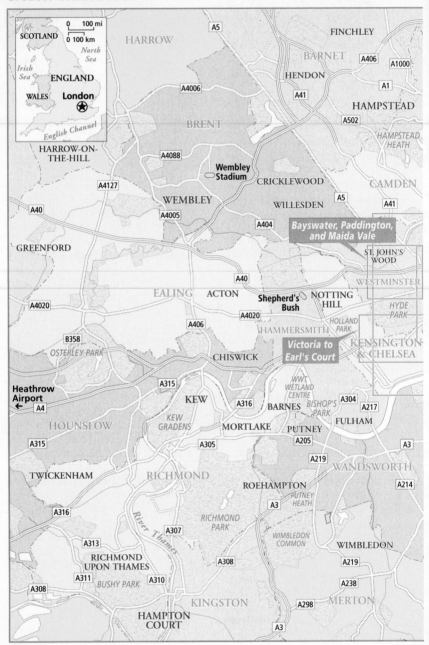

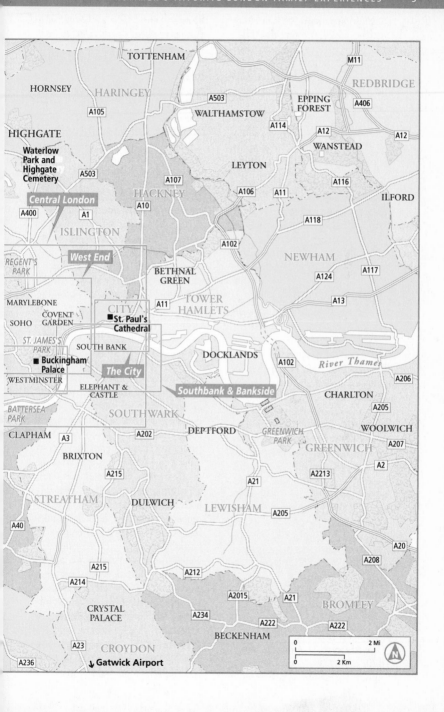

TOTTENHAM

M11

HORNSEY

HARINGEY

REDBRIDGE

A105

A503

EPPING
FOREST

A406

HIGHGATE

WALTHAMSTOW

A114

A12

A12

Waterlow
Park and
Highgate
Cemetery

A503

WANSTEAD

LEYTON

A107

HACKNEY

A116

ILFORD

Central London

A106

A11

A400

A1

A10

A118

ISLINGTON

A102

NEWHAM

West End

BETHNAL
GREEN

A124

A117

MARYLEBONE

REGENT'S
PARK

COVENT
GARDEN

CITY

A11

TOWER
HAMLETS

A13

SOHO

St. Paul's
Cathedral

ST. JAMES'S
PARK

SOUTH BANK

DOCKLANDS

A102

River Thames

A206

Buckingham
Palace

The City

WESTMINSTER

ELEPHANT &
CASTLE

Southbank & Bankside

CHARLTON

A205

BATTERSEA
PARK

SOUTHWARK

GREENWICH
PARK

WOOLWICH

CLAPHAM

A3

A202

DEPTFORD

GREENWICH

A207

BRIXTON

A2

A215

A2213

A21

STREATHAM

DULWICH

LEWISHAM

A205

A40

A20

A215

A208

A214

A212

A2015

A21

BROMLEY

CRYSTAL
PALACE

A234

A222

A222

A23

CROYDON

BECKENHAM

0   2 Mi

A236

Gatwick Airport

0   2 Km

you get snooty, know that a study carried out in 2000 found that London taxi drivers' brains are larger than those of most of their peers, due to their having to remember up to 400 routes within a 9.5km (6-mile) radius of Charing Cross, as part of a competence test known as "The Knowledge." See p. 53.

- **Idling Away Sunday Morning in Greenwich:** Spend the morning browsing the stalls at Greenwich's famous weekend markets, which sell crafts, antiques, books, clothes, and general junk. There's plenty of culture to be had in the neighborhood too, plus a great pub in which to kick back and enjoy a Sunday roast: **Greenwich Union** (56 Royal Hill; ℂ 020/8692-6258), with its spacious and very child-friendly beer garden. See p. 171.

2 The Best Hotel Bets

London accommodations are never a bargain in comparison with their counterparts elsewhere, but the city's hoteliers and B&B proprietors are fast wising up to the needs of visiting families, and services and facilities for kids and their parents are improving by the day.

- **Most Family-Friendly: 22 Jermyn Street** (22 Jermyn St., SW1; ℂ 020/7734-2353), a family-run town house steps from Piccadilly Circus and St. James's Park, is to my mind the most welcoming hotel in town, and that's especially true for parents. The management has thought of everything, it seems, but if you have additional requirements, the friendly but unobtrusive staff will go out of their way to procure it for you. Amenities include free kids' movies delivered to your room or suite with complimentary popcorn, wipe-clean drawing books, musical cassettes with sing-along books, the owner's own lively newsletter highlighting kid-friendly sights and restaurants, and cozy bathrobes for all ages. Staff members will even babysit while parents make use of temporary membership in a trendy health club and pool nearby. See p. 74.

  One Aldwych (1 Aldwych, WC2; ℂ 020/7300-1000), best known as a luxurious destination, is fast accruing a reputation as an unexpectedly family-friendly choice after introducing in-room play boxes, hotel teddy bears, junior-size slippers, bathrobes, pajamas, and the best children's room-service meals I've had. Well-situated for Theaterland, it's also the best option for those who can't do without a pool. See p. 71.

- **Best Neighborhood Option: Europa House** (79a Randolph Ave., W9; ℂ 020/7724-5924) is a collection of spacious serviced apartments in a safe residential area with wide, tree-lined avenues leading down to the picturesque canals of Little Venice, where a barge hosts puppet shows and companies run narrow-boat trips to London Zoo. You'll find an array of family-friendly delis, cafes, and pubs; an organic grocer; and a small 24-hour supermarket nearby, yet the center of London is just a 15-minute bus ride away. Best of all is the 1.4-hectare (3½-acre) enclosed garden to which the apartments have access, with a playground where little ones can make friends with local kids. Inside, the apartments are stylish but practically furnished for parents. See p. 80.

  North of the center, **La Gaffe** (107–111 Heath St., NW3; ℂ 020/7435-8965) is an Italian restaurant and guesthouse in an 18th-century shepherd's house in villagey Hampstead. The charming shops, teahouses, restaurants, and historic pubs of Hampstead High Street and Flask Walk are a few minutes' walk away, as are the wild spaces of Hampstead Heath, full of local families flying kites, swimming in the Lido, and generally running amok. See p. 93.

- **Best Views:** Deluxe rooms and suites on the river side of the **Four Seasons Canary Wharf** (46 Westferry Circus, E14; ℂ 020/7510-1999), east of the center in Docklands, overlook a dramatic sweeping bend of the Thames and as far back as the BA London Eye. Order from the superior kids' room-service menu, then sit in your window and watch boats and ferries chug by. In the morning, enjoy the kids' session in the adjoining infinity-edge pool, which seems to merge with the river outside.

The all-suite **Conrad London** (Chelsea Harbor; ℂ 020/7823-3000) also trades an off-the-beaten track location for awesome views, this time over the surrounding marina and along the Thames towards Westminster. The views (from rooms on the south side only) are especially stunning at night, when Albert Bridge is lit up like a Christmas tree. The suites facing the river also have sizeable balconies on which you can breakfast in fine weather, enjoying a classic London vista of red double-deckers driving over the bridges. You also get an eyeful of swanky yachts from the harborside pool and restaurant. See p. 92 and 78.

- **When Hipness is Important: The Zetter Restaurant & Rooms** (86–88 Clerkenwell Rd., EC1M; ℂ 020/7324-4444) in trendy Clerkenwell combines cutting-edge design with reasonable prices and a relaxed attitude towards kids who dig the funky gadgetry (raindrop-sensitive glass roof, swipecard vending machines, pink lighting in the rooms . . .). Don't miss the long, lazy weekend brunches in the see-and-be-seen restaurant. See p. 89.

- **When Price is No Object:** Belgravia's ultra-chic **Berkeley** (Wilton Place, SW1X; ℂ 020/7235-6000) will blow your budget sky-high, but it's worth it for its outstanding kids' amenities (gift-pack, books, magazines, board games, GameBoy Advance, DVDs, CDs, minibathrobes, and slippers); its jaw-dropping rooftop pool; and its superb restaurants, from the Caramel Room with its chi-chi donuts and cakes, to the Boxwood Café (see below). Parents can repair to the meltingly lovely Blue Bar for some of the best cocktails in town. See p. 75.

The new Pop Art–themed Family Apartment at the five-star **Athenaeum Apartments** (116 Piccadilly, W1J; ℂ 020/7499-3464) is brilliant fun for kids of all ages, with its mirrored Philippe Starck chairs, children's sleeping niche with whiteboards and magnetic games, and vintage-style games console. Parents have the flexibility of using the fully fitted kitchen complete with washing machine, or taking advantage of the hotel services—including 24-hour room service, a modern British restaurant, a lounge for afternoon tea, and a spa. See p. 73.

- **When Price is Your Main Object:** The family-run **Crescent** (49–50 Cartwright Gardens, WC1H; ℂ 020/7387-1515) is virtually unique in its moderate price range in that it offers baby-listening (via baby monitor), highchairs, bathrobes on request and, best of all, access to a private garden square and four tennis courts. It's the best central option for those keeping an eye on their pennies. See p. 69.

- **Best Pool:** It's a close call between the 20m (65-ft.) Thameside infinity-edge pool at **Four Seasons Canary Wharf** (see above), open to kids for 2 hours each morning; and the calm blue 18m (59-ft.) basement pool at **One Aldwych** (see above), where kids are welcome all day. See p. 92 and 71.
- **Best Hotel Restaurant for Kids:** The Berkeley (see above) might be one of the smartest hotels in town, but its **Boxwood Café** restaurant positively embraces children, with a kids' menu of simply prepared seasonal produce such as halibut and farm chicken, plus a Scooby Doo coloring pack. Alternatively, the supertrendy **Zetter Restaurant & Rooms** (see above) offers children's portions of its regional Italian dishes and Sunday brunch treats, and keeps junior diners happy with drawing equipment. See p. 118 and 89.
- **Tops for Teens:** If getting an early night is not your priority, **The Pavilion** (34–36 Sussex Gardens, W2; © 020/7262-0905) is a theatrical joint attracting rock stars, models, and other glam folk who can afford to stay in much more expensive places. The outrageously themed rooms include a *trompe-l'oeil* family room. Don't be surprised if there's a photo shoot going on during your stay; it's that chic. See p. 82.

  Where The Pavilion is raucous, **Myhotel Chelsea** (35 Ixworth Place, SW3; © 020/7225-7500) is sophisticated. This subtly pink-themed hotel was designed according to feng shui principles and offers a pamper room, tarot readers, a library with free soft and hot drinks, DVD movies, XBox games, and an ice cream trolley in summer. It couldn't be better located for teen queens looking to flex some plastic in the fashion emporiums nearby. See p. 79.

- **Tops for Toddlers:** The exemplary, eco-friendly **Rotherhithe Youth Hostel** (20 Salter Rd., SE16; © 020/ 7232-2114) is heaven for under-3s, with activity packs, a kids' library, a toy box, more than 30 board games, some giant games, a blackboard, a PlayStation, a TV lounge, a small and secure garden, and bikes for rent. On rainy days there are treasure trails and quizzes. Parents can rest assured that all the practicalities—highchairs, baby baths, monitors, strollers, cribs, and kids' menus—have been taken care of. The out-of-center location works in your favor—you'll benefit from unrestricted parking, a good nearby park and organic farm, and quirky local attractions. See p. 86.

  The central **Hilton London Metropole** (225 Edgware Rd., W2; © 020/7402-4141) tempts toddlers with weekend splash hours in its pool, toys, and special dishes such as scrambled egg or banana and custard. Parents will appreciate the large, bright, and very reasonably priced family rooms, some with lounge areas, as well as the discount vouchers for London attractions. See p. 81.

3 The Best Dining Bets

British food, a long-standing joke among visitors, has come of age over the last decade or so, to the point where London is now one of the world's gastronomic capitals. Though people don't tend to expect much of the food in a restaurant that sets out its stall as a family-friendly venue, that, too, has changed, and there is now a host of places where you can get wonderful cuisine that keeps both you and the kids happy.

- **Best Family Dining:** The rapid growth of the **Giraffe** empire (36–8

Blandford St., W1; ℂ 020/7935-2333; 10 other branches at press time) is testament to its popularity among London parents—in fact, it's become well nigh indispensable. Bright and stylish with a cheerful world music soundtrack and keen young staff, it boasts a globally inspired menu with something to suit all tastes and moods. See p. 99.

- **Most Kid-Friendly Service:** Staff members at the **Blue Kangaroo** are the essence of unflappable geniality. They have to be—this family restaurant, with its basement softplay areas monitored by CCTV cameras, is almost always cacophonous and crowded. See p. 122.

- **Best Kids' Menu: Carluccio's Caffè** (8 Market Place, W1; ℂ 020/7636-2228; more than 15 other venues) is a bustling all-day Italian eatery with a great-value three-course kids' menu featuring a superior chicken breast with rosemary potatoes, real ice cream, and more. See p. 103.

- **Best Neighborhood Hangout:** West London's **Bush Garden Café & Food Store** (59 Goldhawk Rd., W12; ℂ 020/8743-6372) is a homey lunch bar and organic grocer with a menu of simple kids' favorites, great cakes, and a partly covered garden with a playhouse and toys. See p. 127.

- **Best Outdoor Eating:** You get a real taste of the great outdoors at **Frizzante@CityFarm** (1A Goldsmith's Row, E2; ℂ 020/7739-2266)—it's slap bang in the middle of a farmyard, complete with clucking chickens and a garden with a kids' play area. The homemade Italian cuisine includes all-day breakfast with eggs from those same chickens, great pizzas and pasta dishes, and superb cakes and puddings. See p. 138.

- **Best Park Cafe:** Along with a striking grass-roofed and glass-fronted building, the lovely views of the surrounding royal park and palaces from its wooden terrace make **Inn the Park** (St. James's Park, SW1; ℂ 020/7451-9999) special. It offers diners the choice of upscale cafe fare, including children's lunch sets, or seasonal British cuisine. See p. 113.

- **Best Museum or Gallery Cafe: Camden Arts Centre**'s cafe (Arkwright Rd., NW3; ℂ 020/7472-5516) is a fashionably minimalist but relaxing oasis after the pandemonium of the nearby O2 Centre. Set in a garden, the cafe offers kids' portions of daily specials such as fishcakes, as well as comfort-food faves such as toast with Marmite, brownies, and organic chocolate bars. The art's not bad, either. See p. 129.

- **Best View:** The **Top Floor** at Peter Jones (Sloane Sq., SW1; ℂ 0845/345-1723) is a kid-friendly, non-smoking spot on the sixth story of an excellent Chelsea department store, where you can enjoy 360-degree panoramic views over London as you tuck into breakfast, lunch, pastries, or afternoon tea. Little ones get their own small but perfectly formed menus including non-standard fare such as fisherman's or shepherd's pie with French beans, plus use of a "goodie box" with paper and crayons. See p. 120.

- **Best Breakfast:** The yolk-yellow walls of **Boiled Egg & Soldiers** (63 Northcote Rd., SW11; ℂ 020/7223-4894) make it an outstanding spot on this street of family-friendly eateries. Comforting breakfast favorites include—surprise!—boiled egg with "soldiers" (strips of buttered bread), Marmite and toast, smoked salmon, and Fluffies (hot milk with chocolate foam), and you can eat outside here on sunny mornings. See p. 130.

- **Best Brunch:** With its industrial chic (a marriage of steel, concrete, and exposed brickwork), the warehouse-like ground-floor cafe at **Smiths of Smithfield** (67–77 Charterhouse St., EC1; ☎ **020/7251-7950**) doesn't look like the most promising spot for families, but its weekend brunches draw them from afar. Recline in the leather armchairs or settle at one of the long bench-style tables to tuck into such child-pleasers as waffles with maple syrup, eggs Benedict on English muffins, and corned beef hash with spinach and fried eggs. The fresh Asian juices (ginger, lime, lemon grass, pineapple, and mango) make great pick-me-ups if you're flagging from sightseeing. See p. 132.

- **Best Fish and Chips:** Trendy renovation work hasn't put off the East End taxi drivers who come to **Fish Central** (149–52 Central St., EC1; ☎ **020/7253-4970**), but junior diners are made welcome by the cheery staff, kids' portions, and patio for fine weather. Little extras that single this place out from your average "chippy" include homemade bread, fresh vegetables, and wonderful desserts, but my advice is to stick to the spanking-fresh traditional battered cod or haddock with lip-smacking chips and mushy peas. See p. 136.

- **Best Pizza:** Families return again and again to **Italian Graffiti** (163–5 Wardour St., W1; ☎ **020/7439-4668**) for its superb (and enormous) crisp-based pizzas cooked in a wood-fired oven. Adding to the ambience of this cozy family-run venue are its open fireplaces, its large windows from which you can observe the bustle of Soho, and the big-hearted staff, who might even whisk your kid away to show them how to make pizza. See p. 109.

- **Best Burgers:** Stealing the thunder of Ed's Easy Diner, many branches of which are *not* so child-friendly (p. 137), the new **Gourmet Burger Kitchen** mini-chain (50 Westbourne Grove, W2; ☎ **020/7243-4344;** seven branches) consulted New Zealander celeb chef Peter Gordon when developing its award-winning (and good-value) burgers. These run the gamut from the classic to the exotic ("the Jamaican," with mango and ginger sauce; or "the Kiwiburger," with beetroot, eggs, pineapple, cheese, and relish). Junior incarnations are available, and there are great fries and heavenly shakes See p. 124.

- **Best Sausages:** Another growing chain, **S&M Café** (268 Portobello Rd.; ☎ **020/7359-5361;** three other venues) serves sausage and mash (the "s&m" that make up its name) in a variety of guises, traditional or otherwise, including wild boar, lamb and mint, steak and Guinness, Algerian *harissa* (pepper and tomato sauce), and spinach and cheddar. Lashings of gravy and creamy potatoes complete the picture. Stodgy, old-school puddings are available if you have room to spare. See p. 126.

- **Best Vegetarian Restaurant:** Even hardened carnivores don't miss meat when they dine at **The Place Below** (Cheapside, E2; ☎ **020/7329-0789**), a pretty spot set in the crypt of St. Mary-le-Bow, complete with a courtyard where you can eat when the weather permits. Kids don't get special dishes, but that's not an issue when the menu features such delights as homemade muesli with apples and honey. Yum! See p. 132.

- **Best Fast Food:** Eat in the style of an Indian family at casual, canteen-style **Masala Zone** (147 Earl's Court Rd., SW5; ☎ **020/7373-0220;** and branches in Islington and Soho), serving budget-priced dishes you might find at Indian street stalls, plus thalis and Bombay-style beach snacks. Kids are welcome. You can either order takeout or eat in. See p. 121.

- **Best Asian Food: The Blue Elephant** (4–6 Fulham Broadway, SW6; ℃ 020/7385-6595) wows kids with its junglesque interior of trees, ponds, and waterfalls studded with statues and baroque ornaments; its imaginative Thai fare; and its Sunday buffet brunches with displays of exotic fruit carved into spectacular shapes; as well as free face-painting and sugar-spinning demos. See p. 121.

- **Best Ice Cream:** A London institution dating back to the 1930s and now run by the founder's grandsons, **Marine Ices** (8 Haverstock Hill, NW3; ℃ 020/7482-9003) knows its stuff—its authentic Italian ice cream is smooth and creamy without being too rich or sickly sweet. Try some of the 20-plus flavors by themselves in a wafer cone, or try them embellished with sauces and other toppings in a fluted dish. Good pizzas and pasta dishes are on offer, too. See p. 134.

- **Best Girls' Day Out:** There's no better place to round off a spot of designer-clothes shopping than bewitching **Yauatcha** (15 Broadwick St., W1; ℃ 020/7494-8888), where you can choose between sophisticated dim sum in the basement, and divine cakes and patisseries with an Asian twist in the ground-floor teahouse, accompanied by exotic brews. Chill-out music will help speed you into the relaxation zone. See p. 111.

- **Best Boys' Lunch:** Reserve a "baby-foot" (table football) machine at **Café Kick** (43 Exmouth Market, EC1; ℃ 020/7837-8077) and spend the afternoon enjoying a match or two, stopping to refuel on quality tapas, charcuterie and cheese platters, or sandwiches, washed down with juices, smoothies, or chocolate milk. (For parents there's a great range of beers and cocktails.) Big football matches are screened, too. Kids are welcome till 4pm. See p. 133.

2

Planning A Family Trip to London

Planning a family trip anywhere is a fine art. Overplan, and your vacation can start to resemble a military expedition—or worse, a school outing. Underplan, and you miss out on some great experiences because you're forced to make last-minute decisions without the full facts at your disposal. Tread a fine line and—most importantly—*get kids involved* in the upcoming adventure. Talk about what you'd all like to see and do, taking everyone's wishes and needs into account rather than making assumptions. Remember to maintain enough flexibility to allow room for the *unplanned*.

This chapter guides you through the practical quagmire, and gives you the information you'll need to make your trip as stress-free and easy as possible.

1 Visitor Information

The **British Tourist Board** has a walk-in information center and four smaller offices in London (p. 39), an excellent website (see "Helpful Websites," below), a 24-hour recorded information line (℃ **0906/133-7799**), and offices around the world. (See www.visitbritain.org for the location nearest you.)

For details of **magazines listings,** see p. 57. The best-known, *Time Out,* also publishes some of its information online at www.timeout.com/london. The *Evening Standard*'s website, www.thisislondon.co.uk, has an "Insider's Guide" listing film, music, theater art, restaurant, and pub choices, plus ticket offers and promotions. For information on theater programs and tickets, see p. 247.

HELPFUL WEBSITES The most useful general website for London visitor information is the official Tourist Board site at **www.visitbritain.com**, which lists accommodations, attractions, events, and transport options around the country. It also has "travel tools" such as a route planner, a currency converter, and a brochure-ordering facility. Its little sister, containing more specific information about the city (customized according to where you are from), is **www.visitlondon.com**. Amazingly comprehensive, this site has everything from events listings to recommendations from well-known locals. You can buy the **London Pass** (p. 139); book tickets for shows, concerts, and hundreds of other events; book rooms in hotels and B&Bs (with a best-price guarantee); and even book airline tickets and packages. Its 24-hour TV channel, **London TV** (SKY channel 244), showcases current highlights.

The Tourist Board also has its own kids' site, **www.kidslovelondon.com**, with listings for young visitors and Londoners alike. Another dedicated children's site well worth a browse is **www.show.me.uk**, the offspring of the wonderful **www.24hour museum.org.uk**. The "Show Me" children's site lists 25,000 U.K. museums and galleries (including information on their child-friendliness); has a "By Kids for Kids" section with advice from local children; and features a great event-search engine. "Show Me" also has maps of family-friendly sights and museums, divided into categories such as "scary stuff," "crazy stuff," and "cool stuff."

See also **www.guardian.co.uk/kidsin museums**, which charts the history of the national newspaper's campaign to find the country's most family-friendly museum. The *Guardian*'s kids' travel specialist has her own website, **www.deabirkett.com**, with a handy family travel forum for exchanging tips and views.

The very good **www.londonfreelist.com** has a kids' page with no-cost events and activities; while **www.londonfamilies. co.uk**, **www.londontreasures.com**, and **www.fun4families.org.uk** have suggestions for activities and outings. (The latter also has handy online beginner's guides to visiting art galleries, the theater, and so on.) The non-child-specific but brilliant **www.bbc.co.uk/london/where youlive/** has microsites on London neighborhoods, with information on markets, local restaurants, little-known parks, and more.

More general kids' sites include **www.london.gov.uk/young-london**, **www.familiesonline.co.uk**, **www.child friendly.net** (with handy user reviews), **www.artsandkids.org.uk**, and **www. kidzango.com**. You'll also want to check out **www.takethefamily.com**, a very professional family vacation guide with a London section that includes a hotel-booking facility; **www.family-travel.co.uk**, a highly

rated site with travel advice, news, a notice board, and subscription-based destination reports; **www.babygoes2.com**, with advice, info, tips, location reports and features, shopping resources, and a guide to recommended-by-parents villas and hotels worldwide, with or without child-care; **www.mumsnet.com**, with features, discussions, product reviews, weekend break recommendations, and a facility whereby you can meet other moms in your area; **www.all4kidsuk.com**, a family directory and parent resource site with area-based guides for everything from hotels to toddlers' music classes; and **www.youngtravellersclub.co.uk**, a fast-developing new site providing young children with useful information about other countries.

For help finding your way around, see **www.streetmap.co.uk**; key in the street name, telephone area code, or postal code of the place for which you are looking, and a map of the area with the location circled will appear. Another useful tool is **www.streetsensation.co.uk**, which allows you to "explore" some of the main streets in zone 1, such as Marylebone High Street and Carnaby Street, through scroll-along photographs of their restaurants, pubs, and shops, backed up by listings information. It's not always 100% up-to-date, though, so do check if you're making a special trip.

For information on getting from the airports to central London, go to **www. baa.com**, which also has a guide and terminal maps for Heathrow, Gatwick, and Stansted airports, including flight arrival times, duty-free shops, and airport restaurant locations. For local transport within London, see **www.tfl.gov.uk**.

2 Entry Requirements & Customs

ENTRY REQUIREMENTS

Citizens of the United States, Canada, Australia, New Zealand, and South Africa require passports to enter the United Kingdom, but do not require visas. Irish citizens and citizens of European Union countries need only identity cards. The maximum stay for non–European Union visitors is 6 months. Some Customs officials request proof that you have the means to leave the country (usually a round-trip ticket) and means of support while you're in Britain. (Someone in the U.K. will have to vouch that they are supporting you, or you may be asked to show documents that indicate that you have an income.) If you plan to fly on from the United Kingdom to a country that requires a visa, it's wise to secure the visa before you leave home.

Because of child custody and abduction concerns, applying for children's passports usually requires plenty of documentation. In some cases, the consent of both parents or legal guardians and an in-person appearance by the child(ren) are required during the application process. Consult these websites for complete details: http://travel.state.gov in the U.S., www.ppt.gc.ca in Canada, www.passports.gov.au in Australia, and www.passports.govt.nz in New Zealand.

CUSTOMS
WHAT YOU CAN BRING INTO LONDON

For Non-E.U. Nationals 18 Plus   You can bring in, duty-free, 200 cigarettes, 100 cigarillos, 50 cigars, or 250 grams of smoking tobacco. The amount allowed for each of these goods is doubled if you live outside Europe.

You can also bring in 2 liters of wine and either 1 liter of alcohol over 22 proof or 2 liters of wine under 22 proof. In addition, you can bring in 60cc (2 oz.) of perfume, a quarter liter (250ml) of eau de toilette, 500 grams (1 lb.) of coffee, and 200 grams (½ lb.) of tea. Visitors 15 and over may also bring in other goods totaling £145 ($268); the allowance for those 14 and under is £72.50 ($134). Customs officials tend to be lenient about general merchandise, realizing the limits are unrealistically low.

You can't bring your pet straight to England. Six months' quarantine is required before it can be allowed in. An illegally imported animal may be destroyed.

For E.U. Citizens   Visitors from fellow European Union countries can bring into Britain any amount of goods as long as the goods are intended for their personal use—not for resale.

The current policy for bringing pets into the U.K. from the E.U. is under review. Right now, animals or pets of any kind are forbidden from entering without a long quarantine period.

WHAT YOU CAN TAKE HOME

For U.S. Citizens   Returning **U.S. citizens** who have been away for at least 48 hours are allowed to bring back, once every 30 days, $800 worth of merchandise duty-free. You'll pay a flat rate of duty on the next $1,000 worth of purchases. Any dollar amount beyond that is subject to duties at whatever rates apply. On mailed gifts, the duty-free limit is $200. Be sure to keep your receipts or purchases accessible to expedite the declaration process. *Note: If you owe duty, you are required to pay on your arrival in the United States—either by cash, personal check, government or traveler's check, or money order (and, in some locations, a Visa or MasterCard).*

To avoid paying duty on foreign-made personal items you owned before your trip, bring along a bill of sale, insurance policy, jeweler's appraisal, or receipts of purchase. Or you can register items that can be readily identified by a permanently affixed serial number or marking—think laptop computers, cameras, and CD players—with Customs before you leave. Take the items to the nearest Customs office or register them with Customs at the airport from which you're departing. You'll receive, at no cost, a Certificate of Registration, which allows duty-free entry for the life of the item.

With some exceptions, you cannot bring fresh fruits and vegetables into the United States. For specifics on what you can bring back, download the invaluable free pamphlet *Know Before You Go* online at **www.cbp.gov.** (Click on "Travel," and then click on "Know Before You Go! Online Brochure") Or contact the **U.S. Customs & Border Protection (CBP),** 1300 Pennsylvania Ave., NW, Washington, DC 20229 (© **877/287-8667**) and request the pamphlet.

For Canadian Citizens For a clear summary of **Canadian** rules, write for the booklet *I Declare,* issued by the **Canada Border Services Agency** (© **800/461-9999** in Canada, or 204/983-3500; www.cbsa-asfc.gc.ca). Canada allows its citizens a C$750 exemption, and you're allowed to bring back duty-free one carton of cigarettes, 1 can of tobacco, 40 imperial ounces of liquor, and 50 cigars. In addition, you're allowed to mail gifts to Canada valued at less than C$60 a day, provided they're unsolicited and don't contain alcohol or tobacco (write on the package "Unsolicited gift, under $60 value"). All valuables should be declared on the Y-38 form before departure from Canada, including serial numbers of valuables you already own, such as expensive foreign cameras. Note: The $750 exemption can only be used once a year and only after an absence of 7 days.

For Australian Citizens The duty-free allowance in **Australia** is A$400 or, for those under 18, A$200. Citizens can bring in 250 cigarettes or 250 grams of loose tobacco, and 1,125 milliliters of alcohol. If you're returning with valuables you already own, such as foreign-made cameras, you should file form B263. A helpful brochure available from Australian consulates or Customs offices is *Know Before You Go.* For more information, call the **Australian Customs Service** at © **1300/363-263,** or log on to www.customs.gov.au.

For New Zealand Citizens The duty-free allowance for **New Zealand** is NZ$700. Citizens over 17 can bring in 200 cigarettes, 50 cigars, or 250 grams of tobacco (or a mixture of all 3 if their combined weight doesn't exceed 250g); plus 4.5 liters of wine and beer, or 1.125 liters of liquor. New Zealand currency does not carry import or export restrictions. Fill out a certificate of export, listing the valuables you are taking out of the country; that way, you can bring them back without paying duty. For more information, contact **New Zealand Customs,** The Customhouse, 17–21 Whitmore St., Box 2218, Wellington (© **04/473-6099** or 0800/428-786; www.customs.govt.nz).

3 Money

POUNDS & PENCE

Britain hasn't adopted the euro and is still using the pound (£), made up of 100 pence (written "p"). There are £1 and £2 coins, as well as coins of 50p, 20p, 10p, 5p, 2p, and 1p. Banknotes come in denominations of £5, £10, £20, and £50.

As a general guideline, the price conversions in this book have been computed at the rate of £1 = US$1.90. Bear in mind, however, that exchange rates fluctuate daily.

ATMs

ATMs are found all over London, usually outside banks but also in some larger stores. You'll usually get a better exchange rate using an ATM (currency exchange booths take a huge commission or give an unfavorable rate, or both), but your bank may charge a fee for using a foreign

What Things Cost in London	UK£	US$	Euro€
Taxi Heathrow Airport—center	40–70	76–133	60–105
Heathrow Express train to center, adult	14.00	26.60	21.00
Heathrow Express train to center, child*	6.50	12.40	9.70
Tube Heathrow—central London, adult	3.80	7.20	7.20
Tube Heathrow—central London, child	1.40	2.70	2.10
Single Tube ride, adult (Zone 1)	2.00	3.80	3.00
Single Tube ride, child (Zone 1)	0.60	1.15	0.90
Single bus ride, adult	1.20	2.30	1.80
Single bus ride, child	0.40	0.75	0.60
West End movie ticket, adult	8.50–12.50	16.20–23.80	12.70–18.70
West End movie ticket, child	4.50–10.50	8.60–20.00	6.70–15.70
Local telephone call (per min.)	0.05	0.10	0.08
Margherita pizza at Pizza Express	4.95	9.40	7.40
500ml still water at Pizza Express	1.75	3.30	2.60
500ml still water at small supermarket	0.40	0.75	0.60
Packet of 20 small Pampers at Boots	3.69	7.00	5.50
1 liter ready-mixed infant formula at Boots	1.75	3.30	2.60

*Children's fares apply to 5- to 15-year-olds except where stated otherwise.

ATM. You may also need a different PIN to use overseas ATMs; check in advance with your bank, and make sure you're clear about your daily withdrawal limit.

The most popular ATM networks are **Cirrus/MasterCard/Maestro** (www.mastercard.com) and **VISA** (http://visa.com); check the back of your ATM card to see which network your bank belongs to.

TRAVELER'S CHECKS

Traveler's checks are becoming a thing of the past now that most cities and towns have 24-hour ATMs. But if you prefer the tried and true and don't mind showing an ID every time you cash a check, you can order traveler's checks at Amex (www.americanexpress.com) or Thomas Cook (www.thomascook.com) offices or major banks. Note that exchange rates are more favorable at your destination, and that it's helpful to exchange at least some money before going abroad in case you can't easily get to a bank (which gives better exchange rates than a hotel or shop). When you do change your checks, note the rates and ask about commission fees; it can sometimes pay to shop around.

Keep a record of your traveler's checks' serial numbers separate from the checks so you're ensured a refund in an emergency.

CREDIT CARDS

Most London stores and restaurants take credit cards, but sometimes there is a lower spending limit of £10 ($19) before you can use them. Credit cards are a safe way to carry money and also allow you to withdraw cash at any bank or at their ATM. (You pay interest on the advance the moment you receive the cash.) You now need a PIN both for purchasing with your card and for using an ATM, so if you don't have one, call your credit card company ahead of your trip—it usually takes 5 to 7 business days.

Keep in mind that many banks now assess a 1–3% "transaction fee" on **all** charges you incur abroad (whether you're using the local currency or US dollars). But credit cards still may be the smart way to go when you factor in things like exorbitant ATM fees and the higher exchange rates and service fees you'll pay with traveler's checks.

To report lost or stolen cards, see p. 57.

4 When to Go

A typical London-area forecast for a summer's day predicts "scattered clouds with sunny periods and showers, possibly heavy at times." Summer temperatures seldom rise above 78°F (25°C), nor do they drop below 35°F (2°C) in winter. London, as one of the mildest parts of the country, can be very pleasant in spring and fall. Yes, it rains, but you rarely get a true downpour. Rains are heaviest in November, when the city averages 2½ inches (6.5cm).

For planning purposes, call 📞 **0870/ 600-4242** for the latest forecast, or see www.bbc.co.uk/london/weather. The outlook is quite often wrong, but it's better than a complete shot in the dark.

London's Average Daytime Temperature & Rainfall

	Jan	Feb	Mar	Apr	May	June	July	Aug	Sept	Oct	Nov	Dec
Temp. (°F)	40	40	44	49	55	61	64	64	59	52	46	42
Temp. (°C)	4.4	4.4	6.7	9.4	12.8	16.1	17.8	17.8	15.0	11.1	7.8	5.6
Rainfall (in.)	2.1	1.6	1.5	1.5	1.8	1.8	2.2	2.3	1.9	2.2	2.5	1.9

KIDS' FAVORITE LONDON EVENTS

HolidaysBritish public holidays include New Year's Day (Jan 1), Good Friday and Easter Monday (late Mar or early Apr), May Day (1st Mon in May), spring and summer bank holidays (last Mon in May and Aug, respectively), Christmas Day and Boxing Day (Dec 25 and 26). One or two extra days are added on as holidays if Christmas Day and/or Boxing Day fall on a weekend. For British school vacations, see p. 139.

London's hectic events calendar is continually evolving. I've listed my current favorites below, but always check in advance to make sure an event is still running. Keep an eye out for new events in *Time Out* magazine. The website **www. visitlondon.com** has an excellent month-by-month "Events Diary" and a little sister, **www.kidslovelondon.com**.

Remember that during school vacations, many museums, galleries, and other venues host extra kids' activities—see their websites for details.

January

New Year's Day Parade. This spectacular family procession winds through the heart of London (from Parliament Sq. to Green Park), complete with bands and dance troupes from around the world, clowns, stilt-walkers, dancing dragons, and vehicles of various guises. It sets out as Big Ben strikes noon and takes about 3 hours, passing lots of historical monuments on the way. See www.londonparade.co.uk. January 1.

London International Mime Festival. A 2-week extravaganza of visual theater, this festival sometimes includes puppetry as well as mime, at a variety of venues. Not all shows are suitable for kids; the website has age guidelines. See www.mimefest.co.uk. Second 2 weeks of January.

Charles I Commemoration. This march from the Buckingham Palace end of the Mall to the Banqueting House on Whitehall by cavaliers in 17th-century dress (members of the English Civil War Society) retraces the route that culminated in the public execution of Charles I in 1649. At noon a wreath is laid at the Banqueting House, and a short service is held before the march returns to its starting point. See www. english-civil-war-society.org. Last Sunday in January.

February

Chinese New Year. Don't miss this riotous celebration, with lion and dragon dancers making their way among Chinatown restaurants, firecrackers, live music, and food stalls. The lion dancers and children's fun parade leave Leicester Square at 11:30am and head to Trafalgar Square for the first stage performances. At noon there's a thanksgiving ceremony, at 2pm there are fireworks in Leicester Square, and celebrations and stage performances continue throughout the afternoon. See www.chinatownonline.co.uk. Late January or early February.

Great Spitalfields Pancake Race. Teams of four race up and down Dray Walk (at the Old Truman Brewery on Brick Lane, E1), all the while tossing pancakes to raise money for Save the

Children. It starts at 12:30pm; if you want to take part, you need to dress up and bring your own frying pan. Contact the organizers in advance, via www.alternativearts.co.uk. Shrove Tuesday (last day before Lent).

March

St. Patrick's Day Parade. This family parade showcases many of London's 400,000-strong Irish community. Participants congregate at Hyde Park Corner at 11am, leaving at noon and dispersing at Whitehall at about 3pm. En route, there are concerts in Trafalgar Square, a food market in Covent Garden, and music workshops and a kids' funfair in Leicester Square. See www.london.gov.uk/stpatricksday. March 17.

Oranges and Lemons Service. This famous children's service at St. Clement Danes, the Strand, WC2, serves as a reminder of a nursery rhyme mentioning the "bells of St. Clements," though this church may not be the one in question. Pupils from a local school read the lesson, recite the rhyme, and sometimes play the tune on hand bells. After the service, all kids are given an orange and a lemon on their way out. Call ✆ 020/ 7242-8282. Third week of March.

April

London Harness Horse Parade. This huge parade of working horses takes place around Battersea Park. Wearing traditional brass harnesses and plumes and pulling old carriages, carts, and engines, the horses on display range from Shetland ponies to cart horses. See www.wandsworth.gov.uk. Easter Monday.

Oxford & Cambridge Boat Race. This upstream battle between Oxford and Cambridge universities dates back to 1829. Covering 7km (4¼ miles) between Putney and Mortlake, the race starts just after 3pm and is best viewed from a riverside pub; see www.theo boatrace.org. (*Insider tip:* There's an equally exciting contest, the **Head of the River Race,** that runs the same course in the opposite direction, a week before the university race. This involves more than 400 vessels but draws fewer visitors, making it a better option for those with little kids. See www.horr.co.uk.) Late March or early April.

London Marathon. About 40,000 competitors run from Greenwich Park to Buckingham Palace, watched by a half-million spectators. Bands and street performers line the route, giving the event a festival feel. Aim to reach your chosen vantage point at about 9am to get a good spot. Local kids ages 11 to 17 can take part in the Mini London Marathon over the last 4.25km (2.65 miles) of the course. See www.london-marathon.co.uk. Mid- to late April.

The Queen's Birthday. Elizabeth II's birthday is celebrated with gun salutes in Hyde Park at noon and at the Tower of London at 1pm. See www.royal.gov. uk. April 21.

May

Museums & Galleries Month. Enjoy a month of free entry to national museums and galleries, many of which host special events, workshops, and exhibitions, including family activities, night openings with quizzes, and "Fab Finds," whereby collectors can take items into museums for assessment. The 2005 event introduced 11 new walking trails, which you can download from the website, including a Children's and Family Trail. (Note that the final stop, Pollock's Toy Museum, is sadly now closed.) See www.mgm. org.uk. All of May.

Covent Garden May Fayre and Puppet Festival. This gathering of puppeteers from around the country meets in the garden of St. Paul's Church on Bedford Street, WC2, close to where diarist Samuel Pepys made England's first recorded sighting of Mr. Punch in 1662. The day kicks off with a grand procession led by a brass band at 10:30am, followed by a church service with Mr. Punch in the pulpit, then Punch & Judy shows and puppet shows from noon to 5:30pm, when the event is rounded off by folk music, maypole dancing, clowns, and jugglers. See www.alternativearts.co.uk. Second Sunday in May.

Dulwich Festival. This 10-day program of arts events for all ages in south London includes a children's mystery-film event with quizzes, a kids' literature workshop, a teddy bears' picnic with a tame live bear in Dulwich Park, and a children's art works trail. There are also open artists' studios, choral music, and more. See www.dulwich festival.co.uk. Mid-May.

The Royal Windsor Horse Show. This is one of the country's biggest outdoor horse shows, hosting world-class competitions, including polo matches and stunning equestrian displays. In 2005 it moved to the private gardens and parkland of Windsor Castle, which are off limits to the public the rest of the year. The Queen herself attends, and her husband the Duke of Edinburgh sometimes competes. See www.royal-windsor-horse-show.co.uk. Mid-May.

June

Spitalfields Festival Fringe. This rag-tag of contemporary art events, exhibitions, theater, and more takes place around the Spitalfields/ "Banglatown" area of east London, held in tandem with the Spitalfields Festival of classical and contemporary music. The

National Museum of Childhood in Bethnal Green, the Ragged School Museum, and others host special family activities. Other popular presentations have included an R&B and hip-hop musical, and a theatrical "ode to cinema" (presenting 35 movies from the last 100 years in just an hour) involving mime, puppetry, and masks. See www.alternativearts.co.uk. All month.

Trooping the Colour: On the Queen's official birthday (her actual birthday is Apr 21; see above), the monarch, seated in a carriage, inspects her regiments as they parade their colors. The procession on Horse Guards Parade begins at 11am, but applications for tickets (write to **HQ Household Division,** Horse Guards, Whitehall, London SW1X 6AA, enclosing a self-addressed envelope and International Reply Coupon) must be received by late February. There are also gun salutes in Hyde Park and at the Tower of London. See www.royalgov.co.uk. June 15.

Open Garden Squares Weekend. This event opens up many of London's private garden squares and other gardens to the public for 2 days. Some of the gardens plan special activities for families—Russell Square features music, Punch & Judy shows, falconry displays, painting, and games. See www.myweb.tiscali.co.uk.london.gardens/squares. Early June.

All England Lawn Tennis Championships. This legendary tournament held at Wimbledon is a must for young tennis fans. See p. 258. Late June to early July.

City of London Festival. As well as classical concerts and art installations held in some of London's most stunning structures, including St. Paul's Cathedral and the Lloyd's Building, this festival comprises many free outdoor events throughout the City—they might involve circus acts in Paternoster Square, gospel choirs on the steps of St. Paul's, performance art and jazz in various gardens, and a procession by schoolchildren dressed as ancient Londoners. See www.colf.org. Late June to early July.

Greenwich+Docklands International Festival. Come to this free program for mind-blowing outdoor performances, including aerial theater, giant puppetry, inflatable birds, pyrotechnics, water effects, stilt walking, and music. See www.festival.org. Late June to late July.

Open Air Theatre. Outdoor performances of Shakespeare, light opera, and kids' classics take place in Regent's Park throughout the summer. See www.open airtheatre.org. Late May to mid-Sept.

July

Crystal Palace Park Victorian Weekend. These 2 days of activities deal with the history of the famous Crystal Palace and surrounding park (p. 205), including a Victorian and Edwardian funfair and amusements, brass bands, and guided walks. See www.crystalpalacefoundation.org.uk. First weekend in July.

Music on a Summer Evening. You'll find picnic concerts and fireworks at this annual festival held at Kenwood House and Marble Hill House. See www.picnicconcerts.com. From early July to late August.

Soho Festival. This annual fundraiser in the gardens of St. Anne's Church just off Shaftesbury Avenue boasts live music, food stalls, and a market selling vintage clothes and bric-a-brac. The spaghetti-eating competition and alpine horn blowing are the highlights (the waiters' race is now sadly defunct), but there's plenty of other family fun, which may include a puppeteer and face-painting. See www.thesohosociety. org.uk. Mid-July.

Rise. This free anti-racism, pro-diversity open-air music festival was formerly known as Respect. As well as six stages hosting concerts by big names such as De La Soul and Public Enemy, and lesser-known acts from Asia, Africa, and the Arab nations, it features a comedy tent, slam poetry events, film, dance, art displays, food stalls, a market, an extreme sports zone, and a family area with rides, workshops, kids' theater, and play areas. It's held in a different London park each year. See www.risefestival.org. Mid-July.

Swan Upping. This royal ritual, comprising the annual census (or "counting") of the swan population on parts of the Thames, dates back to the 12th century, when the monarch owned all mute swans—and ate many of them at royal feasts! They were counted to make sure they were not being stolen or killed by other people. The "swan uppers" row upriver for 5 days in skiffs flying flags and pennants. Call ✆ **01628/523030.** Third week of July (different departure points and times).

The Proms. Don't miss the annual Henry Wood Promenade Concerts at the Royal Albert Hall and their overspill into Hyde Park. See p. 249. Mid-July to mid-September.

Toddlerthon. This toddlers' walk for charity (Great Ormond St. Children's Hospital in Bloomsbury) covers over 150m (492 ft.) on Regent's Park athletics track, near London Zoo. See www.toddlerthon.co.uk. Last week in June.

August

South East Marine Week. A program of special events celebrating the marine wildlife of London and its environs, Marine Week boasts activities ranging from arts and crafts, to exhibitions of marine photographs, to sailing with seals. In London there's a "beach party" on the Thames's foreshore. See www.southeastmarine.org.uk. Second week in August.

Kids' Week. Every August, the West End hosts an annual children's program of reduced-price theater tickets and special events. See www.official londontheatre.co.uk/kids/week. Second half of August.

Notting Hill Carnival. This is one of Europe's biggest street festivals, with colorful floats, extravagantly dressed dancers, steel drums, calypso music, concerts, and Caribbean food. It starts around 10am, and crowds are dispersed about 9:30pm. See www.lnhc. org.uk. Usually the last Sunday and Monday of August.

National Playday. This is Britain's biggest celebration of children's play, run by the Children's Society and the Children's Play Council and involving about 100,000 children in a range of events around the country. See www. playday.org.uk. Early August.

Fruitstock. A fantastic free music festival at the Camden end of Regent's Park, Fruitstock features copious kids' entertainments, including a circus top with clown shows and circus skills tuition, a carousel, and swingboats. Music tends toward the jazzy and laid-back, and there's a farmers' market and natural food stalls. Visit www.fruit stock.com. Early August.

September

Trafalgar Great River Race. This colorful, madcap race from Richmond to Greenwich passes many historic landmarks and employs about 250 traditional boats, such as Hawaiian war canoes, Viking longboats, Chinese dragonboats, and naval whalers. Crews hail from all over the world. The best place to watch is between Battersea

Bridge and Tower Bridge. See www.great riverrace.co.uk. First or second week in September.

Regent Street Festival. This day of free family entertainment on the famous shopping street changes every year. In 2004, there was a Victorian fairground; in 2005, the theme was an "English country garden" and a polo showcase with ponies and riders. It always includes picnics, food stalls, live music, and in-store promotions. See www.regent-street.co.uk. Early September.

Brick Lane Festival. This lively street festival celebrates the ethnic diversity of this area of east London, with a world music and dance stage, a curry festival, global food stalls, restaurant specialties, outdoor theater, jugglers, rickshaw rides, a crafts market, a funfair, tours of historic houses, and—especially for kids—stilt-walking workshops, face painting, and bouncy castles. See www.bricklanefestival.com. Second Sunday of September.

The Mayor's Thames Festival. The South Bank from Westminster Bridge to Tower Bridge are taken over by Indian-themed events and displays (including an Indian boat sculpture made from more than 130,000 light bulbs); Japanese dancers and drummers; boat rides; "beach" events; food and crafts stalls; a spectacular night procession, market, and carnival with outlandish floats and costumes; and a fireworks finale at this glorious 2-day multicultural celebration of the river. See www.thamesfestival.org. Mid-September.

Open House. This 2-day event allows access to around 500 architecturally significant buildings normally closed to the public. In 2005 a free kids' pack, *Architective*, was introduced to help children explore the buildings, as well as keep busy with activities. See www.londonopenhouse.org. Mid- to late September.

Horseman's Sunday. At this eccentric event, more than 100 horses are blessed by a horseback vicar outside St. John's Church in Hyde Park Crescent, W2, before being trotted around the neighborhood and through Hyde Park. The event is in remembrance of an open-air service held in the 1060s to protest against the possible closure of local riding schools. Call © 020/7262-1732. Late September.

Tree-Athlon. Inaugurated in 2005 to raise money in urban spaces from London's East End to Ethiopia, this event consists of a 5km (3-mile) run in Battersea Park, followed by a tree "wish" and a seed planting. For non-runners and young kids, there's a 1km (0.5-mile) tree trail walk, a tree identification competition, face-painting, music, and refreshments. See www.tree-athlon.org. Late September.

October

The Big Draw. This festival consists of more than 1,000 drawing events across the country, including the Art on the Square launch in Trafalgar Square, with free creative activities such as hat-, mask-, and costume-making, portraiture, cartooning, and celebrity artists. Other venues have included the Brunel Engine House and Tate Britain. See www.drawingpower.org.uk. All month.

The Baby Show London. Come to this huge parenting event, held at Olympia in west London, to meet celebrity children's experts, buy toys and clothes, test strollers, watch fashion shows, and even book a pampering treatment. For kids there's a day nursery, play zones, and crawling races. See www.thebabyshow.co.uk. Mid-October.

Trafalgar Day Parade. An annual parade by more than 600 sea cadets (naval trainees ages 12–18) from around the country gathers to commemorate Adm. Lord Nelson and his death at the Battle of Trafalgar. The event takes place in Trafalgar Square and includes music by cadet bands, the laying of a wreath, and a short service with hymns. See www.sea-cadets.org. Sunday nearest October 21.

Opening of Parliament. Here's your chance to see the Queen ride in one of her royal coaches from Buckingham Palace to the House of Lords, accompanied by the Household Cavalry. Inside (viewable only on TV), she ensconces herself on the throne and, after some eccentric behavior involving Black Rod (the senior official who summons the House of Commons) having a door slammed in his face, inaugurates the parliamentary year by reading an official speech drawn up by the government, stating its plans for the coming year. See www.parliament. uk. Late October to mid-November (plus shortly after a general election).

Diwali. The 5-day Hindu and Sikh Festival of Lights celebrating the victory of good over evil is celebrated in Trafalgar Square with Bollywood and traditional dance performances, spectacular light displays, and free vegetarian food. Another good place to witness the celebrations is the gorgeous Shri Swaminarayan Mandir temple in north London (www.mandir.org), where rituals include the decorating of shrines, scattering of petals and rice grains, and fireworks. See www.london. gov.uk/mayor/diwali. Dates vary during October and November.

November

Chocolate Week. See p. 122. First week in November.

Guy Fawkes Night. On the anniversary of the Gunpowder Plot (an attempt to blow up King James I and his Parliament, led by Guy Fawkes), huge bonfires are lit to burn effigies of Guy Fawkes. There are also spectacular fireworks displays, food stalls, and more. The best venues at which to wait for the show are Battersea Park, where the fireworks display is set to music and lights; Alexandra Park; and Ravenscourt Park. Check *Time Out*'s website for locations: www.timeout. com/london. November 5 or the nearest Friday or Saturday night.

London-to-Brighton Veteran Car Run. The world's oldest motoring event, the car run involves about 500 pre-1905 vehicles on a 97km (60-mile) run from the southeast corner of Hyde Park to the Brighton seafront. Cars leave in pairs between 7:15 and 8:45am and drive at about 32kmph (20 mph) along Constitution Hill, Birdcage Walk, and Westminster Bridge into south London. Note that the day before the run, there's a concourse on Regent Street where up to 100 of the cars can be seen close up, plus driving demonstrations. See www.lbvcr.com. First Sunday in November.

Lord Mayor's Procession & Show. This journey by the new Lord Mayor of the City of London, in his fairy-tale state coach, runs from Mansion House to the Royal Courts of Justice to pledge allegiance to the Crown. (You can view the pledging by invitation only.) From the street, you can watch the 5.5km (3½-mile) procession being led by the enormous figures of Gog and Magog (the City's traditional guardians) accompanied by floats, bands, and tanks. The parade starts at 10:55am but you should get here much earlier to stake out a place. Queen Victoria Street and the Embankment are good places to watch the Lord Mayor return. Afterwards, there are free walking tours of the City that deliver you to the river in plenty of time for the fireworks finale at 5pm. See www.lordmayor show.org. Second week in November.

Christmas Lights. The famous lights in Regent Street are switched on almost 2 months ahead of the big day, usually by a pop act that performs live in front of the crowd. A less commercialized event takes place on Marylebone High Street in mid-November, with more artistic lights, fireworks, and a street market. See www.regent-street.co.uk. Early November.

December

Christmas Carols on Trafalgar Square. This program of carol concerts by about 30 different choirs is free, but donations go to charity. The singing, which takes place most evenings, is against the backdrop of a traditional Norwegian Christmas tree given by the people of Oslo every year since 1947 in gratitude for Britain's support of Norway in World War II. The tree is lit in a ceremony at the end of November, and remains in the square until "Twelfth Night" (Jan 6). See www.london.gov.uk. Early December until Christmas Eve.

Father Christmas at Harrods. London's most magical Santa's grotto opens well ahead of the festive season (Harrods's Christmas World section actually opens in Aug!), but a visit is a must. Arrive early and expect queues of up to 2 hours, but don't worry—the cheery elves are on hand to keep things merry with singing, dancing, and free lollies and cookies. See www.harrods.com. From early November to Christmas Eve.

Frost Fairs. After a break of nearly 200 years, this famous fair (p. 45) returned to London in 2003. Come to the Bankside area (in front of Shakespeare's Globe) for a day of music, theater, ice sculptures, snow machines, craft and food stalls, and children's workshops, plus a 30-metre ice slide outside the Tate Modern (open until early January). Call © **020/7357-9168** or visit www.visitsouthwark.com. Late December.

International Showjumping Championships. This is one of Europe's top equine events, held in west London. As well as show jumping, you'll see dressage, dog agility performances, displays by mounted police, and a grand finale involving a procession with a Christmas theme. See www.olympia showjumping.com. Mid-December.

New Year's Eve. There's a dearth of organized activities heralding the new year in London, especially where families are concerned. You're best off enjoying a special feast at a child-friendly restaurant such as The Blue Elephant or La Porte des Indes, and saving your energies for the parade the next day (p. 17). December 31.

5 What to Pack

The British consider chilliness wholesome, and try to keep room temperatures about 10° below the American comfort level, so bring sweaters year-round if you tend to get cold. Bring a light jacket, too, for cooler summer evenings.

Aside from common-sense advice about bringing hats, gloves, and scarves in winter, and sturdy, comfy shoes for walking, our best tip is to bring layers of clothing. Carry a jacket in your bag for those all-too-frequent days when you experience 3 seasons in 1 day. The only places you aren't allowed to be seen in normal casual attire are posh hotel restaurants and tea salons, where men will need smart shirts and trousers, and perhaps also sports jackets. Kids shouldn't wear jeans, sneakers, shorts, baseball caps, or other athletic gear.

Lastly, **travel light:** Take water, juice, and snacks to avoid having to pay high prices at convenience stores; wipes (and diapers if needed); and a handful of small toys to fill in long waits at restaurants or when stuck in traffic.

6 Health, Insurance & Safety

TRAVEL INSURANCE AT A GLANCE

Check your existing insurance policies and credit card coverage before you buy travel insurance. You may already be covered for lost luggage, cancelled tickets, or medical expenses. If your standard insurance doesn't cover travel and you decide that you'd like to purchase additional insurance, first ask your travel agent about a comprehensive package, which may be less expensive. The cost of travel insurance varies widely, depending on the cost and length of your trip, your age and overall health, and the type of trip you're taking.

For information in the U.S., contact one of the following popular insurers:

- **Access America** (℃ 866/807-3982; www.accessamerica.com)
- **Travel Guard International** (℃ 800/826-4919; www.travel-guard.com)
- **Travel Insured International** (℃ 800/243-3174; www.travel insured.com)
- **Travelex Insurance Services** (℃ 888/457-4602; www.travelex-insurance.com)

For information in Great Britain, contact the following agency:

- **Columbus Direct** (0845/330-8518; www.columbusdirect.com)

For information in Canada, contact:

- **Travel Guard International** (see U.S. contact information above).

Trip-cancellation insurance helps you get your money back if you have to back out of a trip, if you have to go home early (both of which are more likely if you're traveling with kids than not), or if your travel supplier goes bankrupt. Allowed reasons for cancellation can range from sickness to natural disasters to the State Department's declaration that your destination is unsafe for travel. In this unstable world, trip-cancellation insurance is a good buy if you're getting tickets well in advance—who knows what the state of the world, or of your airline, will be in 9 months? Insurance policy details vary, so read the fine print—and especially make sure that your airline is on the list of carriers covered in case of bankruptcy. For information, contact one of the insurers listed above.

Visitors from most other European countries are covered for **medical care** by the British National Health Service under the E.U. Reciprocal Medical Treatment arrangement, but you must get an E111 form from your social security office before departure. Australian citizens also benefit from a reciprocal agreement between Britain and Medicare. See www.dh.gov.uk for guidance on health treatment for overseas visitors.

Most other non-E.U. nationals need **medical insurance** for all but emergency care. With the exception of certain HMOs and Medicare/Medicaid, your insurance should cover medical treatment—even hospital care—overseas. However, most out-of-country hospitals make you pay bills upfront and send a refund after you've returned home and filed the necessary paperwork. And in a worst-case scenario, there's the high cost of emergency evacuation. If you require additional medical insurance, try **MEDEX International** (℃ 800/527-0218; www.medexassist.com) or **Travel Assistance International** (℃ 800/821-2828; www.travelassistance.com).

STAYING HEALTHY

There are no real health risks while you're traveling in England. For general advice on traveling with kids, read *Your Child Abroad: A Travel Health Guide,* by Dr. Jane Wilson-Howarth and Dr. Matthew Ellis (Bradt).

WHAT TO DO IF YOU GET SICK AWAY FROM HOME

For information on emergency treatments, doctors, and drugstores, see p. 56. If you or your child have an illness impossible to explain quickly and that warrants swift and accurate treatment (such as epilepsy, diabetes, asthma, or a food allergy), invest in a **MedicAlert E-HealthKEY** (*©* **888/633-4298;** www. medicalert.org). This alerts doctors to the carrier's condition and gives them access to their records through a PC or 24-hour response center. The company also has various "Kid Smart" services, including notifying designated family members should your child need emergency treatment in your absence. Alternatively, free membership in the **International Association for Medical Assistance to Travellers** (www. iamat.org) gets you a Traveller Clinical Record providing physicians with your medical history, plus a directory of IAMAT-approved physicians in 125 countries.

Pack **prescription medications** in your carry-on luggage in their original containers with pharmacy labels, otherwise they won't make it through airport security. Also bring along copies of prescriptions in case you or anyone in your family loses their medication or runs out, and carry the generic name of prescription medicines in case a local pharmacist is unfamiliar with the brand name. It's also a good idea to obtain a reference for a London pediatrician in case of a sudden illness. Failing that, your hotel's front desk should be able to put you in touch with a local doctor if any illnesses flare up during your London stay.

7 Words of Wisdom & Helpful Resources

Rule number one is to **hold hands with your child** and not let him or her out of your sight for a second, unless he or she is being supervised by someone you trust. If you have a stroller, fitting a Buggyboard (a board allowing kids to stand on the back of a stroller) is a good idea if you have an older child who can't manage huge walks but doesn't want to sit in their stroller all day, or if you have two kids.

Be especially careful around **intersections**—London is full of aggressive drivers. Always cross at traffic lights or at "zebra crossings," although don't assume that just because it's the law, a driver will stop at the latter—wait until they have slowed down and are motionless before proceeding.

Avoid situations where your child could get swept away in a **crowd,** and with older kids agree on **a place to meet should you get parted**—at the information desk at a museum, for instance. Make sure they have your cellphone number and hotel address on them, with instructions to approach a member of the police force should they not be able to find you. And common sense dictates that kids should be made aware of the importance of **never divulging their names to a stranger,** and that their names should never be visible on their bags or clothing.

For more tips on safety, especially with regard to London neighborhoods, see p. 58.

FOR SINGLE PARENTS

Online, **Single Parent Travel Network** (www.singleparenttravel.net) offers excellent advice, travel specials, a bulletin board, and a free electronic newsletter. **Family Travel Forum** (www.familytravelforum. com) also hosts a single-parent travel bulletin board for tips from fellow travelers.

Within the U.K., the charity **One Parent Families** has lots of travel information and advice on its website (www.oneparentfamilies.org.uk). It also offers members a travel magazine; membership is free for single parents. Their free help line is ℭ **08000/185026**. **Gingerbread** (www.gingerbread.org.uk), a nationwide support organization, lists services for lone parents in London as well as provides holiday and travel suggestions. They have a free advice line at ℭ **08000/ 184318**.

Note that youth hostels (p. 70) offer good rates for single people traveling with kids.

FOR GRANDPARENTS

Mention the fact that you're a senior when you make your travel reservations. Check with your airline (especially America West, Continental, and American) to see if they offer senior discounts; many hotels offer discounts for seniors, too. In most cities, people over the age of 60 qualify for reduced admission to theaters, museums, and other attractions, as well as for discounted fares on public transportation.

Grand Travel (ℭ 800/247-7651; www.grandtrvl.com) deals exclusively with holidays for grandparents and grandkids (mainly ages 7–17), including a combined London-and-Paris trip, and a "Castles, Highlands, and Heather" itinerary from Edinburgh to London, via York, Stratford-upon-Avon, and Bath. **Elderhostel** (ℭ 877/426-8056; www.elderhostel.org), a not-for-profit travel organization, offers study programs for older adults (including art or theater in London), plus a broad range of intergenerational adventures (though none of these are in the U.K. at present).

FOR FAMILIES WITH SPECIAL NEEDS

In theory, all public buildings in Britain should have been wheelchair accessible since October 2004, but many architecturally valuable places have been exempted. That said, most museums and venues now have excellent access and facilities for those with disabilities, and many hotels now have specially adapted rooms. The Tube continues to be an embarrassment, with very few stations with elevators; ask at a station for a map highlighting stations that do have step-free access from street to platform. New-style buses (as opposed to old-style Routemasters; see p. 53) have sliding ramps on the back doors.

Many travel agencies offer customized tours and itineraries for travelers with disabilities. **Flying Wheels Travel** (ℭ 507/ 451-5005; www.flyingwheelstravel.com) offers escorted tours and cruises that emphasize sports and private tours in minivans with lifts. **Accessible Journeys** (ℭ 800/846-4537 or 610/521-0339; www.disabilitytravel.com) caters specifically to slow walkers, wheelchair travelers, and their families and friends.

Holiday Care (www.holidaycare.org.uk) offers holiday and travel information advice for travelers with disabilities, including discounts on accessible rooms at various London hotels for members. Its information line within the U.K. is ℭ **0800/124-9971** (ℭ 020/8760-0072 outside).

8 The 21st-Century Traveler

PLANNING YOUR TRIP ONLINE
SURFING FOR AIRFARES

The "big three" online travel agencies, **Expedia.com, Travelocity.com,** and **Orbitz.com** sell most of the air tickets bought on the Internet. (Canadian travelers should try Expedia.ca and Travelocity.ca; U.K. residents can go for Expedia.co.uk and Opodo.co.uk.) Each has different business deals with the airlines and may offer different fares on the same flights, so it's wise to shop around. Of the smaller travel agency websites, **SideStep** (www.sidestep.com) has gotten the best reviews from Frommer's authors. It's a browser add-on that purports to "search 140 sites at once," but in reality only beats competitors' fares as often as other sites do.

Remember to check **airline websites;** you can often shave a few bucks from a fare by booking online directly through the airline and avoiding a travel agency's transaction fee. For the websites of airlines that fly to and from London, go to "Getting There," below.

Great **last-minute deals** are available through free weekly e-mail services provided directly by the airlines. Sign up for weekly e-mail alerts at airline websites, or check sites that specialize in last-minute deals, such as **Smartertravel.com, Site59. com,** and **Lastminutetravel.com.** For a website listing numerous bargain sites and airlines around the world, go to **www.itravelnet.com**.

If you're willing to give up some control over your flight details, use an **"opaque" fare service** like **Priceline** (www.priceline.com or www.priceline.co. uk) or its smaller competitor **Hotwire** (www.hotwire.com). Both offer rock-bottom prices in exchange for travel on a "mystery airline" at a mysterious time of day, often with a mysterious change of planes en route. The mystery airlines are all major, well-known carriers, and the airlines' routing computers have gotten a lot better than they used to be. But your chances of getting a 6am or 11pm flight are pretty high, and you might find this too inconvenient with kids in tow. Hotwire tells you flight prices before you buy; Priceline usually has better deals than Hotwire, but you have to play their "name our price" game. If you're new at this, the helpful folks at **BiddingFor-Travel** (www.biddingfortravel.com) do a good job of demystifying Priceline's prices and strategies. Priceline also now

offers non-opaque deals that allow you to pick exact flight options.

SURFING FOR HOTELS

Shopping online for hotels is generally done one of two ways: by booking through the hotel's own website, or by booking through an independent agency (or a fare-service agency like Priceline). Internet hotel agencies have multiplied in mind-boggling numbers of late, and you must shop around, as prices can vary considerably from site to site. Keep in mind that hotels at the top of a site's listing may be there for no other reason than that they paid money to get the placement.

Of the "big three" sites, **Expedia** offers a long list of special deals and "virtual tours" or photos of available rooms so you can see what you're paying for. **Travelocity** posts unvarnished customer reviews and ranks its properties according to the AAA rating system. Also reliable are **Hotels.com** and **Quikbook.com.** An excellent free program, **TravelAxe** (www. travelaxe.net), can search multiple hotel sites at once and conveniently lists the total price of the room, including the taxes and service charges. Another booking site, **Travelweb** (www.travelweb. com), is partly owned by the hotels it represents (including the Hilton, Hyatt, and Starwood chains) and is therefore plugged directly into the hotels' reservations systems—unlike independent online agencies, which have to fax or e-mail reservation requests to the hotel, a good portion of which get misplaced in the shuffle. Many of the major sites are undergoing improvements in service and ease of use; in the meantime, it's a good idea to **get a confirmation number** and **make a printout** of any online booking transaction.

In the opaque fare service category, **Priceline** and **Hotwire** are even better for hotels than for airfares; with both, you're allowed to pick the neighborhood and quality level of your hotel before offering up your money. On the downside, many hotels stick Priceline guests in their least desirable rooms. Be sure to go to the BiddingForTravel website (see above) before bidding on a hotel room on Priceline; it features a fairly up-to-date list of hotels that Priceline uses in major cities. For both Priceline and Hotwire, you pay upfront, and the fee is nonrefundable. *Note:* Some hotels do not provide loyalty program credits or points or other frequent-stay amenities when you book a room through opaque online services.

SURFING FOR CAR RENTALS

For booking car rentals online, the best deals are usually found at car-rental company websites, although all the major online travel agencies also offer car rental reservations services. Priceline and Hotwire work well for car rentals, too; the only "mystery" is which major rental company you get, and for most travelers the difference between Hertz, Avis, and Budget is negligible.

INTERNET ACCESS AWAY FROM HOME
WITHOUT YOUR OWN COMPUTER

It's hard nowadays to find a city that *doesn't* have a few cybercafes. Although there's no definitive directory for cybercafes, two places to start looking are **www.cybercaptive.com** and **www.cybercafe.com**. There are very few London streets without a least one Internet cafe. One of the most ubiquitous is **easyInternet** (www.easyeverything.com), with 18 branches in or around the capital at press time. See the website for addresses.

Aside from formal cybercafes, most **public libraries** offer Internet access free or for a small charge. Avoid **hotel business centers** and **Internet kiosks** unless you're willing to pay exorbitant rates.

To retrieve your e-mail, ask your **Internet Service Provider (ISP)** if it has a Web-based interface tied to your existing e-mail account. If your ISP doesn't have such an interface, you can use the free **mail2web** service (www.mail2web.com) to view and reply to your home e-mail. For more flexibility, you may want to open a free, Web-based e-mail account with **Yahoo! Mail** (http://mail.yahoo.com) or **Fastmail** (www.fastmail.fm). Your home ISP may be able to forward your e-mail to the Web-based account automatically.

If you need to access files on your office computer, look into a service called **GoToMyPC** (www.gotomypc.com). The service provides a Web-based interface through which you can access and manipulate a distant PC from anywhere—even a cybercafe—provided your "target" PC is on and has an always-on connection to the Internet (such as with Road Runner cable). The service offers top-quality security, but if you're worried about hackers, use your own laptop rather than a cybercafe computer to access the GoToMyPC system.

WITH YOUR OWN COMPUTER

Wi-Fi (wireless fidelity) is the buzzword in computer access, and more and more hotels, cafes, and retailers are signing on as wireless "hot spots" from where you can get high-speed connection without cable wires, networking hardware, or a phone line (see below). **Boingo** (www.boingo.com) and **Wayport** (www.wayport.com) have set up networks in airports and high-class hotel lobbies. IPass providers (see below) also give you access to a few hundred wireless hotel lobby setups. Best of all, you don't need to be staying at the Four Seasons to use the hotel's network; just set yourself up on a nice couch in the lobby. The companies' pricing policies can be byzantine, with a variety of monthly, per-connection, and per-minute plans, but in general you pay around $30 a month for limited access—and as more and more companies jump on the wireless bandwagon, prices are likely to get even more competitive.

There are also places that provide **free wireless networks** in cities around the world. To locate these free hot spots, go to **www.personaltelco.net/index.cgi/WirelessCommunities**.

If Wi-Fi is not available at your destination, most business-class hotels throughout the world offer dataports for laptop modems, and a few thousand hotels in the U.S. and Europe now offer free high-speed Internet access using an Ethernet network cable. (You can bring your own cables, but most hotels rent them for around $10; call your hotel in advance to see what your options are.)

In addition, major Internet Service Providers (ISPs) have **local access numbers** around the world, allowing you to go online by placing a local call. Check your ISP's website or call its toll-free number and ask how you can use your current account away from home, and how much it will cost.

If you're traveling outside the reach of your ISP, the **iPass** network has dial-up numbers in most of the world's countries. You'll have to sign up with an iPass provider, who will then tell you how to set up your computer for your destination(s). For a list of iPass providers, go to www.ipass.com. One solid provider is **i2roam** (www.i2roam.com; ✆ **866/811-6209** or 920/235-0475).

Wherever you go, bring a **connection kit** of the right power and phone adapters, a spare phone cord, and a spare Ethernet network cable—or find out whether your hotel supplies them to guests.

USING A CELLPHONE

The three letters that define much of the world's **wireless capabilities** are GSM (Global System for Mobiles), a big, seamless network that makes for easy cross-border cellphone use throughout Europe and dozens of other countries worldwide. In the U.S., T-Mobile, AT&T Wireless, and Cingular use this quasi-universal system. In Canada, Microcell and some Rogers customers are GSM, and all Europeans and most Australians use GSM.

If your cellphone is on a GSM system, and you have a world-capable multiband phone such as many Sony Ericsson, Motorola, or Samsung models, you can make and receive calls across much of the globe, including London. Just call your wireless operator and ask for "international roaming" to be activated on your account. Unfortunately, per-minute charges can be high—usually $1 to $1.50 in London.

That's why it's important to buy an "unlocked" world phone from the get-go. Having an unlocked phone allows you to install a cheap, prepaid, removable computer memory phone chip (called a **SIM card**) in your destination. (Show your phone to the salesperson; not all phones work on all networks.) You'll get a local phone number and much, much lower calling rates. Getting an already locked phone unlocked can be a complicated process, but it can be done; just call your cellular operator and say you'll be going abroad for several months and want to use the phone with a local provider.

For many, **renting** a phone is a good idea. (Even world-phone owners will have to rent new phones if they're traveling to non-GSM regions.) While you can rent a phone from any number of overseas sites, including airports and car rental agencies, we suggest renting the phone before you leave home. That way you can give loved ones and business associates your new number, make sure the phone works, and take the phone wherever you go—especially helpful for overseas trips through several countries.

Phone rental isn't cheap. If you don't bring your own, you're better off buying a pre-paid or pay-as-you-go phone in the U.K. Handsets start at about £50 ($95), and you recharge them by buying top-up cards (available from most newsagents and phone shops) in denominations of £10 ($19) and up. Major networks Orange (www.orange.co.uk), Vodafone (www.vodafone.co.uk), and O2 (www.O2.co.uk) have their own shops. Alternatively, there are branches of Carphone Warehouse (www.carphonewarehouse.com) at Heathrow Airport Terminal 2 and Waterloo Station; and a branch of The Link (www.thelink.co.uk) at Gatwick Airport's South Terminal, These companies sell phones on a variety of networks. Make sure you tell your provider that you need a model that can make and receive international calls.

Two good wireless rental companies are **InTouch USA** (✆ **800/872-7626;** www.intouchglobal.com) and **RoadPost** (✆ **888/290-1606** or 905/272-5665;

www.roadpost.com). Give them your itinerary, and they'll tell you what wireless products you need. InTouch will also, for free, advise you on whether your existing phone will work overseas; call ✆ **703/222-7161** between 9am and 4pm EST, or go to http://intouchglobal.com/travel.htm.

For trips of more than a few weeks spent in one country, **buying a phone** becomes economically attractive, as many nations have cheap, no-questions-asked prepaid phone systems. Once you arrive at your destination, stop by a local cellphone shop and get the cheapest package; you'll probably pay less than $100 for a phone and a starter calling card. Local calls may be as low as 10¢ per minute, and in many countries incoming calls are free.

9 Getting There

BY PLANE

Heathrow is a bit closer to central London than Gatwick, but there is a fast train service from both airports to the West End (see "Getting into Town from the Airport," below). **High season** on most airlines' routes to London is usually from June to the beginning of September. **Shoulder season** is from April to May, early September to October, and December 15 to 24. **Low season** is from November 1 to December 14, and from December 25 to March 31.

FROM THE UNITED STATES & CANADA Airlines that fly regularly between the U.S. and London include: **American Airlines** (✆ **800/433-7300;** www.aa.com), **British Airways** (✆ **800-AIRWAYS;** www.britishairways.com), **Continental Airlines** (✆ **800/231-0856;** www.continental.com), **Delta Air Lines** (✆ **800/221-1212;** www.delta.com), **Air India** (✆ **800/223-7776;** www.airindia.com), **Northwest Airlines** (✆ **800/447-3757;** www.nwa.com), **United Airlines** (✆ **800/538-2929;**

www.united.com), and **Virgin Atlantic Airways** (✆ **800/821-5348;** www.virgin-atlantic.com).

Air Canada (✆ **888/247-2262;** www.aircanada.com) flies daily to Heathrow from various Canadian cities.

FROM AUSTRALIA   Qantas (✆ **800/227-4500** or 612/13-13-13; www.qantas.com) and **British Airways** (✆ **800/247-9297;** www.britishairways.com) fly to London from Australia.

FROM SOUTH AFRICA South African Airways (✆ **0861/359722;** www.flysaa.com), **British Airways** (✆ **011/441-8471;** www.britishairways.com), and **Virgin Atlantic Airways** (✆ **011/340-3400;** www.virgin-atlantic.com) fly to London from Johannesburg and/or Cape Town.

GETTING INTO TOWN FROM THE AIRPORT

For information on Heathrow, Gatwick, and Stansted, including travel to and from these airports, and flight arrivals and departures, see www.baa.com.

LONDON HEATHROW AIRPORT

Heathrow (☎ 0870/000-0123) is about 25km (15 miles) west of central London. Terminals 1 and 2 receive the intra-European flights of several European airlines. Terminal 3 receives most transatlantic flights on U.S.–based airlines, and Terminal 4 handles the long-haul and transatlantic operations of British Airways.

Heathrow has two Underground (Tube) stations, the first servicing Terminals 1, 2, and 3. The other, servicing Terminal 4, is closed for extension work until September 2006; until then, there's a replacement bus service from Hatton Cross Tube. It takes up to an hour to get to central London by Tube, with tickets costing £3.80 ($7.20) for adults and £1.40 ($2.70) for kids, making it by far your cheapest option. A quicker and more comfortable choice is the **Heathrow Express** (www.heathrow express.com), which takes you to Paddington Station in 15 minutes (23 min. from Terminal 4). Trips cost £14 ($27) each way in economy class, £6.50 ($12) for kids 5 to 15. You can pre-book tickets online, or get them at self-service machines at Heathrow (also available from travel agents). A taxi from Heathrow is likely to cost £40 to £70 ($76–$133).

GATWICK AIRPORT

Gatwick (☎ 0870/000-2468) is 45km (28 miles) south of London. The fastest way to get to the center is via the **Gatwick Express trains** (www.gatwickexpress.co.uk), which take you to Victoria Station in 30 minutes (35 min. on Sun). The one-way charge in standard class is £12 ($23) for adults, £6 ($11) for kids 5 to 15. A slower but cheaper alternative is the **National Express Airbuses** (www.nationalexpress.com) from Gatwick South Terminal to Victoria coach station (next to Victoria train station), taking 1 hour to 90 minutes. One-way tickets cost £6.20 ($12) for adults, £3.10 ($5.90) for kids 3 to 15. Make sure you don't get on a coach that takes you via Brighton. The airport's official taxi concessionaire, **Checker Cars** (☎ 0800/747-737), charges £77 ($146) for journeys into central London, plus an extra £8 ($15) if you enter the Congestion Charge zone between 7am and 6pm.

LONDON STANSTED AIRPORT

Stansted (☎ 0870/000-0303), located some 65km (40 miles) northeast of London, mostly handles flights to and from the European continent, mainly by budget airlines. The **Stansted Express train** (www.stanstedexpress.com) takes an average of 45 minutes to get to London's Liverpool Street Station, costing £15 ($28) for adults, £7.25 ($14) for kids one-way. There are a variety of coach options, the quickest being the new Terravision services to Liverpool Street Station or Victoria, taking 55 minutes and 75 minutes respectively. Fares are £6.70 ($13) for adults, £4 ($7.60) for kids to Liverpool Street; £8.10 ($15) for adults, £5 ($9.50) for kids to Victoria. A **taxi** to the West End by the official taxi company, **Airport Carz** (☎ 0870/224-5000), will cost about £90 ($171).

LONDON CITY AIRPORT

London City Airport (☎ 020/7646-0000; www.londoncityairport.com), 5km (3 miles) east of the business community of Canary Wharf, and 16km (10 miles) from the West End, receives flights from a number of cities in western Europe and Scandinavia. It runs frequent shuttle buses to Liverpool Street Station; the one-way trip costs £6.50 ($12) adults, £2 ($3.80) kids. You can also use local buses to hook up with the Tube or DLR, but this is trickier. Black cabs into the West End cost £25 ($48).

GETTING THROUGH THE AIRPORT

Generally, you'll be fine if you arrive at the airport **1 hour** before a domestic flight and **2 hours** before an international flight; if you show up late, tell an airline employee and she'll probably whisk you to the front of the line. Bring a **current, government-issued photo ID** such as a driver's license or passport. Keep your ID at the ready to show at check-in, the security checkpoint, and sometimes even the gate. Children under 18 do not need government-issued photo IDs for domestic flights, but they do for international flights to most countries, including Britain.

The Transportation Security Administration (TSA) has phased out **gate check-in** at all U.S. airports. Passengers with e-tickets can still beat the ticket-counter lines by using **airport electronic kiosks** or **online check-in** from your home computer. Ask your airline which alternatives are available, and if you're using a kiosk, bring the credit card you used to book the ticket or your frequent-flier card. If you're checking bags or looking to snag an exit-row seat, you will be able to do so using most airlines' kiosks; again, call your airline for up-to-date information. **Curbside check-in** is also a good way to avoid lines, although a few airlines still ban curbside check-in; call before you go.

Security checkpoint lines are getting shorter, but some doozies remain. If you have trouble standing for long periods of time, tell an airline employee; the airline will provide a wheelchair. Speed up security by **not wearing metal objects** such as big belt buckles. If you've got metallic body parts, a note from your doctor can prevent a long chat with the security screeners. Keep in mind that only **ticketed passengers** are allowed past security.

Federalization has stabilized **what you can carry on** and **what you can't.** The general rule is that sharp things are out, nail clippers are okay, and food and beverages must be passed through the X-ray machine—but that security screeners can't make you drink from your coffee cup. Bring food in your carry-on rather than checking it, as explosive-detection machines used on checked luggage have been known to mistake food (especially chocolate, for some reason) for bombs. The TSA has issued a list of restricted items; check its website (**www.tsa.gov**) for details.

Airport screeners may decide that your checked luggage needs to be searched by hand. You can now purchase luggage locks that allow screeners to open and re-lock a checked bag if hand-searching is necessary. Look for Travel Sentry certified locks at luggage or travel shops and Brookstone stores (you can buy them online at www.brookstone.com). These locks, approved by the TSA, can be opened by luggage inspectors with a special code or key. For more information on the locks, visit www.travelsentry.org. If you use something other than TSA-approved locks, your lock will be cut off your suitcase if a TSA agent needs to hand-search your luggage.

FLYING FOR LESS: TIPS FOR GETTING THE BEST AIRFARES

It's becoming more widely realized that passengers sharing the same airplane cabin rarely pay the same fare—travelers who need to purchase tickets at the last minute, change their itinerary at short notice, or fly one-way often get stuck paying the premium rate. Here are some ways to keep your airfares down.

- If you can book your ticket **long in advance, stay over Saturday night,** or **fly midweek** or **at less-trafficked hours,** you may pay a fraction of the full fare. If your schedule is flexible, say so, and ask if you can secure a cheaper fare by changing your flight plans.
- Keep an eye on local newspapers for **promotional specials** or **fare wars,** when airlines lower prices on their most popular routes. If you can travel in the off season, you may snag a bargain this way.

- Search the **Internet** for cheap fares: Try www.expedia.com, www.travelocity.com, or www.orbitz.com, which can include hotel deals with your fare. Sign up to receive **e-mail notification** when a cheap fare becomes available to your favorite destination. There are also facilities such as www.sidestep.com that compare offers on various sites. Note that even with the major airlines listed above, you can often shave a few bucks from a fare by booking directly through the airline (online).

- **Consolidators,** also known as bucket shops, are great sources for international tickets. Start by looking in Sunday newspaper travel sections; U.S. travelers should focus on the *New York Times, Los Angeles Times,* and *Miami Herald.* **Beware:** Bucket shop tickets are usually nonrefundable or rigged with stiff cancellation penalties, often as high as 50% to 75% of the ticket price. Several reliable consolidators are worldwide and available on the Internet. **STA Travel** (© **0800/781-4040;** www.statravel.com), the world's leader in student travel, offers good fares for travelers of all ages. **Flights.com** (© **516/228-4972;** www.flights.com) started in Europe and has excellent fares worldwide, including to London.

- Join **frequent-flier clubs.** Accrue enough miles and you'll be rewarded with free flights and elite status. It's free, and you'll get the best choice of seats, faster response to phone inquiries, and prompter service if your luggage is stolen, if your flight is canceled or delayed, or if you want to change your seat. With more than 70 mileage awards programs on the market, consumers have never had more options, but the system has never been more complicated—what with major airlines folding, new budget carriers emerging, and alliances forming

(allowing you to earn points on partner airlines). Investigate the program details of your favorite airlines before you sink points into any one.

FLYING WITH KIDS

If you plan carefully, you can make it fun to fly with your kids.

- You'll save yourself a good bit of aggravation by **reserving a seat in the bulkhead row.** You'll have more legroom, your children will be able to spread out and play on the floor underfoot, and the airline might provide bassinets (ask in advance). You're also more likely to find sympathetic company in the bulkhead area, as families with children tend to be seated there.

- Be sure to **pack items for your kids in your carry-on luggage,** from pacifiers to diapers.

- **Have a long talk with your children** before you depart on your trip. If they've never flown before, explain to them what to expect. If they're old enough, you may even want to describe how flight works and how air travel is even safer than riding in a car. Explain to your kids the importance of good behavior in the air— how their own safety can depend upon them being quiet and staying in their seats during the trip.

- **Pay extra careful attention to the safety instructions** before takeoff. Consult the safety chart behind the seat in front of you and show it to your children. Be sure you know how to operate the oxygen masks, as you will be expected to secure yours first and then help your children with theirs. Be especially mindful of the location of emergency exits. Before takeoff, plot out an evacuation strategy for you and your children.

- Ask the flight attendant if the plane has any **special safety equipment for**

children. Make a member of the crew aware of any medical problems your children have that could manifest during flight.

- **Be sure you've slept sufficiently** for your trip. If you fall asleep in the air and your child manages to break away, there are all sorts of sharp objects that could cause your child injury. Especially during mealtimes, it's dangerous for a child to be crawling or walking around the cabin unaccompanied by an adult.

- **Be sure your child's seat belt remains fastened properly,** and try to reserve the seat closest to the aisle for yourself. This will make it harder for your children to wander off—in case, for instance, you're taking the red-eye or a long flight and you do happen to nod off. You will also protect your child from jostling passersby and falling objects—in the rare but entirely possible instance that an overhead bin pops open.

   In the event of an accident, unrestrained children often don't make it—even when the parent does. Experience has shown that it's impossible for a parent to hold onto a child in the event of a crash, and children often die of impact injuries.

- **Try to sit near the lavatory,** though not so close that your children are jostled by the crowds that tend to gather there. Consolidate trips there as much as possible.

- **Accompany children to the lavatory.** They can be easily bumped and possibly injured as they make their way down tight aisles. It's especially dangerous for children to wander while flight attendants are blocking passage with their service carts. It's wise to encourage your kids to use the restroom as you see the attendants preparing to serve.

- Be sure to **bring clean, self-containing compact toys.** Leave electronic games at home. They can interfere with the aircraft navigational system, and their noisiness, however lulling to children's ears, will surely not win the favor of your adult neighbors. Magnetic checker sets, on the other hand, are a perfect distraction, and small coloring books and crayons also work well, as do card games like Go Fish.

- Some airlines **serve children's meals first.** When you board, ask a flight attendant if this is possible, especially if your children are very young or seated toward the back of the plane. After all, if your kids have a happy flight experience, everyone else in the cabin is more likely to as well.

- You'll certainly be grateful to yourself for packing **tidy snacks** like rolled dried fruit, which are much less sticky and wet and more compact and packable than actual fruit. Blueberry or raisin bagels also make for a neat, healthy sweet and yield fewer crumbs than cookies or cakes. Ginger snaps, crisp and not as crumbly as softer cookies, will also help curb mild cases of motion sickness. And don't forget to stash a few resealable plastic bags in your purse. They'll prove invaluable for storing everything from half-eaten crackers and fruit to checker pieces and matchbox cars.

BY CAR

If you plan to take a rented car across or under the English Channel, check with your rental company about license and insurance requirements before you leave.

BY FERRIES FROM THE CONTINENT

There are many "drive-on, drive-off" car-ferry services across the Channel. The most popular ports in France for Channel crossings are Boulogne and Calais, where you can board Stena ferries or hovercraft taking you to the British ports of Dover and Folkestone. For details, see "Sailing To & From Europe," under "By Boat," below.

BY SHUTTLE

The Chunnel carries motor vehicles under the Channel (© **08705/353535;** www.eurotunnel.com) between Calais, France, and Folkestone, U.K., in 35 minutes. You don't even need to book in advance, though you do get better deals if you do, and if you travel during off-peak hours. Prices start at £49 per car one-way, but you'll generally pay much more than that. Note that if you miss your pre-booked train but arrive within 2 hours of it, you are allowed free onto the next available departure.

The A20/M20 links London directly with the Channel ports of Folkestone and Dover (where you'll arrive by ferry; see below).

Note that Eurotunnel has combined with Hertz to offer **Le Swap** (© **08708/ 448844;** www.hertz.co.uk), a package allowing you to exchange a car hired on one side of the Channel for another with the steering wheel on the correct side.

BY TRAIN
FROM THE CONTINENT

Eurostar (© **0870/530-0003;** www.eurostar.com) operates frequent express trains between London's Waterloo Station and Calais, Brussels, Lille, Paris, Disneyland Paris, Avignon, and even the Alps, depending on the time of year.

A return leisure fare between London and Paris in standard class costs from £59 ($112) per adult and £50 ($95) per child 4 to 11 depending on how far in advance you book it and the degree of flexibility you require regarding exchanges or refunds.

BRITRAIL TRAVEL PASSES

Low-cost flights between many cities now mean flying can be cheaper than taking a train, as well as a quicker, though not an environmentally sound, alternative. If you

do plan to get around a lot by train outside London, money-saving BritRail passes allow a child ages 5 to 15 to travel free when accompanied by one adult, with subsequent children traveling at a 50% discount. See www.britrail.net for details or to buy passes. You can also find out the times of British national trains, and book tickets on www.thetrainline.com.

BY BUS

This is your cheapest but slowest and least comfortable means of getting to London from the Continent. If you must, **Eurolines** (© **0870/808080;** www.eurolines.co.uk) is a reputable operator running buses to and from Paris (9 hr.); Amsterdam (12 hr.), and more, with one-way fares starting at just £8 ($15). Its new Eurolines Plus option is a more luxurious service to Paris, with increased legroom, reclining seats, and individual headphones for music and video entertainment.

BY BOAT
CROSSING THE ATLANTIC

Cunard Line (© **800/7-CUNARD;** www.cunardline.com) runs regular luxurious transatlantic cruises on the mighty 13-deck *Queen Mary 2,* launched to great fanfare in 2004. Kid-friendly amenities include a basketball court, a planetarium, play zones for 2- to 7-year-olds and 8- to 12-year-olds, a splash pool, and English nannies. Fares vary according to the season and your cabin grade, with an average 6-day crossing beginning at about £1,050 ($2,000) per person.

SAILING TO
& FROM EUROPE

The shortest sea route between the U.K. and the Continent is the Dover–Calais crossing. You can choose to ride with **P&O Ferries** (© **08705/980333;** www.poferries.com), **Sea France** (© **08705/ 711711;** www.seafrance.com), or **Hoverspeed** (© **0870/240-8070;** www.hoverspeed.com). Ferries take about 75 minutes, Hoverspeeds just under an hour. A long stay (more than 5 days) round trip ferry ticket costs from £90 ($171) for a car and passengers. Hoverspeed prices start at about £60 ($114) for a flexible return for a car and up to five people.

Note that www.ferrybookers.com, a useful one-stop shop for ferries and Eurotunnel (p. 36), often quotes better prices than do the operators themselves. Click on its "Route Info" facility for details of all routes between the U.K.

and France, the Netherlands, Spain, and Ireland.

Ferry Bookers doesn't deal with **Speed-ferries** (© **0870/220-0570;** www.speed ferries.com), a relative newcomer offering low-cost, fast crossings (50 min.) on the slightly longer Dover-Boulogne route. Long-stay returns for a standard car with up to five people cost from £50 ($95). Note that there's a fee of £10 ($19) for bookings made by phone rather than online.

10 Show & Tell: Getting Kids Interested in London

Involving kids in planning your forthcoming adventure is the best way to get them interested. Use this book to show them what they can look forward to in London, whether it be the views over the city from the London Eye Ferris wheel or the new "super-sensing" dinosaur at the Natural History Museum. Also, get them to browse **websites** such as www.kids love.london.com and www.show.me.uk.

Depending on your kids' ages, rent **movies** such as *101 Dalmatians, Finding Neverland, The World is Not Enough, Bridget Jones's Diary* or its sequel, and any of the *Harry Potter* movies, all of which have scenes set in identifiable areas of London.

A good resource for kids ages 3 and up is *The Usborne London Sticker Book,* which has more than 100 color stickers of London sights to peel off and stick down by area, from a double-decker bus to London Bridge, plus a simple map. The same company produces the minipaperback *Book of London,* a children's sightseeing guide with lots of photos, a map, and more than 100 recommended websites. It's suitable for kids about 6 and up.

Another good activity book, this time for those about 7 and up, is *Pop-Up London* (Tarquin), with six main London scenes to create, including St. Paul's Cathedral and the Tower of London, plus

smaller pop-ups. Children 4 and over will enjoy the classic *This is London* by M. Sasek (Universe), a beautifully illustrated tour of London taking in sites as varied as the ravens at the Tower of London and the Billingsgate fishmarket. It was written in 1959 but the recent reprint includes updated London facts.

Young girls might enjoy *Katie in London* (Orchard), which describes how the eponymous heroine and her cousin are taken on a tour of London by a talking stone lion from Trafalgar Square. We meet her again in *Katie and the Dinosaurs,* when she visits the Natural History Museum and befriends a little dinosaur who can't find his way home. In a similar but decidedly more French vein, *Madeline in London* (Picture Puffin) tells of the madcap adventures of a Paris schoolgirl and her classmates in London. By the same publisher, *The Sandal* is the delightful tale of a little girl who leaves her shoe in the British Museum after seeing one that belonged to a Roman child.

Boys might prefer *Adam Sharp 02: London Calling* (Golden Books), in which an 8-year-old supersleuth tries to find out who stole Big Ben. In *The Runaway Ravens of the Royal Tower* (Red Fox), it's the famous birds from the Tower of London that have gone missing, together with a brave young traveler who tried to find them. The reader's job is to find them all via cryptic clues and rhymes.

Some well-known fictional Londoners include *Paddington Bear,* by Michael Bonds (Picture Lions); this is the charming tale of a stowaway Peruvian bear taken in by a couple who find him at Paddington Station. His adventures continue in *Paddington at the Palace,* where he is taken to see the Changing of the Guard. Another visitor to the royal household is Winnie the Pooh, in A. A. Milne's verse collection *When We Were Very Young* (Methuen), which includes the famous ditty, "They're changing guard at Buckingham Palace." Farther south of the palace, Wimbledon Common provides the setting for Elizabeth Beresford's *The Wombles* (Puffin) and its strange creatures.

For older readers, Peter Pan, the little boy who wouldn't grow up, appears as a baby in *Peter Pan in Kensington Gardens* and flies over the rooftops of Bloomsbury in the better-known *Peter Pan and Wendy.* You can get both in one volume (Penguin or Oxford World's Classics).

Also for older kids, *Tales from Shakespeare* (Orion) is an illustrated introduction to works by the Bard. Mid-teens with good reading skills might like to dip into Sir Arthur Conan Doyle's famous *The Adventures of Sherlock Holmes* (Penguin) or even some of Charles Dickens's masterful evocations of Victorian London, including *Oliver Twist, David Copperfield,* and *Great Expectations* (Penguin).

For history, try *The Story of London: From Roman River to Capital City* (A&C Black), featuring the people and events that have shaped the city, with cutaway drawings and buildings, cartoons, and quizzes. The same publisher produces the kid-oriented *Royal London. Britannia: 100 Great Stories from British History* (Orion), which recounts lots of fascinating London lore, such as the story of the princes in the Tower.

Dick Whittington (Ladybird) tells the fairy tale based on the real-life 14th-century Lord Mayor of London, while *The Little Queen* (Hodder) is a beautifully illustrated biography of Queen Victoria for young children. A great historical audiobook for ages 10 and up is *The Fairytales of London Town* (Hodder), with stories, poems, and fairy tales both classic and modern.

Lastly, for arts-mad older kids, *Looking at Pictures* (A&C Black) is an introduction to art for young people, told through the National Gallery's collection.

3

Getting to Know London

When choosing a site for the British Airways London Eye, an observation wheel built to herald the new millennium, planners decreed the center of London to be Jubilee Gardens on the South Bank. But while it's true that the southern bank of the Thames has become the city's cultural heart over the last few years, in many ways London life turns its back on its river. Practically speaking, Trafalgar Square is the city's hub—it's to the statue of Charles I here that British mileposts measure distances to London, and the piazza, now partly pedestrianized, has become the venue for all kinds of cultural celebrations, as well as being home to the National Gallery, storehouse for many of the country's most precious artworks.

Dozens of communities radiate out from Trafalgar Square; each has its own personality, and they are often described as "villages." In fact, if you feel daunted by London's vastness and the almost preposterous choices of things to do, it's a good idea to pick a neighborhood or two and explore them in greater depth, rather than try to cover everything. Marylebone, Little Venice, and Hampstead are particularly great areas for families, so you might want to use these as starting points.

This chapter provides you with a brief orientation to the city's neighborhoods and tells you how to get around London by public transport or on foot. In addition, the "Fast Facts" section helps you find everything for traveling families, from babysitters to late-night pharmacies to medical support.

1 Orientation

VISITOR INFORMATION

The **London Tourist Board** (© 08701/566366; 24-hr. recorded info 0906/133-7799; www.visitlondon.com) runs the walk-in **Britain & London Visitor Centre** at 1 Lower Regent St., SW1 (Tube: Piccadilly Circus), which has booking services for hotels, trains, major attractions, and theater tickets, plus a Transport Desk for Tubes and buses within the city. It also has a "mini-money" book with commission-free money changing, it can deal with VAT refunds, and it boasts a shop selling books, souvenirs, and public Internet access. The Visitors Center is open Monday 9:30am to 6:30pm, Tuesday to Friday 9am to 6:30pm, and Saturday and Sunday 10am to 4pm (June–Sept Sat 10am–5pm). There are additional Tourist Information centers at St. Paul's in the City, at Greenwich, and within the Vinopolis wine attraction on the South Bank, plus there's a small kiosk at Waterloo Station.

PUBLICATIONS

The monthly *Junior* magazine (£3.10/$5.90), sold at larger newsagents, has an excellent "Junior London" section, with children's events and shop listings, close-ups of specific attractions, and features on London areas. *Time Out* magazine (£2.50/$4.75), containing comprehensive listings, comes out every Tuesday and is available at all newsstands and newsagents. As well as coverage of exhibitions, movies, sports events, theater arts, restaurants, and more, it has a "Kids' London" section in its "Around Town" pages.

On a smaller scale, the London edition of *The Guardian* newspaper on Saturday (£1.20/$2.30) comes with a free local listings supplement, **The Guide**. **Where London** is a monthly magazine of listings available in expensive hotel rooms (see www. wheremagazine.com for advance copies or subscriptions).

CITY LAYOUT
AN OVERVIEW OF LONDON

Central London is roughly bounded by Park Lane to the west, Marylebone Road/Euston Road to the north, Gray's Inn Road to the east, and Victoria Street to the south. When suburbanites talk about going "up west," they mean the **West End,** another hazy concept which, although roughly synonymous with "Central London," implies that they have in mind Oxford Street shopping, Soho nightlife, Chinatown's restaurants, the theaters of Covent Garden and the Strand, the cinemas of Leicester Square, or the hotels of Mayfair. Indeed, given that most hotels, restaurants, and major attractions are in this area, it's probably where you'll spend most of your time. On the other hand, many families choose to live outside the center because of high property prices and lack of space, so bear in mind that you'll find a great deal of kids' facilities and community activities in some of the "villages" outside the center.

West of the Center, the upscale neighborhoods of Belgravia, Knightsbridge, and South Kensington have some major stores and attractions, which have brought in their wake a good choice of hotels and eateries. Chelsea, to the south of here, is a family magnet, particularly along the King's Road. Earl's Court is more down at the heel but is fertile hunting ground for budget accommodations, as are Paddington and Bayswater to the north of Hyde Park. Neighboring Maida Vale, Notting Hill, and Holland Park are popular areas with London's wealthier families and hence have good amenities for visitors with kids.

South of the Thames, the South Bank and the riverbank area—stretching east as far as Tower Bridge—is subject to ongoing regeneration and is currently one of the city's cultural hot spots. Hotels and restaurants are burgeoning here, but the rest of south London is patchy, with truly deprived areas as well as real gems worth traveling out of the center for. Back across the river from the South Bank, **the City** with a capital "C" is one of the world's great financial centers, but it's not all glass skyscrapers and sharp suits—this is where London began (it's the original square mile that the Romans called *Londinium*) and it retains much of its historical, architectural, and social interest. Bordering it to the north, Clerkenwell is one of London's most fashionable and vibrant areas, and a surefire hit with teens.

To the east of the City, the sprawling **East End** is another area that, though largely deprived, has a great deal of character and many sights that bear witness to its fascinating history. The business-dominated area of the regenerated Docklands has some surprisingly kid-friendly attractions, restaurants, and accommodations to rival those of the West End.

North London properly begins at Islington, a family area full of great stores and restaurants. Further afield are more bases for young families, including Stoke Newington, and green and lovely Hampstead and Highgate. A little south toward the center,

Primrose Hill is probably London's hippest area, where movie stars and musicians bring up their broods.

FINDING YOUR WAY AROUND

It's not easy finding an address in London, as the city's streets—both names and house numbers—follow no pattern whatsoever. London is checkered with squares, mews, closes, and terraces that jut into, cross, overlap, or otherwise interrupt whatever street you're trying to follow. And house numbers run in odds and evens, clockwise and counterclockwise, when they exist at all—many establishments don't have numbers, though the building right next door does. If you have trouble finding a place, ask someone.

Throughout this book, street addresses are followed by their postal areas, such as SW1 and EC1. The original post office was at St. Martin-le-Grand in the City, so the postal districts are related to where they lie geographically from there. Victoria is SW1, since it's the first area southwest of St. Martin-le-Grand; Liverpool Street is east central of St. Martin-le-Grand, so its postal area is EC1.

If you plan to explore in any depth, you'll need the *London A to Z,* an indispensable map book with a street index, which most Londoners carry around with them. It's available at bookstores and newsstands in various sizes and prices, depending on the exact areas it covers.

LONDON'S NEIGHBORHOODS IN BRIEF

Central London Neighborhoods

Marylebone, Regent's Park & Fitzrovia Marylebone is a fashionable district extending north from Oxford Street to Regent's Park, and west from the largely Middle Eastern Edgware Road to stately Portland Place. Though it's a largely residential area popular with well-off young families as well as poodle-loving old ladies, you're almost certain to come here to visit **Madame Tussaud's** waxworks and the adjoining Planetarium. Its hub is **Marylebone High Street,** colonized over the past few years by an unbeatable selection of kid-friendly stores and eateries, and home to a great Sunday farmers' market. This leads south past the impressive **Wallace Collection** to indispensable department stores such as **Selfridges** and **John Lewis.** Marylebone is a prime area for central accommodations to suit all pockets, from five-star hotels to town-house B&Bs.

At Marylebone's northern extreme lies lovely **Regent's Park,** home to an open-air theater, the London Zoo, and more. To its east, **Fitzrovia,** once a magnet for literary bohemians, was unsuccessfully renamed "Noho" ("north of Soho") a few years back. Though the name did not take, Fitzrovia does resemble a smaller, more laid-back version of Soho with its terraced restaurants, cafes, and bars, many around **Charlotte Street.**

Bloomsbury & Holborn Bloomsbury, bounded roughly by Euston Road to the north, Tottenham Court Road to the west, Gray's Inn Road to the east, and High Holborn to the south, is best known as the erstwhile home of "the Bloomsbury Set" of writers and artists, which included Virginia Woolf and her sister Vanessa Bell. It's still a liberal-thinking, academic area where you'll find the **University of London** and other colleges, many **bookstores,** and the **British Museum,** a repository of treasures from around the globe. The area is not all hard work

Central London

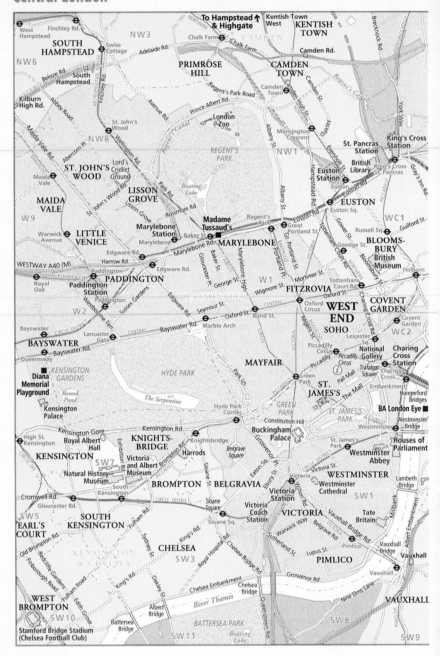

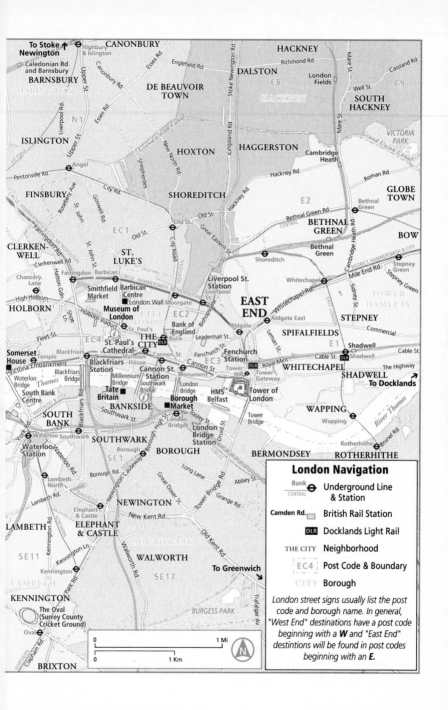

A Right Royal River

Thirty million years ago, before Britain was an island, the Thames was a mere tributary of the Rhine. By A.D. 50 it had changed course and so gave Britain its capital, after the invading Romans established *Londinium* as a port at the highest point of the tide. (It now reaches further inland due to rising sea levels and the fact that Britain is tilting—the Environment Agency says the east coast of Britain is sinking into the sea at a rate of 15cm every century.)

The Romans consolidated the river as an international port (trade with the Continent had started in the Bronze Age), constructing mills, wharves, and bridges. London Bridge was the first crossing, lined with houses and shops; it's been replaced several times—most recently in the 1960s when the previous one was taken apart and shipped to Lake Havasu, Arizona. There are now 14 bridges in central London, the most recent being the Golden Jubilee footbridges built in 2002.

About 100km (60 miles) from the sea, the Thames becomes tidal, flowing "the wrong way" towards its source twice a day as the sea pushes up the estuary. As the tide falls, the foreshore (riverbed) is revealed, and in the mud and shingle you can discover fascinating clues to London's past, including clay tobacco pipes and pottery fragments (see p. 190 for organized "beach-combing" walks).

The Thames was most splendid under the Tudors and Stuarts, when the river-loving monarchs lived in lovely waterside palaces at Hampton Court, Kew, Richmond, Whitehall, and Greenwich, using the waters as a "royal highway." Fittingly, the Thames saw many monarchs' final journeys in the

for the kids, though: **Coram's Fields** is one of the city's best playgrounds, and the neighboring **Foundling Museum** an engrossing testament to a tragic past. This is also one of your best bets for moderately priced hotels and B&Bs in the center, though for good eating options you'll need to stroll a short distance across to Fitzrovia, or down to Soho or Covent Garden.

Holborn (pronounced *Ho*-burn), south of Bloomsbury and east of Covent Garden, lacks major attractions, though **Sir John Soane's Museum** is a favorite among many Londoners and visitors. The history-laden district remains charmingly Dickensian in spirit—the Victorian

author featured the two Inns of Court (where law students perform their apprenticeships and barristers' chambers are located) in some of his novels. Though not traditionally a hotel area, it does have a couple of reasonably priced options that are within walking distance of the heart of the action.

Covent Garden & the Strand
Covent Garden, based around a glorious restored flower, fruit, and vegetable market building, is touristy in parts, trendy in others, but generally great fun. As well as must-see attractions such as **London's Transport Museum, Theatre Museum,** and **Somerset House,** it's the starting point for London's **Theatreland** which, as well as

form of stately funeral processions, including that of Elizabeth I in 1605, and that of Henry VIII in 1547. It's said that during the overnight stop at Syon House (p. 187), his coffin came apart and dogs licked his remains.

Today you can travel the same waters, albeit less regally, on passenger ferries or tourist vessels from Westminster—upriver to Hampton Court via Richmond and Kew, or downriver to the glittering stainless-steel Thames Barrier via Greenwich (p. 155). Alternatively, you can walk all or part of the Thames Path from the river's source at Thames Head down to the Thames Barrier, or wander along the South Bank with its riverside attractions, restaurants, pubs, and shopping malls. (Note that a walk along the Embankment on the other side can be frustrating for little kids because of its high walls.)

Whichever way you travel, wonder at the fact that this river was once so full of fish that London's apprentices became tired of being fed salmon. (That said, a campaign in the 1960s made this one of the world's cleanest urban rivers, supporting more than 115 fish species and many invertebrates, as well as birds such as herons and cormorants.) Picture in your mind's eye the Lord Mayor's processions that took place from the 15th century to the middle of the 19th, the barges covered with gold leaf, some rowed with silver oars. In the 17th and 18th centuries, Frost Fairs were held on the river during winter freezes, complete with fairground amusements and stalls, performing animals, and ox roasts. Today, The Mayor's Thames Festival (p. 22) is a spectacular family-oriented celebration of the river hosting a variety of annual regattas, including the famous Oxford and Cambridge Boat Race (p. 18).

taking up much of **the Strand,** extends along Shaftesbury Avenue as far as Piccadilly Circus. There are also some first-class hotels on the Strand or just off it, and a vast choice of restaurants in the district in general (including a fair number of tourist traps).

Trafalgar Square   The Strand leads to London's biggest piazza, which lacks outdoor cafe terraces at which to linger but does impress you, with its magnificent lion sculptures (which older kids love clambering on), its soaring 56m (185-ft.) column from which Admiral Nelson gazes down, its fountains, and the Fourth Plinth (p. 46). Though the tradition of pigeon feeding in the square has thankfully been banned,

visitors still flock here to get a sense of just *being* in London, as well as to visit the precious artworks of the mighty **National Gallery,** or get creative in the **London Brass Rubbing Centre.** Trafalgar Square has long been a focal point for New Year's revelry, and now hosts celebrations of the city's ethnic diversity, too. Not surprisingly, it's a little too noisy to make it a great place to stay with kids.

Soho & Chinatown   The same goes for this cosmopolitan nightclubber's paradise, bordered by Regent Street to the west, Oxford Street to the north, Charing Cross Road to the east, and Shaftesbury Avenue to the south. There aren't many hotels, anyway, and those that do exist tend to cater for a hedonistic media clientele. Though much of its notorious sex industry has been edged out by fashionable restaurants and boutiques, Soho is also the heart of London's expanding gay scene and may be a little too lively for younger kids. Teens, though, will love Carnaby Street, a key locale universe in the Swinging '60s that became a tourist trap but is newly hip again, with exciting fashion stores. Hamleys, the world-famous toy store, is on the Soho side of Regent Street.

Between Shaftesbury Avenue and Leicester Square is London's **Chinatown,** centered on Gerrard Street. It's small but authentic, and packed with good restaurants.

Piccadilly Circus & Leicester Square Piccadilly Circus, with its giant neon billboard and its statue of Eros, is a postcard cliché if ever I saw one—it's a place where tourists seem to flock when they're not sure what else to do. Largely soulless in spite of some impressive architecture, it draws idle youth with its giant Funland arcade and massive themed restaurants. Nearly as tawdry, but free of cars, buses, and taxis and their concomitant fumes, is **Leicester Square,** which is largely taken up by multiscreen cinemas set in old entertainment palaces, plus various nightclubs.

Hotels here are overpriced and noisy—avoid them like the Plague.

St. James's & Mayfair Though it adjoins the hellish Piccadilly Circus, St. James's, which basks in its royal associations (it's home to **Buckingham Palace** and **Clarence House,** for instance, the official residences of the Queen and her eldest son respectively), has a very "gentlemen's club" feel, with its luxurious shops selling suits and its old-fashioned barber's shops. It's not child-unfriendly, though: The world-renowned department store **Fortnum & Mason** has a good food hall, restaurant, and children's section. No. 22 Jermyn Street is an outstanding, if expensive, area hotel (plus there's a good moderate option, the Sanctuary House Hotel).

North of St. James's, bounded by Piccadilly, Park Lane, Oxford Street, and Regent Street, **Mayfair** is renowned for its hotels—the grandest in London—and its designer clothes shops, art galleries, and glitzy auction houses. Many of them lie along New and Old Bond streets. Attractions tend to be low key—**Handel House Museum** is an example. West towards Park Lane, **Shepherd Market** is an unexpected and rather quaint little village of inns, restaurants, cafes, small shops, and galleries. A few minutes'

The Fourth Plinth

It's confused people for years—that empty plinth at the northwest corner of Trafalgar Square. Why is there no statue on it? The fact is, the plinth, built in 1841, was intended to host an equestrian statue, but funds ran out and for more than a century and a half it was unused. Now, however, it's going to display temporary works by contemporary artists (each for 12–18 months). Keep your eyes open for exciting modern sculptures such as Thomas Shütte's yellow, red, and blue perspex Hotel for the Birds, from summer 2006. Let's hope the pigeons find the accommodations to their taste.

walk away, **Grosvenor Square** (pronounced *Grov*-nor) is nicknamed "Little America" because it's home to the American Embassy, statues of Roosevelt and Eisenhower, and a memorial garden to those who died in the 9/11 terrorist attacks.

West London

South Kensington There's no avoiding this area south of Kensington Gardens if you're with kids—it houses three major museums, all of them extremely child-friendly (the **Natural History Museum, Science Museum,** and **Victoria and Albert Museum**). **Kensington Gardens** to the north also has London's very best play park, the **Diana Memorial Playground. Hyde Park,** with its wonderful boating lake, is a few minutes' walk away. To the west, shoppers come out in full force on **Kensington High Street,** a great spot for eating *en famille.* You're likely to spend a lot of time here, so you might want to make it your base; if so, the area offers moderately priced hotels, B&Bs, and self-catering apartments, plus a youth hostel.

Knightsbridge, Brompton & Belgravia Neighboring Knightsbridge is a top residential, hotel, and shopping district south of Hyde Park. Its best-known attraction is **Harrods,** "the Notre Dame of department stores"; don't miss its extravagant Toy Kingdom. Chi-chi kids' clothing boutiques and other luxury stores abound in Knightsbridge and adjoining Brompton and Belgravia, as do deluxe hotels and apartments.

Westminster, Victoria & Pimlico Westminster, a triangular area south of Buckingham Palace and St. James's Park, bordered by the Thames to the east, has been the seat of the British government since Edward the Confessor. As well as visiting grand historical landmarks such as **Houses of Parliament, Big Ben,** and **Westminster Abbey,** you can inspect **Churchill's Cabinet War Rooms** and walk down **Downing Street** to see **no. 10,** home to Britain's prime minister.

If you're looking for accommodations, **Victoria** just to the south of Westminster has lots of moderately priced and cheap hotels and B&Bs because of the train station, though the area can be noisy. (Be aware, too, that many of the hotels along Belgrave Road are occupied by welfare recipients.) Adjacent **Pimlico,** home to the wonderful **Tate Britain,** is a little less frenetic, and the area as a whole is convenient for day trips out to Windsor and Legoland.

Chelsea This stylish Thames-side district stretching west of Pimlico has always been a favorite of writers and artists, including Oscar Wilde (who was arrested here) and Henry James; more recent residents have included Mick Jagger, Margaret Thatcher, and a host of "Sloane Rangers" (the 1980s name for posh local gals, derived from Sloane Sq.). **King's Road,** which was at the forefront of fashion both in the Swinging '60s (Mary Quant launched the miniskirt here) and at the birth of punk, is now baby central—some days you can hardly move for Bugaboo Frogs. On the upside, kids' boutiques, toy stores, and family-oriented restaurants are more densely packed here than anywhere else in London. The few hotels tend to be upmarket, but be warned that transport is an issue (there's a dearth of Tube stops west of Sloane Sq.).

West Brompton & Earl's Court North of Chelsea, things shift progressively downmarket as you move through **West Brompton,** focused around flower-filled Brompton Cemetery, and into **Earl's Court,** which attracts a youthful crowd (often gay) to its pubs, wine bars, and coffeehouses. You'll only want to stray here if you're looking for B&Bs and budget hotels within a 15-minute Tube ride of Piccadilly.

Bayswater, Paddington, Little Venice & Maida Vale   **Bayswater** and **Paddington,** to the north of Kensington Gardens and Hyde Park, are rather shabby "in between" areas with lots of B&Bs that attract budget travelers. That said, there are some excellent accommodation choices with easy transport links to the West End, and Paddington is currently seeing a lot of regeneration, especially around the "basin" area of canals behind the train station. **Hyde Park** is also handily nearby.

The new canal walkways connect Paddington to delightful **Little Venice** with its floating cafes on boats, its puppet barge, and its family-friendly pubs and restaurant. Little Venice segues into villagey **Maida Vale,** a great family base with surprisingly easy transport links into central London.

Notting Hill   West of Bayswater, Notting Hill has long been popular with wealthy families for its elegant houses set on quiet, leafy streets. Its restaurants, clubs, and bars are some of the trendiest in town. **Portobello Road** is the setting of a famous, funky, street market, and plenty of hip kids' boutiques dot the area. Truly kid-friendly hotel options are nonexistent, however.

Holland Park, Shepherd's Bush & Further West   **Holland Park** immediately west of Notting Hill is an even more exclusive residential neighborhood, popular with families for its lovely eponymous park. Adjoining it, once-scruffy **Shepherd's Bush** is a rapidly gentrifying area, attracting hip new restaurants, cafes, and hotels that appeal to local broods and media types from nearby **BBC Television Studios,** which you can tour.

Shepherd's Bush is the gateway to the western outer reaches of London, worth venturing out to in order to enjoy historical landmarks such as **Hampton Court Palace, Syon House,** and **Osterley House,** as well as green areas such as **Bushy Park** and **Brent Lodge Park.**

South of the River

The South Bank to Rotherhithe Across Waterloo Bridge from the Strand, this area is home to the **South Bank Arts Centre,** the largest arts center in western Europe. Still undergoing large-scale regeneration, it's a vibrant area where you'll always find something going on, whether it's world-class concerts and shows, ad hoc riverside entertainment, or free foyer events and exhibitions. It's not all art, either. Thrills and kid-oriented attractions, from the **BA London Eye** to the **London Aquarium,** mean it has something for the entire family.

The South Bank turns into the exciting **Bankside** area, home to the wonderful **Tate Modern** and numerous other attractions well worth exploring, from the **HMS *Belfast*** to a reconstruction of **Shakespeare's Globe** theater. The hotel scene is blossoming in these districts, and you'll find some interesting family-friendly options offering better rates than more central venues, as well as good places to eat.

Adjoining Bankside, **Borough** and **Bermondsey** are historically rich and colorful areas that, although somewhat off the beaten track, boast ancient inns and markets, including wonderful **Borough Market;** intriguing old wharves and spice warehouses; and small-scale, offbeat attractions like the **Fashion & Textile Museum** and the

Old Operating Theatre, Museum, and Herb Garret.

Rotherhithe to the east of here is a little-known and -explored area that nevertheless boasts the city's most child-friendly youth hostel, a historic pub, and great venues for kids, including **Southwark Park,** an organic city farm; and **Brunel Engine House & Tunnel Exhibition.**

The remainder of south London is a mosaic of quite deprived (but often culturally rich) districts such as **Brixton,** and family enclaves such as **Clapham** and **Balham.** If you don't mind being a 30-minute Tube ride from the West End, you can find some quirky B&Bs and self-catering options here.

One place definitely worth traveling out for in its own right is **Greenwich** to the southeast. Though its palace, Henry VIII's favorite, is long gone, visitors still come for nautical attractions such as the 1869 sea clipper, *Cutty Sark,* and the **National Maritime Museum,** as well as its lovely park, its historical **Royal Observatory** (home to Greenwich Mean Time or GMT, the basis of standard time throughout the world), and its charming market. From here it's not far to spellbinding **Eltham Palace** or the unusual attractions of **Woolwich**—the **Old Station Museum, Royal Artillery Museum,** and stunning **Thames Barrier.**

Other southern venues worth a train ride out of the center include **Dulwich Picture Gallery, Horniman Museum, Crystal Palace Park** with its dinosaur park and the National Sports Centre, and **Croydon Airport Visitor Centre.**

Over to the southwest, **Battersea** is home to a great park complete with children's zoo, plus a flourishing eating scene clustered around Battersea Rise, about 10 minutes from Battersea Park. Just to the west are **Wimbledon,**

Barnes, Richmond, Kew, and **Twickenham,** famous primarily for their green open spaces—**Wimbledon Common, WWT Wetland Centre, Richmond Park,** and **Royal Botanic Gardens.** Wimbledon is also known for its tennis; if you're not here for those glorious 2 weeks in summer, **Wimbledon Lawn Tennis Museum** will have to suffice.

The City & Around

The City The City was where the Roman conquerors first settled, and despite the Great Fire of 1666, the bombs of 1940, and the IRA bombs of the 1990s, it retains some of its medieval character amidst the modern tower blocks. Landmarks include Sir Christopher Wren's masterpiece, **St. Paul's Cathedral,** along with the **Monument to the Great Fire,** and the **Tower of London,** shrouded in legend and gore. The City's 2,000 years of history unfold at the **Museum of London,** while the **Barbican Centre** is a hotbed of culture for all ages.

You'll most likely venture here during the day, although there are some unique places to stay. Be warned, though, that things can go deathly quiet on weekends—and that includes restaurants and cafes. Trendy but atmospheric **Smithfield Market** (into which trucks still rumble through the night, unloading beef carcasses), on the border of the City and Clerkenwell, is your best bet, both for sleeping and dining. **Clerkenwell** itself, home to London's oldest church, St. Bartholomew-the-Great, has been reinvented by the moneyed and fashionable in the last few years, and hot restaurants, clubs, and art galleries continue to spring up.

The East End One of London's poorest regions, the East End extends east from the City walls, encompassing **Spitalfields, Whitechapel, Bethnal Green,** and other districts. That doesn't mean it's not worth visiting—you'll find, among other attractions, the wonderful **National Museum of Childhood** at Bethnal Green, the **Discover** interactive play center, the eclectic **Spitalfields Market,** the explosive **Royal Gunpowder Mills,** good parks, the wild space of **Epping Forest,** and lots of excellent ethnic cuisine (the area has seen successive waves of immigration).

There's a dearth of hotels here, though, except in the **Docklands** district, a business area in which old Thameside warehouses have been converted into chic lofts, entertainment complexes, shops, restaurants, and museums, including the fascinating **Museum in Docklands.** Though it's only a 20-minute ferry ride from Westminster Pier, you may choose to splash out on a first-class hotel here, and enjoy the quiet and first-rate river views.

North London

Islington   Families move here for the spacious houses set on tranquil squares, and though there are few "sights" as such, there are good parks, plus an unbeatable range of offbeat shops and kid-friendly pubs, cafes, and restaurants. It also has well-priced accommodations from where it's no great schlep to the center.

Hampstead   This desirable residential district (Sigmund Freud and D. H. Lawrence lived here, and John Le Carré still does) is a popular day-trip destination among Londoners, both for its splendid **heath** and lovely **Kenwood House,** and its pleasant high street full of chic shops and appealing restaurants, pubs, and tearooms. Though it has very few hotels, there are a couple of homely guesthouse options and a beautifully located youth hostel. As a whole, the area is just 20 minutes by Tube from Piccadilly Circus.

Highgate   This is another choice residential area, particularly on or near **Pond Square** and along High Street. Moody **Highgate Cemetery,** London's most famous burial ground and the final resting place of Karl Marx and other famous figures, is best experienced without children. However, **Waterlow Park,** along with its centerpiece **Lauderdale House,** is one of London's most child-friendly gems. The wild expanses of Highgate Wood are not far away.

The Best of the Rest   Other family enclaves you might like to explore are hippyish **Stoke Newington,** with a good park, nature reserve in an atmospheric old cemetery, and high street filled with organic stores, cafes, and secondhand bookshops. Ultra-hip **Primrose Hill** is home to movie stars, supermodels, and their brats. At sedate **St. John's Wood,** you can enjoy a stately game of cricket on a long summer's day at the world-famous **Lord's.**

2 Getting Around

BY PUBLIC TRANSPORTATION

The London Underground and the city's buses operate on the same system of six fare zones. The fare zones radiate in rings from central zone 1, which is where most visitors spend the majority of their time. Zone 1 covers the area from Liverpool Street in the east to Notting Hill in the west, and from Waterloo in the south to Baker Street, Euston, and King's Cross in the north. To travel beyond zone 1, you need a multi-zone ticket. Note that all single one-way, round-trip, and 1-day pass tickets are valid only on the day of purchase.

Tube, bus, river, and road maps are usually available at all Underground stations, or you can download them from the excellent **Transport for London (TfL)** website:

Travelcard Prices

At press time, the following prices were in effect for up to 7 days. Prices traditionally increase in February.

One-Day Travelcards (no photo card needed)

Zones 1–2, peak times: £6 ($11) adults, £3 ($5.70) kids. Off peak: £4.70 ($8.90) adults, with up to four kids paying £1 ($1.90) each.

Zones 1–3, peak times: £7 ($13) adults, 3.50 ($6.70) kids. No off-peak rates available.

Zones 1–4, peak times: £8 ($15) adults, £4 ($7.60) kids. Off peak: £5.20 ($9.90) adults, with up to four kids paying £1 ($1.90) each.

Zones 1–5, peak times: £10 ($19) adults, £5 ($9.50) kids. No off-peak rates available.

Zones 1–6, peak times: £12 ($23) adults, £6 ($11) kids. Off peak: £6 ($11) adults, £2 ($3.80) kids.

Zones 2–6, peak times: £7 ($13) adults, 3.50 ($6.70) kids. Off peak: £4 ($7.60) adults, with up to four kids paying £1 ($1.90) each.

Family Travelcard, zones 1–2 £3.10 ($5.90), zones 1–4 £3.40 ($6.50), zones 1–6 £4 ($7.60), zones 2–6 £2.60 ($4.90), with kids 5 to 15 paying an extra £0.80 ($1.50), except on weekends and public holidays. (Kids 14 and 15 need an 11×15 photo card to get this price.)

Three-Day Travelcards

Kids 14 and 15 need an 11×15 photo card

Zones 1–2, peak times: £15 ($29) adults, £7.50 ($14) kids. No off-peak rates available.

Zones 1–6, peak times: £36 ($68) adults, £18 ($34) kids. Off peak: £18 ($34) adults, £6 ($11) kids.

Seven-Day Travelcards

Adults need photo cards; kids 5 to 15 need 5×10 or 11×15 photo card.

Zone 1, adults £19 ($35), kids £7.30 ($14).

Zones 1–2, adults £21 ($40), kids £8.60 ($16).

Zones 1–4, adults £30 ($58), kids £14 ($27).

Zones 1–5, adults £36 ($69), kids £16 ($30).

Zones 1–6, adults £40 ($75), kids £17 ($33)

www.tfl.gov.uk/tfl. The website's free Journeyplanner service can help you work out your most direct route. **TfL Information Centers** offering maps, advice, and entry tickets to the Tower of London and Madame Tussaud's can be found at major Tube stations (Piccadilly Circus; Liverpool St.; Heathrow's Terminals 1, 2, and 3; and Heathrow Terminal 4); national rail stations (Euston and Victoria); and bus and coach stations (Victoria and West Croydon; the latter is closed on weekends). Most are open from at least 9am to 5pm. A 24-hour public-transportation information service is also available at © **020/7222-1234.**

TRAVEL DISCOUNTS   If you plan to use public transport a lot, **Travelcards** offer unlimited use of buses; Underground, including the Docklands Light Railway) trains

(DLR; p. 51) except the Heathrow Express; and trams in Greater London. The card can be for a day, 3 days, a week, a month, or a year, and it offers a third off scheduled riverboat service tickets as well. You can get peak and off-peak versions on 1- and 3-day cards; the latter can be used after 9:30am Monday to Friday, and all day weekends and public holidays. They're available from Tube stations, TfL Information Centers, Oyster Ticket Stops, and train stations. For all but 1-day and weekend cards, you need a passport-size photo. You can also get **bus passes.** The **Oyster Card** is a travel smart-card that can store your Travelcard, bus pass, or pre-pay tickets (which cost less than a normal single fare); you can renew any of these online or by phone (📞 **0870/ 849-9999;** www.oystercard.com), or at the places you can buy Travelcards. You can also get carnets (both adults' and kids') of 10 Tube tickets and six bus tickets that cost less than buying individual single fares. Tube stations and TfL Information Centers accept American Express, Diners Club, MasterCard, and Visa. For the **London Pass,** which includes unlimited free transport in addition to access to more than 70 London attractions, see p. 139.

Children under 5 travel free on the Tube, trams, and buses if accompanied by a ticket holder and when not occupying a seat that could be used by a fare-paying passenger. (On buses, no more than two under-5s can travel free with a fare-paying passenger.) On buses alone, travel is free for under-11s. For 11- to 15-year-olds; fares are 40p (76¢); 14- and 15-year-olds need an 11×15 photo card, for which you have to present a European ID card or your passport. Sixteen- and 17-year-olds with a relevant photo card can buy weekly, monthly, or annual Travelcards and bus passes at the children's rate (£4/$7.60 for 7 days).

BY TUBE

The Underground, or Tube, decrepit though it is, is the fastest and easiest way to get around, given the state of London's traffic. With kids it can be a nightmare, however—there are very rarely lifts for those with strollers or little children, staff can mysteriously evaporate into thin air when you need assistance, and escalators are often at a standstill, meaning you'll be subjected to long, steep descents by foot as irate commuters barge past you. If you do have a stroller, especially a cumbersome double stroller like mine, the least you can do is give yourself a head start by picking up a Tube map that marks out the 50 or so stations with access for travelers with limited mobility (that is, step-free access from the street and lifts to the platforms). This may help you plan your journey to some degree. Between the peak hours of 7:30 to 9:30am and 4 to 7pm, you are not supposed to bring unfolded strollers into the Underground.

Note: Mayor Livingstone has pledged to spend at least £18 billion on improving the city's transport system in the lead up to the 2012 Olympics, so the Tube should show improvements over the next few years.

Tube stations are clearly marked with a red circle and blue crossbar. The color-coded route map may look complicated but is actually quite user-friendly once you've got the hang of it. You can transfer as many times as you like, as long as you stay in the Underground and have a ticket covering the zones in which you have traveled. Some of the ticket machines take credit cards and/or notes; others take exact change only. You can also pay at the ticket offices, but there are often queues. The flat fare for one trip within zone 1 is £2 ($3.80), £0.60 ($1.15) for kids. Trips from the central zone to other zones range from £2.30 to £3.80 ($4.40–$7.20), but moneysaving options are available (see the "Travelcard Prices" box above).

When you've bought your ticket or pass, slide it into the slot at the automated gate (if you have a stroller, there's a special staffed gate), and pick it up as it comes through on the other side. Hold onto it—it must be presented when you exit the station at your destination or you'll be fined. Tube hours (about 5am–11:30pm) may come as a bit of a shock to those used to later subway hours, but there are proposals to run trains an hour later on Friday and Saturday (starting an hour later in the morning).

BY BUS

The bus system is slightly cheaper than the Underground and gives you better views of the city, though congested streets mean your trip will inevitably be slower. If you have a stroller, it's often easier to get on a bus than to fight your way down to the Tube; specially designated bays in the middle of the bus are for strollers (make sure you put the brake on), but if someone is already aboard with an unfolded stroller, the driver is supposed to ask you to fold yours (more often than not, they don't). The classic Routemaster buses that you can hop on and off without having to arrive at a stop, but on which you have to fold all strollers, are gradually being phased out by single-level "bendy buses" and low-floor double-deckers that are easier to board and have more space to park strollers.

A bus journey on most routes in London costs £1.20 ($2.30) for adults, 40p (75¢) for kids 11 to 15 (14- and 15-year-olds need a photo card), but you can bring this down by using Oyster Pre-Pay (p. 52) or by buying a carnet or a bus pass (1 day, 7 days, 1 month, or 1 year) at Tube stations or from some newsagents. In central London, before boarding at the stop, you have to purchase tickets at the machines (exact change only), although these have been known to swallow cash without coughing up a ticket. If this happens to you, or the machine is out of order, you don't have any option but to climb aboard, tell the driver, and hope he or she believes you.

Transport for London's Travel Information Centers (listed above) and some Tube stations have bus maps, or you can download one from their website. Don't consider taking a night bus with kids; they get horribly crowded and can be rowdy.

BY TAXI

Black cabs are comfortable and well designed, and some of the drivers are true local characters who'd like nothing better than to offer visitors their own, often eccentric, takes on London life. You can hail a taxi in the street (available if the yellow taxi sign on the roof is lit), go to a cab stand (at major rail, Tube, and bus stations), ask your hotel porter to flag you one, or call for one (© **0871/871-8710**), which incurs a £2 ($3.80) surcharge.

Like passengers in all other cars, cab riders are required to wear **seat belts.** (Your driver won't enforce this rule, though by law it's his or her responsibility and the driver risks a fine of £1,000 ($1,900) if you don't buckle up.) The law regarding **child passengers** is the same for cabs as for cars, which is that in the rear, a child under 3 must use an appropriate child restraint *if available,* while anyone 3 and up must wear an adult seat belt if a child restraint is not available. (This rule is enforced even though most kids under 8 aren't tall enough to use standard seat belts safely; if this bothers you, you'll have to carry your own booster seat around with you.) If you are carrying a tiny baby in a car seat, you will be able to strap your baby in as you do in your car; if you have a single stroller, you can push it right into the taxi and put the brake on. (With a double-stroller, you might have to collapse it, get in, and then unfold it again, or hold your baby or toddler on your knee.)

Fares within Greater London depend on the time of day, the distance traveled, and the taxi's speed, and they are displayed on the meter. There is a £2.20 ($4.20) minimum fare. For an average journey lasting 15 to 30 minutes and covering 6.5km (4 miles), expect to pay about £10 to £14 ($19–$27) during weekdays; you'll pay a bit more at night, on weekends, and during holiday seasons. Though there are no longer extra charges for luggage, you'll pay a £1 ($1.90) surcharge if you come from Heathrow into Greater London. It's recommended that you tip 10% to 15% of the fare.

Minicabs are meterless, often unlicensed, cars—you negotiate the fare in advance—so they're cheaper but riskier, resulting in about 10 sexual assaults a month. Always pre-book a car through a licensed operator (call © **020/7222-1234,** or use the search facility on www.tfl.gov.uk); if you are at all unsure, ask to see the operator's or driver's Public Carriage Office license. Additionally, check that the driver knows your name and destination before you get in, sit in the back, and carry a mobile phone.

BY CAR

Driving is a major headache in London: Traffic is hellish and parking is difficult and expensive. If you do arrive by car, park it and forget about it. (Call your hotel ahead of your trip and inquire if it has a garage and what the charges are, or ask for the name and address of a garage nearby.)

BY BICYCLE

I don't recommend cycling with kids in London's heavy traffic. For off-road bicycle tours, see p. 208.

3 Planning Your Outings

If you've got kids, you won't need me to tell you that getting from A to B often requires planning on a military scale. Factoring sightseeing, bathroom breaks, and snack stops into your plans and remaining flexible enough to cope with the unexpected—whether it be blisters or a national strike—is an epic feat. My advice is to make a plan, with a list of sights you intend to see, details of how you will get between them, and suggestions for pit stops, but don't beat yourself up if it doesn't go according to plan.

FINDING A RESTROOM/PUBLIC TOILET

Anyone who's gotten beyond the diaper stage needs to know where the nearest restroom is at all times, though you can help yourself by ensuring that everyone goes before leaving the hotel or apartment, and on the way out of restaurants and museums. Luckily, most attractions, big or small, have added child-friendly facilities these days, whether it's a fold-down diaper-changing board or toilet stalls big enough for more than one family member.

If you're out and about, there are restrooms at parks and rail stations, many automatically sterilized after each use. Some of the latter may require a couple of coins. Many high-street stores and venues, including some branches of Starbucks and Woolworths, refuse to let anyone use their toilets "for insurance reasons." Department stores (p. 190) are an exception (most have several restrooms). Large branches of bookstore chains like Borders and Waterstone's can be useful, although sometimes you'll need to ask a member of staff to unlock the door for you. Otherwise, major hotel lobbies and restaurants will normally take pity on you if your child really is getting to bursting point. McDonald's is a handy standby.

NURSING MOMS & INFANTS

No one will bat an eyelid if you breastfeed in public in London, whether it be in a restaurant or on public transport. (My second son has been fed on buses, riverboats, and Tube trains as we gallivanted around the city for this guide, as well as in parks and playgrounds.) Should modesty prevail, **John Lewis** department store (p. 222) has a special feeding room in its parents' facility.

FAST FACTS: London

Area Codes See "Telephone Tips" on the inside front cover of this book.

Baby Equipment If you're staying with friends or in a budget apartment that can't provide you with baby equipment, contact **Chelsea Baby Hire** (© 020/8789-9673; www.chelseababyhire.com), which has strollers, stair gates, cribs, foldout beds, highchairs (including portable versions), car seats, and more.

Babysitters All expensive and some moderate hotels will arrange a sitter for you; usually this will be from a reputable outside agency rather than one of their staff members. Most of them use the long-established **Childminders** (© 020/7935-2049; www.babysitter.co.uk), who you can also contact directly. They charge £6.80 ($13) per hour during the day and £5.20 to £6.40 ($10–$12) per hour at night, with a 4-hour minimum. You either have to be a member, which costs £49 ($93) per year for evening sitters, £59 ($112) for day and evening sitters; or you must pay a £10 ($19) booking fee each time you use a sitter in a hotel. You must also pay reasonable transportation costs. Temporary nannies can be arranged.

Business Hours The major high street banks are generally open Monday to Friday 9:30am to 3:30pm, though some of the bigger branches stay open until 5:30pm, and a few are open on Saturday morning. Most have 24-hour ATMs outside, though some close for a few hours at night. Restaurants in London tend to stay open all day from late morning on, or earlier if they serve breakfast; fewer and fewer open for set lunch and dinner hours. Stores generally open at 9am or 10am and close at 5:30pm or 6pm, or 7pm or 8pm on Wednesday or Thursday. On Sunday, many shops open for 6 hours (the maximum), from 10am to 4pm or 11am to 5pm. Many malls stay open until at least 8pm, and many supermarkets and superstores stay open from 8am until 10pm or 11pm Monday to Saturday, plus Sunday as above. Many large supermarkets (generally out of the center) are now open 24 hours except Sunday. Some shops open on public holidays, but banks are closed. All shops are closed on Christmas Day (Dec 25), and some shops are closed on New Year's Day (Jan 1).

Climate See "When to Go," in chapter 2.

Currency See "Money," in chapter 2.

Dentists For dental emergencies, call **Eastman Dental Hospital** (© 020/7915-1000; Tube: King's Cross or Chancery Lane).

Doctors Call © **999** in a medical emergency. Some hotels have physicians on call. You can also contact the private **Doctorcall** (© 07000/372255), which charges a £85 ($162) callout fee up to 6pm, £95 ($181) thereafter (extra on public holidays). If you're worried about any aspect of your health or your child's, you can get free advice by calling **NHS Direct** at ℂ 020/0845-4647; they will tell you if you need to see a medical practitioner and provide you with contact details, but you have to pay for the latter unless your country has reciprocal arrangements with the U.K.

Drugstores Every police station has a copy of the names of late-hour chemists (dial 0 and ask the operator for the local police). One of the most central late-opening stores is **Bliss Pharmacy,** 5 & 6 Marble Arch, W1 (ℂ **020/7723-6116;** Tube: Marble Arch), open daily from 9am to midnight. See also **Boots the Chemist,** p. 234.

Electricity The British current is 240 volts, AC, so you'll need a converter or transformer for U.S.-made electrical appliances, as well as an adapter that allows the plug to match British outlets. Some (but not all) hotels supply them for guests. If you've forgotten one, you can buy a transformer/adapter at most branches of **Boots the Chemist** (p. 234).

Embassies & High Commissions See www.fco.gov.uk for the contact details of all embassies and high commissions. The **U.S. Embassy** is at 24 Grosvenor Sq., W1 (ℂ **020/7499-9000;** www.usembassy.org.uk; Tube: Bond St.). The **Canadian High Commission** is also in Grosvenor Square, at MacDonald House no. 1 (ℂ **020/7258-6600;** http://canadaonline.about.org). The **Australian High Commission** is at Australia House, Strand, WC2 (ℂ **020/7379-4334;** www.australia. org.uk; Tube: Charing Cross or Aldwych). The **New Zealand High Commission** is at New Zealand House, 80 Haymarket, SW1 (ℂ **020/7930-8422;** www.nz embassy.com; Tube: Charing Cross or Piccadilly Circus). The **French Embassy** is at 58 Knightsbridge, SW1 (ℂ **020/7073-1000;** www.ambafrance-uk.org; Tube: Knightsbridge). The **German Embassy** is at 23 Belgrave Sq., SW1 (ℂ **020/ 7824-1300;** www.german-embassy.org.uk; Tube: Hyde Park Corner). The **Italian Embassy** is at 14 Three Kings Yard, Davies St., W1 (ℂ **020/7312-2200;** Tube: Bond St). The **Irish Embassy** is at 17 Grosvenor Place, SW1 (ℂ **020/7235-2171;** Tube: Hyde Park Corner).

Emergencies For police, fire, or an ambulance, dial ℂ **999.**

Holidays See "When to Go," in chapter 3.

Hospitals The **University College Hospital,** Cecil Flemming House, Grafton Way, WC1 (ℂ **020/7387-9300;** Tube: Warren St.) is recommended by GPs as having the casualty department to which they would bring their own children in an emergency. Many other London hospitals also have accident and emergency departments.

Legal Aid In every case in which legal aid is required by a foreign national within Britain, the British Tourist Authority advises visitors to contact their embassy.

Mail A 10g airmail letter or a postcard to North America or Australia costs 47p (90¢), with mail generally taking about a week. A 10g airmail letter or a postcard to continental Europe costs 42p (80¢); mail generally takes about 5 days. See "Post Offices," below, for locations.

Maps See "Finding Your Way Around," under "Orientation," earlier in this chapter.

Money & Credit Cards See also "Money," in chapter 2. The main American Express office is at 30–31 Haymarket, SW1 (© 020/7484-9600; Tube: Piccadilly Circus). Full services are available Monday to Saturday from 9am to 6pm. On Sunday from 10am to 5pm, only the foreign-exchange bureau is open.

For **lost or stolen credit cards,** file a report at the nearest police station; then call the relevant company. For **Amex,** call © 01273/696933; for **Visa,** call your issuing bank or © 0800/891725; for **MasterCard** call © 0800/964767; for **Diners Club** call © 08700/110-0011.

If you need emergency cash over the weekend when banks and American Express offices are closed, you can have money wired to you via **Western Union** (© 0800/833833; www.westernunion.com).

Newspapers & Magazines The serious British dailies are *The Guardian, The Independent, The Times,* and *The Daily Telegraph;* all have online versions. On Sunday, the Guardian's sibling, *The Observer,* is strong on culture. *Metro* is a free daily London newspaper available at Tube stations, with news, features, reviews, and events; it's published by the same group as the *Evening Standard,* another local that is sold at all newsagents, at newsstands, and from vendors posted near Tube stations and the like. For events listings, the weekly *Time Out* magazine (published each Tues) is unrivalled.

Copies of the *International Herald Tribune, USA Today, Le Monde, Die Tageszeitung,* and most major international newspapers and magazines, are sold at many newsagents and newsstands, especially around the main transport terminals and tourist centers.

Police In an emergency, dial © 999 (free).

Post Offices To find a post office close to you, call © 08457/223344 and give them your postal code (p. 13); or check out www.postoffice.co.uk. London's main post office is just off Trafalgar Square at 24–28 William IV St., WC1 (© 020/7484-9307; Tube: Charing Cross). It's open Monday to Friday 8:30am to 6:30pm and Saturday 9am to 5:30pm. Other post offices and post-office branches are open Monday to Friday from 9am to 5:30pm and Saturday from 9am to 12:30pm (some close for an hour at lunchtime).

Pubs No alcohol can be served to anyone under 18. Children under 16 aren't allowed in pubs, except in certain rooms, and only when accompanied by a parent or guardian.

Radio **BBC Greater London Radio** (94.9) is one of the best stations to listen to while you're in the capital. Between midday and 3pm, Robert Elms presents a lively magazine show including fascinating facts and oddities about London, and featuring guests from the fields of arts, entertainment, media, and politics. **LBC** (97.3) is another local station with news and London-based chat, while **KISS FM** (100) is a capital-based dance music station.

Countrywide 24-hour radio channels include **BBC Radio 1** (104.8), with new music, live studio sessions, concerts, and festival broadcasts; **BBC Radio 3** (between 90 and 92), with classical music, jazz, world music, drama, and arts discussions; **BBC Radio 5 Live** (909 or 693), with live news and sports; **Virgin Radio** (105.8) for classic and current rock 'n' roll; and **XFM** (104.9) for the best guitar music, alternative dance, and hip-hop. (XFM was instrumental in introducing acts such as The White Stripes and Franz Ferdinand in the U.K.) Classical buffs listen to **Classic FM** (100–102), which is an active participant in Kids' Week (p. 247) and has released a chart-topping *Music For Babies* double CD. **Jazz FM** (102.2) is the place for jazz, blues, and big-band music.

Especially for kids, **BBC7,** one of the BBC's new digital radio networks (available on digital radio, on TV sets, and via the Internet), has a new daily kids' show, **Big Toe Radio Show,** with news, sports, music, interviews, a reporters' club, science, and stories. It's broadcast live from 4 to 6pm, but you can listen to it at any time at www.bbc.co.uk/bbc7/bigtoe. **Little Toe Show** is a story hour from 7 to 8am daily (again, you can listen to stories at any time on the website). **Capital Disney** is a dedicated digital kids' channel with music from big acts and up-and-comers, news and reviews, famous guests, games, competitions, DVD and game reviews, and features for and by children; you can listen online at www.capitaldisney.co.uk. **Capital FM** (95.8) itself is a pop and rock station.

Safety Pockets of luxury rub shoulders with deprived areas even in London's center, so stay cautious and alert at all times, and if you feel in the slightest degree uneasy, leave the area at once.

The usual common-sense tips apply: Don't leave money or valuables on display on your person, and be especially wary of **pickpockets** in confined public spaces such as the Tube. At an **ATM,** don't allow yourself to be distracted by anyone while making your transaction. **Muggings** occur anywhere, even on seemingly innocuous residential streets, so don't walk alone **after dark,** especially in unlit open spaces such as parks (most are locked, anyway). You may also want to avoid the **Tube** late at night, when people start to spill out of pubs.

Homelessness is a big problem in London, as in many major urban centers. Many **derelicts** sit by ATMs, hoping for handouts; few are threatening, but steer clear of any obviously under the influence of drink or drugs. A particular area to steer clear of in this respect is the top of **Charing Cross Road** around the Centrepoint building. **King's Cross,** though currently being regenerated in preparation for the northern extension of the Eurostar link, is another seedy and rough area to avoid. You'll probably also want to steer clear of **Soho** and **Piccadilly Circus** late at night, when there's lots of drunken leering and swaggering.

There has been a definite upswing in the police presence on the streets and in public parks of late, partly in response to the terrorist attacks of July 2005, but also in a bid to crack down on "antisocial behavior." That said, and not wishing to be a scaremonger, I have to stress that there is a disturbing number of mentally ill individuals on the city's streets (the result of a misguided "Care in the Community" campaign to close down mental institutions), and you need to be on your guard. You'll want to report any incidents to the nearest police station if you can. The most central station is **West End Central Police Station** at 27 Saville Row, W1 (© 020/7434-1212). The website www.met.police.uk lists the others borough by borough. All stations are open 24 hours a day. Alternatively, report a crime on the **Crimestoppers line,** © 0800/555111.

Taxes There is a 17.5% national **value-added tax (VAT)** added to all hotel and restaurant bills, which is included in the price of many items you purchase; see p. 219 for refund protocol.

Airport departure taxes, which are always subject to change but are about £10 ($19) for flights within Britain and the European Union; and £20 ($38) for flights to the U.S. and other countries, are usually included in air tickets, but check in advance.

Taxis See "Getting Around," earlier in this chapter.

Telephone See "Telephone Tips" on the inside front cover of this book for more information on dialing to, from, and within London.

Toll-free numbers: Numbers beginning with 0800 are toll-free within the U.K. except from mobile phones, but calling a 1-800 number in the U.S. from England costs the same as an overseas call.

There are three types of **public pay phones:** those taking only coins, those accepting only phone cards, and those taking both phone cards and credit cards. **Phone cards** are available in three values: £5 ($9.50), £10 ($19), and £20 ($38), and are reusable until the total value has expired. Those sold at post offices give you free calls on Saturday between noon and midnight to selected countries. You'll also find £5 ($9.50) E.U. phone cards, allowing cheap calls to the U.K.

See "The 21st-Century Traveler" in chapter 2 for information on using a cellphone.

Time Zone Most of the year, Britain is 5 hours ahead of the time observed on the East Coast of the United States, though because the U.S. and Britain observe daylight savings time at slightly different times of year (Britain puts its clocks forward by an hour the last Sun in Mar, and back by an hour on the last Sun of Oct), there's a brief period (about a week) in the spring when London is 6 hours ahead of New York. Most European Union countries are an hour ahead of the U.K.

Tipping In **restaurants,** service charges of 15% to 20% are usually added to the bill. Sometimes this is clearly marked; if in doubt, ask. If it isn't included, it's customary to add 15% to the bill unless service was lousy (or even if service was included—pay for catering staff is terrible here). **Hotels** often add a service charge of 10% to 15% to most bills. In smaller B&Bs, the tip isn't likely to be included, so tip people who performed special services, such as for the person who served you breakfast. Or you can ask that 10% or 15% be added to the bill and divided among the staff. Tip chambermaids £1 ($1.90) per day (more if you've made their job extra-difficult). It's standard to tip taxi drivers 10% to 15% of the fare. Barbers and hairdressers expect 10% to 15%. Tour guides expect about £3 ($5.70), although it's not mandatory. Theater ushers don't expect tips.

Transit Information See "Getting Around," earlier in this chapter.

Water London's water is safe to drink. Tap water is free in restaurants, so be sure to ask for it if you don't want to pay for bottled water.

Weather Call ℂ **0870/600-4242** for current weather information, or see www.bbc.co.uk/london/weather.

4

Family-Friendly Accommodations

First the bad news: London is an expensive and overcrowded city, so hotel rooms here can seem small and overpriced in comparison with their equivalents elsewhere. It's especially difficult to find acceptable options at the budget end of the scale. Very cheap rooms here tend to be a tight fit for two, and won't accommodate a rollaway or sometimes even a crib. For that reason, it's important that you are crystal-clear about your needs when making a booking, and that if you need a triple or "family" room, you ask for it.

The good news is that, since the turn of the century, the number of hotel rooms in London increased by more than 10,000, and is set to increase by a further 11,500 by 2008. These extra rooms are often in no-frills **chain hotels,** it's true, but don't overlook these as a family option—they may not be the most stylish or charming, but they do offer decent, clean accommodations in great central locations or in farther-flung but quieter districts. And you'll know what to expect rather than just hoping for the best. I've reviewed some chain hotels where the locations merited checking out. Otherwise, see the "Chain Gang" box on p. 67 for suggestions.

An increasingly popular alternative to hotels for families with young kids or teens is **serviced apartments,** which offer space, flexibility (to eat out or cook a meal), and relative value for the money.

(Prices can end up as little as £50/$95 per person per night for five-star options.) A good-value, chain name in this field is the Europe-wide Citadines Apart'hotels (p. 67). For more self-catering apartments, see the suggestions throughout this chapter, or check out www.london 4rent.com, which specializes in high-end properties but includes cheaper options.

Of course, if you're willing and able to fork over the money, London's historic **grand hotels** can't be beat for cachet and atmosphere; some are snooty but others are surprisingly welcoming towards young guests, and these are the ones focused on in this guide. At the other end of the luxury spectrum, some of London's **designer boutique hotels** have realized that style need not preclude a child-friendly attitude. It's worth bearing in mind that top-end hotels are especially keen to accommodate families when business travelers go home, and they often offer special weekend rates.

Down the scale somewhat, **B&Bs** can be great places to stay with kids, each offering a true "home away from home" in a foreign city, and more personal touches than any hotel can provide. Those outside the center often offer excellent rates, increased space, and proximity to some of London's natural areas, such as Hampstead Heath. You do get breakfast—often a fully cooked English version that will set everyone up for an entire day of sightseeing. (**Hotel break-**

fasts—as opposed to those at B&Bs—tend to be enormously expensive; you're better off seeking out a local cafe.)

The London Bed & Breakfast Agency Ltd. (© 020/7586-2768; fax 020/7586-6567; www.londonbb.com), London B&B (© 800/872-2632 in the U.S.; 619/531-1179 local; fax 619/531-1686; www.londonbandb.com), and Uptown Reservations (© 020/7351-3445; fax 020/7937-6660; www.uptownres.co.uk), are all reputable agencies that can arrange B&B accommodations in private homes, plus some self-catering apartments; family rooms cost about £135 ($256).

Lastly, real budget accommodations come in the form of London's youth hostels, which often offer family rooms (p. 70).

RESERVATION SERVICES Various websites offer hotel and apartment discounts. Three of my favorites are www.londonnights.com, www.londontown.com, and www.smoothhound.co.uk. In my experience, though, rooms booked on the Internet don't always come up to scratch—they can be tiny, for instance, or in inferior parts of the hotel (the hotels themselves are usually uninspiring chains, too). It's therefore essential that you clarify, when booking, that your accommodations should be large enough. Note also that booking through such websites can be time-consuming and frustrating, as the hotels you choose may not have the special offers available on the type of room you need.

A NOTE ABOUT PRICES The price categories provided below divide up as follows: Very Expensive means a family of four pay more than £250 ($470) per night, Expensive means a bill of £175 to £250 ($330–$470), Moderate means £100 to £175 ($190–330), and Inexpensive less than £100 ($190). Unless otherwise stated, published prices are rack rates. Many of them, particularly in the case of expensive hotels, don't include the government-imposed VAT (value-added tax) of 17.5%, so check when booking, as this can add a hefty slab to your bill. Always ask for a better rate, particularly at the first-class and deluxe hotels (B&Bs generally charge a fixed rate), and check the hotels' websites for special online rates.

RESERVE IN ADVANCE It's common sense that those with children in tow should always book accommodations in advance, especially during the peak season (roughly Apr–Oct). Most hotels and B&Bs offer nonsmoking rooms—ask for one when you book. All very expensive and some lower-category hotels offer babysitting services, but because these are generally outsourced from reputable agencies, they require 24 hours' notice. If you need a crib or highchair, reserve one in advance, too, as most hotels have limited numbers.

For a description of London neighborhoods (including those likely to have accommodations suitable for you and your family), see p. 41.

If you've a late flight in or an early flight out, you might need to stay near an airport. Websites www.airporthotels4less.co.uk and www.holidayextras.co.uk offer good discounts, especially on three-bed and family rooms. Otherwise, Hilton London Heathrow Airport (© 020/8759-7755) and Hilton London Gatwick Airport (© 01293/518-080; www.hilton.com) are expensive but have pools to keep little ones occupied; the former is part of Terminal 4 and has a glass wall facing the runways. At Stansted Airport, a new Radisson SAS (© 01279/661012; www.stansted.radissonsas.com) is linked to the airport via a walkway, which boasts great runway views and a pool. Rates range from moderate to expensive, depending on when you stay and whether you get an online deal. More options are listed below.

1 Central London

MARYLEBONE, REGENT'S PARK & FITZROVIA
VERY EXPENSIVE

The Landmark ★ *Finds*   The *pièce de résistance* of this impressive Victorian railway hotel (it's actually joined to Marylebone Station by an ornate walkway) is its 15m (49-ft.) semi-ozone pool and bubbling whirlpool, which children love. (Because this is such a large hotel, however, their pool does get busier than many pools elsewhere.) Another highlight is the fabulous eight-story atrium through the middle of the building, home to the Winter Garden restaurant, where kids get their own menus, and highchairs are provided. The Winter Garden is also a fine setting for a traditional afternoon tea or a Sunday jazz brunch. Staff are extremely friendly, and with Edgware Road so close at hand, it's no surprise that Middle Eastern guests are well catered to, with Arabic menus, Arabic TV channels, and yummy, child-pleasing Middle Eastern specialties as part of the outstanding room service.

The traditionally decorated guest rooms are some of the biggest in the capital, and their large windows make them seem airier still. This is especially noticeable in the marble bathrooms with their deep tubs, walk-in showers, twin sinks, and separate WC. One of the best options for families is to book a twin-bedded room, since the beds are queen-size and can sleep two people each. For a little more parental privacy, Studio Suites have the same bed set up but the seating area is partially separate (through an archway). Up a few notches are the two-bedroom deluxe suites with kitchenettes, or the presidential suites with full kitchens and Jacuzzis. Watch for family packages, such as the Family VIP Pass offering a free day's entry to more than 50 attractions with a deluxe room, and off-season promotions. For very young kids, a whole range of amenities, from pacifiers, diapers, and toiletries to babywalkers, are just a phone call away.

When booking, be sure to state whether you want a room facing the main road, the internal atrium, or the station. The latter rooms are quieter, but double glazing throughout means that all rooms are peaceful (though there's the occasional shudder from Tube trains passing right beneath). *Insider tip:* Marylebone Station has an excellent little community of shops for everyday needs, including a newsagent, a Marks & Spencer Simply Food store where you can stock up on breakfast and snack fare, a great bagel stand, and a specialist cheese outlet.

222 Marylebone Rd., NW1 6JQ. ℂ 020/7631-8000. Fax 020/7632-8080. www.landmarklondon.co.uk. 299 units. £255–£455 ($485–$864) double; from £495 ($940) suite. Children under 14 stay free in parent's room. Rollaway beds £60 ($114); cribs free. AE, DC, MC, V. Tube: Marylebone. **Amenities:** 2 restaurants; bar; indoor pool; spa; gym; concierge; business services and IT center; boutique; hair and beauty salon; 24-hr. room service; massage; babysitting; laundry service; same-day dry cleaning; nonsmoking rooms. *In room:* A/C, TV w/pay movies; VCR/DVD players on request, PlayStations; dataport, minibar, hair dryer, safe.

The Langham ★★   The Langham has history with a capital H and opulence to match. London's first purpose-built grand hotel (it was opened by the Prince of Wales in 1865, and some of its corridors were designed to allow two ladies wearing crinolines to walk side by side), it was frequented by Mark Twain and Oscar Wilde, among others, until World War II left it in tatters. Used by the BBC as offices and broadcasting studios, then restored by the Hilton group in the 1980s, it became independent again in 2004, but the feel is still very much that of the British Empire at its apogee, with some rooms designed by Harrods, no less (think chintz). The family

In the Swim

A splash about in the pool is a great way of burning off energy or relaxing before or after a hard day's sightseeing. My favorite pool is at the **Four Seasons Canary Wharf** (p. 92), which has an infinity edge that can almost make you believe you're swimming in the Thames, which it overlooks. It's technically part of the adjoining health club, but kids get their own session from 9 to 11am every morning. At 20m (66 ft.), it's also the biggest pool of the hotels reviewed in this guide.

One Aldwych (p. 71) and **The Langham** (p. 62) both have smallish but swanky basement pools; **The Landmark** (p. 62) has a less plush but perfectly good version. If you need a view, **The Berkeley**'s (p. 75) extravagant Roman-themed rooftop pool has the benefit of a retractable roof for fine days, and great views over surrounding Knightsbridge, while the **Conrad London** (p. 78) looks onto a yacht-filled marina. **The Savoy**'s (p. 72) cute little pool is tucked away deep within the hotel (in an atrium above the Savoy theater), which means you're very likely to have it to yourself; kids adore the inbuilt Jacuzzi.

If you're on a budget, the sparkling-clean pool at **Crown Moran** (p. 94), set beneath a lovely atrium, is exceptional given the low rates. More centrally, **Hilton Metropole** (p. 81) has a decent pool (it's the most functional of the lot) with a dedicated splash hour at weekends.

---

rooms are very large, with two queen-size beds and space for a rollaway; rollaways and cribs can also be accommodated in a standard double, and there are interconnecting rooms too. Those staying in the more expensive Langham Club (a plush rear section with more contemporary styling and a more private feel, where guests enjoy late checkout, and a lounge area serving complimentary breakfast, afternoon tea, canapés, and evening drinks) get cute little bathrobes, but practicalities aren't overlooked either, including spare nappies and non-slip bathmats. For a truly special occasion, book the Infinity Suite—London's most expensive. It boasts two bedrooms, two bathrooms, two dressing rooms, a drawing room with stunning views over the lovely All Souls church opposite, a kitchen, and an "infinity bath" with changing colors (you hit a button to keep the one that suits your mood).

The West End with its vast array of eating and entertainment options lies quite literally at your doorstep, but with all the cocooning on offer here you might not want to leave. There's a health club and spa with a 16m (52ft) pool atmospherically set in a former bank vault (with no time restrictions on children's use), a whirlpool, and seven beauty treatment rooms, although the £7 ($13) a day membership (£4/$8 for kids, although they don't charge for toddlers) seems pretty steep given what you're paying for the rooms. There are also two bars—one polo-themed and one Russian (offering more than 100 vodkas)—the dramatic Edwardian-style Palm Court, providing the perfect sybaritic setting for traditional afternoon tea, as well as breakfast and snacks, and Memories restaurant, a great place to feast on British fare with a Continental twist. Both restaurants have highchairs, and children's portions can be cooked to order. There are also a few kids' basics on the room service menu.

Insider Tip: Check the website for special offers and seasonal rates that make this a good family base, especially in August.

Where to Stay in Central London

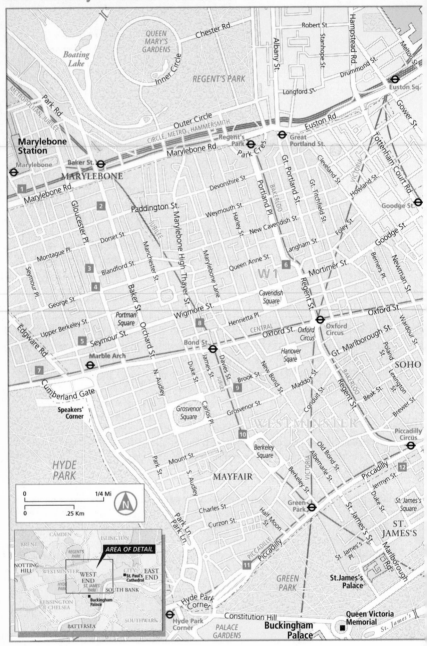

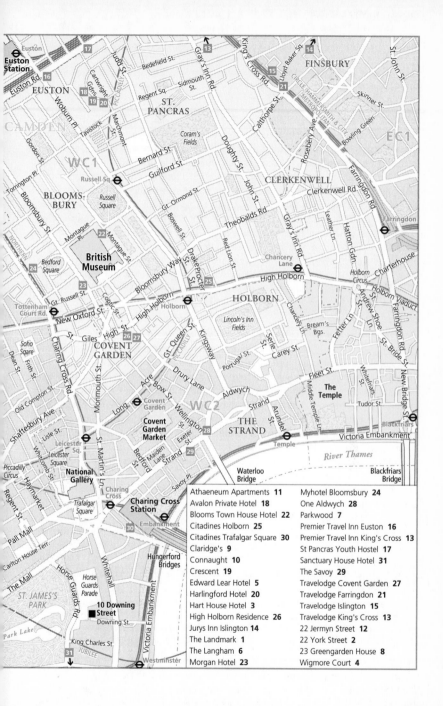

Athaeneum Apartments **11**	Myhotel Bloomsbury **24**
Avalon Private Hotel **18**	One Aldwych **28**
Blooms Town House Hotel **22**	Parkwood **7**
Citadines Holborn **25**	Premier Travel Inn Euston **16**
Citadines Trafalgar Square **30**	Premier Travel Inn King's Cross **13**
Claridge's **9**	St Pancras Youth Hostel **17**
Connaught **10**	Sanctuary House Hotel **31**
Crescent **19**	The Savoy **29**
Edward Lear Hotel **5**	Travelodge Covent Garden **27**
Harlingford Hotel **20**	Travelodge Farringdon **21**
Hart House Hotel **3**	Travelodge Islington **15**
High Holborn Residence **26**	Travelodge King's Cross **13**
Jurys Inn Islington **14**	22 Jermyn Street **12**
The Landmark **1**	22 York Street **2**
The Langham **6**	23 Greengarden House **8**
Morgan Hotel **23**	Wigmore Court **4**

1C Portland Place, W1B 1JA. (C) 020/7636-1000. Fax 020/7323-2340. www.langhamhotels.com/langham/london. 429 units. £255–£415 ($484–$788) double; £425 ($807) family room; from £345 ($655) suite. Rollaway beds £70 ($133); cribs free. AE, DC, MC, V. Tube: Oxford Circus. **Amenities:** Restaurant; 2 bars; indoor pool; health club; spa; sauna; concierge; business center; salon; 24-hr. room service; massage; babysitting; laundry service; same-day dry cleaning; nonsmoking rooms. *In room:* A/C, TV/VCR w/pay movies, dataport, minibar, safe.

EXPENSIVE

22 York St. ★★ *Finds*   The sheer homeliness of this wonderful little Georgian town house B&B comes as something of a shock given its location just a couple of minutes from the roar of Baker Street. Guest rooms really couldn't be more appealing, with their gorgeous rug-strewn wooden floors, French antique furniture, and soft quilts. In the delightful breakfast room, guests congregate around a long curved table to enjoy a specially selected continental breakfast and to exchange sightseeing tips (a highchair can be provided). A pleasant lounge offers satellite TV, along with complimentary tea and coffee. Of the 20 rooms, two are triples (one double and one single bed), and three are family rooms (one double and two single beds). There's no elevator, and the owner is keen that parents take into account the stone staircases and other hard surfaces.

22 York St, W1U 6PX. (C) 020/7224-2990. Fax 020/7224-1990. www.btinternet.com/~michaelcallis. 20 units. £100 ($190) double; £141 ($268) triple; £120 ($228) w/child under 5 staying for free in single; £188 ($357) family room; £160 ($304) w/child under 5 staying free in the single. Cribs free. Rates include Continental breakfast. AE, MC, V. Tube: Baker St. **Amenities:** Babysitting; all nonsmoking rooms. *In room:* TV, dataport, hair dryer.

MODERATE

Hart House Hotel ★   This friendly, family-run hotel in an impressive Georgian town house has refreshingly spacious rooms, given its central location between Hyde Park and Regent's Park and its keen prices. There are rooms for three-person families (one double and one single bed) and four-person families (one double and two single beds), but some of the other rooms can accommodate foldout beds. The decor is neutral and easy on the eye, beds are comfortable enough—though you may need to ask for extra pillows—and the en suite bathrooms are roomy, spruce, and modern, with either a shower or a tub. Morning replenishment in the pleasant basement dining room (there's one highchair, but the hotel's small enough for that not to matter) includes a buffet of cereals, juice, and toast, together with a hearty English breakfast. Be warned that some of the staff have somewhat shaky English, so you may have to repeat yourself. The only two downers here are the lack of a lift (elevator); and the hotel's location on an extremely busy street. However, the noise of traffic isn't enough to rouse you from your slumber.

It's worth noting that if you're flying into Heathrow, the Airbus brings you directly to Gloucester Place in about an hour. Also, special deals are sometimes available out of season, making this excellent find even more of a bargain. If it's full, **Georgian House Hotel** nearby at 87 Gloucester Place ((C) **020/7935-2211**) is a similar but slightly cheaper option.

51 Gloucester Place, W1U 8JF. (C) 020/7935-2288. Fax 020/7935-8516. www.harthouse.co.uk. 16 units. £105 ($199) double; £130 ($247) triple; £150 ($285) quad. Rollaway beds £10 ($19); cribs free. Rates include English or continental breakfast. AE, MC, V. Tube: Marble Arch or Baker St. **Amenities:** Babysitting; laundry service/dry cleaning; all nonsmoking rooms; rooms for those w/limited mobility. *In room:* TV, dataport, beverage-maker, hair dryer.

Wigmore Court *Value*   This welcoming establishment stands out not only for its fair prices given its central location, but for its well-maintained, self-catering kitchen and laundry facilities—a real boon for families traveling on a tight budget. Set in an historic building that has played host to the likes of the Duke of Gloucester and William

The Chain Gang

Though the bulk of their clients are business travelers, some of the big hotel chains offer superb family rates if you don't mind absence of character and an impersonal feel. **Citadines** Apart'hotels (✆ **0800/376-3898** within U.K.; www.citadines.com) consist of reasonably priced, basic studios and apartments in which guests can enjoy free standard hotel services (such as a breakfast lounge and babysitting services) and options adding to the flexibility of self-catering amenities (including a dishwasher and bottlewarmers) and laundry facilities. In London, you'll find them in the City, South Kensington, Holborn, and Trafalgar Square—the latter has two-person studios with rollout/sofa beds, four-person apartments with a double bed in the bedroom and a pullout/sofa bed in the lounge area, and six-person duplex apartments with two double beds and a pullout/sofa bed. It's an absolute steal for the area, at about £150 ($285) for a four-person apartment. (Book through the website and you might get yourself an even better deal.)

Premier Travel Inn (✆ **0870/242-8000**; www.premiertravelinn.com), a new amalgam of Travel Inn and Premier Lodge, has more than 450 budget hostelries around the country, including 11 in the capital: County Hall (p. 86), Tower Bridge, Southwark, Putney Bridge, Docklands, Kew, Kensington, King's Cross, Euston, Wembley, and Beckton in the East End. The best things about this chain are that family rooms are charged at the same rate as standard doubles, and kids under 10 get free breakfasts (it's cheap for those 10 and over, too). The family rooms sleep up to two adults and two children under 15 (in a double bed and a pullout/sofa bed), plus a child under 2 in a cot. Twin rooms have one double and one pullout, but if they're the same price, why skimp on space? It's easiest to book rooms online, but note that you're expected to pay for rooms on arrival, to prevent "check-out delays."

"No chandeliers, just comfy beds" promises the **Travelodge** chain of 240 budget hotels around the U.K. (✆ **0870/191-1600**; www.travelodge.co.uk), which is slowly being spruced up to make the decor more modern, bright, and generally appealing. If you want to stay in the center or not far from it without paying through the nose (check for stunningly good online offers), this is a decent bet—newish openings include Covent Garden (p. 73), King's Cross, Islington, and Farringdon. There are more branches in Battersea, Kew, Docklands, and other locations. As at Premier Travel Inns, family rooms accommodating up to two adults and two kids under 16 cost the same as doubles, and kids under 10 eat free at breakfast. Older kids and parents can help themselves at a plentiful buffet for a modest sum. Low-priced "Breakfast-to-Go" bags are available day and night. Again, as at Premier Travel Inns, you settle upon arrival, to "avoid check-outs." *Insider tip:* If you book online, print out your form and take it along with you in case of any discrepancies over rates.

Pitt, the hotel is subject to a more-or-less continuous improvement program. Take your pick from "triples" (with one double and one or two single beds), quads, five-bed rooms, or a family "suite" (one huge room carved up into two, with its own fridge) suitable for those with older kids. All but one single and one double have their own bathrooms; the majority come with tub/shower combos. Be aware that there's no lift (elevator), and that the front rooms can be noisy. Breakfasts aren't copious but are fine for all but the most ravenous.

23 Gloucester Place, W1H 3PB. ✆ 020/7935-0928. Fax 020/7487-4254. www.wigmore-court-hotel.co.uk. 18 units. £98 ($186) double; £120 ($228) triple, £130 ($247) quad. MC, V. Tube: Marble Arch. **Amenities:** Guest kitchen; coin-op washers and dryers. *In room:* TV, dataport, beverage-maker.

INEXPENSIVE
Edward Lear Hotel   A long-popular budget choice, this hotel was once the town house of Victorian artist and limerick writer Edward Lear, whose illustrated works punctuate the walls. Rooms here aren't huge or particularly inspiring, and the area can be pretty hectic (ask for one of the back rooms if this bothers you), but the price is right and the staff is friendly. Triples come with shared facilities (shower only) or with a tub and toilet; family rooms have either shower only, or a tub and toilet. Cribs can be provided, and there are highchairs in the dining room. The **Parkwood** (✆ **020/7402-2241**), across the Edgware Road in Bayswater, run by the same people and just a few steps from Hyde Park, is a similar spot, with a gallery of paintings by visiting kids.

28–30 Seymour St., W1H 5WD. ✆ **020/7402-5401.** Fax 020/7706-3766. www.edlear.com. 31 units, 12 with bathroom. £50—£89 ($94–$169) double; £59–£99 ($112–$188) triple; £74–£105 ($141–$199) family room. Children under 2 stay free in parent's room. Cribs free. Rates include English breakfast. MC, V. Tube: Marble Arch. **Amenities:** Free Internet access in guest lounge. *In room:* TV w/pay movies, dataport, beverage-maker.

BLOOMSBURY & HOLBORN
VERY EXPENSIVE
In addition to the hotels listed below, there's **Myhotel** just off Tottenham Court Road; see Myhotel Chelsea, p. 79.

EXPENSIVE
Blooms Town House Hotel   A welcoming 18th-century town house with a country-house feel, this hotel is ideal for lovers of tradition who are traveling with older kids. In winter you can huddle round the fireplace together, with your choice of newspapers, books, and board games from the library. In summer, the walled garden overlooking the British Museum is a pleasant sanctuary where you can enjoy drinks, afternoon tea, and light meals. The dining room, which has highchairs, can serve a special kids' menu by advance request, although the standard fare is child-friendly enough, including the likes of traditional fish and chips. Up to four people can fit in the family room, which is basically a spacious double with an extra bed added, and room for a cot. There's also a spacious and bright junior suite with plenty of room for four. Both the family room and junior suite come with lovely garden views. Bathrooms are small- to medium-size and elegant, with well-maintained showers and tubs.

7 Montague St., WC1B 5BP. ✆ 020/7323-1717. Fax 020/7636-6498. www.bloomshotel.com. 26 units. £159–£169 ($302–$321) double; £195 ($370) family room, £220 ($418) suite. Children under 16 share parent's room at 50% of cost (except infants in cribs). Cribs free. AE, DC, MC, V. Tube: Russell Sq. **Amenities:** Restaurant; whisky bar; 24-hr. room service; IT facilities; laundry service/dry cleaning; nonsmoking rooms. *In room:* Satellite TV, beverage-maker, hair dryer, trouser press.

MODERATE

Crescent ★ *Finds*   The warmth of this excellent little family-run hotel is attested to by its many loyal fans, who return again and again for its comfortable rooms, reasonable prices, and a host of little touches that make it virtually unique in this price range—bathrobes on request, baby-listening according to staff availability, highchairs in the breakfast room and, best of all, for kids needing to burn off excess energy, access to a private garden square and to four recently renovated tennis courts (staff can loan out rackets and balls). Certain staff members are proud to now babysit the grandchildren of those who first stayed here in their own youth. Rooms are fairly plain but clean and pleasant; all but some of the singles are en suite. There's no lift, but ground-floor rooms are available. The English breakfasts are robust enough to keep you going all day, and there's a pleasant quiet lounge for hot drinks and snacks.

49–50 Cartwright Gardens, WC1H 9EL. ℂ 020/7387-1515. Fax 020/7383-2054. www.crescenthoteloflondon.com. 27 units. £91 ($173) double; £100 ($190) triple; £110 ($209) family room. Kids under 2 stay free in parent's room. Cribs free. MC, V. Tube: Euston or Russell Sq. **Amenities:** Tennis courts; babysitting. *In room:* TV, beverage-maker, hair dryer, iron, safe.

Harlingford Hotel ★ *Value*   On the same quiet garden square as the Crescent and similar in price, the Harlingford is altogether different in feel. A makeover in 2003 gave it a stylish contemporary vibe, with neutral backgrounds embellished with rich, deep reds, purples, and greens. That said, the character of this trio of Georgian town houses has been left intact—right down to the steep staircases and lack of lift (there are some easy-access rooms on the ground floor). All rooms have fair-sized, modern bathrooms, and there are a couple of cots and highchairs. Rollaways and interconnecting rooms are not available, but there are triples and quads. As at the Crescent, guests can use the garden square and its tennis courts.

61–63 Cartwright Gardens, WC1H 9EL. ℂ 020/7387-1551. Fax 020/7387-4616. www.harlingfordhotel.com. 43 units. £95 ($180) double; £105 ($199) triple; £110 ($209) quad. Cribs free. Rates include English or continental breakfast. AE, MC, V. Tube: Euston or Russell Sq. **Amenities:** Tennis courts. *In room:* TV, beverage-maker, hair dryer.

Morgan Hotel   Like all popular places, the family-run Morgan has had its detractors, but after undergoing a thorough refurbishment in early 2005, it's spick-and-span again, with new air-conditioning and bright (if small) bathrooms in all rooms. Its secret weapon, and what sets it apart from rivals, is its separate annex on the same street, with competitively priced apartments with galley kitchens. All have one bedroom, a bathroom, a living room, and a kitchenette, though one of them can sleep four people (the bedroom has one double and two single beds), and three can sleep three people. Unfortunately, these are no insider secret and you'll need to book well in advance to secure one, especially in summertime. Massive English breakfasts are served in a light and airy basement space, where highchairs can be provided. *Insider tip:* Ask about special offers for families with small children, and note that the back rooms with views over the mighty British Museum are quieter.

24 Bloomsbury St., WC1B 3QJ. ℂ 020/7636-3735. Fax 020/7636-3045. www.morganhotel.co.uk. 21 units. £95–£105 ($180–199) double; £130 ($247) triple; £170 ($323) 3-person apt; £210 ($399) 4-person apt. Rates include full English breakfast. MC, V. Tube: Tottenham Court Rd. *In room:* AC, TV, voicemail, dataport, kitchen in suites, hair dryer, safe.

INEXPENSIVE

In addition to the below reviews, there's a youth hostel suitable for kids, including under-3s, on Euston Road (p. 70).

Putting the Youth in Youth Hostels

Yes, there are downsides to staying in a hostel. You might share the venue with a noisy school party; you normally have to share bathrooms; and sometimes you'll have to vacate the hostel at certain times of day while they clean. But youth hostels are a much underrated and under-utilized budget option for families—if you don't mind going back to basics, that is. The special family rooms (for those with children over 3) don't exactly scream glamour, but two bunk beds are comfy enough (bed linen and duvets are provided but no towels), and there's always a washbasin. Cots and highchairs are available in hostels welcoming under-3s. Best of all, self-catering kitchens, present in all but a few hostels, allow you to save money on eating out. Most hostels also offer cooked meals, with special menus for children under 10—this is great for little ones who can rapidly tire of having to sit around in proper restaurants. There are also laundry facilities in most, and a couple even boast gardens of their own where your youngsters can let off steam.

If you're traveling with over-3s, it's worth asking a particular hostel not designated for families about staying there, since some may have bunk-bed rooms that can be booked by families for their private use. And some hostels now have en-suite rooms, often with single or double beds, if you want a little more privacy. Single parents aren't forgotten either—a discount is available when booking a family bunk-bed room.

All hostels have family games and activities, from board games to kite-making. Most also have a game room with the likes of pool, table tennis, and arcade games—perfect for when you return from sightseeing and want to relax while the kids make friends.

Membership is required for all those wishing to stay at a youth hostel. At press time, this cost £28 ($53) for two-parent families and £14 ($27) for single parents, with under-18s free. This can be arranged at the time of booking, or you can visit www.yha.org.uk for information.

Britain's Youth Hostels Association, which celebrated its 75th birthday in 2005, has more than 220 hostels countrywide. One hundred are suitable for children and 70 have been deemed appropriate for children under 3. Five of these are in London—**St. Pancras Hostel** at 79–81 Euston Rd., NW1 2QS (© **020/7388 9998,** or 0870/770-6044 within U.K.; www.yha.org.uk), is convenient for transport links. **Hampstead Heath Hostel,** 4 Wellgarth Rd., NW11 7HR (© **020/8458 9054,** or 0870/770/5846 within U.K.; www.yha.org.uk), comes with an enclosed little garden and is conveniently located by the heath. **City of London Hostel,** at 36 Carter Lane, EC4V 5AB (© **020/7236-4965,** or 0870/770/5764 within U.K.; www.yha.org.uk), is located virtually opposite St. Paul's in an old choirboy school. **Baden-Powell House,** 65–67 Queen's Gate, SW7 5JS (© **020/7584 7031,** or 0870/770-6132 within U.K.; www.yha.org.uk), is close to such major museums as the Natural History museum.

The best in the city, however, is Rotherhithe Youth Hostel; it's reviewed separately later (p. 86).

Avalon Private Hotel   Don't come to the Avalon expecting luxury, and you won't be disappointed. But for the price, this is a more-than-acceptable option. It offers access to the same garden square and tennis courts as the Crescent and the Harlingford. It also has a pleasant reading room overlooking the square, filled with guidebooks and maps so you can plot your adventures. Top-floor rooms, often filled with students, are reached via steep stairs, but bedrooms on the lower levels have easier access. The triples have either three single beds or a double and a single, while "quads" have a double bed and either two or three singles. A handful of units have tiny shower rooms; all units have basins. Reserve online and you'll net yourself a good savings.

46–47 Cartwright Gardens, WC1H 9EL. ℭ 020/7387-2366. Fax 020/7387-5810. www.avalonhotel.co.uk. 27 units £56–£82 ($108–$156) double; £66–£95 ($127–$180) triple; £75–£104 ($144–$198) quad. Children under 16 pay £5 ($9) if sharing parent's room. Rates include English breakfast. AE, DC, MC, V. Tube: Euston or Russell Sq. **Amenities:** Outdoor tennis court. *In room:* TV, beverage-maker, safe.

High Holborn Residence *(Finds*   Make like a student at one of the venerable London School of Economics' residence halls, which offers B&B accommodations to individuals and families during summer vacation (mid-Aug to late Sept). One of six halls in a number of decent locations, this is handy for the shops and theaters of Covent Garden, the museums of Bloomsbury, and the varied entertainments of the South Bank. Most rooms are en suite triples with telephones, but some of the twin-bedded doubles have shared bathrooms. As you'd expect, given the context, the decor and furnishings tend towards the functional, but rooms are clean, bright, and airy. Linen and towels are provided (and changed every 3 days). Guests can make use of the bar, TV lounge, game room with pool table, self-catering kitchenette, and launderette.

178 High Holborn, WC1V 7AA. ℭ 020/7107-5737. Fax 020/7107-5735. www.lse.ac.uk/collections/vacations. 494 units. £49–£70 ($93–$133) twin; £80 ($152) triple. Price includes buffet-style continental breakfast. MC, V. Tube: Holborn. **Amenities:** Bar; kitchenette; game room; launderette; TV lounge.

COVENT GARDEN & THE STRAND
VERY EXPENSIVE

One Aldwych ✦✦✦   Boy, do these guys know how to make you feel welcome! (Rumor has it they're paid more than their peers at other hotels, which helps explain why they're so obliging.) This stunning conversion of a former newspaper headquarters is very adult in feel, with simple but chic guest rooms with contemporary furnishings, crisp white linens, and luxurious bathrooms with all-natural toiletries and mini-TVs. But don't let the fanciness put you off—One Aldwych more than welcomes kids through its impressive doors, offering an in-room play box of toys and games; complimentary teddy bears; a glass of milk and cookies, milkshake, or fruit cocktail, depending on age; slippers and bathrobes for those 7 and up; pajamas for 4- to 13-year-olds; and bottlewarmers on request. Special weekend rates and packages that include premium tickets to the *Lion King* are also available.

Wooden cots and very comfy rollaways can be placed in rooms from the deluxe category and up (standard doubles, called Aldwych Rooms, are tiny) but, best of all, for those with sizeable wallets, are the executive suites with two or three bedrooms, some with kitchenettes with full-size fridges and microwaves, some with dining rooms, and some with private gyms. Other rooms have fabulous views over Waterloo Bridge and the National Theatre. Parents can take advantage of the excellent 24-hour babysitting service to relax in the double-height lobby bar; enjoy a three-course meal followed by a classic movie in the luxurious leather screening room (mostly Fri, Sat, and Sun evenings); work out in the state-of-the-art, 24-hour gym; or sweat it out in the sauna rooms. Kids won't be able to resist the divine 18m (59-ft.) basement pool, complete with underwater music. Luckily, it's not crowded, so no one will mind if the kids splash about a bit (water wings are provided).

Eats-wise, children's portions and highchairs are available in the two modern European restaurants (Axis and the more informal mezzanine-level Indigo), while the room service menu has a well-thought-out children's section available until 11pm. Breakfast might include toast with peanut butter and bananas; or blueberry pancakes with maple syrup and bacon; the rest of the day, little ones can enjoy dishes that eschew the pasta bias of many kids' menus in favor of dishes like pan-fried organic salmon with mashed potatoes. *Insider tip:* If you don't want to pay for a full breakfast, the Cinnamon Bar, which is part of the hotel but has a separate entrance, serves delectable cookies, muffins, and juices, as well as great espressos for flagging parents.

1 Aldwych, WC2B 4RH. ✆ 020/7300-1000. Fax 020/7300-1001. www.onealdwych.com. 105 units. £335–£405 ($636–$770) double; from £530 ($1,007) suite. Children under 16 stay free in parent's room. Rollaway beds £65 ($124), free for under-16s; cribs free . AE, DC, MC, V. Tube: Covent Garden or Temple (closed Sun). **Amenities:** 2 restaurants; 2 bars; indoor pool; gym; treatment rooms; sauna and steam room; concierge; 24-hr. room service; massage; babysitting; laundry service; same-day dry cleaning; nonsmoking rooms, movie-screening room. *In room:* A/C, TV/VCR w/pay movies, CD player and free CD library, fax, dataport, minibar, hair dryer, safe.

The Savoy   The Savoy's hidden gem when it comes to kids is its lovely little atrium pool situated above the 19th-century Savoy Theatre. Vastly expanded over the years, the Savoy is a bit of a warren now, with endless corridors and lifts that only take you to certain floors. Some guest rooms are spruce and relatively newly done, others are beginning to look a little worn, although the traditional furniture, quirky features, and Art Deco touches give them a very English character, and the marble bathrooms are excellent (watch out for slippery floors, though). New owners promise a £30 million ($48 million) loving overhaul by 2006, including opening the main restaurant (currently used as a breakfast room, albeit one with stunning Thames views).

Special family accommodations come in the form of two-bedroom units with one king-sized bed and two twins. Unfortunately, these lack the stupendous river views of the south-facing rooms, making them darker and less attractive; if your heart is set on a view, you need to ask for a river junior suite to be converted into a family room with interconnecting doors or by adding extra beds. Alternatively, travel cots and rollaways can be placed in double rooms.

Children's amenities include complimentary soft toys on arrival, bathrobes and slippers, kids' TV channels and videos, and highchairs. Luxury picnics can be provided for family excursions, and the concierge can arrange tickets and transport. The famous **Savoy Grill** is a formal dining option; teenagers may prefer the "chic American diner" feel of **Banquette,** where they can tuck into burgers, fishcakes, and good old English shepherd's pie while spying on celebrities going in or out of the classy hotel entrance below. A fun new kids' room-service menu, available upon request, features dishes like Humpty Dumpty and All His Men (boiled egg and soldiers—strips of buttered toast), and Captain Pugwash's Supper (fish fingers).

Back to that pool, though—like many London hotel pools, it's rarely used, so during the day you might find you have the run of it. Water wings can be provided, though it's not very deep, and the Jacuzzi corner is huge fun for kids and adults.

The Strand, WC2R 0EU. ✆ 020/7836-4343. Fax 020/7240-6040. www.fairmont.com. 263 units. £199–£329 ($378–$625) double; £399–£769 ($758–$1,461) family accommodations; from £439 ($834) suite. 1 child under 12 can stay free in parent's room. Rollaway beds free, cots free. AE, DC, MC, V. Tube: Charing Cross or Covent Garden.

Amenities: 4 restaurants; 2 bars; health club; sauna; spa; indoor pool; massage; business center; 24-hr. room service; babysitting/child-minding; laundry service/dry cleaning; nonsmoking rooms; rooms for those w/limited mobility. *In room:* A/C, TV/VCR, dataport, minibar, beverage-maker (for extra fee); hair dryer, safe.

INEXPENSIVE

Travelodge *Value*   A well-located branch of the nationwide budget chain (see "The Chain Gang" on p. 67), this Travelodge is an especially good choice if you want to catch some shows—it's located on the fringes of Theatreland. The hotel has just undergone a massive, much-needed refurbishment that has left it more spruce and inviting—rooms remain functional, but at these prices, they should. The once-terrible bathrooms, some of which are shower-only, have been greatly improved. There's also a fresh-looking bar-cafe serving light snacks and pizzas, although with so many great eating options nearby, it's hard to imagine why you'd stay in, unless you get totally worn out from the equally great neighborhood shopping.

10 Drury Lane, WC2B 5RE. (℃) 020/7208-9988. Fax 020/7831-1548. www.travelodge.com. 153 units. £85 ($161) double or family room. Cots free. AE, DC, MC, V. Tube: Covent Garden. **Amenities:** Bar-cafe; nonsmoking rooms. *In room:* TV, beverage-maker, hair dryer (on request).

ST. JAMES'S & MAYFAIR
VERY EXPENSIVE

In addition to the below hotels, there's a **Four Seasons** hotel (p. 92) on Park Lane.

Athenaeum Apartments ★★ *Finds*   The Athenaeum, a five-star hotel with old-fashioned, rather chintzy rooms, has a secret—four Georgian town houses with apartments lie around the corner from the main building, containing some of London's best choices for family stays. These rooms are decorated in a variety of styles to suit all tastes, but those with kids should book the special Family Apartment. This pop art spectacular is a feast for the eyes, with its mirrored Philippe Starck chairs, seats resembling giant computer keys, child-size table, plasma screen TVs, and bathrooms tiled with reflective stainless-steel bricks. Kids sleep in their own gorgeous little niche off the living room, complete with funky building blocks, a games console that doubles as a coffee table, (with nostalgia-inducing games such as Space Invaders), and a welcoming bag with a sticker book, a teddy bear, and a bath duck. Potties and strollers can be supplied free of charge.

Practical as well as appealing, all rooms come with full kitchens, washing machines, and highchairs on request. Guests can chose to fend for themselves or avail themselves of the hotel services—including 24-hour room service (featuring an extensive kids' menu), a modern British restaurant, a lounge for afternoon tea and relaxing (there's even a resident tasseographer, or tea-leaf diviner, to read guests' futures), a whisky bar, a sumptuous spa (without a pool, sadly), and an incredibly helpful long-standing concierge named Donald. There's even a grocery shopping service, though small supermarkets are nearby if you prefer to handle the shopping, and the kitchen can provide hampers for picnics. (Hyde Park is mere steps away.) The apartments do lack the views overlooking Green Park and the river enjoyed by the hotel rooms, but the spaciousness of the apartments more than makes up for the lack of view.

There are further swanky one- and two-bedroom contemporary apartments at the Athenaeum's sister property, **23 Greengarden House,** a 15-minute walk away in Marylebone; guests there (over-12s) can use the hotel spa. *Tip:* American guests should ask about the special pound-for-dollar rate, which offers a very good value.

116 Piccadilly, W1J 7BJ. (℃) 020/7499-3464. Fax 020/7493-1860. www.athenaeumhotel.com. 33 units. From £299 ($568). Rollaway bed £35 ($67), crib free. Rate includes continental or English breakfast. AE, DC, MC, V. Tube: Green

Park. **Amenities:** Restaurant; bar; spa; business services; hair salon; 24-hr. room service; massage; babysitting; laundry service; same-day dry cleaning; free CD loan; nonsmoking apartments. *In room:* A/C, TV/DVD/CD player w/pay movies, dataport, minibar, hair dryer, trouser press, iron, safe.

22 Jermyn Street ★★★ *(Finds)*   Of all the accommodations that made it into this guide, this town-house hotel, run by the same family for nearly a century and reinvented as an upscale boutique hotel in 1990, is the most welcoming where families are concerned—there's nothing, it seems, that the discreet, knowledgeable staff haven't thought of, whether it's candies and musical cassettes with sing-along books, or practicalities such as safety features, baby thermometers, baby baths, changing mats, and bottlewarmers. They'll even bring you nappies (Brit-speak for diapers) should you run out, and staff will babysit, although they'll provide agency staff if you prefer. The owner produces a brilliant newsletter detailing the city's best sights and restaurants (as well as a comprehensive general London guide on the latest happenings in the arts world, theaters, and so on).

Families have the choice of two-bedroom suites or of paying an extra charge for a comfy queen-size sofa bed to be set up in a one-bed suite (there are also five double rooms). There's no dining room, but there is a good and varied room-service menu featuring kid-friendly fare, all of which can be made in smaller portions. Entertainment includes a 14-channel satellite TV, an extensive complimentary video library (with free popcorn, salted and sweet), GameBoys, and books to read or draw in and then wipe clean. After soaking in the deep tubs, little ones can wrap up in a one of the child-sized bathrobes, available for all ages.

My one caveat is that the hotel is subject to inevitable round-the-clock noise since it's close to Piccadilly Circus. ***Insider tip:*** If you're heading out for a walk in nearby St. James's Park (p. 204), ask the kitchen for bread or croissants for the ducks, geese, and pelicans.

22 Jermyn St., SW1Y 6HL. ⓒ 020/7734-2353. Fax 020/7734-0750. www.22jermyn.com. 18 units. £210 ($399) double; from £295 ($560) suite; from £505 ($960) 2-bedroom suite. Sofa bed £50 ($95), cot free. AE, DC, MC, V. Tube: Piccadilly Circus. **Amenities:** Access (over-18s) to nearby health club with swimming pool £15 ($29); concierge; business services; 24-hr. room service; physical therapy and massage; babysitting; same-day laundry service; same-day dry cleaning; nonsmoking rooms. *In room:* TV/VCR w/pay movies, dataport, minibar; safe.

MODERATE

Sanctuary House Hotel   This small hotel, set above a pub famous for its award-winning traditional beers, may not sound like the most family-friendly option, but its weekend rate, inclusive of continental breakfast, is a superb bargain in this part of town. The rooms are a bit chintzy and they're not huge, but each can accommodate one rollaway bed and one crib (for which you have to supply your own bedding). The adult beds (king-size four-posters in the superior rooms) are extremely comfortable, and the small bathrooms have both a tub and shower. Rooms are on the first to fifth floors (there's a lift), away from the bustle of the ground-floor Ale & Pie House (owned by the Fuller's brewery), which offers old-style British dishes such as Welsh lamb (most available in half-portions), and has a highchair and a nonsmoking section. Note, however, that kids aren't allowed in on Thursday and Friday nights, when the pub gets too busy (it's tiny).

There are further good-value Fuller's pub-hotels on the South Bank. The Mad Hatter has interconnecting rooms for families; and Ealing, 15km (10 miles) from Heathrow airport , has The Fox & Goose, with a patio garden.

33 Tothill St., SW1H 9LA. ℭ **020/7799-4044.** Fax 020/7799-3657. www.sanctuaryhousehotel.co.uk. 34 units. £99–£150 ($188–$285) double. Children under 12 stay free in parent's room. Rollaways free; cribs free. Rate includes continental breakfast. Fri–Sun. AE, MC, V. Tube: St. James's Park. **Amenities:** Restaurant/bar; nonsmoking rooms. *In room:* A/C, TV, dataport, beverage-maker, iron (on request), trouser press.

2 West London

SOUTH KENSINGTON
MODERATE
There's also a **Citadines Apart'hotel** here (p. 67).

Swiss House Hotel ★★★ *Value*   Welcomes don't come much more genuine than at this excellent-value little ivy-clad B&B, which prides itself on its "child-friendly focus and attitude." The concierge is a mine of information on family eating options and outings, and can help arrange them for you. All rooms, including the triples and quads, are en suite (warning: bathrooms are minuscule). The quiet back units overlook leafy private gardens. They're plain but tastefully decorated and boast wooden floors and fireplaces (the common parts are more rustic in feel). The top rooms are worth avoiding if you don't like stairs (there's no lift), and they have poor water pressure, too. The continental breakfasts are very good if not huge, and highchairs can be provided in the cozy breakfast room, where you can linger over the papers and listen to music if you like. (There's a free coffee machine.)

171 Old Brompton Rd., SW5 0AN. ℭ **020/7373-2769.** Fax 020/7373-4983. www.swisshousehotel.com. 15 units. £97–£114 ($184–$217) double; £132 ($251) triple; £147 ($279) triple. Kids under 3 stay free in parent's room. Rollaway beds free, cribs free. Continental breakfast included. AE, DC, MC, V. Tube: Gloucester Rd. **Amenities:** Travel desk; laundry service; dry cleaning; nonsmoking rooms. *In room:* TV, beverage-maker, hair dryer, safe.

KNIGHTSBRIDGE, BROMPTON & BELGRAVIA
VERY EXPENSIVE
The Berkeley ⭐   Though set inside a 1970s building, the ultra-smart Berkeley has maintained architectural elements from a previous hotel on the site, especially in the stunning Blue Bar with its outstanding cocktails and non-snooty staff. Kids will probably prefer the Caramel Room with its catwalk-inspired treats, including Jimmy Choo buns and Diane von Furstenberg puffs. Part of the Maybourne group, this Art Deco-meets-French Classical hotel offers all the standard kids' amenities, plus a welcoming gift-pack, a selection of books and board games, kids' magazines with the morning newspaper, an in-room GameBoy with a choice of games, family DVDs and CDs, and mini bathrobes and slippers. If you want a luxury picnic to take on your day out, the kitchen will be only too happy to oblige. If, however, you want to hang out at the hotel, a top-floor health club and spa boasts a breathtaking Roman-themed pool with a roof that can be retracted in fine weather for lovely views.

Families will be most comfortable in one of the luxurious two-bed suites (perhaps the Park Suite with its kitchenette, guest room, and view over Hyde Park), but rollaways can be provided in some other rooms. Make sure you get a sitter in order to sample Marcus Wareing's celebrated cooking at the world-class Pétrus restaurant. If you dine with the kids, the more informal but still luscious Boxwood Café (p. 118) is the hotel's best option, presided over by the famously fiery Gordon Ramsay. Alternatively, there's a kids' room-service menu featuring the usual suspects (pizza, chicken nuggets, spaghetti bolognese), plus treats such as marshmallow knickerbocker glory (an elaborate ice-cream sundae).

Where to Stay from Victoria to Earl's Court

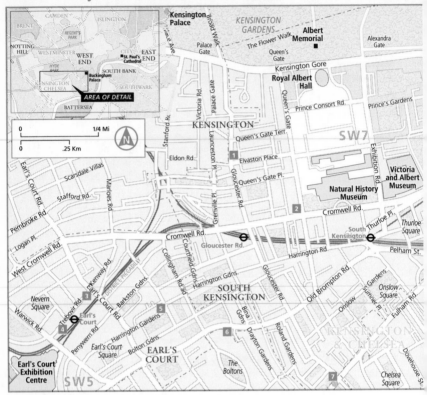

In Mayfair you'll find the Berkeley's sister hotels, **The Connaught** with its "country house" feel, and the Art Deco masterpiece **Claridge's**. Both offer the same kids' amenities. However, neither has a pool, which it's not unreasonable to expect at these prices.

Wilton Place, SW1X 7RL. (C) **020/7235-6000.** Fax 020/7235-4330. www.theberkeleyhotellondon.com. 217 units. £329–£479 ($625–$910) double; from £529 ($1,005) suite. 1 child under 12 stays free in parent's room. Rollaway £75 ($143) for over 12s, crib free. AE, DC, MC, V. Tube: Knightsbridge or Hyde Park Corner. **Amenities:** 3 restaurants; bar; rooftop swimming pool; health club and spa; 24-hr. room service; concierge; babysitting; laundry service/dry cleaning. *In room:* A/C, TV/DVD/CD w/pay movies, dataport, minibar, hair dryer, safe.

Cheval Apartments   There's a negotiable minimum 7-night stay at these contemporary apartments, but you'll probably want to extend your sojourn rather than check out early. These apartments are ideal for shopaholic teens eager to flex your plastic in the nearby Harvey Nichols or Harrods, or for science or natural history buffs looking forward to checking out the big museums. But younger kids don't go unheeded—cots, highchairs, and stair gates are provided, and staff members can set up babysitting or nanny services. A booklet provides suggestions for nearby child-friendly eateries and helpful phone numbers, and the modern, fully fitted kitchens contain a welcome hamper of bread, milk, butter, tea, and coffee.

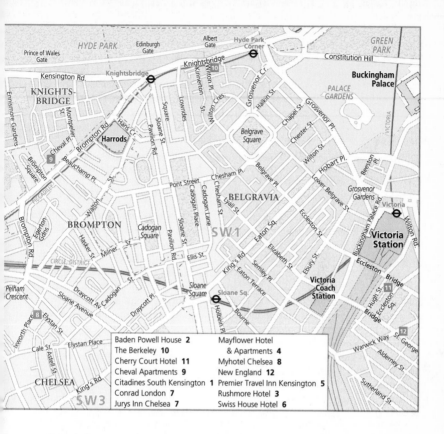

Baden Powell House 2	Mayflower Hotel
The Berkeley 10	& Apartments 4
Cherry Court Hotel 11	Myhotel Chelsea 8
Cheval Apartments 9	New England 12
Citadines South Kensington 1	Premier Travel Inn Kensington 5
Conrad London 7	Rushmore Hotel 3
Jurys Inn Chelsea 7	Swiss House Hotel 6

Space isn't an issue here—separate bedrooms, living rooms, kitchens, and dining rooms may make the apartments bigger than your own home. And there's no need to worry about tidying up: Maid service comes daily at your convenience. The "apartments" consist of two- and three-bed interior-designed flats, town houses, and courtyard houses in modern buildings. What you get for your money includes fine china, flatscreen TVs (in some), and an overall feel of modern luxe in a palette of neutrals and chocolate browns. Rates include free health-club access. *Insider tip:* If you have little kids, don't go for a town house, as these are tall and narrow, and you'll soon get tired of the stairs.

150 Brompton Rd., SW3 1HX. ℭ 020/7225-3325. Fax 020/7581-2869. www.chevalgroup.com. 30 units. £1,495–£1,750 ($2,840–$3,325) 2-bed apt per week; £1,750–£1,875 ($3,325–$3,562) 2-bed house; £2,075–£2,195 ($3,942–$4,170) 3-bed apt; £2,350 ($4,465) 3-bed house. Cribs free. AE, DC, MC, V. Tube: Knightsbridge. **Amenities:** Health club access; babysitting; laundry service; same-day dry cleaning (weekdays). *In room:* A/C (most), TV w/VCR or DVD, dataport, kitchen, hair dryer, safe, iron, trouser press (most).

VICTORIA & PIMLICO
MODERATE
New England ✦ The number of repeat customers speaks for itself at this long-established family-run hotel in a lovely stucco-fronted Georgian corner house. It's

located on a long street leading from behind Victoria Station towards the river. Unlike many hotels in its category, this one has a lift (elevator). Additionally, the whole place was overhauled in the last few years. All rooms are bright and spruced up, with en suite bathrooms with power showers. Triples normally have three single beds, and quads have two large doubles. Beds are handcrafted and supremely comfortable. Customers praise the friendly, helpful staff. Though cots or highchairs aren't provided, many people with babies do stay here, and staff members are happy to store milk in the kitchen. My only complaint is the rather small portions at breakfast. *Insider tip:* Make sure you check the website to enjoy special promotional rates.

20 St. George's Dr., SW1V 4BN. ℂ 020/7834-1595. Fax 020/7834-9000. www.newenglandhotel.com. 25 units. £95–£99 ($180–$188) double/twin; £129 ($245) triple; £139 ($264) quad. Rates include breakfast. MC, V. Tube: Victoria. **Amenities:** All nonsmoking rooms. *In room:* TV, dataport, hair dryer.

INEXPENSIVE
Cherry Court Hotel *(Value)*   A bargain base for hard-core sightseers who don't intend to spend much time in their hotel, this friendly cheapie has been run by the Patel family for more than a quarter of a century. It's set in a Victorian terraced house in a surprisingly tranquil side street, given its location close to the transport hub of Victoria Station. The rooms, though small and basic (well, what did you expect at these prices?) are clean and, incredibly for this price, have air-conditioning and en suite showers and toilets, though the latter are tiny, too. A further bonus is the outside patio area at the rear. For those with kids, there are triples, a quadruple, and a basement "family room" for five, all with double and single beds. The Patels go out of their way to provide visitors with information on the environs, and offer free Internet access in the reception area. There's no dining room, but a perfectly adequate basket of fresh fruit together with biscuits, a cereal bar, and a carton of juice is brought to your room each day.

23 Hugh St., SW1V 1QH. ℂ 020/7828-2840. Fax 020/7828-0393. www.cherrycourthotel.co.uk. 12 units. £55–£60 ($104–$114) double/twin; £80 ($152) triple; £100 ($190) quad; £120 ($228) family room for 5. AE, MC, V. Credit card payments incur a 5% surcharge. Tube: Victoria. **Amenities:** All nonsmoking rooms. *In room:* A/C, TV, dataport, beverage-maker.

CHELSEA
VERY EXPENSIVE
Conrad London *(★)*   This member of the Hilton's luxury tier is blandly modern in feel, but the views over Chelsea harbor and the Thames from one side of the hotel make it special. Views from the other side—over the Chelsea Design Center and the London roofscape—ain't bad either, but these rooms lack balconies (a real rarity in London) on which you can enjoy drinks or room service on a fine day. You're paying for space here—the 160 suites, four floors of which are nonsmoking, all have a hall, sitting room, bedroom, bathroom (with scald-proof taps on tub and basin), and two TVs. Some suites are interconnecting (mostly on the non-river side), but up to two children can share a sofa bed in a parent's suite. Alternatively, splurge on a small, medium, or large penthouse suite, all of which have huge balconies with awesome views. The big ones also boast four-person tubs for family soaks, plus a sauna.

When the kids get fed up with in-room video games (younger kids can play with a welcoming teddy bear), there's a 17m (56-ft.) pool to keep them out of mischief, though you'll have to supervise since it doesn't have a shallow end. Recommendations for nearby sights and activities are also on hand. Sunday brunch in the light-filled

Mediterranean/Asian restaurant Aquasia with its summer terrace is popular with local families, who come to linger over the roasts and copious buffet. It has a good kids' menu (also available from room service) featuring the likes of tomato soup with croutons, and baked beans on toast.

Note: The hotel's off-the-beaten track location isn't the best for public transport (the nearest Tube is a 20-min. schlep), so if you don't have a car, you must factor in the cost of cabs.

Chelsea Harbor, SW10 0XG. (©) 020/7823-3000. Fax 020/7351-6525. www.conradlondon.com. 160 units. From £330 ($627) suite. Kids under 12 stay free in parent's room. Rollaways free; cribs free. AE, DC, MC, V. Tube: Fulham Broadway. **Amenities:** Restaurant; bar; swimming pool; fitness center; sauna; solarium; concierge; tour desk; business services; shop; hair salon; 24-hr. room service; massage; babysitting; laundry service; same-day dry cleaning; nonsmoking rooms. *In room:* A/C, TV w/pay movies, dataport, beverage-maker, hair dryer, safe.

Myhotel Chelsea ⭐   "Where *Sex in the City* meets *Brideshead Revisited!*" shrieks the website, but this hotel is a lot more subtle than it lets on. Located a few minutes' stroll from the shopping meccas of King's Road and Harrods, it should particularly appeal to teenage girls, who might also be tickled to learn that the hotel was designed according to Chinese *feng shui* principles, said to ensure harmony, balance, and energy flow. The excellent beds certainly go some way towards improving your sense of well-being, as does the "Pamper Room" with its Eastern overtones, complete with mood-enhancing treatments and Aveda products. Everything in the hotel—with the exception of grumpy bar and room-service staff, if you're unlucky (they obviously haven't been sampling the treatments)—is designed to induce calm so you kick back and forget about the outside world. If that's not enough, the assistance of palmists, tarot readers, and life coaches can be requested.

Family accommodations include extra beds or interconnecting rooms. Standard doubles are roomy enough to hold a cot but have showers, not tubs; superior doubles vary in size but can accommodate both an extra bed and a crib. It's worth the step up in price to a studio double, which has a separate seating area and two flatscreen TVs so you and the kids can go your own ways. Or blow your life's savings on the largest Thai Suite, which has its own stainless-steel kitchenette and steam room. Downstairs, the attractive conservatory-style library offers free Internet access, soft and hot drinks, DVD movies, and X-Box games. The bar is a relaxing place in which to browse the papers over fruit smoothies, luscious cocktails, finger food, afternoon teas, and more. (In summer, an "ice cream van" circulates daily at 4:30pm.)

There's a larger and older but newly renovated Myhotel in Bloomsbury, with a more Asian *moderne* feel.

35 Ixworth Place, SW3 3QX. (©) 020/7225-7500. Fax 020/7225-7555. www.myhotels.com. 45 units. £250–£280 ($475–$532) double; £360 ($684) studio double; £450 ($855) Thai Suite. Rollaway beds £30 ($57); cots free. AE, DC, MC, V. Tube: Sloane Sq. **Amenities:** Bar; exercise room; treatment room; 24-hr. room service; massage; babysitting; laundry service; same-day dry cleaning; nonsmoking rooms; library. *In room:* A/C, TV/DVD/CD player, X-Box, dataport, beverage-maker, hair dryer, safe, trouser press.

MODERATE

Jurys Inn Chelsea *(Value)*   Jurys Inn hotels won't get your pulse racing—they're very airport-loungey in look and atmosphere—but their fixed-rate standard rooms, which can accommodate up two adults and two children in comfort, are an exceptional value. In addition, promotional rates mean that you can get a double en suite room with a foldout sofa bed for as little as £65 ($123)—a massive bargain, and one that warrants an inexpensive rating. The cost is especially astonishing given the chi-chi marina location of this hotel. Still, you don't actually get river views from the rooms, and it's a 20-minute walk to the nearest Tube stop (though there's a public parking lot nearby). Breakfast and dinner (average international fare) are served in the modern restaurant, where highchairs are provided. There's also a cafe and a bar. Other Jurys Inns can be found in Islington (p. 93) and Heathrow.

Imperial Rd., Imperial Wharf, SW6 2GA. ℭ **020/7411-2200**. Fax: 020/7411-2444. www.jurys-london-hotels.com. 172 units. £110 ($209) double. Cribs free. AE, DC, MC, V. Tube: Fulham Broadway. **Amenities:** Restaurant; bar; cafe; laundry and dry cleaning; nonsmoking rooms. *In room:* A/C, TV, dataport, beverage-maker, hair dryer.

WEST BROMPTON & EARL'S COURT
MODERATE
Mayflower Hotel & Apartments ⭐ *Value*   A rare star on a street of dispiriting B&Bs, the Mayflower comes with en suite rooms that stand out from the crowd with their chunky wooden furniture and colorful but tasteful bedspreads and cushions—some are almost designer in feel. The bathrooms, though diminutive and shower-only, are exceptional at this price. Rooms include some truly appealing triples and quads, and guests should be aware that they may be available at special offers of 30% or more off the full tariffs quoted below—check the website for details. Families staying longer than a night or 2 should inquire about the nearby one- and two-bed serviced apartments.

26–28 Trebovir Rd., SW5 9NJ. ℭ **020/7370-0991**. Fax 020/7370-0994. www.mayflowerhotel.co.uk. 48 rooms, 35 apts. £125 ($237) double; £145 ($275) triple; £169 ($321) quad; £170 ($323) standard 1-bed apt; £230 ($437) luxury 2-bed apt. Cribs free. Children under 2 stay free in parent's room. Rates include continental breakfast (at hotel). AE, MC, V. Tube: Earl's Court. **Amenities:** Laundry service; same-day dry cleaning; nonsmoking rooms. *In room:* TV, beverage-maker; hair dryer and iron on request.

INEXPENSIVE
Rushmore Hotel ⭐ *Value*   Heaven knows how this long-standing budget option keeps its prices so keen, but if you don't mind being out in rather shabby Earl's Court, this friendly, family-run little town-house B&B can't be beat. Guest rooms, though relatively small, are clean and utterly charming given this category, with original features and nicely appointed shower rooms. The conservatory dining room, with its limestone floor, terra-cotta urns filled with cacti, and wrought-iron furniture, is a lovely place to enjoy a complimentary, if undersized, continental breakfast.

11 Trebovir Rd., SW5 9LS. ℭ **020/7370-3839**. Fax 020/7370-0274. www.rushmore-hotel.co.uk. 22 units. From £68 ($129) double/twin; from £78 ($148) triple; from £82 ($156) family/quad. Cribs free. Rates include continental breakfast. AE, DC, MC, V. Tube: Earl's Court. **Amenities:** Laundry service; nonsmoking rooms. *In room:* TV, beverage-maker, hair dryer.

BAYSWATER, PADDINGTON & MAIDA VALE
EXPENSIVE
Europa House ⭐⭐⭐   There's no question in my mind that these are the top serviced apartments in London for those visiting with kids, mostly because of the delightful 1.4-hectare (3.5-acre) private garden they overlook—the garden is enclosed, so you can be assured it's safe. A little play park at the garden's center offers swings and slides, where your children can get to know local youngsters. Staff members have handy items you can borrow to make the best of good weather, such as a picnic rug and a little play tent. What you lose in terms of distance from the city center, is made up for in countless other ways: the ample space within the apartments, the brilliant range of nearby facilities (a 24-hr. supermarket and an organic grocery; wonderful restaurants, delis, and pubs; and a library), and the 10-minute proximity of Little Venice, with its floating cafes, puppet barge (p. 250), and boat trips to the London Zoo (p. 143).

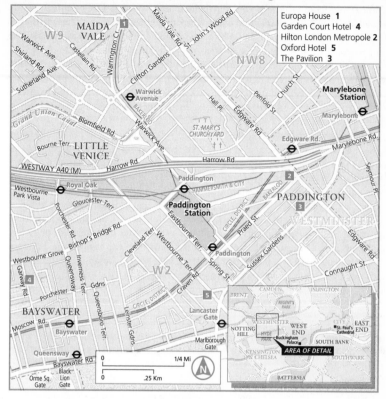

The largely modern decor proves that style can be achieved on a budget; you wouldn't guess, unless you check the labels, that much of the gear is from IKEA. Little extras to make parents' lives easier include highchairs; kids' bowls, cups, cutlery, and bibs; a couple of funky toys; changing mats; toilet steps; and socket covers. You'll be most comfortable in one of the 10 one- and two-bedroom apartments, although if you've a small child in a cot, the one-bedroom flat will be plenty big enough. The kitchens are well appointed and contain "welcome packs" of organic groceries. The marble bathrooms are roomy (there are two in the two-bedders). The deluxe apartments are a bit swankier (bamboo flooring, more luxurious fabrics, and so on).

My only quibbles are the lack of bathrobes and fancy toiletries, which it's not unreasonable to expect at these prices. Otherwise, the place gets gold stars all round.

79a Randolph Ave., W9 1DW. ✆ 020/7724-5924. Fax 020/7724-2937. www.westminsterapartments.co.uk. 13 units. £150 ($285) 1-bed apt. £225–£275 ($427–$522) 2-bed apt. Cribs free. AE, DC, MC, V. Tube: Maida Vale. **Amenities:** Babysitting; laundry service; dry cleaning. *In room:* A/C (in deluxe apts), TV/VCR with free video loan, hi-fi stereo, dataport, full kitchen, hair dryer, safe.

MODERATE–EXPENSIVE

Hilton London Metropole *(Value* Though all Hilton hotels are family-friendly to some degree, this one stands out—and not only because of its monstrous facade. To start, it's just a 5-minute walk from Hyde Park and Oxford Street, and it has a nice

13m (41-ft.) pool with a regular splash hour on weekends. (This can get awfully crowded on weekends, though.) . The bright family rooms ("Deluxe Plus") with their floor-to-ceiling windows can fit up to seven people if necessary, on two double beds and two sofa beds, making this an amazing value for larger broods. Some of these rooms also come with fantastic views over London, plus a lounge area. Alternatively, you can get connecting rooms for two to four people. Lovely contemporary suites each come with a double bedroom, a lounge with a sofa bed, a dining area, and a bathroom with a separate shower. A few self-contained luxury apartments each come with a large double bedroom, a fully fitted kitchen, and a lounge area.

After checking in, kids are given a welcome pack telling them what's on offer here, and detailing their restaurant and room-service menus. The ground-floor lounge bar and the informal Mediterranean/Asian restaurant, Faimma, lack atmosphere, it has to be said, though the latter has a good-value "Planet Hilton Refuelling Menu" with fun dishes such as Flaming Meteorites (meatballs topped with spaghetti hoops and fries), as well as special toddlers' platters such as scrambled eggs or banana and custard. Kids under 5 also eat free with adult guests, but you should beware the drink prices, which can bring the cost rocketing up again. Alternatively, if your kids are 12 or over, whiz up to the 23rd floor, where they will coo at the views from the newly opened Nippon Tuk restaurant, a more sophisticated option serving noodles, tempura, and sushi.

225 Edgware Rd., W2 1JU. ℂ 020/7402-4141. Fax 020/7724-8866. www.hilton.com. 1,052 units. £118–£130 ($224–$247) double; £158–£190 ($300–$361) family room; from £350 ($665) suite, £450 ($855) family apt. 2 children up to 12 stay free in parent's room (in West Wing only; half-price in other rooms). Rollaway beds are free (for certain categories of rooms and suites only); use of cribs free as well. Some rates include continental breakfast. AE, DC, MC, V. Tube: Edgware Rd. **Amenities:** 2 restaurants; bar; indoor pool; health club and shop; concierge; business center; convenience store and souvenir shop; hair salon; 24-hr. room service; babysitting; laundry service; same-day dry cleaning; nonsmoking rooms. *In room:* A/C, TV/VCR w/video games and pay movies, PlayStations, dataport, minibar (fridge for £5/$9.50 a day, plus £50/$95 deposit), beverage-maker, hair dryer, trouser press, iron (on request), safe.

MODERATE

Garden Court Hotel   This popular, family-oriented hotel has been run by the same clan for more than half a century, and their devotion to their art comes through in the details. A refurbishment of the listed 1870 town houses in 2004 means there's a new lift taking you to the bright, clean, and comfortable rooms, all of which are non-smoking. The lounge, with its comfortable leather armchairs, is a calm place to enjoy complimentary tea, coffee, and hot chocolate, though fine weather will have you spoilt for choice between the hotel's pretty paved garden or the leafy Victorian garden square on which it is set. Singles to triples come either en suite or with shared facilities; the three family rooms (one double and two single beds) are en suite. It's best to check exactly what you're getting when you book, as the terms "triple" and "family room" seem to be used interchangeably at times. Note that not all rooms can accommodate the travel cot provided, so this needs to be discussed in advance, too. A wide-ranging buffet breakfast is perfect for grazing or for picky kids. The hotel is near Whiteleys shopping center, which has activities for children of all ages, including Gymboree sessions and an eight-screen cinema complex.

30–31 Kensington Gardens Sq. W2 4BG. ℂ 020/7229-2553. Fax 020/7727-2749. www.gardencourthotel.co.uk. 40 units. £64–£92 ($122–$175) double/twin; £84–£114 ($160–$217) triple; £135 ($256) family room. Crib use free. Rate includes continental breakfast. MC, V. Tube: Bayswater. **Amenities:** Garden; all nonsmoking rooms. *In room:* TV; hair dryer.

The Pavilion   A boho, raucous little joint sure to hit the spot with rebellious teens—as long as you're not counting on getting them to bed early—the Pavilion caters to flocks of rock 'n' roll and fashion hipsters who come for the atmosphere rather than the ultra-low prices. Transformed from an ordinary B&B by a former model and his sister, it has a number of quirkily themed rooms, including the Honky Tonk Afro Room (inspired by *Starsky & Hutch*), the Enter the Dragon Asian Room, and the hippyish Flower Power Room. Although they're on the small side, the rooms (all en suite, with very good showers) do include a *trompe-l'oeil*-themed family room for two adults and two kids. Don't be surprised if a photo shoot is in progress during your stay, or if you bump into Leonardo di Caprio or a Duran Duran on the stairs. Just don't let the kids make a bid for the Phone Queen title, won by model Miriam Fernandez in 2004 after notching up a call bill of nearly £1,000 ($1,900).

34–36 Sussex Gardens, W2 1UL. (C) **020/7262-0905.** Fax 020/7262-1324. www.pavilionhoteluk.com. 30 units. £100 ($190) double/twin; £120 ($228) triple; £130 ($247) family room. Rates include continental breakfast. AE, DC, MC, V. Tube: Edgware Rd. **Amenities:** Laundry service; same-day dry cleaning; drinks on room service. *In room:* TV.

INEXPENSIVE

For the **Parkwood Hotel,** see p. 68.

Oxford Hotel   If your budget isn't elastic enough to get you into some of the truly excellent moderately priced accommodations in this area, then this is a good alternative, with staff who genuinely seem to do their best not to compromise on quality despite the budget rates. Set on a side street leading right down to the wide green spaces of Hyde Park, it's just a few minutes' walk from Paddington Station, into which high-speed trains whiz from Heathrow airport. The street is quiet enough by day but can get a little rowdier at night, especially in summer when local restaurants put tables outside and drinkers spill out of the pubs. The interior stairs can be a little creaky (there's no lift). The rooms are clean if uninspiring, and—remarkably at this price—have en suite toilets and shower rooms (tiny ones, admittedly), as well as microwave ovens. Some are triples and some are four-person family rooms, which are more generously proportioned than you might imagine, given the price. Breakfasts are not a high point—you'd do better finding a local cafe. Rather handily, there's a launderette virtually opposite the hotel, which offers its own, less expensive, laundry service.

13 Craven Terrace, W2 3QD. (C) **020/7402-6860.** Fax 020/7262-7574. www.oxfordhotellondon.co.uk. 21 units. £66 ($125) double/twin; £76 ($144) triple; £83 ($158) family room. Rates include continental breakfast. AE, DC, MC, V. Tube: Lancaster Gate or Paddington. **Amenities:** Laundry service; dry cleaning. *In room:* TV, fan, microwave oven, beverage-maker, hair dryer, trouser press.

HOLLAND PARK, SHEPHERD'S BUSH & FURTHER WEST
VERY EXPENSIVE

K West Hotel & Spa   Once upon a time, this long building with its endless corridors was filled with BBC offices, and you might still see the odd TV presenter checking in or out or enjoying a drink in the lobby bar—the BBC's HQ lies nearby. Now a huge designer hotel located in a still shabby but increasingly trendy neighborhood, K West (part of the posh Landmark group) is clearly banking on the rapid gentrification of the area after the imminent completion of a vast new transport, shopping, and media complex, which will include new train, Tube, and bus stations. And though you're a little way out of the center, you're well placed for the green spaces of Holland Park, Kensington Gardens, and Ravenscourt Park (p. 204) as well as Portobello market (p. 231), and closer than you think to the major museums of South Kensington. Oxford Street is a mere 15-minute bus ride away in a straight line.

The deluxe room, billed as "the room that thinks it's a studio apartment," is a good option for families, though the double sofa beds aren't so comfortable (in contrast to the exquisite handmade super-kings). Embassy suites don't have sofa beds but do boast kitchenettes and large dining tables; K Suites are the top choice, with separate living areas and Philippe Starck bathrooms. The spa, slated for refurbishment at the time of my last visit, is a calm, adult-only zone with luscious treatment rooms. Staff are friendly and laid-back, and don't seem to mind kids running amok. Children under 12 can eat for free in the restaurant, Kanteen, and get free room service; the eclectic-modern food is such a great value, it's reason enough to make it your base. *Insider tip:* If you want a PlayStation 2, mention it when booking, as they can only be used in certain rooms.

Richmond Way, W14 0AX. ℂ 020/7674-1000. Fax 020/7674-1050. www.k-west.co.uk. 222 units. £205–£305 ($390–$580) double; from £355 ($675) suite. Kids under 12 stay free in parent's room. Cribs free. AE, DC, MC, V. Tube: Shepherd's Bush (Central Line). **Amenities:** Restaurant; bar; exercise room; spa; quiet room w/free Internet access; free mobile phone loan; 24-hr. room service; babysitting; same-day laundry service; same-day dry cleaning; non-smoking rooms. *In room:* A/C, TV/DVD w/film hire, PlayStation on request (some rooms), dataport, beverage-maker, hair dryer, iron, trouser press, safe.

MODERATE

Fish Court & Georgian House ⭐
It's virtually impossible to feel the weight of English history more fully than at these historic rental properties overseen by the Landmark Trust, an architectural rescue and preservation charity—they're on the grounds of Hampton Court Palace itself (p. 181) which, together with most of the courtyards, guests are free to wander at any time. (The atmospheric public rooms are accessible during normal opening hours.) Fish Court, a pastry chefs' dwelling on the first and attic floors of the service wing, sleeps up to six people in one double-bedded room, one twin-bedded room, and two rooms with one single bed apiece. Each unit has two bathrooms with a tub, plus a kitchen, a dining room, and a large living room. The Georgian House, in a former palace kitchen, sleeps up to eight over three floors (ground–2nd), in a double bedroom, two twin-bedded rooms, and two single rooms, and also has two bathrooms and a private walled garden.

Both properties are furnished with simple, comfortably worn furniture, and have modern bathrooms and kitchens. Georgian House has a dishwasher, but neither has washing machines, alas. They don't have TVs, either; instead you get jigsaw puzzles, large-scale maps denoting local footpaths, and a logbook in which to write down your experiences. Each property has its own history album that tells of the building's past and its restoration. Linen and towels are provided, except for the cribs. Rental periods can range from a weekend to 3 weeks, and note that off-peak rates can put both options in the moderate category, especially midweek in winter, while high-summer prices nudge them into the very expensive bracket. Central London is a mere 35 minutes away by train, making this a great base between Heathrow and the City.

Hampton Court Palace, E. Molesey, Surrey, KT8. ℂ 01628/825925. Fax 01628/825925. www.landmarktrust.co.uk. 2 units. Fish Court from £614 ($1,167) for 4-night midweek stay in winter, to £1,947 ($3,699) for 1 week in high summer. Georgian House from £668 ($1,269) for 4-night midweek stay in winter, to £2,398 ($4,556) for 1 week in high summer. Cribs free. DC, MC, V. Train: Hampton Court. **Amenities:** Access to grounds; housekeeper. *In room:* Kitchen.

3 South London

SOUTH BANK TO ROTHERHITHE
EXPENSIVE

London Bridge Hotel This fairly luxurious hotel on the buzzing south bank of the Thames is situated in a perfect spot for river strolls, checking out shows at the nearby Unicorn Theatre, and lazy mornings spent tasting the delights of the nearby Borough farmers' market (p. 233). Although this historically fascinating area can be hectic, double-glazing on the windows keeps out street noise. Families are most comfortably accommodated in the large, traditionally styled classic deluxe rooms, with a king-size bed and sofa bed, but if you're on a budget and don't mind being a bit more squashed, cots and rollaway beds can be placed in about 10 of the standard doubles. Up a notch, there are also three serviced apartments situated next to the hotel and sharing its facilities, each with a double room and a twin room, a large sofa bed, two bathrooms, and a kitchen. (Note that there's no lift here.) Highchairs are available in the colonial Malaysian restaurant, where children's portions can be arranged (the same goes for room service), while a more adult-friendly restaurant serves modern Mediterranean cuisine, as well as breakfast. As this book went to press, there were plans to upgrade the classic rooms to a more contemporary design.

8–18 London Bridge St., SE1 9SG. (C) 020/7855-2200. Fax 020/7855-2233. www.londonbridgehotel.com. 138 units. £99–£195 ($180–$370) double; £179–£270 ($340–$513) studio suite for up to 4; £325 ($617) apt sleeping up to 6. Children under 12 stay free when sharing parent's room; 12 and over stay free but pay for breakfast. Rollaways free; cribs free. Rate includes free continental or English breakfast for adults at weekends (children pay £4 supplement for continental, £7 for English). AE, DC, MC, V. Tube: London Bridge. **Amenities:** Restaurant; bar; free access to nearby health club; 24-hr. room service; babysitting; laundry service; dry cleaning; nonsmoking rooms. *In room:* A/C, TV w/pay movies, dataport, minibar, beverage-maker, hair dryer, safe, trouser press.

Southwark Rose ★ *(Finds)* This funky modern hotel is exceptional both for its price range (it only just tips over into the expensive category, but special promotions will almost certainly net you a moderate rate) and for its prime location on a quiet street a few steps from the river and the Tate Modern. Combining boutique-style decor (leather fittings and bright splashes of color against a neutral background) with functionality, it's a useful address for its spacious, spotless family suites (a double in one room and a double sofabed in the other) equipped with good (though shower-only) bathrooms and kitchenettes. Doubles are on the small side but have room for a crib. A business lounge offers free faxing and photocopying, complimentary drinks and snacks, and Internet access. Breakfasts are a bit steeply priced but offer lots of choices; otherwise, prices in the lovely top-floor restaurant, which serves child-friendly modern and traditional food ranging from marinated chili prawns to fish and chips, are good by London standards. Get here before the rest of the world finds out, but be warned that the modern artwork in the lobby can be borderline risque.

43–47 Southwark Bridge Rd., SE1 9HH. (C) 020/7015-1480. Fax 020/7015-1481. www.southwarkrosehotel.co.uk. 84 units. £140 ($266) double; £185 ($351) family suite. Cribs free. MC, V. Tube: London Bridge. **Amenities:** Restaurant; bar; gym; sauna; business lounge; laundry and dry-cleaning service; nonsmoking rooms. *In room:* A/C, TV, dataport, beverage-maker, hair dryer, iron, safe.

MODERATE

A Fullers' pub-hotel, **The Mad Hatter,** 3–7 Stamford St., SE1 ((C) **020/7401-9222**), is located on the South Bank.

INEXPENSIVE

Bankside House   A superbly sited (and enormous) London School of Economics residence hall offers summer accommodations to visitors (early July to mid-Sept) within the shadow of the glorious Tate Modern. All of the basic but bright and airy rooms, bar a few singles, are en suite, and room-only rates here are a fabulous bargain. You have the option of adding on a meager £3 to –£3.50 ($5.70–$6.65) per person for an English or continental breakfast, and adding a further £12 ($23) per person for breakfast and dinner combined. (There are no self-catering facilities—the one drawback to this venue.) Other handy amenities are washing machines, tea- and coffee-making facilities, a bar, and a game room; unusually for accommodations in this price bracket, telephones come with all rooms. Larger families should note that there's another LSE property, **Butler's Wharf Residence** (⟨C⟩ **020/7955-7575**), in the fascinating former spice warehouse area west of here past Tower Bridge, with mainly five- and six-bed flats, rentable by the night or week, at rock-bottom prices.

24 Sumner St., SE1 9JA. ⟨C⟩ **020/7955-7575**. Fax 020/7955-7676. www.lse.ac.uk/collections/vacations. 833 units. £55 ($104) twin; £68 ($128) triple; £74 ($141) quad. MC, V. Tube: Southwark. **Amenities:** Dining room; bar; game room; laundry facilities. *In room:* Hand basin.

Premier Travel Inn County Hall *(Value)*   Luxury hotels would give their right arm for this chain hotel's plum location on the riverfront, within steps of the London Eye, and in fact it shares its impressive building (the former County Hall) with a far more expensive Marriott, as well as with the London Aquarium. Charm and character are not what you pay for here, but at these prices and in this spot, who cares? That said, this is one of PTI's "Metro" hotels, which means you get little extras such as a satellite TV, hair dryer, and dataport. As with other Premier Travel Inns (p. 67), family rooms (which have a double bed and a pullout/sofa bed for up to two adults and two kids) are the same price as standard doubles.

County Hall, Belvedere Rd., SE1 7PB. ⟨C⟩ **0870/238 3300**. Fax 020/7902-1619. www.travelinn.co.uk. 313 units. Mon–Thurs £87 ($165) double or family room; Fri–Sun £85($161). Kids under 15 stay free in parent's room. Cribs free. AE, DC, MC, V. Tube: Waterloo or Westminster. **Amenities:** Restaurant; bar; some nonsmoking rooms. *In room:* TV, beverage-maker, hair dryer (on request), iron (on request).

Rotherhithe Youth Hostel ⭐ *(Finds)*   Embracing kids, including under-3s, with open arms, this modern, solar-powered hostel provides a calm, comfortable base in a surprising but not unpleasant location well away from the center of town on the way to historic Greenwich. As well as practicalities such as highchairs, baby baths, monitors, strollers, and travel cribs (for which you need to bring linen), it offers a children's library, a toy box, more than 30 board games, giant-size games, a blackboard, a PlayStation, a TV lounge, and a small and secure brick-paved garden. All young visitors receive a free activity pack, discounted attraction tickets, self-guided local tour books and pamphlets, and rainy-day activities such as hotel treasure trails and quizzes. Bikes for both adults and kids can be rented for £10 ($19) per day.

The majority of the two-, three-, four-, six- and ten-bedded rooms have bunk beds. (Some have river views, too.) All rooms are en suite so you don't share bathrooms. They're spotless upon your arrival but, since you don't get daily maid service, it's up to you how grubby they get; bed linen is provided but not towels. Breakfast and dinner (with kids' menus) can be provided, as can picnic lunches, though there's a kitchen for those who want to cook. Local attractions include Southwark Park, the city's oldest municipal park, remodeled in 2001; the organic Surrey Docks farm; the Brunel

Where to Stay on the South Bank & Bankside

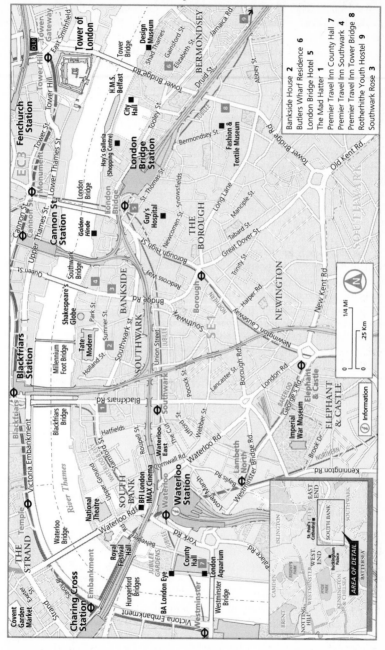

Bankside House **2**
Butlers Wharf Residence **6**
London Bridge Hotel **5**
The Mad Hatter **1**
Premier Travel Inn County Hall **7**
Premier Travel Inn Southwark **4**
Premier Travel Inn Tower Bridge **8**
Rotherhithe Youth Hostel **9**
Southwark Rose **3**

Engine House & Tunnel Exhibition (p. 160); and the historic *Mayflower* pub where the Pilgrims moored prior to their history-changing voyage (kids' portions are available). Another boon is that street parking in this area is free and unrestricted.

20 Salter Rd., SE16 5PR. Ⓒ 020/7232-2114, or 0870/770-6010 within U.K. only. Fax 020/7237-2919. www.yha.org.uk. 70 units. £42 ($81) twin; £63 ($119) triple; £83 ($157) quad. Cribs free. Rates include English or continental breakfast. DC, MC, V. Tube: Canada Water or Rotherhithe. **Amenities:** TV lounge; Internet access; *bureau de change;* self-catering kitchen; cycle store; laundry facilities; all nonsmoking rooms. *In room:* No phone.

STREATHAM & BALHAM
MODERATE

Ambleside Family B&B   Far from the madding crowd, this welcoming Swedish/English family-run B&B is situated in a splendid 1880s red-brick dwelling in a calm and verdant conservation area about a half-hour's Tube ride from central London. For families (up to five people), there's a large room with two comfy sofas, a "double" bed (linked twins), a sleeping loft with two single beds, masses of cupboard space, and a balcony, although for safety reasons this is not suitable for infants and very young children. The decor is flowery without being intrusive. Communal areas include a plush dining room, a library (there's free broadband Internet access for guests), and a lovely garden with a patio area where the kids can make friends with the resident cat. The friendly owners will meet you at the station, or you can park in their driveway. Note that single-night stays incur a £10 surcharge per room, but there's a discount for stays lasting more than 4 nights. The continental breakfast is good but the hours it's served (8–9am) are rather restrictive.

34 Ambleside Ave., SW16 1QP. Ⓒ 020/8769-2742. Fax 020/8677-3023. www.bednbrek.com. 3 units. £60 ($114) twin/double; from £25 ($48) per person per night for family room depending on occupancy. Rate includes continental breakfast. Tube: Tooting Bec. **Amenities:** Free Internet access; all nonsmoking rooms. *In room:* TV, video (in family room), beverage-maker (in family room); hair dryer, library.

The Coach House *Value*   If you're looking for charming accommodations and don't mind being somewhat removed from the action, this ivy-clad former Victorian coachhouse, lovingly converted into self-contained accommodations for up to five people, may well be for you. The main bedroom boasts a rustic, oak beam structure, with French windows looking onto the garden. It also has an en suite bathroom, plus one double and one single bed. The second room has twin beds and its own WC and shower room. You'll have to ask in advance if you need a crib and highchair. The Coach House does have its own kitchen, but while the owners don't mind if you make snacks and heat ready-made meals, they discourage full-scale cooking. A five-course dinner with the hosts is available by arrangement, though this is for over-16s only, so you may have to get a sitter. Otherwise, there are fashionable restaurants aplenty in this family suburb, and central London lies some 30 minutes away by Tube. You probably won't be able to resist the breakfasts (organic if required, for a small surcharge) served in the main house, when the hostess happily shares her local knowledge with guests. The lack of a washing machine is a pain, although there's a launderette just a few minutes' walk away. Note that there's normally a minimum 3- or 5-night stay depending on the time of year.

2 Tunley Rd., SW17 7QJ. Ⓒ 020/8772-1939. Fax 0870/133-4957. www.chslondon.com/ch. 1 unit. £100–£165 ($190–$313) depending on occupancy. Crib free. Rate includes English or continental breakfast. AE, MC, V. Tube: Balham. **Amenities:** All nonsmoking rooms. *In room:* TV, radio, hair dryer.

RICHMOND
MODERATE

The Victoria   A highly regarded and very child-friendly gastropub close to Richmond Park (p. 203), the Victoria boasts a handful of simple but highly stylish en suite double bedrooms, two of which can be turned into twins and two of which have space enough for a travel cot or camp bed. The beautifully firm queen-size beds are dressed with 100% Egyptian cotton bed linen, and the showers are excellent. The out-of-the-ordinary breakfasts include home-baked muffins and handmade *pannetone* (Italian fruitcake), while coffee, organic juices, and baked goods are available all morning and afternoon. In the Spanish-inspired restaurant, the weekend lunch menu always features some simple dishes suitable for children, such as chicken club sandwiches with fries, with kid-size portions available and highchairs provided. The location, on a residential street, is peaceful—rooms are in a separate building across from the gastropub, so they avoid noise. Best of all is the large walled garden on the grounds, with tables outdoors in summer and a children's play area.

10 W. Temple Sheen, SW14 7RT. © **020/8876-4238.** Fax 020/8878-3464. www.thevictoria.net. 7 units. £99 ($187) double. Rollaways £10 ($19); cribs £10 ($19). Price includes English breakfast. AE, MC, V. Train: Richmond. **Amenities:** Restaurant; bar; all nonsmoking rooms. *In room:* TV, flatscreen PC with free broadband Internet access.

4 The City & Around

THE CITY
MODERATE

There's a **Citadines Apart'hotel** close to the Barbican arts center; see p. 67.

Princelet Street ⭐   This Landmark Trust rental property (p. 84) rests in a restored Huguenot silk weavers' house in the historically fascinating Spitalfields area just east of the City. Though a crib is provided (without linen), this is a better bet for those with older kids, as the four-story layout means lots of stairs for you to heft a baby up and down. Accommodating six people, it has one double room and two twin-bedded rooms, two bathrooms and a shower room, a sitting room, a dining room, and a study. The well-stocked kitchen is handily fitted with both a dishwasher and a washing machine. Although there's no TV, there's an enclosed paved garden and plenty to keep you entertained nearby—the house is right on the doorstep of trendy Spitalfields Market, which sells everything from books and records to clothes, crafts, and organic food (p. 235). The house is also just off Brick Lane with its vibrant ethnic festivals (p. 22), Indian restaurants, and Sunday junk market; but it's far enough away to lay claim to a quiet street. The Museum of Childhood (p. 146) is within easy reach, too. Beware, if you have your own car: Parking is difficult in the area.

13 Princelet St., E1. © **01628/825925.** Fax 01628/825925 www.landmarktrust.co.uk. 1 unit. From £580 ($1,102) for 4-night midweek stay in winter to £1,213 ($2,305) for 1 week in high summer. Crib free. DC, MC, V. Tube: Aldgate E. **Amenities:** Private garden; housekeeper. *In room:* Kitchen and kitchen equipment (utensils, dishes, and pots and pans).

CLERKENWELL
VERY EXPENSIVE

The Zetter Restaurant & Rooms   This refreshingly unpretentious "boutique" hotel recognizes that cutting-edge design doesn't have to mean designer prices or preclude younger guests. Though this isn't primarily a "family hotel," teens love the bright-red spiral staircase up through the dramatic five-story atrium of the former Victorian warehouse, and the automatically opening raindrop-sensitive glass roof, plus the hotel's trademark gadgetry, including the swipecard vending machines in hallways, selling everything from cameras to champagne, and the pink lighting option in guest rooms. Staff members take a relaxed and informal attitude towards families, but be aware that rooms are small—for a crib you'll need a deluxe corner room or a studio. For older kids you can pay for an extra bed, available only in deluxe corner rooms, or book interconnecting double and twin rooms. A family of four nudges this otherwise surprisingly good-value option into the "very expensive" bracket.

Within the rooms you'll find such individual touches as wallpaper art, vintage and designer furniture, secondhand classic novels, hot-water bottles with hand-knitted covers, and walk-in showers. The top-floor studios have outdoor decks. The long weekend brunches (till 3pm) in the modern Italian restaurant are very popular with families, offering half-size portions of such child-tantalizing fare as avocado toast with pancetta; and ricotta pancakes with chestnut honey, butter, banana, and crème fraîche.

86–88 Clerkenwell Rd., EC1M 5RJ. 🕐 020/7324-4444. Fax 020/7324-4445. www.thezetter.com. 59 units. £130–£230 ($247–$437) double; £265–£329 ($503–$625) studio. Rollaways £30 ($57); cribs free. AE, MC, V. Tube: Farringdon. **Amenities:** Restaurant; 24-hr. room service; babysitting; laundry service; same-day dry cleaning; non-smoking rooms; free digital music library. *In room:* A/C, interactive TV w/pay movies and CD/DVD player, dataport, minibar, beverage-maker (in rooftop studios), safe.

MODERATE

Cloth Fair   Another Landmark Trust rental property (p. 84), the Cloth Fair resides in a Georgian house overlooking the yard of one of the rare churches that survived the Great Fire of London. Sleeping up to four people in one double room and two single-bedded rooms over two floors (the 1st and 2nd), it also provides a crib for babies. (You'll need to bring your own linen.) There are two bathrooms, one with a tub, the other with a tub and shower; and a modern kitchen, though unfortunately there isn't a washing machine. Situated in the hip Smithfield meat-market district with its great bars, cafes, and restaurants, it's handy for the Barbican arts complex (p. 242) and the Museum of London (p. 168); it's also only a 15-minute walk or so from Covent Garden to the west. High-summer prices nudge this up into the expensive category.

45 Cloth Fair, EC1 🕐 01628/825925. Fax 01628/825925 www.landmarktrust.co.uk. 1 unit. From £552 ($1,049) for 4-night midweek stay in winter to £1,384 ($2,630) for 1 week in high summer. Crib free. DC, MC, V. Tube: Barbican. **Amenities:** Housekeeper. *In room:* Kitchen and kitchen equipment.

Francis Rowley Court   A useful option for single parents traveling with kids, this City University flat, available year-round, comprises three single rooms, each with a TV set, lounge, fully equipped kitchen, and a bathroom with a shower. Linen and towels are provided, as is a small hospitality pack. The best thing about this flat is its location in the heart of trendy Clerkenwell, just minutes from the Barbican and the hip Smithfield meat-market area. Be warned that the place gets booked up quickly, so reserve well ahead.

16 Briset St., EC1M 5HD. 🕐 020/7040-5500. Fax 020/7040-8592. www.city.ac.uk/ems. 1 unit. £96 ($182) for all 3 rooms. DC, MC, V. Tube: Farringdon. **Amenities:** Kitchen. *In room:* TV, no phone.

INEXPENSIVE

Rosebery Hall   This London School of Economics university hall offers rooms during the summer vacation (early July–late Sept), as well as—quite unusually for this type of accommodation—at Christmas (mid-Dec to early Jan) and Easter (mid-Mar to late Apr). Though it inevitably attracts young backpackers, it's also popular with families on a budget. As with the other residences, the rooms are basic but well maintained and

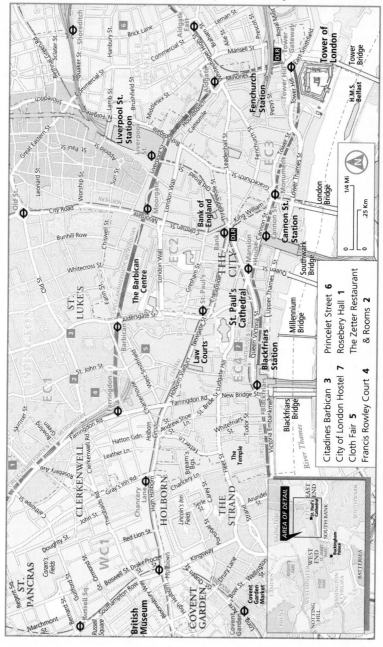

Citadines Barbican **3**
City of London Hostel **7**
Cloth Fair **5**
Francis Rowley Court **4**
Princelet Street **6**
Rosebery Hall **1**
The Zetter Restaurant & Rooms **2**

comfortable; here there are singles, twins, and triples, with all but some of the twins sharing bathroom facilities. The shared shower rooms are clean and spruce, and don't get overcrowded; and there are washbasins in all guest rooms.

Other communal amenities include kitchenettes, beverage-making facilities, washing machines, a bar, and a game room; there are phones in all rooms. The modern building is on the fringes of fashionable Clerkenwell and only a few minutes' walk from all the shops and restaurants of Islington's cosmopolitan Upper Street. If these don't tempt you, you can have breakfast on the patio outside.

90 Rosebery Ave., EC1R 4TY. ☎ 020/7107-5850. Fax 020/7107-5875. www.lse.ac.uk/collections/vacations. 435 units. £48–£58 ($91–$110) twin; £60 ($114) triple; £5 ($9.50). Christmas and New Year supplements. Price includes English or continental breakfast. MC, V. Tube: Angel. **Amenities:** Bar; kitchenette; beverage-makers; game room; launderette; TV lounge.

DOCKLANDS
VERY EXPENSIVE

Four Seasons Canary Wharf ★★★ *Finds*   This is the kind of place where the doorman addresses you by name, and where your kids are greeted with cookies and sweets laid out on a blackboard with a personal welcome message. But practicalities aren't forgotten either, whether it be diape bins in the bathroom or child-sized clothes hangers in the vast wardrobes. Other complimentary baby and children's amenities include bathrobes and slippers, activity bags, PlayStation games, DVDs, and bottles and child-proofing equipment if required. Basically, if it's not there and you need it, just call down and the peerless staff will go out of their way to get it to you post-haste. But the real reason to make this eastern outpost of the Four Seasons your base is that kids 6 months and up and can enjoy use of the truly stunning adjoining Holmes Place 20m (66-ft.) infinity-edge pool overlooking the Thames between 9 and 11am each morning. (Parents can also use its gym, hydrotherapy pools, and spa rooms throughout the day.) And then there are the awesome views from the deluxe rooms on the river side of the hotel, from which you can see as far as the London Eye.

Families are generally accommodated in suites or in interconnecting standard rooms, although very comfortable rollaways and superior metal cribs with colorful bed linen (no tacky travel cots here!) are available free of charge in standard rooms. At breakfast, kids can tuck into such treats as "Monkey Madness" banana pancakes with maple syrup, and at lunch and dinner, they'll be served the likes of "Scuba Diver's" organic fish croquette. Children's room service is offered until 11pm. On the minus side, you might find the bar area and Quadrato restaurant a bit lacking in atmosphere—fine for a business meeting but not somewhere you'd want to hang out with the family. In addition to these amenities, the Canary Wharf Four Seasons offers complimentary kids' toiletries and baby products, plus balloons, candy, and chocolates.

While it seems like a fair trek from the heart of town, the Four Seasons is just 20 minutes by stress-free ferry ride from the heart of London (the boat docks at Canary Wharf Pier in front of the hotel). The central Four Seasons on the fringes of Mayfair is more traditional in decor, and boasts views over Hyde Park. In 2005, this location introduced a teen concierge to help older kids with their visits.

46 Westferry Circus, E14 8RS. ☎ 020/7510-1999. Fax 020/7510-1998. www.fourseasons.com/canarywharf. 142 units. £310–£360 ($589–$684) double; from £650 ($1,235) suite. Children under 18 can share parent's room for free. Rollaways free; cribs free. AE, DC, MC, V. Tube: Canary Wharf. **Amenities:** Restaurant; bar; indoor pool; indoor tennis court; fitness center; access to spa, concierge; business services; 24-hr. room service; massage; babysitting; laundry service; same-day dry cleaning; nonsmoking rooms. *In room:* A/C, TV/DVD w/pay movies, PlayStation (pay by hour); dataport, minibar, hair dryer, safe.

5 North London

ISLINGTON

MODERATE

Jurys Inn Islington *Value*   As with its Chelsea sibling (p. 79), Jurys Inn Islington might not be the most exciting choice around, but it does offer exceptional value with its fixed-rate double en-suite rooms with foldout sofa beds. At this most central branch, you have the option of paying an extra £10 ($19) to upgrade to a more spacious room. You're only a short bus hop from Oxford Street and a few minutes' walk from both hip Clerkenwell and the restaurant and shops of Islington's Upper Street and Camden Passage. Best of all, the hotel is huge, so you're almost guaranteed a room.

60 Pentonville Rd., N1 9LA. (*) 020/7282-5500. Fax 020/7282-5511. www.jurys-london-hotels.com. 229 units. £109–£118 ($207–$224) double. Cribs free. AE, DC, MC, V. Tube: Angel. **Amenities:** Restaurant; bar; discounts at nearby health club and gym; laundry and dry cleaning; nonsmoking rooms. *In room:* A/C, TV, dataport, beverage-maker, hair dryer.

INEXPENSIVE

Kandara Guesthouse   A cozy and child-friendly B&B in a tranquil conservation area about a 10 minutes' walk of Islington Green and 15 minutes from Highbury Fields (p. 206), the Kandara Guesthouse has been run by the same family for more than half a century. Rooms are relatively plain but light and appealing, and the shared shower-rooms/WCs (there's generally one between two guest rooms, plus a couple of extra WCs) are pleasant and well maintained. Rooms include triples with either one double and one single bed, or three single beds; and family rooms with one double and two single beds. It's advisable to book cribs and highchairs ahead. The cooked breakfasts, vegetarian and otherwise, use top-rate ingredients and are worth an early awakening.

68 Ockendon Rd., N1 3NW. (*) 020/7226-5721. Fax 020/7226-3379. www.kandara.co.uk. 11 units. £51–£62 ($97–$118) double/twin; £64–£72 ($122–$137) triple; £70–£76 ($133–$144) family room. Cribs free. Rate includes English breakfast. AE, MC, V. Tube: Highbury and Islington. **Amenities:** Nonsmoking rooms; cycle store. *In room:* TV, beverage-maker.

HAMPSTEAD

MODERATE

La Gaffe *Value*   This Hampstead institution oozes quaintness, combining an Italian restaurant, a wine bar, and accommodations in what was once an 18th-century shepherd's house. Bedrooms are cozy though a little chintzy, some with four-poster beds; all are en suite and comfortable for those worn out from romps on the famous heath nearby. The compact family room is an especially great value, since along with a four-poster bed, a shower room, an attached single room, and a washing machine, it has just about enough space for another fold-out single bed. There's a charming patio for warm weather and a conservatory for less clement times. The Italian restaurant serves up generous helpings of classics such as gnocchi in a tomato and mushroom sauce with fresh basil.

107–111 Heath St., NW3 6SS. (*) 020/7435-8965. Fax 020/7794-7592. www.lagaffe.co.uk. 18 units. £95 ($180) double/twin; £125 ($237) family room. Rollaway free; crib free. Rate includes continental breakfast. AE, MC, V. Tube: Hampstead. **Amenities:** Restaurant; bar; all nonsmoking rooms. *In room:* TV, beverage-maker, hair dryer.

Hampstead Village Guesthouse   The very antithesis of the chain hotel experience, this child-welcoming and informal B&B in a Victorian house close to Hampstead Heath is popular with families for its self-contained studio flat, which comprises a very large room with its own corner kitchenette, shower, and toilet. It normally has a double bed and two singles, but there's room for another single if needed. All rooms have phones. Facilities for tots include highchairs, cots, and toys, and there's a resident hound, Marley, to keep them entertained. The decor throughout is homey in a "lived-in" bohemian way, mixing antique and handmade furniture (including comfortable beds), books, and knickknacks. When the weather permits, you can enjoy a tranquil and leisurely cooked breakfast in the garden. The B&B is a bit difficult to find, so get clear directions to avoid wandering around with cranky kids.

2 Kemplay Rd., NW3 1SY. ℃ 020/7435-8679. Fax 020/7794-0254. www.hampsteadguesthouse.com. 9 units. £75–£90 ($143–$171) double; £145–£170 ($276–$323) studio according to occupancy. Cribs free. AE, MC, V. (5% surcharge on credit cards.) Tube: Hampstead. **Amenities:** All nonsmoking rooms. In room: TV, small fridge, beverage-maker, hair dryer, iron, hot-water bottle.

CRICKLEWOOD
MODERATE
Crown Moran Hotel ★★★ *Finds*   Here you'll find an unexpected burst of genuine Irish hospitality 20 minutes north of the center—this is a largely Irish area, and the hotel is part of a mini-chain with other properties in Dublin and Cork. Formerly one of London's oldest and most colorful pubs, it was converted into a hotel complex in 2003 and, true to the spirit of Irish conviviality, the older building houses five bars ranging from quiet lounges to happening spots with live music and DJs. All offer casual dining and snacks throughout the day (the daily specials are a very good value); or you can eat more formally in the King Sitric restaurant, which offers a fusion of modern Irish and international cuisine, such as traditional smoked salmon with Irish soda bread and capers. The Sunday lunches (the King Sitric sets up a play area for the occasion) and weekend brunches are popular with local families, and there are kids' menus and highchairs. But you may not have any space left after your scrumptious full Irish breakfast (including bacon, sausages, traditional black-and-white pudding, egg, and toast), which is included in the room rate (full English is also available).

Accommodations-wise, cots can be set up free in the standard double rooms. If you have older children, book one of the 15 family rooms with one double and one single bed. The impeccably clean rooms, in an ultra-modern annex, are all large and stylishly appointed for the price, with exceptional bathrooms complete with big tubs and luxurious toiletries. And I haven't even mentioned the 12m (39-ft.) pool, sauna, steam room, and gym yet. If you're still dubious about the area (it's not a looker, granted—think industrial Brooklyn), take a peek at the map to see how close you are to the northern end of lovely Hampstead Heath. Buses run from right outside direct to Marble Arch, and there are two Tube stations nearby. If you have a car, there's even free parking at the hotel. Look out for city break offers and special rates on the website, which make this wonderful place even more of a bargain.

142–52 Cricklewood Broadway, NW2 3ED. ℃ 020/8452-4175. Fax 020/8452-0952. www.crownmoranhotel.co.uk. 116 units. £102–145 ($200–275)) double; £115–165 ($218-313) family room. Cribs free. Rates include full Irish breakfast. AE, MC, DC, V. Tube: Kilburn. **Amenities:** Restaurant; cafe; 5 bars; swimming pool; health club; concierge; travel desk; currency exchange; business facilities; 24-hr. room service; babysitting/baby listening; laundry; dry-cleaning; nonsmoking rooms. In room: A/C, satellite TV, voicemail, Internet access, beverage-maker, trouser press, iron, safe.

5

Family-Friendly Dining

London has gone from culinary laughingstock to one of the world's food capitals in a relatively short space of time. Part of its appeal is its cosmopolitanism—you can enjoy about every cuisine under the sun here, from Moroccan to Vietnamese. However, "Modern British" has also made its mark (classic fare souped up with flavors and techniques from around the world), and traditional British cooking—such as bangers and mash, shepherd's pie, apple crumble, and custard—has made a comeback. The attendant stuffiness has gone out of the restaurant scene, including dress codes, and the emphasis now is on healthful food, variety, and flexibility in a relaxing environment.

All of this is great news for families, but it means that the competition for space in this chapter was fierce. As a result, many places you'd expect to see here might not be reviewed. You don't need to be told about such global chains as **Planet Hollywood, TGI Friday,** and **Hard Rock Cafe**—suffice it to say that I've been there and I won't be going back in a hurry. Just because a company sets out to woo kids doesn't mean there aren't better places to go.

Don't assume that a place offering a **kids' menu** is the best option: Children quickly get bored of choosing among chicken nuggets, pasta, and pizza. It's possible to order imaginatively from adult menus, either by selecting from the starters and sides, or by consulting the

staff on dishes in child-sized portions. Children also love the social aspect of sharing a lot of smaller dishes with their parents: Restaurants serving Lebanese *meze* and Spanish tapas are ideal for this sort of family dining.

This guide focuses on places where you can get good food and a genuine welcome without breaking the bank, though London is a very expensive city when it comes to dining out. Venues classified as **"Inexpensive"** are those in which a family of four can conceivably eat and drink for less than £35 ($67), but these are in short supply. At restaurants classified as **"Moderate,"** a meal should cost you £35 to £60 ($67–$114), and this is the category on which this guide focuses. Anything upwards of that is **"Expensive."** If these figures make your vacation seem impractical, consider staying someplace with self-catering facilities, whether it be an apartment or a youth hostel. Or take packed lunches or picnics out with you (p. 115) as often as possible.

Other good ways to save money are to **breakfast** in a cafe rather than at your hotel, and to take advantage of early-evening **pre-theater menus,** or of **"lunch" deals,** which often go on till 5 or 6pm. You probably want to feed the kids early anyway, and you can always order room-service snacks after they've hit the sack.

Afternoon teas are an alternative for those who want to eat early, serving kiddy-pleasing fare such as finger sandwiches, scones, and cakes (leaving parents to enjoy a civilized dinner after the children are asleep). Yet these are not a money-saving option, with an average cream tea costing upwards of £20 ($38) at a posh hotel, such as **The Ritz** (150 Piccadilly, W1; *©* **020/7493-8181**), **Claridge's** (p. 118) and the **Dorchester** (Park Lane, W1; *©* **020/7629-8888**), which is one of the last places in London serving old-fashioned high teas (substantial meals that can replace dinner; dishes include scrambled eggs and smoked salmon). Note that you have to book about 6 weeks ahead for The Ritz, even though there are five sittings daily. Posh hotels are usually the best places in which to enjoy teas, although the cafe-restaurant **The Wolseley** is an atmospheric newcomer that attracts celebrities in droves.

Pubs are often good places to find relatively inexpensive, home-cooked food. Many **"gastropubs"** (converted pubs serving upscale food, often Modern British) welcome families, although you'll pay more in such establishments. Some pubs don't allow children at all, but many have certification allowing kids in between specific hours (usually not after 9:30pm), when accompanied by an adult. The best way to find out is to ask; www.pubs.com also offers guidance on family-friendly pubs in London.

If in doubt, head for an **Italian** restaurant. Whether it be a family-run trattoria or an Italian-inspired chain such as Pizza Express (p. 110), they generally ensure a warm welcome and convivial family atmosphere; simple, child-pleasing food; and fair prices.

HOURS   It's a rare London restaurant or cafe that closes for Sunday these days (though you'll find some fish specialists closed on Mon); Christmas is the only time when a number of places close. Many now serve food throughout the day, without a break between lunch and dinner, especially when they pride themselves on catering to families. Hours of service are listed in the descriptions below.

RESERVATIONS   Most places, except pubs, cafes, and fast-food joints, prefer or require reservations, and you nearly always get a better table if you book ahead. For famous or very trendy places, you might need to reserve weeks in advance, but even if you haven't, it's worth trying to get in if you are in the area.

TAXES & TIPPING   All restaurants and cafes are required to display the prices of their food and drink in a place visible from outside. Charges for service, as well as any minimums or cover charges, must also be made clear. For advice on tipping, see p. 59.

1 Restaurants by Cuisine

$ = Inexpensive; $$ = Moderate; $$$ = Expensive

AFTERNOON TEA

Café in the Crypt (Trafalgar Square, $, p. 112)

The Original Maids of Honour ✸ (Kew, $, p. 131)

The Refectory@Southwark Cathedral ✸ (Southwark, $, p. 128)

Yauatcha (Soho & Chinatown, $$, p. 111)

AMERICAN

Big Easy (Chelsea, $$, p. 119)

Harlem Soul Food ✸✸ (Bayswater, $, p. 124)

Rainforest Café ✸ (Piccadilly Circus & Leicester Square, $$, p. 109)

Smollensky's on the Strand ✸ (Covent Garden & the Strand, $$, p. 107)

Sticky Fingers (Kensington, $$, p. 114)

Texas Embassy Cantina (Trafalgar Square, $$, p. 112)

ASIAN (MIXED)

Tiger Lil's (Islington, $, p. 135)

Yellow River Café ✹ (Islington, $, p. 135)

BELGIAN

Belgo Centraal (Covent Garden & the Strand, $, p. 107)

BREAKFAST

Bluebird Restaurant (Chelsea, $$$, p. 118)

Boiled Egg & Soldiers (Clapham, $, p. 130)

Café Mozart ✹ (Hampstead, $, p. 137)

Lazy Daisy Café ✹ (Notting Hill Gate, $, p. 126)

Smiths of Smithfield ✹✹ (Clerkenwell, $$, p. 132)

BRITISH(MODERN)

Boxwood Café ✹✹ (Belgravia, $$$, p. 118)

The Engineer ✹ (Camden Town, $$, p. 133)

Julie's Restaurant & Bar ✹✹ (Holland Park, $$$, p. 127)

Quod Restaurant & Bar ✹ (Piccadilly Circus & Leicester Square, $$, p. 108)

BRITISH (TRADITIONAL)

Porter's English Restaurant ✹ (Covent Garden & the Strand, $$, p. 107)

S&M Café ✹✹ (Ladbroke Grove, $, p. 126)

BURGERS

Babes 'n' Burgers (Ladbroke Grove, $, p. 124)

Ed's Easy Diner ✹✹ (Hampstead, $, p. 137)

Gourmet Burger Kitchen ✹✹ (Bayswater, $, p. 124)

CHINESE

Royal China ✹ (Marylebone, $$, p. 102)

Yauatcha (Soho & Chinatown, $$, p. 111)

CREPES

La Galette (Marylebone, $, p. 103)

My Old Dutch Pancake House (Bloomsbury, $, p. 104)

FRENCH

Chez Kristof ✹ (Hammersmith, $$$, p. 121)

Le Bouchon Bordelais ✹✹ (Clapham, $$$, p. 130)

Lou Pescadou ✹ (West Brompton, $$, p. 120)

GLOBAL

The Blue Kangaroo ✹✹✹ (Fulham, $$, p. 122)

Giraffe ✹✹✹ (Marylebone, $$, p. 99)

The Naked Turtle (Richmond, $$, p. 131)

GREEK

Lemonia (Primrose Hill, $$, p. 133)

INDIAN

The Ginger Garden ✹✹ (The City, $$, p. 131)

Masala Zone ✹ (Earl's Court, $, p. 121)

Veeraswamy (Mayfair, $$, p. 114)

ITALIAN

Bar Italia (Soho & Chinatown, $, p. 112)

Buona Sera at the Jam ✹✹✹ (Chelsea, $, p. 120)

Carluccio's Caffè ✹✹✹ (Fitzrovia, $, p. 103)

Frankie's Italian Bar & Grill ✹ (Knightsbridge, $$, p. 118)

Frizzante@City Farm ✹✹ (Hackney, $, p. 138)

La Famiglia ✹✹ (Chelsea, $$, p. 119)

La Spighetta ✹✹ (Marylebone, $$, p. 102)

Loco Mensa (South Bank, $$, p. 128)

Locanda Locatelli ✹ (Marylebone, $$$, p. 99)

Metrogusto ★★★ (Islington, $$$, p. 134)

Quod Restaurant & Bar ★ (Piccadilly Circus & Leicester Square, $$, p. 108)

The River Café ★★★ (Hammersmith, $$$, p. 122)

JAPANESE

Wagamama ★ (Bloomsbury, $, p. 105)

KOSHER

Blooms ★★ (Golders Green, $$, p. 137)

LEBANESE

Fresco (Bayswater, $, p. 123)

LUNCH & SNACKS

Bar Italia (Soho & Chinatown, $, p. 112)

Boiled Egg & Soldiers (Clapham, $, p. 130)

Bush Garden Café & Food Store ★★ (Shepherd's Bush, $, p. 127)

Café Mozart ★ (Hampstead, $, p. 137)

Café in the Crypt (Trafalgar Square, $, p. 112)

Lazy Daisy Café ★ (Notting Hill Gate $, p. 126)

The Original Maids of Honour (Kew, $, p. 131)

The Refectory@Southwark Cathedral ★ (Southwark, $, p. 128)

Smiths of Smithfield ★★ (Clerkenwell, $$, p. 132)

Zoomslide Café (Piccadilly Circus & Leicester Square, $, p. 109)

MEDITERRANEAN

Draper's Arms ★★ (Islington, $$, p. 135)

Sarastro ★ (Covent Garden & the Strand, $$$, p. 105)

MEXICAN

Café Pacifico (Covent Garden & the Strand, $, p. 108)

MODERN EUROPEAN

Bank Aldwych ★ (Covent Garden & the Strand, $$, p. 105)

Bluebird Restaurant (Chelsea, $$$, p. 118)

The Prince Alfred & Formosa Dining Room ★★ (Maida Vale, $$, p. 123)

MOROCCAN

Original Tagines ★★ (Marylebone, $$, p. 102)

PIZZA & PASTA

Italian Graffiti ★★ (Soho & Chinatown, $$, p. 109)

PORTUGUESE

Lisboa Patisserie (Ladbroke Grove, $, p. 126)

SEAFOOD

Café Fish (Piccadilly Circus & Leicester Square, $$, p. 108)

fish! ★★ (Southbank, $$, p. 128)

Fishworks ★★ (Marylebone, $$$, p. 99)

Lou Pescadou ★ (West Brompton, $$, p. 120)

SPANISH/TAPAS

Café Kick (Shoreditch, $$, p. 133)

THAI

The Blue Elephant ★★ (Fulham, $$$, p. 121)

Thai Pavilion ★ (Soho & Chinatown, $$, p. 110)

TURKISH

Sofra (Mayfair, $, p. 114)

VEGETARIAN

Manna ★ (Primrose Hill, $, p. 134)

The Place Below ★★ (The City, $, p. 132)

World Food Café ★ (Covent Garden, $, p. 108)

VIETNAMESE

Green Papaya (Hackney, $, p. 138)

2 Central London

MARYLEBONE, REGENT'S PARK & FITZROVIA
EXPENSIVE

Fishworks ★★ SEAFOOD   This second but most central London branch of an award-winning fish restaurant/fishmonger chain—the other is in Chiswick—gets madly busy on evenings, so if you don't have a reservation for dinner, get here at six on the dot. In the bright, modern surrounds, you can choose from a well-judged menu of classic seafood dishes, or splurge on the freshest oysters, a monster shellfish platter, or a whole fish from the shop counters up front. Kids can get a half-portion of anything on the menu for half-price, or choose from their own menu of fishcakes or—highly recommended and totally unlike the frozen stuff—fish fingers. Fries aren't part of the deal; instead there are superior side orders such as braised fennel or potatoes with butter and fresh mint. If you're in a hurry or think the little ones might get fidgety, make sure the dish you're ordering doesn't take long to cook, although your server will probably proffer this information. (Ours couldn't have been more concerned to keep the kids happy.) *Insider tip:* If you're trying to keep the bill down and don't want to order starters, ask for the appetizer of gorgeous fresh-made *taramasalata* (dip made from fish roe, olive oil, garlic, and breadcrumbs). It comes with a couple of extra dips and enough bread to keep everybody munching while you wait for your mains, and is a real bargain at £1.95 ($3.70). A new branch opened in Islington (© 020/7354-1279) in late 2005, and there's now a Fishworks bar at Harvey Nichols in Knightsbridge.

89 Marylebone High St., W1. © 020/7935-9796. www.fishworks.co.uk. Highchairs, kids' menu. Reservations recommended. Main courses £8.50–£25 ($16–$40); kids' dishes £4.95 ($9.40) or half-price from rest of menu. AE, MC, V. Tues–Fri noon–2:30pm and 6–10:30pm; Sat and Sun noon–10:30pm. Tube: Baker St.

Locanda Locatelli ★ ITALIAN   A few years down the line, this is still one of the most glamorous addresses in town, although complaints about slow service haven't let up. Ever since celeb chef Giorgio Locatelli fumed to the press about the sniffy attitude of many British restaurateurs towards kids, you can at least count on a typical Italian welcome here (and the most stylish highchairs in town, clad in beige leather so as not to jar with the rest of the sleek decor). Before the restaurant opened, its staff received special training in keeping junior diners happy, including inviting them into the kitchen to see their desserts being prepared. Food-wise, you're about as far from nuggets and pizza as possible. There's no kids' menu as such, but the kitchen will rustle up kid-friendly goodies such as homemade spaghetti with tuna balls, and desserts like chocolate and banana beignets. The sublime adult fare includes the likes of tagliatelle with kid goat ragù and white chocolate soup with pistachio ice cream. Locatelli's fellow TV chef and "domestic goddess" Nigella Lawson is said to regularly bring her offspring for lunch here, which is the greatest endorsement you can get, but just be warned about those infamous waits—if you've got a fidgety kid, this place may not be for you. On the other hand, as of September 2005, it extended its opening hours to embrace Sunday lunch and dinner—a great time for family dining.

8 Seymour St., W1. © 020/7935-9088. www.locandalocatelli.com. Highchairs. Reservations required. Main courses £20–£29 ($37–$55). AE, MC, V. Mon–Thurs and Sun noon–3pm and 7–11pm; Fri and Sat noon–3pm and 7–11:30pm. Tube: Marble Arch.

MODERATE
Giraffe ★★★ GLOBAL   This is the kind of restaurant every parent wishes you had at the end of your street: bright but stylish in decor, with a funky world music soundtrack,

Where to Dine in Central London & Clerkenwell

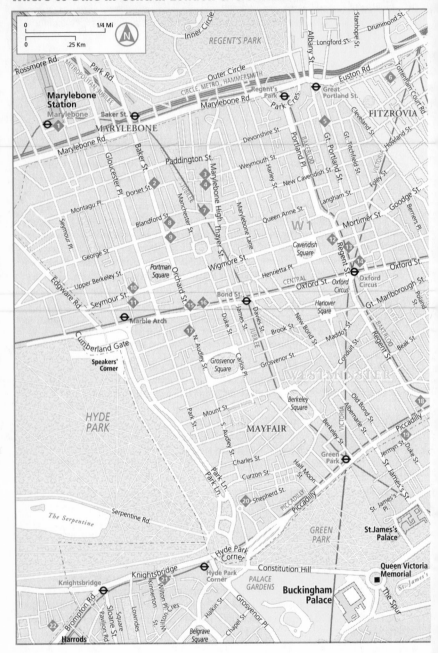

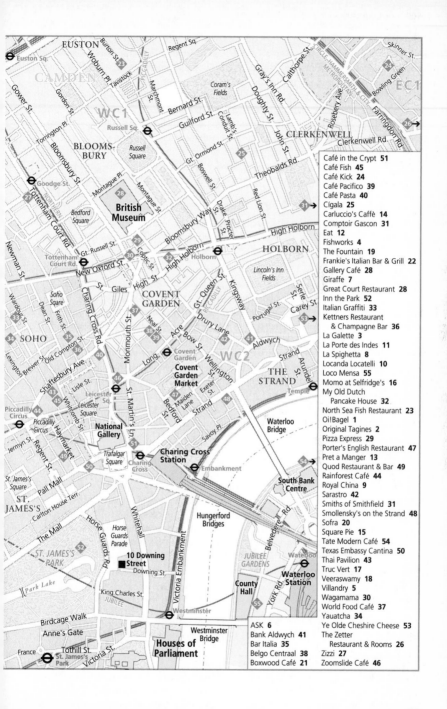

cheerful and endlessly patient young staff, a good-value kids' menu, and an eclectic, globally inspired main menu on which everyone is guaranteed to find something to suit their mood, from tasty southeast Asian curries to burgers and excellent fries. Best of all, if you're not feeling virtuous enough to join the kids in the luscious fruit smoothies or steaming mugs of hot chocolate with melting marshmallows, you can pick from a superb range of cocktails (from chocolate martinis to a killer Bloody Mary), beers, and wines by the glass or bottle. Each of the 11 (and growing) nonsmoking branches of this "herd" is well situated for family activities, be it kite-flying on Hampstead Heath, petting animals at Battersea Park Children's Zoo, or catching some culture at the Royal Festival Hall. There's even a location at Heathrow airport now. *Insider tip:* Weekend brunches are superb but can be hellishly busy; weekdays are quieter, and you can take advantage of special deals for both kids and adults. Note also that Giraffe opens early, making it a great breakfast option.

36–8 Blandford St., W1. ✆ 020/7935-2333. www.giraffe.net. Kids' menu, highchairs. No reservations Sat and Sun lunch. Main course £6.95–£11 ($13–$21). Kids' deal Mon–Fri £4.95 ($9.40) for main, dessert, and smoothie or juice. AE, MC, V. Mon–Fri 8am–11pm, Sat 9am–11pm, Sun 9am–10:30pm. Tube: Baker St.

La Spighetta 🟊🟊 ITALIAN   This excellent restaurant, easily overlooked in its basement location beneath a sushi bar, is well worth seeking out for its simple, well-priced Italian fare and friendly staff, who are happy to organize kids' portions of unfamiliar but addictive dishes such as Sardinian *malloreddus* (shellfish-shaped pasta) with homemade sausage and tomato sauce. The northern Italian–style pizzas here are something else, whether it's the sophisticated (wild boar prosciutto, rocket, and goats' cheese dressing) or the gimmicky (half-calzone, half-pizza); the semi-open kitchen allows you to watch them being made. The dessert list is heavy on the booze, but servings of real ice cream won't leave anyone feeling cheated.

43 Blandford St., W1. ✆ 020/7486-7340. www.spighetta.co.uk. Highchairs. Reservations recommended. Main courses £13–£16 ($24–$30). AE, MC, V. Mon–Thurs noon–2:30pm and 6:30–10:30pm; Fri and Sat noon–2:30pm and 6:30–11pm; Sun 12:30–3pm and 6:30–10pm. Tube: Baker St.

Original Tagines 🟊🟊 MOROCCAN   This cozy little restaurant on a quiet road off Baker Street lures you in with its tempting aromas and warm North African decor. You'll be glad you succumbed: The food is divine, from traditional starters such as hummus, and *b'stilla* pastries (filled with pigeon, lemon-flavored eggs, and almonds), to full-blown dishes like couscous Imperial loaded with lamb, chicken, *merguez* (spicy North African sausage), and vegetables. Many of the *tagines* (stews) are cooked with fruit—lamb with caramelized pear, for instance, or chicken with prunes and almonds—and go down very well with kids, who can get smaller portions. Best of all, though, are the divine desserts—don't leave without at least sharing a bowl or two of the rice pudding with orange blossoms. *Insider tip:* The set lunches are a good bargain.

7a Dorset St., W1. ✆ 020/7935-1545. www.originaltagines.com. Highchairs. Reservations recommended. Main courses £9.50–£12 ($18–$23). MC, V. Mon–Fri noon–3pm and 6–11pm; Sat 6–11pm. Tube: Baker St.

Royal China 🟊 CHINESE   Relocated since 2004 from its previous, smaller site farther up the street, the Royal China has eschewed its former rather 1970s slick black decor in favor of something a little more up to date. The look is still luxurious, but don't be put off—this place is surprisingly accommodating for kids, even the very young, and the chefs don't mind if you order off-menu. (They may embellish an order of, say, plain omelets, with pork, so do say if you are vegetarian.) Even more remarkably, given the notoriously indifferent service of many Chinese restaurants in London, those with babies may find them being whisked off for a tour of the kitchens or passed around the cooing staff while you enjoy their meal, which may include meaty pan-fried eggplant with minced shrimp or subtly flavored salted prawns with vegetables. Make sure the little ones save space for the delicious desserts, such as chilled mango pudding. Despite its cavernous size, this place is hugely popular, especially for the dim sum brunches (the best in London, some say), so try to book ahead. Prices are very reasonable, given the West End location. Note that there are further branches in Queensway, St. John's Wood, and Docklands; the last has an open-air seating area overlooking the river.

40–42 Baker St., W1. ℂ 020/7487-4688. wwww.royalchinagroup.co.uk. Highchairs. Reservations recommended. Main courses £7.50–£32 ($14–$61). AE, MC, V. Mon–Thurs noon–11pm; Fri and Sat noon–11:30pm; Sun 11am–10pm. Tube: Marble Arch.

INEXPENSIVE

Carluccio's Caffè ★★★ *Value* ITALIAN   If you don't like bustle, don't come to one of Carluccio's hectic all-day eateries. You'll miss out, though—despite being a rapidly growing chain (there are about 20 branches total, most of them in London), Carluccio's is a breath of fresh Italian air. This most central branch, in a quiet square just a few steps from Oxford Circus, is very useful if you're shopping in the West End. All of the authentic regional dishes offered in the bright, modern space are on the smallish side, making them ideal for hungry kids (prices are in keeping with the size), but smaller portions of many of the dishes are available. There's also a wonderful, great-value "Per I Piccoli" menu, starting off with *grissini* and a soft drink; progressing to your choice of a superior plate of cold meats, chicken breast with rosemary potatoes, or spaghetti dishes; and finishing with a scoop of ice cream. Highlights of the main menu are the rich wild mushroom soup studded with pancetta, and homemade spinach and ricotta ravioli with butter and sage. Staff don't mind if you're just here to linger over a thick Florentine chocolate drink. As you'd expect from an Italian operation, the staff are also marvelous with kids. ***Insider tip:*** Come for an early lunch to avoid the sussed-up office hordes (you can't book during the day), and to get an outside table that will really make you feel you're on vacation if the sun is shining.

8 Market Place, W1. ℂ 020/7636-2228. www.carluccios.com. Kids' menu, highchairs. Reservations for evening tables only. Main courses £4.95–£11 ($9.40–$21), kids' menu £4.50 ($8.60). AE, MC, V. Mon–Fri 7:30am–11pm; Sat 10am–11pm; Sun 10am–10pm. Tube: Oxford Circus.

La Galette CREPES   It's handy to know about this place, just off the northern end of Marylebone High Street, serving authentic, child-pleasing, savory buckwheat Breton pancakes from morning to late evening. Variations can be as simple or as complex as you like—try one plain with Normandy butter; or another *super complète* with ham, cheese, egg, onion, and mushrooms; then a basic dessert crepe with lemon and sugar or a more fanciful confection with caramelized apple and crème chantilly. Non-galette options include *hors-d'oeuvres* such as country terrine with toast and cornichons, good peasant salads, sorbet, and ice cream. Parents shouldn't miss the traditional accompaniment to galettes—a *bolée* (porcelain cup) of Breton or Normandy cider.

56 Paddington St., W1. ℂ 020/7935-1554. www.lagalette.com. Highchairs. No reservations for groups of less than 6. Main-course galettes £3.50–£8.20 ($6.70–$16). AE, MC, V. Mon–Fri 9:30am–11pm; Sat and Sun 10am–11pm. Tube: Baker St.

BLOOMSBURY & HOLBORN

Although this is a good area for budget accommodations, restaurants tend to be touristy, overpriced, and of poor quality. That said, various decent chains (p. 110)

Food on the Go: Takeouts & Deliveries

Staying in an apartment is a good way to save money on restaurant bills, but you don't want to spend the entire time slaving over a hot stove. The following are some noteworthy choices for takeout service:

Basilico: This award-winning, five-strong Italian chain, with branches in Hampstead, Islington, Fulham, Clapham, and Richmond, has won plaudits for its handmade pizzas baked in wood-fired brick ovens. Its salad and juices are first-class, too, and delivery is free for orders over £10 ($19). ℂ **0800/ 3162656;** www.basilico.co.uk.

Deliverance: This is a very handy service for families who can't agree on what kind of cuisine they want: It offers European, North African, and Asian fare, which means Dad can have good old English shepherd's pie, Mom can have a Thai stir-fry with sticky rice, and Junior can feast on outstanding pasta dishes such as penne with organic smoked salmon and baby spinach. Note that if you order via the website, you must enter your full postal code such as W1H 4NE); otherwise the system will try to spit you out. ℂ **0800/ 019-1111;** www.deliverance.co.uk.

Room Service: This outfit can deliver meals from more than 80 London restaurants to your apartment or hotel within about an hour. Restaurants include Ed's Easy Diner, Planet Hollywood, and Sticky Fingers. Request a brochure online, or order directly through the website. ℂ **020/7644-6666;** www.roomservice.co.uk.

have outlets here, including **Strada** on Great Queen Street; **Pizza Express** on Coptic Street, High Holborn, and Southampton Row; **Ask** on Southampton Row; and **La Porchetta** on Boswell Street. The British Museum also has a variety of good eating options in its atmospheric **Great Court** (p. 129). For a fashionable but family-friendly Spanish restaurant, try **Cígala** (p. 194). Order a traditional "chippie" at **North Sea Fish Restaurant** (p. 194).

INEXPENSIVE

My Old Dutch Pancake House CREPES   This clean and airy space sparingly decorated with Dutch-themed posters has been going strong for years, so it's clearly doing something right—filling diners with its wide range of genuine Dutch pancakes, which are slightly thicker than crepes. Pancakes range from savory vegetarian options; to home classics; to specials such as the highly recommended Amsterdammer with smoked bacon, apple slices, and maple syrup; to sweet confections served relatively plain (with vanilla sugar and slices of lemon) or wondrously and teeth-rottingly over-the-top (for instance, with banana, sultanas, coconut, and cacao sauce). All are served on enormous traditional blue and white tableware. You can also get salads; oddities such as *bitterballen* (a traditional starter made of breadcrumbs, onions, cheese, and garlic, served with sour cream), waffles, and other desserts. There's no kids' menu, but this is definitely a sharing kind of place; portions are huge so three pancakes should be enough for four unless you're ravenous. There are other branches on the King's Road in Chelsea and in Ealing, W5.

132 High Holborn, WC1. © 020/7242-5200. Highchairs. Main courses £6–£8.95 ($11–$17). AE, MC, V. Mon–Sat noon–11:30pm; Sun noon–10:30pm. Tube: Holborn.

Wagamama ★ *Value* JAPANESE   This phenomenally successful stable of noodle joints based on Japanese ramen bars is a great place for an inexpensive and convivial family meal—they're so noisy and hectic, nobody bats an eyelash if your kids decide to raise the roof. Eating takes place at long communal tables with bench seating, which adds to the fun while it discourages you from lingering. (This is fast food, after all—in fact, the dishes arrive so quickly there's barely time for kids to make use of the crayons and paper provided.) Kids love being able to see the chefs at work and are fascinated by the electronic handhelds with which the waitstaff punch orders and zap them through to the kitchen. The side dishes and mains (there are no starters) are brought out as soon as they're ready, which means some members of the party get their order before others; share what's brought out and don't worry about who ordered what. The emphasis is on "positive"—healthy—fare, and the punchy noodle dishes (in soup, in sauces, or cooked on a griddle) certainly put a spring in your step, as do the zingy fresh-squeezed juices. Kids 10 and under enjoy their own keenly priced "mini-menu" of three scaled-down noodle dishes and one chicken-and-rice dish, which go down well supplemented with yummy steamed duck, chicken, prawn, or vegetable dumplings with dipping sauces. At the time of writing, there were 20 branches of Wagamama in London, including Marylebone, Camden, Kensington High St., Covent Garden, Leicester Square, Islington; and the Royal Festival Hall on the South Bank.

4a Streatham St., WC1. © 020/7323-9223. www.wagamama.com. Kids' menu, highchairs. Reservations not accepted. Main courses £5.75–£9.60 ($11–$18); kids' dishes £2.75–£3.95 ($5.20–$7.50). AE, MC, V. Mon–Sat noon–11pm; Sun 12:30–10pm. Tube: Tottenham Court Rd.

COVENT GARDEN & THE STRAND

Many restaurants in this theater district exist purely to sell substandard fare to unwary tourists, but there are also some very fine choices here, some of them offering good-value pre-theater menus, including the restaurants at swank hotel One Aldwych (p. 71).

EXPENSIVE

Sarastro ★ MEDITERRANEAN   This flamboyant place, which bills itself as "the show after the show," is a great spot for a celebration meal—it's laid out like an opera house, with rich draperies, theatrical knickknacks, and even a number of gilded opera boxes in which diners can sit. It's trashy, but enjoyably so. Families are best off coming for the Sunday "opera cabarets," which kick off at 1:30pm. For £20 ($37) per person, or half that for kids, you can watch performances by young talent and students from leading opera houses, including the Royal Opera and English National Opera nearby, while enjoying a three-course menu that includes Turkish/Greek hors d'oeuvres such as cheese *borek* (stuffed filo pastries), mains such as Anatolian-style lamb and, for dessert, a choice of fresh fruit or *sekerpare* (a pastry cooked in honey sherbet and topped with pistachios).

126 Drury Lane, WC2. © 020/7836-0101. www.sarastro-restaurant.com. Reservations recommended. Main courses £8.50–£16 ($16–$30). AE, DC, MC, V. Daily noon–midnight. Tube: Covent Garden.

MODERATE

Bank Aldwych ★ MODERN EUROPEAN   This airy modern restaurant, with its Coney Island murals, bright funky furniture, and startling chandelier made of 3,000 glass slates and covering the entire ceiling (it takes a week to clean, with people working through the night), is a pleasure to visit at any time, but hip young families flock here for the relaxed Sunday brunches lasting till 5pm, when kids can doodle away at a table set up in the corner while parents sit back and enjoy the live jazz and Modern European food. The menu ranges from light dishes such as risotto, or eggs on toast, to hefty roasts, fish, and more. Kids get their own two-course menu featuring the likes of chipolatas (long thin sausages) and mash, fish and chips, linguine, sticky toffee pudding, and milkshakes. Most dishes are well cooked and tasty, but avoid the uninspiring Caesar salad. There is also an interesting range of breakfast choices during the week. Note that there's a Westminster sister restaurant with a smaller kids' menu, but it's closed on Sunday.

1 Kingsway, WC2. © 020/7379-9797. www.bankrestaurants.com. Kids' menu, highchairs. Reservations recommended. Main courses £13–£21 ($30–$40); kids' menu £7.25 ($14). AE, DC, MC, V. Mon–Fri 7.30–11am, noon–3pm, and 5:30–11:30pm; Sat 11:30am–3:30pm and 5:30–11pm; Sun 11:30am–5pm Tube: Holborn.

Food on the Go: Sandwiches & Snack Stops

There'll be days when you don't have the time, money, or inclination to sit down for a full lunch, especially if you're dining out in the evening. If it's just a sandwich you're looking for, one of the best chains is **Pret a Manger** (298 Regent St.; © **020/7932/5219;** www.pret.com), with scores of branches selling its handmade, no-additives sandwiches, plus sushi, salads, pastries, and desserts. High points are the crayfish with rocket salad and the carrot cake. Also first-class are the juices and smoothies. A similar but slightly less ubiquitous place is the simply named **Eat** (319 Regent St.; © **020/7637-9400;** www.eatcafe.com), with great handmade sandwiches (try the tuna crunch), pies, salads, and desserts. This is also a fine spot for a cheap breakfast, whether it be muesli with fruit, or bacon butties (bacon sandwiches, usually with sliced white bread).

Bagel aficionados can get your fix at **Oi!Bagel** (© **020/7723-7321;** www.oi bagel.co.uk), which has branches at Marylebone Station, W1; in the West One Shopping Centre on Oxford Street, W1; and elsewhere. Their fresh handmade bagels come in a variety of guises; the breakfasts and lunch boxes serving four to five people (£10–£20/$19-$38) are a particularly great option for families. If you're in the East End, it's worth seeking out the almost legendary (and much cheaper) **Brick Lane Beigel Bake** (159 Brick Lane, E1; © **020/7729-0616**), open round the clock and producing more than 7,000 bagels a night, which you can enjoy filled with smoked salmon, salt beef, chopped liver, and more. Prices range from just 15p to £1.50 (25¢–$2.85). Other traditional Kosher breads are sold there, too.

For something a little more hearty, **Square Pie** (© **020/7377-1114;** www.squarepie.com) sells traditional and modern pies at Spitalfields Market, Selfridges' food hall, and Canary Wharf. Choose from classics such as steak and mushroom, or from more adventurous takes such as jerk chicken with sweet potato. Prices start at about £5.95 for a takeout pie with gravy, great mash, and mushy or garden peas. It's also worth knowing about the family-size "Take Me Home and Bake Me" pie.

Porter's English Restaurant ✿ TRADITIONAL BRITISH   This is a firm family favorite for its traditional, and calorie-laden, English food—think lamb and apricot pie, beef with herb dumplings, and the kind of stodgy desserts you imagine are served up at British boarding schools. Kids under 12 get their own menu of hearty fare such as sausage, mash, and beans, but make sure they save room for the old-fashioned desserts such as trifle and syrup sponge pudding. They also get their own great cocktails, including one made from orange juice, ginger ale, and strawberry syrup. The traditional English teas are another reason to visit—just make sure not to come dressed in your tightest trousers. Decor-wise, you may have hoped for something a little more classy given that it's owned by the Earl of Bradford. Still, kids are entertained by tacky touches such as the old porter's cart dangling from the ceiling. Note also that the restaurant offers deals combining dinner with a trip on British Airways' London Eye, or with West End shows such as *Mary Poppins* and *The Lion King*.

17 Henrietta St., WC2. ✆ 020/7836-6466. www.porters.uk.com. Reservations recommended. Main courses £9.95–£16 ($19–$30); kids' main courses £6 ($11). AE, DC, MC, V. Mon–Sat noon–11:30pm; Sun noon–10:30pm. Tube: Covent Garden.

Smollensky's on the Strand ✿ AMERICAN   This is one of those places you expect to hate but come away from feeling grateful it exists, even if you wouldn't want to come here more than once in a while. It's touristy, sure, but the American diner-style food is actually very good, especially the steaks, and there's a special kids' menu (with pizza, ravioli, hot dogs, mini-steaks, desserts, and cocktails). Come on the weekend, ideally, when there's a "Family Fun Day" noon through 4pm, boasting a play area involving clowns, face-painting (for £3/$6), goody bags, and competitions. And don't leave without sharing one of the popular chocolate brownies. There are other branches at Tower Bridge (with great views), Canary Wharf, Hammersmith, and Twickenham, but they're not so kiddy-oriented. There are plans to modernize the decor here in 2006.

105 The Strand, WC2. ✆ 020/7497-2101. www.smollenskys.com. Kids' menu, highchairs. Reservations recommended. Main courses £8.25–£20 ($16–$38); kids' main courses about £4.95 ($9.40). AE, DC, MC, V. Mon–Wed noon–11pm; Thurs–Sat noon–12:30am; Sun noon–5:30pm and 6:30–10:30pm. Tube: Covent Garden.

INEXPENSIVE

Belgo Centraal BELGIAN   The food here has slipped a notch or two in recent years, but Belgo is still a fun place to bring the kids, who find it entertaining that the waiters dress in monks' habits (presumably a reference to the Trappist-brewed beers served here). The descent to the basement in the clanking industrial lift is a thrill, and the beer hall atmosphere a laugh. Where parents are concerned, the main draw is that two kids ages 12 or under eat from the mini-Belgo menu, for each adult who orders a main course from the a la carte menu. The kids can choose from rotisserie chicken with apple sauce, pork and leek sausages with mash, and deep-fried cod in breadcrumbs, followed by homemade ice cream. For adults, the mainstay of the menu is mussels and fries, cooked in a variety of sauces, but there are other traditional Belgian dishes for those who aren't fans of sea critters, including *waterzooï* (chicken in creamy sauce) and wild boar sausages with *stoemp* (mash with cabbage). There's another branch, Belgo Noord, in Camden.

50 Earlham St., WC2. ✆ 020/7813-2233. www.belgo-restaurants.co.uk. Kids' menu, highchairs. Reservations recommended. Main courses £9–£18 ($17–$34); kids' menu free with adult main course. AE, DC, MC, V. Mon–Thurs noon–11pm; Fri–Sat noon–11:30pm; Sun noon–10:30pm. Tube: Covent Garden.

Cafe Pacifico *(Value)* MEXICAN   They didn't go light on the Latino theme when they set this place up a quarter of a century ago, but big and loud is sometimes just what you want when dining *en famille,* together with ample portions of gutsy cooking (and, for parents, great margaritas). If you're not sure what you fancy or are unfamiliar with Mexican food, the Degustación del Pacifico combines a taco, an enchilada, and a quesadilla, served with guacamole, sour cream, rice, and beans—a couple of hungry kids could share one of these. Alternatively, the great-value kids' menu comprises soft drink, juice, or milk; main course (quesadilla with melted cheese, guacamole, and sour cream; chicken nuggets; or fish fingers with fries), and ice cream or sorbet. The charming staff members are always keen to offer suggestions.

5 Langley St., WC2. *(C)* 020/7379-7728. www.cafepacifico-laperla.com. Kids' menu, highchairs. No reservations Fri or Sat. Main courses £8–£16 ($16–$30); kids' menu £2.75 ($5.20). AE, MC, V. Mon–Sat noon–11:45pm; Sun noon–10:45pm. Tube: Covent Garden.

World Food Café *(★)* VEGETARIAN   This lovely, light-filled, and friendly cafe serves inexpensive veggie and vegan snacks and lunches from around the globe to a world-music soundtrack. You'll find everything from Mexican chili to Thai yellow curry to Indian thalis to Middle Eastern *meze.* The owner is a travel writer and photographer, and many of the recipes have been picked up during his perambulations; they're good enough to have spawned a cookbook. There's no kids' menu, but most of the food is colorful and appealing to junior palates. If they only want a snack, kids can tuck into such healthy delights as mango and cardamom ice cream and fruit *lassis,* while watching the activity in the semi-open kitchen or peering down into the hippie haven of Neal's Yard below. Try to come off peak, though, as it can get very busy.

14 Neal's Yard, WC2. *(C)* **020/7379-0298.** Highchairs. Main courses £5–£8 ($9.50–$15). MC, V. Mon–Fri 11:30am–4:30pm. Tube: Covent Garden.

PICCADILLY CIRCUS & LEICESTER SQUARE
MODERATE

Café Fish SEAFOOD   This relaxed fish joint is split into a ground-floor rapid-service canteen with wooden benches and long tables (perfect if you need a quick bite before catching a show), and a more leisurely first-floor restaurant. If you can't make it to the coast, this is the next-best place to try British seaside classics such as cockles and whelks, or the catch of the day, simply chargrilled or pan-roasted, although there's plenty of more sophisticated fare, such as pan-fried sea bass with crevette linguine. Kids get their own menu featuring cod and chips, fishcakes, or pasta, plus ice cream with chocolate sauce and a soft drink of their choice. You can also get good deals for two-course pre- or post-theater dinners combined with tickets to shows.

36–40 Rupert St., W1. *(C)* 020/7287-8989. www.santeonline.co.uk. Highchairs. Reservations recommended. Main courses £8.75–£15 ($17–$29); kids' menu £5.95 ($11). AE, DC, MC, V. Mon–Sat noon–11pm; Sun noon–9pm. Tube: Piccadilly Circus.

Quod Restaurant & Bar *(★ Value)* MODERN BRITISH/ITALIAN   Quod is a godsend in an area where affordable, non-touristy restaurants are like gold dust. The kids' menu doesn't offer anything out of the ordinary (spaghetti with tomato sauce, or hamburger or chicken nuggets with chips, followed by ice cream), but it is a fantastically good value. If your child would prefer something more inspired, a starter portion from the pasta and risotto menu, such as potato gnocchi with cherry tomatoes and basil, will only set you back a couple of pounds more. Adults can enjoy everything from classic lasagna to roast belly of pork with Oxford black pudding. If you're on a tight budget, time your visit to take advantage of the pre-theater menu, available from 4 to 7pm Monday to Saturday and 5 to 7pm Sunday. This is also a handy spot for pastries and drinks from 10am during the week, or for afternoon tea from 3 to 5:30pm (except Sun), and it's so big (it's in a former banking hall) that you're never likely to have trouble getting a table. The eye-catching outsize portraits adorning the walls, showcasing contemporary British and modern artists, add drama.

57 Haymarket, SW1. © 020/7925-1234. www.quod-london.co.uk. Kids' menu, highchairs. Main courses £8.35–£18 ($16–$34); kids' menu £3.95 ($7.50). AE, DC, MC, V. Mon–Fri 10am–midnight; Sat noon–midnight; Sun 5–10:30pm. Tube: Piccadilly Circus.

Rainforest Café ☆ AMERICAN   It's your parental duty to take your offspring to one of these jungle-themed extravaganzas at some juncture, so you may as well grit your teeth and get used to the idea. Actually, if you enter into the spirit of things, it can be good fun—unless if you have a child of a nervous disposition, in which case you're better off staying away (many have to be whisked out in a hurry). Most kids, though, love the animatronic, growling wildlife and quickly get used to the rather disconcerting tropical storms that rumble over your heads as you sample gimmicky-sounding but reasonable fare such as Rasta Pasta (pappardelle—flat pasta—with chicken and walnut pesto) and Major Mojo Bones (sticky BBQ ribs). The Rainforest Rascal menu is a whole lot more expensive that most kids' menus, but the range of choices is unusually wide, and—surprisingly—half of the main courses are organic. There are also heaps of goodies thrown in to keep the kids occupied while you wait. If you're trying to stick with healthy options, stay away from the kids' smoothies, which taste overwhelmingly sugary. Otherwise, save the good intentions for tomorrow and get your teeth around some of the immensely gooey desserts. You have to pass through the ground-floor shop on your way in and out, but the merchandise turns out to be both good-quality and fairly priced. *Insider tip:* Avoid weekends at all costs, when reservations aren't taken and you can expect to queue for up to 2 hours.

20–24 Shaftesbury Ave., W1. © 020/7434-3111. www.therainforestcafe.co.uk. Kids' menu, highchairs. Reservations ("priority seating requests") recommended Sun–Fri. Main courses £9.95–£16 ($19–$30). Kids' menu £10 ($19). AE, DC, MC, V. Mon–Wed noon–10pm; Thurs and Fri noon–8pm; Sat 11am–8pm; Sun 11:30am–10pm. Tube: Leicester Sq.

INEXPENSIVE
Zoomslide Café *Finds* LUNCH & SNACKS   This funky cafe in The Photographers' Gallery offers a respite from the fury of surrounding Leicester Square and Covent Garden. You'll feel instantly calmer as you step into the airy, whitewashed space and peruse items in the chiller at the front, which include sandwiches, freshly made salads (available in portions to suit both kid and adult appetites), and home-made cakes. Afterwards, you can settle at one of the communal tables (I've never known it to be busy, so you won't get any elbows digging into you) and enjoy the photography, which is displayed here as well as throughout the gallery itself.

5 Great Newport St., WC2. © 020/7831-1772. www.photonet.org.uk. Highchairs. Main courses £2-£5 ($3.80–$9.50). No credit cards. Mon–Wed and Sat 11am–5:30pm; Thurs 11am–7:30pm; Sun noon–5:30pm. Tube: Leicester Sq.

SOHO & CHINATOWN
MODERATE
Italian Graffiti ☆☆ PIZZA & PASTA   People return again and again to this cozy family-run venue for its superb (and enormous) crisp-based pizzas, which are cooked in a wood-fired oven. Adding to the ambience are the open fireplaces, in which fires flicker when the weather is inclement; the large windows from which you can observe

The Chain Gang

With almost 100 branches in every nook and cranny of the capital and a couple of hundred more around the country, **Pizza Express** (30 Coptic St., WC1; ℭ 020/7636-3232; www.pizzaexpress.com) has obviously been getting it mostly right over the past 40 years, though no one disputes that you'll get better, more Italian pizzas elsewhere. What you come here for, really, is familiarity and consistency—everyone has their favorites among the 20-plus classic pizzas, the handful of pasta dishes and salads, and the desserts (nicely expanded as part of birthday celebrations in 2005). Staff members are definitely more on the ball in some branches than others, but kids are always kept out of mischief with a pack of games and activities. Kids don't have their own menus because the bigwigs in charge think they feel more grownup if they're allowed to choose from the adult menu (they may have a point), but virtually any dish can be customized to take individual likes or whims into account. Kids' portions are provided (the pizzas aren't so huge, though—most kids will be able to tackle one). You're unlikely to spend more than £50 ($95) for a reasonably hungry family of four, including drinks. Unusually for a chain (especially such a large one), the branches are individual in feel, often because they're housed in an interesting old building that has retained some of its original features (in the case of the Bloomsbury branch, a dairy with old tiling).

Not content with the spread of its empire, Pizza Express owns the **Café Pasta** mini-chain (184 Shaftesbury Ave.; ℭ 020/7379-0198), as well as outlets at Covent Garden, Belsize Park, and Richmond); it's another reliable stop-off for pizzas and pasta. Weirdly, it embraces the swank **Kettner's Restaurant & Champagne Bar** (29 Romilly St.; ℭ 020/7734-6112; www.kettners.com), one of the oldest restaurants in town, opened in 1867 by Napoleon III's chef and still

the bustle of Soho; and the big-hearted staff, who sometimes whisk kids away as honored guests to show them how to make pizza. Portions are enormous (a starter would suffice as a main course for an adult, never mind a child), so be conservative when you order or you won't have time for traditional desserts such as pannacotta and cassata.

163–5 Wardour St., W1. ℭ 020/7439-4668. Highchairs. Reservations recommended. Main courses £7–£15 ($13–$29). AE, DC, MC, V. Mon–Fri 11:45am–3pm and 5:45–11:30pm; Sat 11:45am–11:30pm. Tube: Oxford Circus.

Thai Pavilion ★ *Finds* THAI It's worth calling ahead before visiting this slightly chintzy but very likeable Soho Thai to check that the second-floor Sawasdee Room isn't booked by a party—kids love the novelty of sitting on the traditional floor cushions and eating from low tables. If it's full, or if you have a baby or toddler in a highchair and thus need to sit at a full-height table, ask to be seated in the first-floor dining room, where little ones enjoy watching the waterfall and peering down at the bustle on Shaftesbury Avenue. Refreshingly, the kids' menu here isn't limited to European or American standards—although they can get fish or grilled chicken with fries if they so desire. There are also starters of chicken satay sticks, spring rolls, and potato with sesame seeds, as well as mains of chicken tempura with ketchup or mild yellow boasting gilded mirrors and a grand piano—here you can enjoy similar pizzas as well as classy but well-priced seafood, burgers, and all-day breakfasts.

Other Italian-inspired chains worth knowing are **Est Est Est** (57 Upper St., N1; © **020/7359-9198**; www.estestest.co.uk; plus outlets on Chiswick, Wandsworth, and Wimbledon), where kids can wear chefs' hats and assemble their own pizzas. **ASK** (48 Grafton Way, W1; © **020/7388-8108**; www.ask central.co.uk;) has more than 20 branches. Its slightly more upmarket sibling **Zizzi** (33–41 Charlotte St., W1; © **020/7436-9940**; www.zizzi.co.uk) has 13 other branches; **La Porchetta** (141 Upper St., WC1 (© **020/7288/2488**), has three other branches); and **Strada** (4 St. Paul's Churchyard, EC4; © **020/ 7248-7178**; www.strada.co.uk), has more than 20 branches.

Non-Italian family-oriented chains include **Tootsies** (107 Old Brompton Rd., SW7; © **020/7581-8942**; www.tootsiesrestaurants.co.uk; with 13 other branches), which is strong on burgers and organic kids' dishes but leaves something to be desired in the service department; and **Café Med,** some of which, as we went to press, were being turned into new "U.S. Collection" restaurants (including **Hudson Grill** at 184a Kensington Park Rd., W11; and **Brooklyn Bar & Grill** at 320 Goldhawk Rd., W6). Other chains are staying, as is the branch at 21 Loudoun Rd., NW8; © **020/7625-1222;** and a new Café Med slated to open on Campden Hill Road off Notting Hill Gate. Regardless of the name, all will continue to offer more or less the same kids' menu (quality burgers, popcorn chicken, and salmon fishcakes, plus a soft drink and dessert, for about £5 ($9.50).

For reviews of noodle chain **Wagamama,** the globally inspired **Giraffe,** and bustling Italian **Carluccio's Caffè,** see p. 105, 99, and 103.

chicken curry served with rice. For dessert, mango mousse is offered alongside sorbet and ice cream for an additional £2 ($3.80). The main menu has a wide range of fresh light soups, salads, curries, and stir-fries at decent prices, given the central location. There's another location, Thai Pavilion East, designed by a modern architect and also offering a kids' menu, which is handy for a visit to the Imperial War Museum.

42 Rupert St., W1. © 020/7287-6333. www.thaipavilion.com. Kids' menus, highchairs. Reservations recommended. Main courses £6.35–£13 ($12–$25); kids' menu £6 ($11). AE, MC, DC, V. Daily noon–11:30pm. Tube: Piccadilly Circus.

Yauatcha AFTERNOON TEA/CHINESE   If you've got a budding Carrie Bradshaw as a daughter, a visit to this almost unspeakably chic restaurant is a must—you can almost imagine Sarah Jessica Parker and her *Sex in the City* cohorts sitting at one of the designer tables surrounded by shopping bags. Depending on what time of day it is, and on your level of hunger, you can choose between sophisticated dim sum in the basement with its tropical aquarium running the entire length of the bar, and divine cakes and patisseries with an Asian twist in the ground-floor teahouse, accompanied by exotic brews. Customers have complained of snooty service and of being rushed (there's a strict 90-min. table allocation), but most people agree the food is worth it. Avoid the crowds by coming for a late breakfast or afternoon tea.

15 Broadwick St, W1. ℰ 020/7494-8888. Reservations essential. Dim sum dishes around £4 ($7.60); set tea £19 ($38). Mon–Sat 9am–11pm; Sun 9am–10:30pm. AE, MC, V. Tube: Piccadilly Circus.

INEXPENSIVE

Bar Italia ITALIAN/LUNCH & SNACKS   This classic Italian cafe, here since 1949 and a Soho institution, is a great place to bring soccer-mad kids. Even if they don't support one of the Series A league teams whose matches are screened, the atmosphere during a game is electric. The rest of the time, the bar is visited all hours of the day and night by a cast of Soho characters, some arriving on their Lambrettas or Vespas (the bar has its own scooter club, which meets every Sunday at 6pm—anyone is welcome to attend), who enjoy good panini, pizzas, juices, and coffees. Kids are welcome, but try to avoid very busy times, as the place is cramped to say the least (indoor seating is scarce, and generally consists of high stools, while the handful of outdoor tables are hotly fought over). By the way, the blue plaque on the outside wall beside the first-floor window bears witness to the fact that inventor John Logie Baird lived and worked here—indeed, this is where he first demonstrated a fully working TV prototype to members of the scientific community. So you get a double whammy of history for your money.

22 Frith St., W1. ℰ 020/7437-4520. www.baritaliasoho.co.uk. No reservations. Panini/pizzas about £3.50–£9 ($6.70–$17). Mon–Sat 24 hr.; Sun 7am–4am. AE, DC, MC, V. Tube: Leicester Sq.

TRAFALGAR SQUARE
MODERATE

Texas Embassy Cantina AMERICAN   This is another loud but proud (read: heavily themed) joint with a cheerful vibe that appeals to family groups—parents can survey the mayhem over the rims of some of the best margaritas in London, while kids get crayons to entertain them while they wait for taco dinners, hot dogs, or more from a pleasingly varied children's menu. For dessert (£2/$3.80) there's ice cream, with or without apple pie. The adult dessert menu, featuring the likes of *sopaipillas* (Mexican pastries made with cinnamon and honey), chocolate peanut-butter-cup pie, and Key lime pie, is far more interesting. The waitstaff is friendly, if not always up to the mark when it comes to speaking English—you might find yourself explaining something more than once.

1 Cockspur St., SW1. ℰ 020/7925-0077. www.texasembassy.com. Kids' menu, highchairs. Reservations recommended. Main courses £8–£19 ($15–$36); kids' main courses £4.75 ($9). Mon–Wed noon–11pm; Thurs–Sat noon–midnight; Sun noon–10:30pm. AE, DC, MC, V. Tube: Charing Cross.

INEXPENSIVE

Café in the Crypt AFTERNOON TEA/LUNCH & SNACKS   It's not the food that draws people to this award-winning cafe, but the atmosphere—as the name suggests, you're in the crypt of a church, complete with centuries-old stone pillars and brick vaulted ceilings. It's all very Gothic, perhaps even spooky in feel, yet relaxing — you'd never guess you are seconds away from the bustle of Trafalgar Square. Any potential traffic sounds are soothed away by classical music. Full meals, snacks, and afternoon teas are available from a self-service counter, with most dishes prepared daily on-site. Note that as well as a brass rubbing center on-site (p. 185), the crypt houses a gallery hosting changing exhibitions of painting and photography. Call ahead, since at press time the church had entered a huge building project that may see temporary closures in 2006. *Insider tip:* If you have a child in a stroller, you'll find it easier to get into the cafe from inside the church (though there's still no lift) than down the narrow stairs leading directly into the cafe from the street.

St. Martin-in-the-Fields, Trafalgar Sq., WC2. (✆ 020/7766-1100. www.stmartin-in-the-fields.org. Highchairs. Main courses £6–£9 ($11–$17). Mon–Wed 10am–8pm; Thurs–Sat 10am–11pm; Sun noon–8pm. No credit cards. Tube: Charing Cross.

ST. JAMES'S & MAYFAIR
EXPENSIVE

The Fountain restaurant at upper-crust department store Fortnum & Mason is famed for its ice-cream sundaes (p. 221).

Park Life

As well as providing the city's best picnicking spots, London's parks are graced with wonderful and family-friendly restaurants and cafes, all of them with terraces that take advantage of fine weather. One of the best is **Inn the Park** (✆ 020/7451-9999; www.innthepark.co.uk), which opened in St. James's Park (p. 204) in 2004. Set in a striking grass-roofed building and affording views of Duck Island and the surrounding palaces from its decked veranda, its posh restaurant area offers both upscale cafe fare, including children's lunch sets, and seasonal British cuisine. Come for bacon sandwiches, afternoon tea, a warming glass of some of the best hot chocolate in town, or a family winter feast of whole roast organic goose with caramelized Gloucester apples (both lunch and dinner are served). Note that they sell hampers in the summer, for picnics in the park.

In west London, the newly renovated and expanded cafe in the pavilion in the center of **Queen's Park** (✆ 020/8960-6946; p. 204) is a real haven for local families, with a kids' menu of simple dishes such as rarebit for £3 ($5.70); treats such as Portuguese custard tarts and mugs of hot chocolate with whipped cream, marshmallows, and sprinkles; and plenty of space for them to run around. For moms and dads, the breakfast menu runs from homemade muesli with yogurt and honey to full English, and there are daily specials for lunch. Come during the week to take full advantage of the light and airy space, although at lunchtimes it still gets chaotic (and muddy if it's raining).

South of the river, **Cicero's on the Common** in Clapham (2 Rookery Rd., SW4; ✆ 020/7498-0770) is a friendly, slightly hippyish spot for veggie food. Children and animals are welcome. You can sit inside amidst lanterns, or outside in the courtyard, to enjoy the wholesome breakfasts, cakes, salads, and lunch specials. A little further south, **Brixton Beach Cafe** (✆ 020/7274-6276) at Brockwell Lido (p. 214), which derives its name from the fact that this Art Deco outdoor pool is known locally as Brixton's Beach, is a child-friendly place to cool down over snacks and drinks.

Lastly, in north London, on Hampstead Heath, the charming **Brew House** in an old stable block adjoining historic Kenwood House (p. 142) is a gorgeous spot for breakfasts, lunches, cakes, and afternoon teas, especially when the sun lights up its huge terraced garden.

MODERATE

Veeraswamy INDIAN   Britain's oldest Indian restaurant, established in 1926 and graced, over the years, by Charlie Chaplin, Marlon Brando, and Indira Gandhi, was revamped in the 1990s and lost some of its shabby colonial-style charm. That said, the vibrant purple walls and gold-leaf decoration make it a welcoming spot. It's still a great place for a family meal, particularly on Sunday, when there's a good-value, three-course lunch of Indian family favorites for £16 ($30). For kids whose taste buds don't yet welcome such treats, there's an accompanying under-12s three-course menu of nonspicy dishes such as fish fingers, burgers, and ice cream. The pre-theater menu (to 6:30pm Mon–Sat) is also worth checking out. Highlights of the North and Western Indian menu are Malabar lobster curry with fresh turmeric and unripe mango, tandoori baby squid filled with cod and, for dessert, Gujarat *shrikand* (saffron-flavored strained yogurt with berries). It's run by the same folks who run Masala Zone (p. 121); they also own a couple of other award-winning (but more adult) Indian restaurants.

Mezzanine Floor, Victory House, 99 Regent St. (entrance on Swallow St.,) W1. ℂ 020/7734-1401. Kids' menu (Sun), highchairs. Reservations recommended. Main courses £14–£23 ($27–$44); kids' 3-course menu (Sun) £8 ($15). AE, DC, MC, V. Mon–Fri noon–2:30pm and 5:30–11pm; Sat 12:30–3pm and 5:30–11pm; Sun 12:30–3pm and 5:30–10:30pm. Tube: Piccadilly Circus.

INEXPENSIVE

Sofra *Value* TURKISH   This Middle Eastern chain has downsized over the last couple of years, after over-energetic expansion, but it still offers one of central London's best bargains in the form of the exceptionally well-priced set lunches (to 6pm). For just £7.95 ($15) you get two courses that might include a mixed *meze* plate for starters, and *köfte* (meatballs), salmon with bulgur risotto, sea bass, or moussaka for the main. You'll probably spend a bit more once you see the extensive desserts menu, which features baklava, fruit crumble, brownies, and such oddities as tahini ice cream. This branch is in a delightful, villagey part of Mayfair known as Shepherds Market; there are four more, equally pleasant spots situated in Marylebone, St John's Wood, Covent Garden, and Clerkenwell, plus the very central sibling **Özer** (Langham Place, W1), offering a kids' menu with the likes of *köfte* or chicken and chips for a fiver ($9.50).

18 Shepherd St., W1. ℂ 020/7493-3320. Highchairs. Main courses £7.45–$16 ($14–$30). Daily noon–midnight. AE, MC, V. Tube: Green Park.

3 West London

KENSINGTON & SOUTH KENSINGTON

The "Big Three" **museums**—the Victoria & Albert, Natural History Museum, and Science Museum—contain some of the most family-friendly cafes and restaurants in this area. You can also get a great afternoon tea in the gorgeously atmospheric **Orangery** restaurant behind Kensington Palace, or snacks at **Café Boardwalk,** by the Diana Memorial Playground (p. 207). A picnic in Kensington Gardens is another option.

MODERATE

Sticky Fingers AMERICAN   Co-owned by Bill Wyman, formerly of The Rolling Stones, Sticky Fingers excels in its assault on the ears and the eyes, unless you happen to love creaky old rock tunes and garish memorabilia. Many teens do, and that's why you're more likely than not to end up here at some point. Luckily, the kitchen does a

Tips Moveable Feasts

Some of the best places to shop for exciting picnic fare are department-store food halls. Two of the most famous are Harrods and Fortnum & Mason (p. 221). Good, non-messy ideas for outdoor eating are the great bread, cheeses, dips, chunky Spanish-style omelets, cakes, and bottles of concentrate (elderflower is lovely for summer). A cooler box is essential; you may already have one for car journeys, but if you don't want to invest in one, most supermarkets now sell cooler bags that will see you through a picnic or two. Many hotels will also provide hampers for you with a little advance notice.

If you're heading to Hyde Park, try **Selfridges'** wonderful food hall (p. 222) or, 2 minutes' walk away, the splendid **Truc Vert** (42 N. Audley St., W1; ℂ 020/7491-9988), a deli and brasserie selling top-notch charcuterie and farmhouse cheeses, as well as superior picnic fare—sandwiches on artisanal bread, a daily quiche, and great chocolate-orange brownies. On the other side of Kensington Gardens, **Clarke's** (124 Kensington Church St., W8; ℂ 020/7221-9225; www.sallyclarke.com) is famous for its fresh baked breads, and also sells amazing pastries, tarts, cakes, pizza, and focaccia, plus jams, jellies, pickles, and chutneys.

Farther east and very handy for Regent's Park, **Villandry** (170 Great Portland St., W1; ℂ 020/7631-3131; www.villandry.com) is another gourmet food store with a restaurant and bar tacked onto it. Most of the ready-prepared items at the takeaway counter come directly from its own kitchen, while everything in the bakery is produced with organic flour, from the walnut bread, cheese straws, and buttery croissants to the Mexican wedding cookies and to-die-for orange-scented cheesecake. This is food worth getting fat for. If you're in too much of a hurry to browse, call ahead for a seasonal hamper.

Less obvious places to picnic in the capital are Thames Barrier Park to the east of the City (p. 155), and Postman's Park close to St. Paul's Cathedral and the Museum of London (p. 168). For the latter, stop off at **Comptoir Gascon** close to Smithfield market (63 Charterhouse St., EC1; ℂ 020/7608-0851), which sells unbelievable French pâtés, cold meats, cheeses, pastries, breads, cakes, jams, honeys, and more. Don't miss the chocolate-covered walnuts. Alternatively, get veggie takeout from **The Place Below** (p. 132).

very creditable job of turning out the obligatory fajitas, steaks, ribs, fries, and onion rings, plus a somewhat expensive kids' menu featuring pasta dishes, burgers, and shakes. During weekend lunch, a face painter and a magician keep kids entertained. Avoid the place during the evening, though, when the cocktail crowd takes over.

1a Philimore Gardens. ℂ **020/7938-5338.** www.stickyfingers.co.uk. Kids' menu, highchairs. Main courses £7.25–£20 ($14–$38); kids' menu £7.50 ($14) Mon–Sat 11am–11:30pm; Sun 11am–11pm. AE, MC, DC, V. Tube: High St. Kensington.

Where to Dine from Knightsbridge to Earl's Court

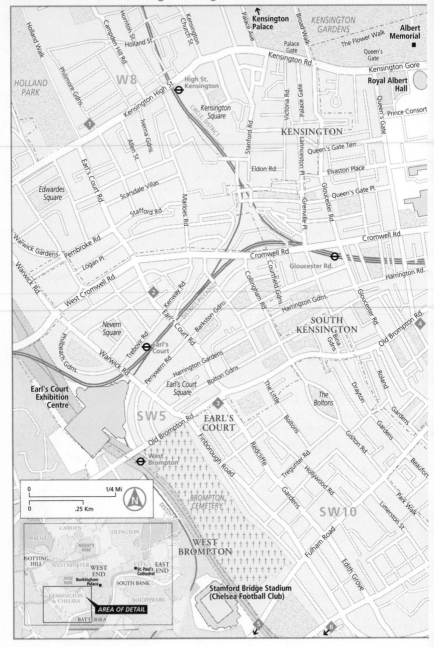

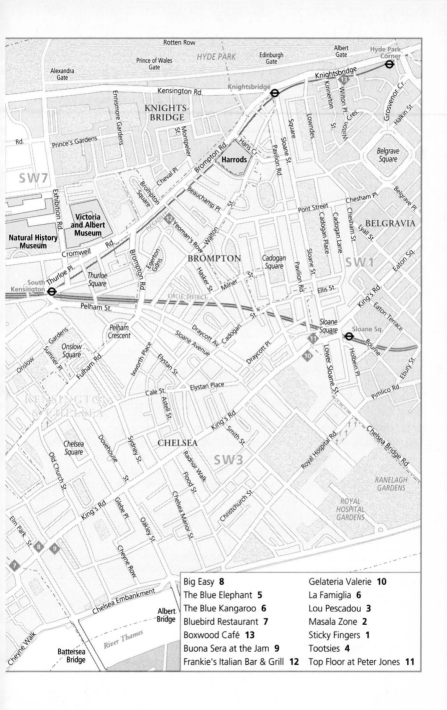

Big Easy **8**	Gelateria Valerie **10**
The Blue Elephant **5**	La Famiglia **6**
The Blue Kangaroo **6**	Lou Pescadou **3**
Bluebird Restaurant **7**	Masala Zone **2**
Boxwood Café **13**	Sticky Fingers **1**
Buona Sera at the Jam **9**	Tootsies **4**
Frankie's Italian Bar & Grill **12**	Top Floor at Peter Jones **11**

KNIGHTSBRIDGE, BROMPTON & BELGRAVIA

EXPENSIVE

Boxwood Café ★★ MODERN BRITISH   When is a cafe not a cafe?—when it's the Boxwood Café at the super-plush Berkeley hotel in Belgravia (p. 75), with its handmade silver- and gold-leaf wallpaper, and its stone floor with mother of pearl ground into it. Although overseeing chef Gordon Ramsay—he of the famously fiery temper—supposedly banned his own four kids from his eponymous restaurant at Claridge's because he didn't want them to grow up as food snobs, here children are welcomed with open arms. It seems a bit inconsistent, but who are we to argue? On arrival, each kid gets a Scooby Doo pack of crayons and coloring paper. The changing kids' menu may not sound that exciting—roast breast of farm chicken and chips or pasta, tomato sauce, and grated Gruyère cheese, for example—but, as with the standard dishes, the emphasis is on the best of seasonal British produce, prepared simply and without fanfare. Adult highlights have included a starter of fried oysters with fennel and lemon, and for the main course macaroni and cheese with roasted porcini mushrooms. Roast loin of suckling pig with cocotte potatoes and grain mustard sauce are backed up by equally comforting side dishes such as fried onion rings and creamed spinach. Don't deny yourselves the Valhrona hot chocolate fondue with marshmallows, banana, and biscotti for dessert.

The Berkeley, Wilton Place, SW1. ✆ 020/7235-1010. www.gordonramsay.com. Kids' menu, highchairs. Reservations required. Main courses £14–£28 ($27–$53); kids' menu £7.50 ($14). Mon–Fri noon–3pm and 6–11pm; Sat and Sun noon–4pm and 6–11pm; Sun noon. AE, MC, V. Tube: Hyde Park Corner.

MODERATE

Frankie's Italian Bar & Grill ★ *Finds* ITALIAN   This upmarket Italian place, opened in 2004, resulted from a collaboration between championship jockey Frankie Dettori (who already had his own supermarket pizza line) and "bad boy" chef Marco Pierre White. The look is glitzy—outsize glitter balls, a leather-look ceiling, and mirrored walls—but the emphasis is on casual, Italian-style family dining, especially during weekend lunches, when kids take over the place, and a magician does table rounds. Kids also get their own menu, featuring fishcakes, burgers, and spaghetti bolognese. However, the crisp-based pizzas are the real draw here—the basil, cherry tomato, and fresh mozzarella demonstrate how simple things can work best when top-rate ingredients are used. They're on the pricey side, but kids can share one, supplemented by deep-fried courgette batons. There are also a handful of perfectly decent pasta dishes and grills, as well as fab desserts, among them an unforgettable pavlova (meringue with marshmallow-y inside).

3 Yeoman's Row. ✆ 020/7590-9999. Kids' menu (weekends), highchairs. Reservations recommended. Mains £10–£15 ($10–$29); kids' menu (weekends only £6.50/$13. Mon–Fri noon–2:30pm and 6–11pm; Sat and Sun 1–4pm and 6–11pm. AE, MC, V. Tube: Knightsbridge.

CHELSEA

EXPENSIVE

Aquasia restaurant in the Conrad London hotel (p. 78) is popular among local families for its Asian/Italian buffet brunches in a waterside setting.

Bluebird Restaurant   BREAKFAST/MODERN EUROPEAN   This enormous, stylish, and highly convivial space attracts young Chelsea families in droves, particularly on weekends, when leisurely brunches (noon–4pm) include a strong kids' menu that might be a smaller serving of the roast of the day, tomato macaroni, or fish and chips. The best thing about the brunches is the sheer wealth of choices you have—you can refuel relatively cheaply on items from the bakery section, including American pancakes with maple syrup and vanilla ice cream, or on traditional brunch dishes such as eggs Benedict (available in both starter and main-course sizes, so it's another option for the kids). Or go whole hog on a superior roast of the day (on my last visit, it was seared Loch Duart salmon with caper butter) or on a decadent seafood plateau from the crustacean bar. It's the same for drinks—chocolate and hazelnut milkshakes and mixed-berry smoothies vie for your attention with classic cocktails and jugs of sangria. The restaurant is part of a "gastrodome" with a good ground-floor cafe serving breakfasts, lighter meals, and afternoon teas; a large delicatessen; a cookware store; and a flower market. Though bird motifs punctuate the decor, the Bluebird is actually named for a brand of sports car that broke the world land speed record in the 1920s—this building, once Europe's biggest motor garage, is thought to have been where the model was assembled.

350 King's Rd., SW3. © 020/7559-1000. www.conran.com. Kids' menu, highchairs. Reservations recommended. Main courses £9.50–£30 ($18–$56); kids' menu £6.25 ($12). AE, DC, MC, V. Mon–Fri 12:30–3pm and 6–11:30pm; Sat noon–3:30pm and 6–11pm; Sun noon–3:30pm and 6–10pm. Tube: Sloane Sq.

MODERATE

Big Easy AMERICAN This barbecue-and-crab shack prides itself on its down-home, American cooking, which means lots of steak and seafood served in trencher-like portions. If it works for princes William and Harry, or for Sheryl Crow, it'll probably work for you—not least because children are made really welcome. To start with, they get crayons, coloring sheets, and paper, with the resulting artwork entered into a competition that's sometimes displayed in the gallery section. Then there's the Urchins' menu of burgers, hot dogs, ribs, and fish fingers, accompanied by fries and a soft drink; alternative beverages are fresh juices, ice cream shakes, sodas, and kiddie cocktails. It's worth considering the Grand Appetizer Platter, large enough for four or even six people to share—a sociable way to start a meal. Note that the good-value two-course "Lunch on the Run" takes place till 5pm during the week.

322–4 King's Rd., SW3. © 020/7352-4071. www.bigeasy.uk.com. Kids' menu, highchairs, booster seats. Main courses £9.40–£20 ($5–$11); kids' menu £4.95 ($9.40). AE, MC, V. Mon–Thurs noon–11:30pm; Fri noon–midnight; Sat 11am–midnight; Sun 11am–11pm. Tube: Sloane Sq.

La Famiglia ★★ ITALIAN Run by a father-and-daughter team, this wonderfully unpretentious and welcoming Tuscan restaurant has remained down-to-earth despite attracting a higher-than-average quotient of celebs. On Sunday you can almost believe you're in Italy, the family ambience is that strong—indeed, the cheerful, blue-painted exterior and quaint, partly tiled dining room with its black-and-white photographs and family portrait make you feel like you've stepped into someone's home while vacationing in Tuscany. The seasonal dishes, based on recipes handed down through the generations, are as far from standard trattoria fodder as you can imagine: In spring or summer (when you can sit out in the large garden), you might try Florentine-style tripe with tomatoes, onion, and Parmesan; salami cooked with lentils; or fresh home-made pasta with turnip tops. There's no kids' menu, but many of the dishes, especially the pasta, can be served as half-portions. Note that there's a newer Clapham offshoot, **Grano,** which serves favorites from the parent restaurant, but also offers great pizzas, plus a "small people's" menu.

7 Langton St., SW10. ☏ 020/7351-0761. www.lafamiglia.co.uk. Highchairs. Reservations recommended evenings and Sun. Main courses £11–£21 ($6–$40). Daily noon–2:45pm and 7–11:45pm. Tube: Fulham Broadway.

INEXPENSIVE

Buona Sera at the Jam ★★★ (Finds) ITALIAN   The novelty value of this well-located and extremely friendly Italian restaurant lies in its diminutive size—that may sound like a nightmare for those with kids, but little ones just love climbing the bunk bed–style ladders up to the tables under the roof (which feel both more secluded and more roomy than those at ground level). Staff have to ascend and descend the ladders several times over the course of the meal, especially when laden with plates. Don't come at peak times, though, or you'll have a long wait for one of these "cabins in the sky," which have the added attraction of your own control of your lighting and music volume. Kids can have any of the authentic pizzas, risottos, pastas, and fish or meat dishes for half-price, which makes it a rare good-value spot if you're shopping on King's Road. If the selections don't appeal to your kids, the charming, endlessly patient staff will cater to reasonable off-menu requests.

289a King's Rd., SW3. ☏ 020/7352-8827. Main courses £6.50–£12 ($12–$23). Highchairs. AE, MC, V. Tues–Fri noon–3pm and 6pm–midnight; Sat and Sun noon–midnight. Tube: Sloane Sq.

WEST BROMPTON & EARL'S COURT

MODERATE

Lou Pescadou ★ FRENCH/SEAFOOD   Lou Pescadou is a rare bright star in the culinary desert of West Brompton, with a loyal local following that proves you're on to a good thing. Here you can relax over a ceramic jug of chilled white wine while the kids admire the nautical decor. The kids' own menu features fish, chicken, and vegetarian

---

What's in Store?

Department stores (see chapter 9) can be great, family-friendly places in which to grab a bite: Most have several cafes and restaurants catering to a range of pockets, as well as parent facilities and toy sections right nearby. An outstanding example is the **Top Floor at Peter Jones** (Finds) (Sloane Sq., SW1; ☏ **0845/345-1723;** www.johnlewis.com), where breakfast, lunch, pastries, or afternoon tea come complete with panoramic views over the capital. The kids' menu features excellent home cooking such as fisherman's or shepherd's pie with French beans, all at pleasing prices (£2.50–£3.95/$4.80–$7.50). Young visitors can help themselves from a goodie box of paper and crayons; adults can enjoy anything from eggs Benedict to seared salmon with Thai red cabbage. On your way in or out, the nursery and toy departments are as good as you'd expect from this little sister of John Lewis, but note that although the store is open on Sunday, the restaurant is closed.

For an altogether more exotic experience, **Momo at Selfridges** (400 Oxford St, W1; ☏ **020/7318-3620;** www.selfridges.com) is an offshoot of the hip Moroccan restaurant within the fashionable Oxford Street department store. Kids love the souk atmosphere of this tearoom and restaurant. The *meze*-style menu means you can order lots of smaller dishes for tasting, although staff are happy to provide special dishes such as breaded chicken with fries, or small bowls of couscous with meat. The futuristic Kids Zone (toys and clothing) is one floor up.

---

dishes, accompanied by good fries and followed by ice cream. The French take their food very seriously, so you can expect top-notch fish soup with *aioli* (garlic mayo) or main courses such as scallops Provençal. In fact, it's so authentic, the highly attentive staff even answer the phone in French.

241 Old Brompton Rd., SW5. ℂ 020/7370-1057. Kids' menu, highchairs. Reservations recommended. Main courses £8–£15 ($15–$29); kids' menu £5.50 ($10). AE, DC, MC, V. Mon–Fri noon–3pm and 7pm–midnight; Sat and Sun noon–3pm and 6:30pm–midnight. Tube: Earl's Court.

INEXPENSIVE

Masala Zone ⭐ *Finds* INDIAN   This third branch of the casual, canteen-style Indian (the others are in Soho and Islington) opened in April 2005 and is a useful budget eatery in an area known for its inexpensive accommodations but poor restaurant options. Despite the keen prices, the food is totally authentic—much of it is the type of thing you might find at Indian street stalls. Don't miss the Bombay-style beach snacks or the brilliant *thali* plates, which combine lots of little dishes, dips, and accompaniments for an average of £8 ($15) and are perfect for sharing. At lunch you can order salads and sandwiches, too. You can either eat in or take out.

147 Earl's Court Rd., SW5. ℂ 020/7373-0220. www.realindianfood.com. Highchairs. No reservations. Main course £6–£12 ($11–$23). MC, V. Tube: Earl's Court.

HAMMERSMITH & FULHAM

For the **Old Ship Inn** with its riverside terrace, see p. 198.

EXPENSIVE

The Blue Elephant ⭐⭐ THAI   This well-known Thai restaurant (part of a global chain with outposts in Paris, Beirut, Bangkok, and other cities) wows kids with its junglesque interior of trees, ponds, and waterfalls studded with statues and baroque ornaments. Kids like the imaginative dishes and—most of all—its Sunday buffet brunches with displays of exotic fruit carved into spectacular shapes, free face-painting, and sugar-spinning demos. The buffets cost £22 ($42) for adults, half that for kids, with no limit on the amount of times you can refill your plate. Last orders are taken at 3:30pm, but you're welcome to stay till 5pm. The standard menu, which includes such adventurous fare as Running Crocodile (stir-fried crocodile meat with chili, basil, and hearts of palm) and *mieng kahm* (betel leaves filled with dried shrimp, roasted peanuts, lime, and ginger) is handily coded so you can see at a glance how hot each dish is. There are plenty of non-spicy options for kids. Note that the Blue Elephant's Indian sibling, **La Porte des Indes** in Marylebone, hosts a similar Sunday brunch with kids' entertainment, plus live jazz, and cooking demonstrations, at the same price. Football fans might be interested in the special Saturday lunch menu for those coming to catch a game at nearby Chelsea FC stadium.

4–6 Fulham Broadway, SW6. ℂ 020/7385-6595. www.blueelephant.com. Reservations recommended. Main courses £10–£28 ($19–$53). AE, DC, MC, V. Mon–Fri noon–2:30pm and 7pm–midnight; Fri and Sat noon–2:30pm and 6:30pm–midnight; Sun noon–3:30pm and 7–10:30pm. Tube: Fulham Broadway.

Chez Kristof ⭐ FRENCH   The younger sibling of a couple of fashionable and highly successful eastern European restaurants, Chez Kristof offers classy but comforting French classics with a twist, such as *choucroute* with honey-glazed ham hock. On my last visit, "Les Petits" kids' lunch menu offered upscale burgers and frites and spaghetti Bolognese, as well as interesting cocktails like apple and elderflower fizz. This menu is gradually being revised, however, to include healthier dishes made from

The Sweetest Thing

If you're in town the first week of November, you're in luck—this is **Chocolate Week** (www.chocolateweek.co.uk), when chocoholics can enjoy a host of activities around the city, including chocolate afternoon teas, competitions, exhibitions, special window displays, a family chocolate carnival at Hampstead Theatre, and scores of tastings. In 2005 the event embraced the first World Chocolate Awards.

Alternatively, some of London's most interesting candies are the traditional Indian and Pakistani confections that can be sampled daily at the top of Tottenham Court Road, on Drummond Street, NW1. Try **Ambala Sweet Centre** (no. 112-4; ☎ 020/7387-3521) and **Gupta Sweet Centre** (no. 100, ☎ 020/7380-1590).

---

organic ingredients. It's best to bring the family for Saturday or Sunday lunch, when food is served till 4pm. If there's a group of you with older kids, you can book the private screening room downstairs, where a library of children's movies is available. (The restaurant has an affiliation with Disney around the corner, and movies are frequently open to the public in the screening room.) *Insider tip:* The adjoining deli with its long shared dining room, around which local mums congregate with their babies and kids, is open for more casual dining from 8am on weekdays, 8:30am weekends. Set lunches are available that should bring the cost down.

111 Hammersmith Grove, W6. ☎ 020/8741-1177. www.chezkristof.co.uk. Kids' menu (lunch), highchairs. Main courses £12–£17 ($22–$31); kids' menu £6 ($11). AE, MC, V. Mon–Fri noon–3pm and 6–11:15pm; Sat noon–4pm and 6–11:15pm; Sun noon–4pm. Tube: Hammersmith.

The River Café ★★★ ITALIAN   Few people would disagree that this famous Thameside spot serves the best Italian food in London—millions of cookbook sales and the required advance booking (1 or 2 weeks) nearly 20 years after it opened are proof, should you need it. The converted 19th-century warehouse, designed by Sir Richard Rogers, husband of co-owner Ruth, offers a stunning view of the expansive lawn area and the river beyond it from the floor-to-ceiling windows. In summer you can sit outdoors on a lovely big terrace (try to get a shaded table under the trees). It all makes for a memorable family eating experience. The food lives up to the hype: Fresh market ingredients sourced from France and Italy, along with homegrown produce, are used to concoct the likes of smoked eel with fresh horseradish and crème fraîche (heavy, fermented cream). There's no kids' menu, but the amiable staff go out of their way to prepare something to please everyone, whether it be simple pasta with cheese or tomato sauce for toddlers, or an adaptation of one of the existing dishes for older kids.

Thames Wharf, Rainville Rd., W6. ☎ 020/7386-4200. www.rivercafe.co.uk. Highchairs. Reservations required. Main courses £26–£31 ($49–$59). AE, DC, MC, V. Mon–Thurs 12:30–3:30pm and 7–11pm; Fri and Sat 12:30–3:30pm and 7–11:20pm; Sun 12:30–3:30pm. Tube: Hammersmith.

MODERATE

The Blue Kangaroo ★★★ GLOBAL   This unique venue is the only place I know of in London that combines full-on children's facilities—in this case, an entire basement area given over to soft play areas for three different age groups up to age 7—with a menu of high-quality, "proper" food that won't leave grownups feeling hard up. A huge plasma screen in the ground-floor restaurant means you can keep an eye on your kids as they run riot downstairs (a 90-min. session costs £3–£4.50/$5.70–$8.60, depending on the child's age; those under 9 months go free). If you'd rather supervise them more closely, the basement has a cafe area and a counter selling good cakes and drinks. It's all very flexible, in that kids can eat upstairs with you and then wander off when they've had enough of your company, or you can eat downstairs while they play and you chat, browse the stash of newspapers and magazines, or—football fans are you listening?—watch Sky Sports. The kids' menu is a good value at around £5 ($9.50) for the likes of scrambled eggs with cheese and toast, and penne with creamy chicken, plus a soft drink; you can also get vegetable sides for just £1 ($1.90). More organic dishes were being added at our last visit. Adults get tons of choices; I can recommend the lovely butternut risotto (which a child might enjoy in a starter portion) and the wild mushroom tagliatelle. Every Sunday a traditional lunch roast is served with Yorkshire pudding, potatoes, and vegetables. Note that there are weekly activities (music classes, art parties, balloon modeling) plus special events such as Valentine's and Halloween discos and storytelling/book signings. Note, too, that the place is open for late breakfasts. The waitstaff are the essence of unflappable geniality.

555 King's Rd., SW6. ℭ 020/7371-7622. www.thebluekangaroo.co.uk. Kids' menu, highchairs. Reservations recommended on weekends. Main course £6.95–£16 ($13–$30); kids' menu £4.95 ($9.40). AE, MC, V. Daily 9:30am–8:30pm. Tube: Fulham Broadway.

BAYSWATER, PADDINGTON & MAIDA VALE
MODERATE
The Prince Alfred & Formosa Dining Room ★★ *Finds* MODERN EUROPEAN
One of the most colorful pubs in London, the Prince Alfred occupies a hip modern space that's retained its wonderful Victorian features—etched glass, carved mahogany, and five separate "snugs" divided by wooden partitions. These snugs were created to segregate drinkers from different social strata in the 19th century—each has its own entrance from the street, as well as half-height doors into neighboring snugs through which the cleaners gained access. If you come for an early-evening meal (before 6pm) when the more minimalist restaurant area is closed and the pub as a whole isn't busy, staff should let you have a snug to yourself, which makes for a lovely, private venue for a family meal. The menu outside the main restaurant hours is compact but tasty and comforting fare—sausages and mash, mushroom risotto, sticky toffee pudding, that kind of thing. Make sure to order some of the gorgeous bread to nibble with your soft drinks or real ale, served with dipping bowls of rich olive oil and balsamic vinegar. In the restaurant, the calf's liver, lamb shank, and duck always go down well, and this is a great place for a Sunday roast, which you can walk off with a stroll along the canal banks of Little Venice just a couple of minutes away.

5a Formosa St., W9. ℭ 020/7286-3287. Highchairs. Reservations recommended (restaurant). Main courses £8.50–£18 ($16–$34). AE, MC, V. Mon–Sat noon–11pm; Sun noon–10:30pm. Tube: Warwick Ave.

INEXPENSIVE
Fresco *Finds* LEBANESE   This little Middle Eastern diner is so good, you almost want to keep it a secret. There's nothing fancy about it—its charm lies in its breezy staff and fantastically fresh, cheap food, much of which is displayed in a cabinet upfront so you can see what you're getting. Kids are very welcome; there's no separate menu for them, but this is exactly the sort of cuisine that is suited to family eating, especially if some of you are into veggies and some are carnivores. Among the choices

are wraps, hummus, baba ganoush, falafel, and gooey baklava: your best option by far is to order a *meze* plate, so that you can try a bit of everything. The massive choice of fresh juice combinations is worth stopping by for even if you're not hungry. There are less than a dozen tables, but if it's crowded, you can get takeout for a picnic in nearby Hyde Park.

25 Westbourne Grove, W2. © 020/7221-2355. Highchairs. Main courses £6–£10 ($11–$19) Mon–Sat 9am–11:30pm; Sun 9am–10:30pm. MC, V. Tube: Bayswater.

Gourmet Burger Kitchen ★★ BURGERS   London's burger scene took a massive stride forward when this chain took flight a couple of years back—the classic and exotic combinations (simple beef burgers, a Jamaican version with mango and ginger sauce; a Kiwiburger with beetroot, egg, pineapple, cheese, and relish; and a chorizo-and sweet-potato number) were designed by New Zealand chef Peter Gordon, who had already made his mark on the London dining scene with the much-missed, now-closed Sugar Club. Despite this illustrious pedigree, and although they are made from the finest, freshest ingredients (including artisan-made sourdough buns and juicy Aberdeen Angus Scotch beef), prices here are refreshingly low—partly because diners order and pay at the bar, which keeps costs down. Kids enjoy watching the chefs at work in the clearly visible kitchens. There are junior incarnations of the chicken burger, plus great fries and heavenly shakes (the lime should not be missed). At press time there were seven other branches, in Chiswick, Fulham, Battersea, Putney, Richmond, West Hampstead, and Belsize Park.

50 Westbourne Grove, W2. © 020/7243-4344. www.gbk.co.uk. Kids' menu, highchairs. Reservations not accepted. Main courses £5–£8 ($9.50–$18), kids' menu £3.95 ($7.50). MC, V. Mon–Fri noon–11pm; Sat 11am–1pm; Sun 11am–11pm. Tube: Bayswater.

Harlem Soul Food ★★ AMERICAN   This trendy place serving "soul food redefined New York style" gets a little too raucous for families at night, when a DJ takes to the decks from 9pm (it's owned by the famous record producer Arthur Baker). It's at its laid-back best during the day, when you can take your time over excellent and fairly priced breakfast and brunch dishes, including homemade granola; pancakes with blueberries, pecans, cinnamon, or other toppings; and a monster Harlem Downtown Brunch of sausage patties, bacon, Boston beans, tomatoes, home fries, and eggs any style. The lunch menu of burgers, steak sandwiches, salads, and more is supplemented by a good-value kids' menu comprising buttermilk fried chicken and Harlem fries, a classic burger, fish and chips, or macaroni and cheese, finished off with buttermilk pancakes with maple syrup. In 2005 a second branch opened in Brixton, SW9.

78 Westbourne Grove, W2. © 020/7985-0900. www.harlemsoulfood.com. Kids' menu. Reservations recommended. Main courses £2.50–£14 ($4–$26); kids' menu £4.95 ($9.40) AE, DC, V. Daily 10:30am–midnight. Tube: Notting Hill Gate.

NOTTING HILL GATE & LADBROKE GROVE
INEXPENSIVE

Babes 'n' Burgers *Overrated* BURGERS   As the name implies, there's not a great deal that's subtle about this burger bar, which opened toward the end of 2004 in the hope of snaring trendy young local parents as well as visitors to Portobello Market. It's largely succeeded, if weekend queues are anything to go by, although not because of the unexceptional organic burgers and home-grown fries. What people really come for is the supervised play area at the back of the small dining room, where you can park your youngster, keeping an eye on him or her from CCTV monitors on the larger tabletops. Giant plasma screens elsewhere relay MTV or big soccer games at low volume, and on

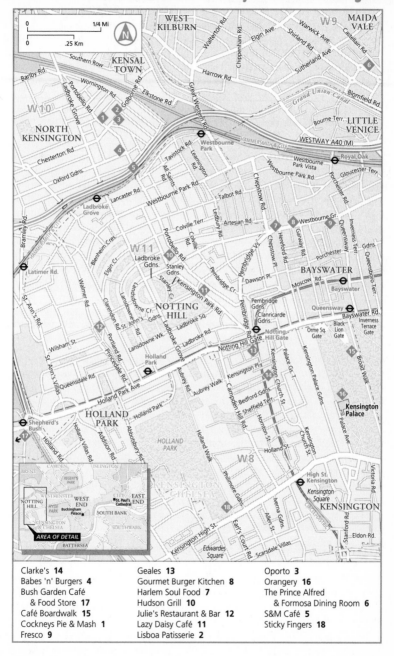

Clarke's **14**
Babes 'n' Burgers **4**
Bush Garden Café
  & Food Store **17**
Café Boardwalk **15**
Cockneys Pie & Mash **1**
Fresco **9**

Geales **13**
Gourmet Burger Kitchen **8**
Harlem Soul Food **7**
Hudson Grill **10**
Julie's Restaurant & Bar **12**
Lazy Daisy Café **11**
Lisboa Patisserie **2**

Oporto **3**
Orangery **16**
The Prince Alfred
  & Formosa Dining Room **6**
S&M Café **5**
Sticky Fingers **18**

Friday afternoons the toy area shows kids' movies. Back to the burgers, though—they come in beef, chicken, or tofu incarnations, available with extra bacon, cheese, or avocado; the regular size is small enough for kids, while hungrier adults will probably have to double up. Kids can also get their own burgers, as well as the like of haddock fingers with crudités or just plain beans on toast. Brunch dishes such as chicken Caesar salad are also featured on the main menu. Some of the staff lend new meaning to the word "unfocused," which takes some doing in this laid-back area of town.

275 Portobello Rd., W11. ⓒ 020/7727-4163. www.babesnburgers.com. Kids' menu, highchairs. Main courses £3.50–£8.50 ($6.70–$16), kids' menu £1–£4 ($1.90–$7.60). MC, V. Mon 9:30am–11:30am; Sun 11:30am–10:30pm. Tube: Ladbroke Grove.

Lazy Daisy Café ⭐ *(Finds* BREAKFAST/LUNCH & SNACKS   There's no sweeter place in London to bring your kids, especially if they're tiny, than this petite cafe hidden behind a sunny little courtyard—a perfect place for kids to play in fine weather. The decor inside is child-friendly, with a toy corner and a baby-changing facility that boasts free wipes and toddler-height sinks. The waitstaff is totally at ease with tots running (or crawling) around; they even welcomed my oldest into the kitchen, where he helped sweep the floor (way to go, boy!). Food ranges from sandwiches and excellent cakes via all-day breakfasts and brunch fare to lunch soups, quiches, jacket potatoes, salads, and pasta dishes; there are also kids' meals (such as fish fingers and beans), reduced-size portions, and organic baby food. Just don't come on weekends, when the entire parent brigade of Notting Hill shows up.

59a Portobello Rd., W11. ⓒ 020/7221-8416. Kids' menu, highchairs. Reservations not taken. Lunch dishes £5 ($9.50), kids' menu £1.95–£3.50 ($3.70–$6.70). Mon–Sat 9am–5pm; Sun noon–2:30pm. No credit cards. Tube: Notting Hill Gate.

Lisboa Patisserie PORTUGUESE   It's almost obligatory, when shopping at Portobello Market (p. 231), to stop off at this authentic Portuguese patisserie for a *pastei de nata* (an Lisbon egg custard tart with a singed top). There's a wide range of other cakes if you feel like branching out, including *castanha de ovo* (a wobbly egg cake) and orange and coconut tarts. If you need something filling before progressing to the sweet stuff, sandwiches and rolls are good and cheap. Coffee is served in glasses, in the Iberian way. This is a bit of a Portuguese enclave, so if Lisboa gets too crowded (which it often does—it has far too many tables for the restricted space), **Oporto** at no. 62a is a similar option, with the advantage of a highchair for those with babies. Note that Lisboa also has a traditional deli at no. 54, selling fresh-baked bread, cheese, olives, and more, as well as other patisseries in Camden, Chelsea, and Lambeth.

57 Golborne Rd., W11. ⓒ 020/8968-5242. Cakes and pastries from about £0.50 ($0.95). No credit cards. Mon–Sat 8am–8pm; Sun 8am–7pm. Tube: Ladbroke Grove.

S&M Café ⭐⭐ TRADITIONAL BRITISH   Don't be scared by the name—there's no kinkiness about this growing diner chain, which serves what it terms "the world's number one comfort food" (sausage, that is, along with mash) in a variety of guises, and even caters to vegetarians. Depending on your mood and the daily specials, you can choose from the likes of Lincolnshire lamb and mint, spicy Tunisian, and mushroom and tarragon sausage, with kids getting their own portions (or fish fingers or chicken nuggets if they prefer, with beans or peas), plus a glass of juice and a dish of chocolate or vanilla ice cream. The best part of the deal is that you don't have to stick to one type, but can combine up to three varieties of sausage on one plate. The mash is a fluffy bowl of heaven, the gravy—you get a choice, including sweet tomato and basil—perfectly seasoned. Other mains are toad-in-the-hole (sausage baked in Yorkshire pudding), steak-and-kidney pie, fishcakes, and salads. It's unlikely you'll have room for one of the old-school desserts, but a steamed hot chocolate pudding is worth sharing. Don't miss the great soft drinks either, including Victorian lemonade and Seville orange jigger. The diner is also open for breakfast, from bacon sandwiches to full English. The cafe premises are pleasingly down-to-earth; the branch on Essex Road in Islington, N1, is worth visiting for its original 1920s interior. There is a further branch near Spitalfields Market, and more are surely to come.

268 Portobello Rd. (*C*) 020/7359-5361. www.sandmcafe.com. Kids' menu, highchairs. Main courses £5.95–£7.95 ($11–$15); kids' menu £4.95 ($9.40). DC, MC, V. Mon–Thurs 9am–11pm; Fri and Sat 9am–11:30pm; Sun 9am–10:30pm. Tube: Ladbroke Grove.

HOLLAND PARK, SHEPHERD'S BUSH & FURTHER WEST
EXPENSIVE
Julie's Restaurant & Bar ★★ MODERN BRITISH   Lord knows parents need to treat themselves once in a while, and this is a good place for it. Perennially fashionable Julie's is the unlikely home of one of London's first restaurant nurseries, which is in operation on Sunday between 1 and 4pm. Kids ages 2 to 12 are served their meal (either organic roast chicken with roast potatoes and vegetables, fresh organic pasta with tomato sauce, or house sausage with homemade chips and vegetables, followed by sorbet or ice cream, plus a soft drink) with the parent's first course, before being whisked away to be entertained by the fully qualified staff. The adult set-price menu, available as two or three courses, offers the likes of fresh Dublin Bay prawns with chili mayo; roast beef; lamb, pork, or chicken with accompaniments; seared salmon and, to round it all off, chocolate Bailey's cream mousse or warm apricot rice pudding. At about £85 ($162) per family of four, including drinks, it's a surprisingly good value given the quality of the food, the sumptuous surrounds (the romantic space is divided up into a number of cozy rooms, including a plush white conservatory with a removable roof for summer, a former forge with twinkling fairy lights, and the atmospheric Gothic Room with its tables tucked into alcoves), and the childcare element.

135 Portland Rd., W11. (*C*) 020/7229-8331. www.juliesrestaurant.com. Kids' menu (Sun), highchairs. Sun set menu, 2 courses £22 ($42), 3 courses £26 ($53); kids' menu £10 ($19) including nursery. AE, MC, V. Mon–Fri 12:30–2:45pm and 7:30–11:15pm; Sat 7:30–11:15pm, Sun 12:30–3pm and 7:30–10:15pm. Tube: Holland Park.

INEXPENSIVE
Bush Garden Café & Food Store ★★ LUNCH & SNACKS   This homely lunch bar and organic grocer offers a menu of simple kids' favorites such as beans, eggs or Marmite on toast, great cakes (some of them from trendy bakery Konditor & Cook), and a friendly staff. There's also a partly covered garden complete with a playhouse and toys, in which the kids can run riot while you enjoy homemade sandwiches, soups, quiches, and daily hot specials, plus fresh juices and smoothies. (If parenthood has left you feeling a little frazzled, ask for a shot of wheatgrass to perk you up.) Despite the low prices, you might find that portions outstrip your appetite. The garden is equipped with heaters to extend the fun into the cooler months. There's space for strollers by the baby-changing toilets.

59 Goldhawk Rd., W12. (*C*) 020/8743-6372. Highchairs, kids' menu. Lunch dishes around £4 ($7.60); kids' menu £1.50 ($2.90). MC, V. Mon–Sat 8am–6pm. Tube: Goldhawk Rd.

4 South London

SOUTH BANK TO ROTHERHITHE

MODERATE

fish! ★★ SEAFOOD   This is the original restaurant and sole survivor of a chain that over-expanded and imploded pretty rapidly, and it's all the better for being a stand-alone restaurant again. Stunningly situated beneath the railway arches of Borough Market, it's a theatrical space in which diners sit around a central open kitchen to watch the chefs strut their stuff. (On a sunny day, though, it'd be a crime not to sit out on the lovely decked terrace.) Kids love the drama, the crayons and paper provided, and the very good children's menu. This basically consists of spaghetti tuna bolognese, or strips of fish or chicken breast with fries, a soft drink, and ice cream, but—unlike in many places—it's very flexible, so they can get you new potatoes or mash instead of fries, and small filets of swordfish, cod, or certain other fish in season. Adults can go for classics such as fish, chips, and mushy peas or for more exotic dishes such as Thai crab cakes. The best option, though, is to try one of the catches of the day, steamed or grilled; your waiter will advise you on which of the five sauces will do it the most justice. Strangely, prices seem to have dropped a tad since this place opened in 1999, which makes it a relative bargain. It's also the only restaurant I know of with a mom's menu, clarifying what kind of fish they can eat before and during pregnancy and while breastfeeding.

Cathedral St., Borough Market, SE1. © 020/7407-3803. www.fishdiner.co.uk. Kids' menu, highchairs. Reservations recommended. Main courses £9.95–£17 ($19–$32); kids' menu £6.50 ($12). AE, MC, V. Daily 11:30am–11pm. Tube: London Bridge.

Loco Mensa ITALIAN   A relative newcomer situated behind the County Hall building (making it a handy address after a morning spent riding the BA London Eye and visiting the London Aquarium), Loco is part of a mini-chain that also embraces **Loco Locale** (neighborhood restaurants in Fulham and Blackheath) and **Loco Pronto** in Borough Market, selling Italian street food to go. It's not the greatest Italian food in the world, granted, but I can't fault any of the dishes I've ordered. On a recent visit, my waitress was an absolute delight, especially given the rowdiness of the kids in the party (whether she'd have been as calm had the place been fuller is a moot point). In any event, there's a sofa and coffee table corner where staff seem happy enough to let kids play between courses. The children's menu is rather limited (there's just spaghetti bolognese or pizza Margherita, soft drinks, and ice cream), You may prefer to order a selection of starters to share with your kids: the white bean, rosemary, and garlic purée with crostini, for instance; or the cherry tomato focaccia. Pizzas are available by the square from the pizza counter, too, or you can order starter portions of nearly half the pasta or risotto dishes. Desserts are excellent: I know three little boys who were made very happy by the chocolate and hazelnut tart.

3b Belvedere Rd., SE1. © 020/7401-6734. www.locorestaurants.com. Kids' menu, highchairs. Main courses £7.95–£15 ($15–$29); kids' menu £5.95 ($11). AE, MC, V. Mon–Fri noon–10:30pm; Sat and Sun 10am–10:30pm. Tube: Waterloo.

INEXPENSIVE

The Refectory@Southwark Cathedral ★ *Finds* AFTERNOON TEA/LUNCH & SNACKS   This atmospheric choice opened as part of this small Gothic cathedral's millennium celebrations, and combines a bright modern dining space with original concrete vaulting. The arches are embellished with tiles based on Roman originals in the churchyard wall, and changing artworks are displayed. It's a bit of a local secret that's worth knowing about for its well-priced, home-cooked snacks, lunch fare, and afternoon teas, including pastries, salads, and noodles (which can be served in kids' portions upon request). The soup and cakes are particularly great—don't miss the almost legendary lemon pancake torte. In fair weather there's a gorgeous cobbled courtyard, just steps from the river, and occasional summer barbecues. Alternatively, buy picnic supplies at nearby Borough Market, a gourmet food haven (p. 233), and

Meals in Museums

Before setting out in search of a child-friendly eatery, it's always worth finding out what's on offer right under your nose—most of London's museums and galleries are top-notch when it comes to family facilities, right down to their restaurants and cafes, many of which I've mentioned or described in the relevant reviews in chapter 6, "Exploring London with Your Kids." You might pay a little more to eat on-site, but it's usually worth it for the sheer convenience.

One of my favorites is the **Tate Modern Café** (© 020/7401-5014; www.tage.org.uk) on level 2 of the brilliant contemporary art museum dramatically sited in a former power station on the South Bank (p. 177). This takes full advantage of its Thameside setting, offering diners great river views while they plough through breakfasts, lunches, afternoon tea, and light evening meals. Especially popular with kids (who get crayons to create their own mini-masterpieces in homage to the artworks they've seen) are the organic raspberry and white chocolate muffins, and the carrot and pineapple cake with orange sauce.

In a 2004 assessment of children's food at some of Britain's top tourist attractions, the British Museum (p. 158) scored highly, especially in the self-service **Gallery Café** with its kids' lunchboxes, and in the more posh **Great Court Restaurant** (© 020/7323-8990; www.thebritishmuseum.ac.uk) nestled beneath the stunning glass-and-steel roof of the Great Court and overlooking the famous 19th-century Reading Room. Serving morning coffee, hot and cold lunches, afternoon tea, and dinner (the Great Court remains open later than the museum itself), it offers kids smaller portions of any main course for half-price (about £4.50–£6/$8.60–$11), or a good penne pasta or pizza followed by chocolate mousse for £4.95 ($9.40). *Insider tip:* Book an early lunch table on a weekday and you save 20% on your bill (you'll need to take along a printout of the website offer).

A more offbeat choice is the cafe at **Camden Arts Centre** (© 020/7472-5516; see p. 174), a fashionably minimalist but relaxing oasis after the pandemonium of the nearby O2 Centre (p. 255), with a garden and kids' portions of daily specials such as fishcakes, as well as comfort food faves such as toast with Marmite, brownies, almond *cantucci* (cookies), and organic chocolate bars. The art's not bad, either, although check what's on ahead of your visit, as some of the shows can be a little risqué.

eat your food in the lovely, lavender-scented cathedral gardens in the company of local office workers. The cathedral's worth a look, too, with its bronze of Shakespeare (whose brother Edmund was buried in an unknown grave here) and stained-glass window with scenes from some of his plays.

Montague Close, SE1. ℂ 020/7407-5740. www.southwark.anglican.org/cathedral. Highchairs. No reservations. Main courses about £5 ($9.50). MC, V. Daily 10am–5pm. Tube: London Bridge.

BATTERSEA & CLAPHAM

Though you're unlikely to stay in this area, there is a very child-friendly enclave around Northcote Road and Battersea Rise, with lots of family-oriented eateries—perfect after a day out in Battersea Park 10 minutes' walk away—including branches of **Giraffe** (p. 99) and **Gourmet Burger Kitchen** (p. 124).

EXPENSIVE

Le Bouchon Bordelais ★★ *Finds* FRENCH A relatively long-standing neighborhood brasserie, Le Bouchon Bordelais has been given a shot in the arm by its new co-partner, super-chef Michel Roux (whose dad and uncle opened the legendary Le Gavroche in Soho). But its main appeal for parents is the free nursery during weekend lunches (by request on other days)—a rare commodity in a restaurant of this quality. After speeding through their own fairly conventional but high-quality and extremely good-value menu (fish fingers, chicken breast, or Cumberland sausage with peas, fries or mash, and salad *coquillettes* (shell-shaped pasta) with ham, plus a soft drink and an ice cream), little ones ages 1 to 9 can go make mischief in a supervised play area amply stocked with games, coloring books, and videos. Meanwhile, adults can tuck into well-executed French classics such as lobster soup, snails in garlic and parsley butter, foie gras, steak frites with sauce béarnaise, and—Atkins dieters look away—profiteroles with vanilla ice cream and chocolate sauce. In fine weather there are tables outdoors on a terrace. The adjoining bar is a great place for French breakfast and brunch dishes, including *viennoisseries* (breakfast rolls) and *croques* (grilled cheese on toast); for cheapish lunches such as omelets, fish cakes, steak baguettes, and Toulouse sausage with mash; or for lighter dinners. There's a branch, Le Bouchon Lyonnais, on nearby Queenstown Road; it doesn't have a nursery but is a fun place to watch Wimbledon French and English rugby and football matches.

5–9 Battersea Rise, SW11. ℂ 020/7738-0307. www.lebouchon.co.uk. Kids' menu, highchairs. Reservations recommended. Main courses £12–£25 ($23–$32); kids' menu £4.95 ($9.40). AE, MC, V. Mon–Sat noon–11pm; Sun 12:30–10:30pm. Train: Clapham Junction.

INEXPENSIVE

Boiled Egg & Soldiers BREAKFAST/LUNCH & SNACKS This tempting spot is at its sunny best at breakfast or at brunch when the comforting favorites include—surprise!—boiled egg with toast soldiers, Marmite and toast, pancakes and muffins, and Fluffies (hot milk with chocolate foam), in which you can indulge at the outside tables on sunny mornings. In fact, you can get breakfast all day long, so there's no need to rush here. The decor is characterized by bold strokes of color, the staff are friendly and tolerant of kids, and parents can treat themselves to steak sandwiches, smoked salmon, champagne. and cocktails, should the nursery fare not appeal.

63 Northcote Rd., SW11. ℂ 020/7223-4894. Highchairs. Main courses £5–£10 ($8–$19). No credit cards. Mon–Sat 9am–6pm; Sun 10am–5pm. Train: Clapham Junction.

WIMBLEDON, RICHMOND & KEW

For **The Victoria** in Richmond, see p. 89.

MODERATE

The Naked Turtle *Finds* GLOBAL   With its singing waitresses, cartoon sketches of turtles on its vibrant red walls, and spacious front deck and rear sun-trap garden, this friendly little place feels like an offbeat neighborhood hangout. The food could almost be an afterthought, but instead it continues the zany theme—expect bison steaks with black cherry sauce, zebra steak with chocolate sauce, and the renowned specialty, Roo Platter, comprising "bites" of kangaroo, crocodile, and ostrich with dipping sauces. (There's also less outlandish fare such as seafood with pasta and filet steak for the faint-hearted.) The live jazz nights are great for teens, with occasional vocals by the same lovely waitresses, some of whom are trained classical singers. On weekends, when kids ages 12 and up get free lunches (and face painting), there are traditional roasts. Prices are on the high side, but remember that you're not paying extra for the entertainment. (They do appreciate tips though, which supposedly go towards their singing lessons.)

505 Upper Richmond Rd. W., SW14. © 020/8878-1995. www.naked-turtle.com. Highchairs. Reservations recommended on weekends. Main course £8–£15 ($15–$29), kids free Sat and Sun lunch. AE, MC, V. Daily noon–midnight. Tube: Richmond.

INEXPENSIVE

The Original Maids of Honour *Finds* AFTERNOON TEA/LUNCH & SNACKS The word traditional takes on a whole new dimension when describing this cozy tea-room with its oak paneling and leaded-glass windows, situated across the street from the Royal Botanic Gardens (p. 188). Set up in the 18th century to sell the famous Maids of Honour cake (a sort of minicheesecake with puff pastry thought to have been named by Henry VIII when he saw Anne Boleyn and other maids of honor eating them at his royal palace at Richmond), it's now run by the fifth generation of the same family. It's one of those places where you can find something to suit your mood or appetite at any time of day: Breakfast pastries, baguettes and open-face sandwiches, full roast lunches, and—best of all—traditional afternoon teas featuring delightfully light scones with dollops of clotted cream, butter, and jam; cream cakes; and Maids of Honour. A bargain compared with the teas served at swanky London hotels, teas here can be enjoyed on the terrace in the summer.

288 Kew Rd., TW9. © 020/8940-2752. www.newens.co.uk. Highchairs. Afternoon tea £6.25 ($12). MC, V. Mon 9am–1pm; Tues–Sat 9:30am–6pm. Tube: Kew.

5 The City & Around

THE CITY

City restaurants tend to cater to expense-accounters; this is the business district, after all. However, there are some colorful (and cheaper) options worth seeking out while you're exploring the area. For **Ye Olde Cheshire Cheese** pub, see p. 195; for **Bevis Marks** in the country's oldest synagogue, see p. 197.

MODERATE

The Ginger Garden ★★ *Finds* INDIAN   This unique space—close to the Tower of London—nestles up to the Café Spice Namaste, one of Britain's finest Indian restaurants, of which it is a part. The restaurant itself is set in a 19th-century courthouse where warrants were once issued for Jack the Ripper; the imposing historic facade contrasts with the bright decor of pinks, purples, and gold. It's a lovely spot for Bombay snacks, naan wraps, panini, and experimental dishes cooked on an outdoor tandoor, amidst a setting of Parsee murals, mosaics, hot colors (saffron, cinnamon, and kasbah blue), tropical plants, and decking. Child-friendly items include sizzler sticks of lamb, chicken *tikka*, and vegetables; also try the duck *tikka*, mango, and cheddar sandwiches. Ingredients are organic where possible. Note that, for obvious reasons, the garden is open in summer only. (There are heaters and canopies for cooler or wetter days.)

Magdalen Passage, E1. ⓒ 020/7488-9242. www.cafespice.co.uk. Highchairs. Snacks about £5–£11 ($9.50–$21). AE, DC, MC. V. Mon–Fri noon–9pm. Tube: Tower Hill.

INEXPENSIVE

The Place Below ★★ *(Value)* VEGETARIAN   Heavy on atmosphere, The Place Below is set in the Norman crypt of St. Mary-le-Bow, one of Sir Christopher Wren's best churches and the one by which Cockneys are defined. (To make the cut, you need to have been born within earshot of its bells, which you can hear for 30 min. before major services or on special occasions such as the Lord Mayor's Parade; see p. 22). Kids love to watch the speedy juicing machine produce a glass of beautifully scented Valencia orange juice, while parents can enjoy what must be the cheapest cup of real coffee in the City, at just £0.80 ($1.50) if purchased with breakfast. The latter consists of porridge with maple syrup and cream, homemade muesli with apples and honey, or croissants and pain au chocolate from Comptoir Gascon (p. 115). Sandwiches are a highlight: Try the grilled field mushroom with garlic butter and Camembert, or aubergine salad with dill pickle and tahini dressing. *Insider tip:* you get a full £2 ($3.80) off the main hot dish, salad, or quiche of the day if you have an early or late lunch (11:30am–noon or 1:30–2:30pm), though they're cheap enough as they are. There's a courtyard with outdoor tables; or any dish can be sold as takeout—perhaps for a picnic in Postman's Park (p. 198).

Cheapside, EC2. ⓒ 020/7329-0789. www.theplacebelow.co.uk. Main courses £5–£5.50 ($9.50–$11). MC, V. Open Mon–Fri 7am–3pm. Tube: St. Paul's.

CLERKENWELL

For **The Zetter Restaurant & Rooms,** see p. 89.

MODERATE

Smiths of Smithfield ★★ BREAKFAST/LUNCH & SNACKS   With its industrial chic (steel, concrete, and sand-blasted brickwork), the warehouselike ground-floor cafe at this three-story restaurant, bar, and club doesn't look like the most promising spot for families, but its weekend brunches draw them in from afar to feast on the likes of eggs Benedict on English muffins. It's also a great spot for breakfast or lunch any day of the week, including big breakfasts served all day. (Smaller versions might be waffles with maple syrup, or fresh fruit salad with yogurt, muesli, and honey.). Alternatives include imaginative hot and cold sandwiches, salads, meat pies, and a daily soup, using organic ingredients where available. There's almost an embarrassment of choices, although I discourage you from ordering the porridge (on the other hand, don't miss the fresh-squeezed Asian juice with ginger, lime, lemon grass, pineapple, and mango). The atmosphere is laid-back, with leather armchairs and sofas, or seating at long, bench-style tables.

Sunday bunch is also available in the fairly expensive top-floor Restaurant with its views over the City. The second-floor Dining Room is a more relaxed spot, offering Modern European dishes at surprisingly fair prices (£11/$20 for a main course).

67–77 Charterhouse St., EC1. ℂ 020/7251-7950. www.smithsofsmithfield.co.uk. Highchairs. Main courses £3.50–£8.50 ($6.70–$16). AE, DC, MC, V. Daily 7am–11pm. Tube: Farringdon.

SHOREDITCH
MODERATE

Café Kick SPANISH/TAPAS   Kids are welcome till 4pm at this "babyfoot" bar, where you can hire a foosball table and spend the afternoon enjoying a match or two, stopping to refuel on quality tapas, charcuterie and cheese platters, salads, or sandwiches, washed down with juices, smoothies, or chocolate milk (for moms and dads there's a great range of beers and cocktails). If you're feeling up for some teamwork, share a large Kick Platter of Spanish cheeses, cured meats, salad, and bread, supplemented by tapas dishes such as bruschetta or chorizo with roasted peppers.

43 Exmouth Market, EC1. ℂ 020/7837-8077. www.cafekick.co.uk. Main courses £4–£7 ($7.60–$1). MC, V. Mon–Sat noon–11pm; Sun noon–11:30pm. Tube: Farringdon.

DOCKLANDS

This largely business district has a string of family-friendly restaurants along the riverside, some with attractive terraces lit up by fairy lights in the trees; they include branches of **Royal China** (p. 102) and **Zizzi** (p. 111).

6 North London

CAMDEN TOWN & PRIMROSE HILL
MODERATE

The Engineer ✿ MODERN BRITISH   One of London's original "gastropubs" (old boozers converted into chic modern pub/restaurants), The Engineer remains one of its best. It offers kids a first-rate menu of free-range ham, battered fish, or free-range poached egg (served with choice of wonderful baked fries, sautéed spinach, or mash). Or your kids can order penne with tomato sauce, followed by organic Rocombe Farm ice cream. In return, The Engineer asks that young ones stay at the table, since this is quite a small, closely packed, and bustling environment. (The staff helps them keep their end of the deal by handing out crayons and coloring books.) Parents enjoy more complex dishes such as aromatic baby chicken with plum sauce and cucumber relish—Modern British with more than a hint of Pacific Rim. If that all sounds too fancy, come for a relaxed summer breakfast in the gorgeous garden with its orange trees and lilac bushes; the choices extend from a fresh fruit plate, homemade beans on toast, or waffles, to a full English breakfast. Make sure to ask for a highchair when you book, as they can be in short supply.

65 Gloucester Ave., NW1. ℂ 020/7722-0950. www.the-engineer.com. Kids' menu, highchairs. Main courses £10–£16 ($20–$30); kids' menu £5.95–£6.95 ($3–$4). MC, V. Mon–Sat 9am–11pm, Sun 9am—10:30pm. Tube: Camden Town.

Lemonia GREEK   I'd hazard a guess that many people who pitch up at this taverna do so in the hope of seeing local celebs such as Kate Moss or Jude Law and their respective broods chowing down on plates of grilled *halloumi,* fish croquettes, or *keftedakia* (that's deep-fried minced chicken to you and me). Be that as it may, Lemonia is unpretentious in both setting and food, and this is a long-standing favorite among families, who come to share vast *meze* platters and juicy kabobs, or to sample more sophisticated dishes such as octopus salad, red mullet, or quail. Vegetarians won't feel hard up here, with the stuffed peppers and other meat-free offerings. The staff

Ice Time

It's no surprise that the best ice creams in town are to be had at an Italian joint—namely **Marine Ices** (8 Haverstock Hill, NW3; ✆ **020/7482-9003**), a 1930s institution now run by the founder's grandsons. Its 20-plus flavors, smooth and creamy without being too rich or sickly sweet, are sold simply in wafers (savor them as you stroll to nearby Primrose Hill), or in fluted dishes embellished with sauces and other toppings. Good pizzas and pasta dishes are on offer, too.

A good second is **Gelateria Valerie** (9 Duke of York Sq., SW3; ✆ **020/7730-7978**), a new ice-cream cafe opened in Chelsea by one of London's best cake houses, Patisserie Valerie (p. 233), with a huge choice of fantastic Italian-style *gelato* (try pistachio or Nutella) and a terrace well placed for people-watching on fashionable King's Road. Or try **The Fountain** restaurant in Fortnum & Mason (p. 221) on Piccadilly for awesome sundaes.

copes with it all admirably, though you'd be best advised to avoid weekends, when madness descends. (You'll probably have to wait for a table in spite of booking and despite its size.) Weekday lunchtimes, you can take advantage of excellent-value two- and three-course menus. Hope for a sunny day, when tables spill out of the conservatory onto the sidewalk, inducing a real holiday atmosphere.

89 Regent's Park Rd., NW1. ✆ 020/7586-7454. Reservations essential. Main courses £9–£14 ($17–$26). DC, MC, V. Mon–Sat noon–3pm and 6–11:30pm. Tube: Chalk Farm.

INEXPENSIVE

Manna ✪ VEGETARIAN   This multi-award-winning vegetarian restaurant, one of the oldest in Europe, has an ardent following for its exciting, globally inspired dishes made from mainly organic produce. You might enjoy a banana leaf parcel containing smoked tofu, lotus roof, and mizuna or a bowl of *pho* (spicy Vietnamese noodle soup). Follow one of these dishes with the baked rhubarb on hazelnut meringue, served with pomegranate seeds. The kitchen is more than happy to provide reduced-priced kids' portions on request, though some dishes are more suited to this than others—the daily pasta is a handy fallback. As all dishes are prepared fresh to order, there can be a bit of a wait when it's busy, although the friendly staff members don't take it badly if you ask them to speed things up a little because of the kids. (Staff don't like them wandering around after things start to get busy at about 7:30pm.) It's just a shame that Manna is not open for lunch other than on Sunday.

4 Erskine Rd., ✆ 020/7722-8028. www.manna-veg.com. Highchairs. Reservations recommended. Mains £9.25–£13. MC, V. Mon–Sat 6:30–11pm; Sun 12:30–3pm. Tube: Chalk Farm.

ISLINGTON

EXPENSIVE

Metrogusto ✪✪✪ ITALIAN   "We are an Italian restaurant!" exclaimed the proprietor when I asked if he could provide kids' dishes, going on to explain that the lack of tablecloths in his attractive dining room with its bright modern artworks was calculated to avoid "dramas." Indeed, in spite of the brilliantly executed progressive Italian fare served here (think guinea fowl in hazelnut and saffron sauce with beetroot, or grilled venison with cinnamon sauce and chickpea fritters), this is a very child-friendly spot with a real neighborhood feel. Pasta and risotto dishes are more classic—fettuccine might come with sour cream and wild mushrooms, maltagliati with smoked ham,

sage, and Parmesan—but parents (or kids) are encouraged to discuss their requirements with the very obliging waiting staff. A simple plate of pasta with tomato, fresh
basil, and mozzarella, for instance, will cost £7.50 ($14); or the kitchen can prepare a
rice-based dish. Don't let them overdo it, though, as the desserts are a marvel, and emi-
nently suitable for kids—thin apple tart with Parmesan ice cream, for example.

13 Theberton St., N1. ℂ 020/7226-9400. www.metrogusto.co.uk. Highchairs. Reservations recommended. Main
courses £11–£17 ($21–$32). AE, MC, V. Mon–Thurs 6:30–10:30pm; Fri and Sat noon–3pm and 6:30–11pm; Sun
12:30–3pm. Tube: Angel.

MODERATE

Draper's Arms ⭐⭐ MEDITERRANEAN   A beautiful, bright, bohemian-feeling
gastropub on a quiet street in an affluent family area, Draper's attracts its fair share of
minor local celebs, who like to spread out on the fashionably worn leather sofas or sit
in the cute paved garden. (There's a smarter restaurant area upstairs, which does have
the advantage of being nonsmoking.) The menu, which changes every month and
includes lighter lunch dishes, is eclectic to say the least—burgers, steak sandwiches,
and brunch dishes such as eggs royale are offered alongside the likes of chilled squash
and fresh ginger soup. Kids' portions are provided—risotto, fishcakes, and toad-in-
the-hole are favorites—and if you snare one of the front or rear sofa areas, little ones
have lots of room to play on the low coffee tables. Sunday brunches are a highlight—
try bubble and squeak (a dish made from leftover roast vegetables, often served with
cold roast) with poached egg; or a full veggie breakfast of creamed mushrooms, halloumi cheese, fries, eggs, tomatoes, beans, and toast, which should set you all up for
a romp on nearby Highbury Fields (p. 206).

44 Barnsbury St., N1. ℂ **020/7619-0348.** www.thedrapersarms.co.uk. Highchairs. Reservations recommended
(restaurant). Main courses £7.50–£15 ($14–$29). Mon–Sat noon–3pm and 7–10pm; Sun noon–3pm and
6:30–9:30pm. Train: Highbury and Islington.

INEXPENSIVE

Tiger Lil's ⟨Value⟩ ASIAN   This shrinking chain (it now only has this branch and one
in Clapham) remains a good bet when the kids are restless and in need of diversion,
which it provides in the form of flaming woks used by the chefs to stir-fry the ingredients, sauces, and garnishes chosen by the diners (staff are trained to guide kids
through the selection). As well as special chopsticks, each child gets a badge; a large
placemat with word games, puzzles, jokes, and more; and returnable pick-up sticks.
They love having their own cocktail menu, too, with the likes of Red Dragon (strawberry, banana, and ice cream) and Ancient Temple (ginger ale, passion fruit, and
grenadine). Under-5s eat free with an adult, and under-12s eat for little more than £5
($9.25), including a stir-fry bowl, a soft drink, and an ice cream. Adults can take
advantage of a "Try it All" three-course deal for less than £12 ($23).

270 Upper St., N1. ℂ 020/7226-1118. www.tigerlils.com. Kids' menu, highchairs. Main course £7.90 ($15), kids'
menu £5.60 ($11). AE, MC, V. Mon–Thurs 6pm–midnight; Fri noon–3pm and 6pm–midnight; Sat and Sun noon–mid-
night. Tube: Highbury and Islington.

Yellow River Café ⭐ ⟨Value⟩ ASIAN   Star-chef Ken Hom has long been an advocate
of encouraging kids to eat healthy food—a principle he puts into practice in this chain
of family-friendly modern restaurants, which serve very reasonably priced southeast
Asian and regional Chinese food. (This is the lone London branch.) Kids are usually
delighted with their own cute bento boxes containing prawn crackers, a starter, a main
course, and noodles or steamed rice. Much of the menu is tempting, including starters

of *pakoras* (potato fritters with cucumber and yogurt dip) or sesame prawn toast; mains of lemon-grass chicken with pieces of fresh mango; and desserts such as lotus crepe with ice cream. Drinks-wise, the kids can sample luscious smoothies and lassis, and parents can choose from tropical thirst-quenchers such as mango daiquiris.

Only in London

A trip to Britain wouldn't be complete without at least one **fish and chip supper**, laced with salt and malt vinegar and accompanied by pickled onions, mushy peas, and/or pickled eggs (although I still contend that they're best enjoyed on the seafront, straight from the paper they were wrapped in; for Whitstable, see p. 268). Many of London's fish and chip shops have gone downhill of late. If in doubt, look for ones with London taxis parked outside, as the city's cabbies have an unerring instinct for good-quality, good-value haunts. One such spot is **Fish Central** (149–52 Central St., EC1; ✆ 020/7253-4970), with cheery staff, kids' portions, and a patio for fine weather. It's been trendified of late, and offers little extras you won't see in a run-of-the-mill "chippy" (such as homemade bread, fresh vegetables, fish soup, pasta dishes, and wonderful desserts), but you're best off sticking to the spanking-fresh traditional battered cod or haddock with lip-smacking chips and tasty mushy peas. Another option a little farther into the center is **North Sea Fish Restaurant** in Bloomsbury (p. 194).

One of the longest-standing and most famous chippies, **Geales** in Notting Hill Gate (2 Farmer St., W8; ✆ 020/7727-7528) has been serving first-rate cod, haddock, and plaice since before World War II, plus fishcakes, fish pie, salmon, skate, oysters, and even caviar. Kids are welcome (and get their own menu), but vegetarians should be warned that the fish (not the fries) is cooked the traditional way, in beef dripping. The place is great on a balmy summer evening, when they open the big front windows.

A little more of an acquired taste than fish and chips, the eels sold at London's few surviving traditional **pie and mash shops** are eaten cold and jellied, or warm in a stew, with a splash of vinegar or parsley "liquor." Sounds hideous, doesn't it? If you can't bring yourself to try this most working-class of dishes, come to a shop anyway, for the mash, the beef and gravy pies, and—most of all—the surroundings. Dating from the 19th or early 20th century; the shops are atmospheric, family-fun places boasting their original tiled walls, wooden benches, and marble-topped tables. A meal of this kind will cost you little more than a fiver ($9.50). One of the best (and most central) is **M Manze** on the South Bank (87 Tower Bridge Rd., SE1; ✆ 020/7407-2985; www.manze.co.uk), established in 1902 and also serving veggie pies. The non-related **Manze's** at 76 Walthamstow High St., E7 (✆ 020/8520-2855), is a good place to fill up after a visit to another East End institution—the greyhound racing at Walthamstow Stadium (p. 258). In west London, try **Cockneys Pie & Mash** at 314 Portobello Rd., W10 (✆ 020/8960-9409).

206 Upper St., N1. 📞 **020/7354-8833**. www.yellowrivercafes.co.uk. Kids' menu, highchairs. Main courses £5.95–£9.50 ($11–$18), kids' bento box £5 ($9.50). Mon–Fri noon–3pm and 6–11pm; Sat noon–11:30pm; Sun noon–10:30pm. Tube: Highbury and Islington.

HAMPSTEAD & GOLDERS GREEN
MODERATE

Blooms ✪✪ KOSHER   You don't get much more traditional than this kosher deli-restaurant with its family atmosphere and wonderful staff, some of whom have worked here for decades (perhaps they even remember the visits by Charlie Chaplin and Frank Sinatra). The food is everything you'd expect of a place this iconic, from the faultless hors d'oeuvres of chopped liver, egg, and onion; gefilte fish; or chicken soup with matzo; to mains such as *gedempte* (braised) meatballs. "Kiddies" are very well catered-to with a high-quality menu of turkey schnitzels, hot dogs, burgers, or pasta, all served with fries and a soft drink and followed by ice cream. If you're in a hurry to get to the nearby Heath, stop at the deli instead for salt beef sandwiches, potato salad, and a few treats from the pickle bar, as well as *lockshen* pudding (egg noodle pudding).

130 Golders Green Rd., NW11. 📞 **020/8455-1338**. www.blooms-restaurant.co.uk. Kids' menu, highchairs, Main courses £7.50–£18 ($14–$33), kids' menu £6.95 ($13). AE, DC, MC, V. Mon–Thurs and Sun noon–10:30pm; Fri noon–3pm. Tube: Golders Green.

INEXPENSIVE

Café Mozart ✪ BREAKFAST/LUNCH & SNACKS   There's no finer spot to warm up after a gusty morning on the Heath or a performance in Waterlow Park (p. 253) than this charming cafe with its cozy outdoor terrace warmed by heaters (a better bet than the rather cramped interior). Come for breakfast and brunch in a variety of styles (English, Parisienne, and vegetarian to name just three), be it pancakes, sandwiches, or eastern European dishes such as *schnitzel Holstein* (chicken escallops) or beef goulash. Or forget all of those in favor of the real standout here—handmade European cakes and cookies, including *mohn torte* (with poppy seeds) and vanilla *kipfel* (walnut cookies with jam). Moms and pops can accompany the treats with a range of luxurious coffees and teas, or with beers, wines, or champagne. For Junior there are babycinnos (frothy milk sprinkled with chocolate) and winter warmers such as hot cranberry juice, in addition to the more usual soft drinks.

17 Swains Lane, N6. 📞 **020/8348-1384**. Highchairs. Cakes £1.10–£2.50 ($2.10–$4.80); main courses £2.95–£7.95 ($5.60–$15). MC, V. Mon–Fri 8am–10pm; Sat and Sun 9am–10pm. Tube: Archway.

Ed's Easy Diner ✪✪ BURGERS   Not all branches of this popular retro American diner (based on Los Angeles's Apple Pan Diner) are child-friendly—the original one in Soho, in particular, is tiny and cramped, and staff seem to think that by studiously ignoring people with kids, they will drive them away (actually, they're not wrong). On the other hand, I couldn't be a bigger fan of this large branch in the O2 entertainment mall (p. 255)—it's perfectly located for refueling before or after visiting the Children's Gallery of International Art, expending energy at Gymboree (p. 216), or catching a movie in the multiplex cinema. It's corny on the surface, sure—there's a jukebox playing rock 'n' roll, lots of hokey signs adorning the walls, and a heavily themed decor, but the burgers really are top-notch, as are trimmings such as onion rings and shakes (the banana and peanut butter malted should be on anyone's "last meal" list). The under-12s Junior Bites menu of burgers, hot dogs, or chicken filets, all served with the excellent fries, will cost you about £5.50 ($10) if you add a Mini Moo shake or a Baby sundae on top. There are further branches in Piccadilly Circus, Covent Garden, Chelsea, and the Bluewater shopping mall (p. 238).

255 Finchley Rd., NW3. ✆ **020/7431-1958.** www.edseasydiner.co.uk. Kids' menu, highchairs. Main courses £4.45–£7.95 ($8.50–$15), kids' menu £3.95 ($7.50). AE, MC, V. Daily 11am–11:30pm. Tube: Finchley Rd.

BETHNAL GREEN & HACKNEY
INEXPENSIVE

Frizzante@CityFarm ★★ ITALIAN   A true curiosity, this is a genuine Italian cafe set slap bang in the middle of a farmyard, complete with clucking chickens and a garden with a kids' play area, as well as a handful of outdoor tables. The superbly simple homemade fare, cooked by chefs from three different regions of Italy, includes all-day weekend breakfasts with eggs from those same chickens, great pizzas and pasta dishes, and superb cakes and puddings. Kids' portions can be laid on as required, with pasta dishes costing about £2.50 ($4.70). All of the fruit and vegetables used are organic. Try to coincide your visit with some of the many activities run at the farm, including animal feeding (daily at 4pm), parent's and kids' pottery classes (Wed), music and movement classes for under-4s (Thurs and Fri), and massages for adults (Thurs). And stock up on your way out with farm produce (those eggs again) or cakes; this makes for a handy picnic stop on the way to the National Museum of Childhood.

Hackney City Farm, 1A Goldsmith's Row, E2. ✆ **020/7739-2266.** www.hackneycityfarm.co.uk. Highchairs. Main courses £4–£7 ($7.60–$13). No credit cards. Tues–Fri 10:30am–4:30pm, Sat and Sun 10:30am–5:30pm. Tube: Cambridge Heath.

Green Papaya VIETNAMESE   Of the numerous good Vietnamese restaurants and canteens in this area, Green Papaya stands out for its lovely garden, where you can eat in good weather (in summertime they string up fairy lanterns). It's almost impossible to choose from the large menu of modern but authentic Vietnamese dishes, but prices are so low you can afford to spring for a whole host of little starter dishes to share. (Try the green papaya or banana flower salads or the *banh xeo* pancakes filled with meat or vegetables.) From the mains, rice noodle soup with fishcake is a surefire winner with most kids. Note that all dishes are prepared to order, so come for an early dinner or expect to wait a bit. Though there aren't desserts, you can stop off at one of the nearby Vietnamese supermarkets if you need a sweet fix.

191 Mare St., E8. ✆ **020/8985-5486.** www.greenpapaya.co.uk. Highchairs. Main course £5–£8 ($9.50–$15). DC, MC, V. Mon–Sat 5–11:30pm. Tube: Bethnal Green.

6

Exploring London
With Your Kids

Even those who live here never get to the bottom of this inexhaustible city and all it has to offer, and I've had to be brutal when it comes to what and what not to list. The upside of this is that, on the whole, only the really stellar attractions have made it into the book. The sections on **"Suggested Itineraries"** and **"Top Attractions"** should help you prioritize.

Children's prices generally apply to those ages 5 to 16, with under-5s usually going free. **Opening hours** can change at short notice, so it's essential that you call ahead if you're making a special sightseeing trip with your kids. All museums are closed on Good Friday, December 24 to 26, and New Year's Day. Most venues close on bank holidays, around Christmas and New Year's, and in some cases in May.

During British **school vacations** (which are staggered across the country but broadly consist of a 2-week Easter break in April, a 6-week summer break from late July to early September, and a 3-week Christmas break from mid-December to early January, plus 1-week "half-term" breaks in February and in October), major attractions get crowded and queues lengthen. On the other hand,

during these periods many venues feature special **kids' activities,** so they can be good times to visit. If your trip does coincide with a British school vacation, check websites ahead of time, and book activities if required.

If you plan to see lots of sights, a **London Pass** (www.londonpass.com) may be worth investing in. It offers free admission to 54 attractions in and around London, fast-track tickets to some, and a pocket guidebook. The transport option offering unlimited free travel on buses, the Tube, and trains across all six zones after 9:30am is highly recommended. One-day passes are available, as are passes for 2, 3, or 6 consecutive days, with prices varying accordingly; a 6-day pass with transport option costs £94 ($179) for adults, £53 ($101) for kids 5 to 15. Note, however, that prices quoted don't include the VAT (value-added tax).

Another money-saving option is **www. london2for1.com**, which offers two-for-one ticket offers on many of London's top attractions when you're traveling by train or by Tube; it also offers deals on restaurants, hotels, and theater tickets.

SUGGESTED ITINERARIES

If You Have 1 Day

If you have only a day, get a stunning overview of the city's vast sprawl and some of its most famous monuments (St. Paul's Cathedral, Buckingham Palace, Westminster Abbey) from a gleaming glass pod on the giant **London Eye** Ferris wheel. If you're not suffering from jet lag, you can then take younger kids to stroke sting rays at the **London Aquarium,** or older kids on a short walk downriver to see the art at the impressive **Tate Modern,** with its award-winning children's audio tour and its discovery trails. Family-friendly lunch options in the area include Loco Mensa behind the London Eye, and The Cafe on Level 2 of the Tate Modern.

Spend the rest of the afternoon taking a languid **riverboat cruise down to Greenwich,** passing beneath the sparkling-new Millennium Footbridge and historic Tower Bridge; enjoying views of the Tower of London, the Canary Wharf towers, and more; and disembarking on the *Cutty Sark,* a 19th-century clipper.

Arriving back at Embankment Pier, you're well placed for **Trafalgar Square** or **Leicester Square,** with their big, brash family eating options, such as Texas Embassy Cantina and Rainforest Cafe.

If You Have 2 Days

Day 1 Spend Day 1 as above.

Day 2 Head for South Kensington and choose between the huge, ultra-kid-friendly **Natural History Museum** and the **Science Museum,** which both offer exhibits, interactive displays, and activities to delight and fascinate all ages. Each has enough to occupy a brood for the entire day, as well as a variety of child-pleasing lunch options.

If you don't spend the whole day at one or both of the museums, browse away the afternoon at **Harrods'** mighty Toy Kingdom, taking in a performance at its kids' theater, and peeking into its legendary pet store. Grab dinner ingredients in Harrods' legendary food halls, or walk or catch a cab to the King's Road with its excellent range of restaurants that welcome kids, including Bluebird and The Blue Kangaroo (with its CCTV-monitored play zone).

If You Have 3 Days

Days 1–2 Spend Days 1 and 2 as above.

Day 3 Begin your day at the conservation-conscious **London Zoo,** lunching at its wonderful cafe or stopping off at one of the appealing eateries that dot Regent's Park as you stroll down to Marylebone. There are play parks here, too, if the kids need a stretch.

After lunch, grit your teeth and take the kids to the trashy but irresistible (to kids, at least) **Madame Tussaud's** wax museum and its adjoining planetarium. It you want to do something a little more educational, take the Tube or a taxi to the **British Museum,** whose special tours and trails help younger visitors get a handle on its vast collections.

Have dinner at one of the great family-oriented restaurants clustered around villagey Marylebone High Street, such as Fishworks or Giraffe. If you're coming from the British Museum, there's a nearby branch of Wagamama. For those who haven't had your fill of culture, it's only a few minutes' walk to **Theaterland** with its big-budget West End shows.

If You Have 4 Days or More

Days 1–3 Spend Days 1, 2, and 3 as above.

Day 4 Head east to the City, London's birthplace, and to **St. Paul's Cathedral,** where you can view the tombs of such greats as Lord Nelson and the Duke of Wellington, marvel at the weird acoustics of the Whispering Gallery, and take in panoramic views. It's a short walk from there to atmospheric **Smithfield** meat market, with its buzzing restaurants and cafes, including Smiths of Smithfield (p. 132).

Now walk to the **Museum of London** to learn how the city grew and weathered such disasters as the Great Fire and the Black Death. With smaller kids, it's worth the journey farther east to the splendid **National Museum of Childhood** at Bethnal Green. A good dinner option near the Museum of

London is the branch of **Pizza Express** dramatically straddling the road beneath it. If you'd prefer to eat in Bethnal Green, try one of the authentic Vietnamese canteens lining Kingland Road and its side streets.

If the Weather's Hot

There's no better place to spend a sweltering summer's day than **Hyde Park** and **Kensington Gardens.** Younger kids (and parents) can cool their feet in the beach cove at the stunning Diana Memorial Playground; older ones like floating their boats and feeding the birdlife on the Round Pond, or investigating the Princess of Wales Memorial Fountain (alas, paddling is not permitted).

Have lunch at one of the waterside cafes, or picnic in the park, then spend a few lazy hours cruising The Serpentine in a paddleboat or rowboat, or even go swimming in it. Use one of the informal sports fields for laid-back games of Frisbee or cricket if you can summon up the wherewithal.

It's a short taxi or bus ride to the breezy canals of **Little Venice,** where dinner options include the charming Prince Alfred pub. Afterwards, those with older kids can enjoy a performance in the unique **Puppet Theatre Barge** (p. 250 in chapter 10).

If the Weather's Cold

Journey west out of the city center to Syon House and its two tropical animal attractions, **London Butterfly House** and **Tropical Forest.** If those don't warm up the kids sufficiently, an indoor adventure playground is located on the grounds, too.

Have a long lunch in Richmond at, for instance, Canyon or the Victoria, before heading back to central London to embrace the cold at one of its seasonal **outdoor ice rinks.** The loveliest rink is in the courtyard of Somerset House. It's a short hop from there to

Porter's English Restaurant, where steamed puddings with custard will warm you up again.

If You Have a Sitter

One of London's most romantic spots is leafy **Highgate Cemetery** (© 020/ 7435-2062), a Victorian graveyard where beautifully elaborate, angel-bedecked tombs peek from behind trees and rosebushes. Many of the graves on either side of its wandering pathways are those of historical figures, including Karl Marx and poet Christina Rossetti. Seek refreshments at nearby **Flask** (© 020/8340-7260), a lovely villagey pub with cellars where highwayman Dick Turpin is said to have hidden, and where 18th-century painter William Hogarth was a regular.

Head back to central London, to Holborn and the wonderfully eccentric **Sir John Soane's Museum,** which can be better appreciated without kids in tow—particularly on the first Tuesday of the month, when the architect's house is candlelit from 6 to 9pm.

Your dinner options are myriad, but if it's summer you'll want to head to a Shakespeare performance at the gorgeous **Open-air Theatre** in **Regent's Park.** Be sure to bring a Fortnum & Mason Picnic Package (© 08700/ 601811), which for £200 ($380) gets you two seats and a hamper filled with the likes of duck stuffed with apricots and pistachios, crème brûlée, gourmet cheeses, and white wine. If it's winter, the beautiful Art Deco **Gordon Ramsay at Claridge's** (© 020/7592-1373), presided over by the rambunctious Michelin-starred chef, is an adult paradise where you can enjoy delectable fare such as velouté (white sauce) of portobello mushrooms with truffle chantilly. (*Insider tip:* If this stretches your budget a bit far, go at lunchtime and enjoy their substantial selections on the set menu.) I also have a soft spot for

Soho's **Andrew Edmunds** (📞 020/7437-5708), which is a considerably cheaper option. The cooking might not reach Ramsay's heights, but the atmosphere couldn't be better suited to an intimate dinner.

Night owls who want to carry on into the wee hours should head to **Ronnie Scott's** (📞 020/7439-0747), a world-famous jazz joint in Soho.

1 Kids' Top 10 Attractions

British Airways London Eye ★★★   **All ages.** The world's biggest observation wheel and fourth-tallest structure in the city offers half-hour "flights" at a pace slow enough to make it suitable for even the smallest kids. Built to mark the millennium, it's said to be at the current dead center of London. The 32 glass pods (each holding 25 people) afford stunning panoramic views—even when the weather is less than perfect—of the Thames bridges, the Queen's garden at Buckingham Palace, Hampstead Heath to the north, and Windsor Castle to the west. You can buy a "miniguide" for £3 ($5.70) from the gift shop to help you identify landmarks. Queues can be horrendous during weekends and school vacations, especially on clear days, so book in advance if possible—you can only do this online, 14 days ahead, but you do get a 10% discount (phone bookings are same-day only). Strollers must be folded before boarding the Eye, but a free baby-carrier loan is available, and there are baby-changing facilities by the customer services desks inside County Hall. You must arrive 30 minutes before your flight to collect your tickets and board; allow about 30 minutes for the ride itself.

Millennium Jubilee Gardens, SE1; ticket office inside County Hall 📞 0870/500-0600. www.ba-londoneye.co.uk. Admission £12.50 ($23.75) adults, £10 ($19) seniors, £6.50 ($23.35) children 5 to 15. Feb–Apr and Oct–Dec daily 9:30am–8pm, May, June and Sept daily 9:30am–9pm; July and Aug daily 9:30am–10pm. Tube: Westminster or Waterloo.

Hampstead Heath ★★   **All ages.** A much-loved and gloriously wild expanse of park, woods, heath, meadows, and ponds offers a taste of the countryside just 6.5km (4 miles) from the city center. Londoners come here to stroll, jog, swim, sunbathe, fly kites, picnic, play in the adventure and traditional playgrounds, fish, and enjoy incredible views from its summit at Parliament Hill—on a clear day you can see St. Paul's Cathedral and as far as Kent from here. Sports facilities include an athletics track, tennis courts, a pétanque (lawn bowling) pitch, and a bowling green. Golders Hill Park, part of the Heath's northern extension, has a small children's zoo featuring animal-feeding. The Heath's wildlife includes breeding kingfishers and meadow brown butterflies. Funfairs are frequently held, as are events such as nature-spotting walks. Summer vacation brings free puppet shows. A Heath diary is worth getting (at no charge) from the **Superintendent's Office** (📞 020/8348-9908).

On the Heath's northern fringe lies **Kenwood House** (📞 020/8348-1286; www.english-heritage.org.uk), a country home revamped by architect Robert Adam in 1764. It contains period furniture and paintings by Turner, Gainsborough, and others. Admission is free. It's open April to September daily 10am to 6pm; October daily 10am to 5pm; and November to March daily 10am to 4pm. Children's activities (mainly free) include an annual Easter Egg hunt, a St. George's Day Dragon Trail, kite-making days or weekends, bat-spotting evenings, and butterfly-spottings followed by craft sessions. The Brew House cafe is a kid-friendly spot for breakfast, lunch, or coffee and cakes, with a large garden for sunny days. On the shore of Kenwood's lake, you can sit beneath the stars and enjoy symphony concerts and fireworks on summer evenings (www.picnicconcerts.com), but be warned that tickets sell out well ahead.

You can even swim on the Heath, in the newly refurbished Parliament Hill Lido or the Heath Ponds, which were originally brick pits (p. 214). (One is for both men and women, and two are single-sex.) The traditional playground at Parliament Hill also has a paddling pool. You'll want to spend a half-day to a day here.

Hampstead, NW3. ℭ 020/7485-4491. www.cityoflondon.gov.uk. Free admission. Open 24 hr. (Golders Hill Park, the Kenwood Estate, the Hill Garden, and the Pergola close before dusk.) Tube: Belsize Park. Hampstead, or Golders Green.

Horniman Museum ★★★   All ages.
This delightfully quirky museum contains 350,000 objects collected by a Victorian tea trader, from torture instruments used in the Spanish Inquisition and a giant overstuffed walrus to outsize model insects, displays of live insects, and a small aquarium (feeding time is Wed noon–12:30pm). The museum's main anthropology, natural history, and musical instrument displays inspire a program of temporary exhibitions and free events and activities. These include interactive puppet theaters and discovery boxes; storytelling relating to objects in the galleries; arts and crafts sessions; Science Week events; Caribbean dance; World Music workshops; African drumming; and nature exploration. There's also a new drop-in "Under-5s Book Zone" where families can read together; free half-hour family-friendly tours of the gallery on Tuesday and Thursday; and education packs with trails and activity sheets for family use.

If it all gets overwhelming, repair to the cafe, which overlooks a lovely Victorian conservatory and 6.5 hectares (16 acres) of gardens, where you'll find a nature trail and an animal enclosure holding rabbits, goats, and turkeys. All exhibition spaces and facilities are stroller accessible. Allow a half-day to see everything.

100 London Rd., SE23. ℭ 020/8699-1872. www.horniman.ac.uk. Free admission except for major temporary exhibitions. Daily 10:30am–5:30pm. Train: Forest Hill.

London Zoo ★   All ages.
A zoo without elephants doesn't seem quite right—a few years ago, London Zoo's were shipped off to enjoy the greater space at the zoo's sister establishment, Whipsnade Wild Animal Park (p. 264), 48km (30 miles) outside London. Pachyderms or not, this remains one of the world's best-run and most conservation-conscious zoos, with giraffes, lions, tigers, a Reptile House with popular handling sessions, a children's zoo with a "touch paddock" and advice sessions on looking after small pets, and a celebrated new B.U.G.S. biodiversity exhibition, where you can watch white-coated men in little rooms growing trays of Polynesian snails and the like. Adults will appreciate the shaded walkways and the zoo's famous architecture; its 12 listed buildings include the dramatic 1960s Snowdon Aviary and the 1930s Penguin Pool (no longer in use; the penguins have a brand-new habitat). The large, bright, main cafe has thought of everything when it comes to kids, from a buggy park, to tons of highchairs, to a parent and baby unit where you can heat bottles, to a well-considered choice of refreshments, from organic juices, baby foods, and croissants, to full meals. Plenty of other pit stops are dotted around the zoo (some are closed out of season), including merry-go-rounds and fun rides galore, and a highly rated shop without rip-off prices. Be aware that some enclosures may be locked 15 minutes or so in advance of the main zoo's closing time, so don't leave the best till last. The last zoo admission is an hour before closing time. Note that online booking saves you 10% on ticket prices.

West End Attractions

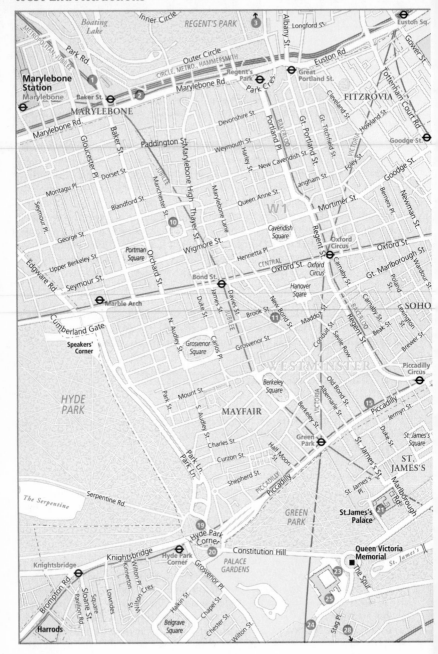

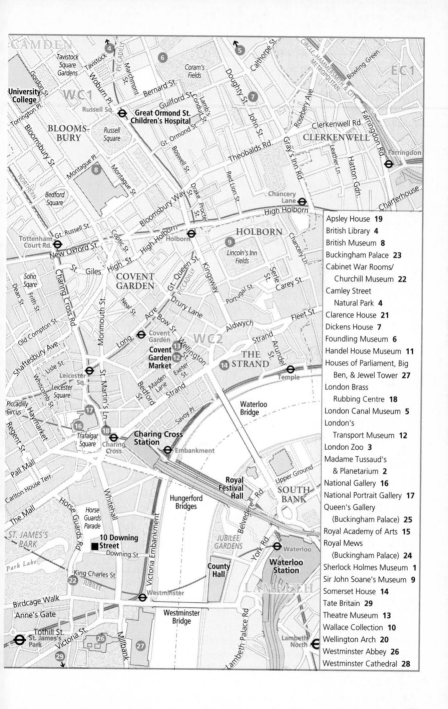

Apsley House **19**
British Library **4**
British Museum **8**
Buckingham Palace **23**
Cabinet War Rooms/
  Churchill Museum **22**
Camley Street
  Natural Park **4**
Clarence House **21**
Dickens House **7**
Foundling Museum **6**
Handel House Museum **11**
Houses of Parliament, Big
  Ben, & Jewel Tower **27**
London Brass
  Rubbing Centre **18**
London Canal Museum **5**
London's
  Transport Museum **12**
London Zoo **3**
Madame Tussaud's
  & Planetarium **2**
National Gallery **16**
National Portrait Gallery **17**
Queen's Gallery
  (Buckingham Palace) **25**
Royal Academy of Arts **15**
Royal Mews
  (Buckingham Palace) **24**
Sherlock Holmes Museum **1**
Sir John Soane's Museum **9**
Somerset House **14**
Tate Britain **29**
Theatre Museum **13**
Wallace Collection **10**
Wellington Arch **20**
Westminster Abbey **26**
Westminster Cathedral **28**

Insider tip: Combine a visit here with a canal trip via the London Waterbus Company (p. 178) to get reduced-price entry and forgo queues. You'll need a half-day to a day to see the zoo's full offerings.

Outer Circle, Regent's Park, NW1. ℂ 020/7722-3355. www.londonzoo.co.uk. Admission £14 ($27) adults, £12 ($23) seniors and students; £11 ($20) children 3–15, £45 ($86) family ticket (2 adults and 2 children or 1 adult and 3 children). Jan 1–Mar 6 and Oct 31–Dec 31 (except Christmas Day), 10am–4pm; Mar 7–Oct 23, daily 10am–5:30pm; Oct 24–30, daily 10am–4:30pm. Tube: Regent's Park or Camden Town.

National Museum of Childhood (Museum of Childhood at Bethnal Green) ★★★ **All ages.** This toys and games museum, the winner of a 2004 London Tourist Board poll on the best-loved children's attraction, will delight those of all ages. An outpost of the V&A (p. 172), it looks stuffy from the outside, but inside, the three-story central atrium makes for a wonderfully light and airy space in which children can run around to their hearts' content. There's so much going on, in fact, that they might not even notice the permanent glass cabinets filled with more than 6,000 items, including gorgeous dolls in period costume, dolls' houses, puppets, toy soldiers, trains, and much, much more, such as the temporary exhibitions on topics like Beatrix Potter. Special video consoles allow visitors to see the out-of-reach objects in action. Other areas allow children to dress up, enjoy giant board games, read books, and play with toys. As if this weren't enough, there are endless activities for kids of all ages, including interactive storytelling sessions, art workshops, and weekend softplay for the under-5s (£1.80/$3.40; 40-min. session). Older children and parents interested in social history will enjoy serious-minded but fascinating temporary exhibitions such as "Children at Work." A permanent gallery is dedicated to London's East End communities; it includes Vietnamese water puppets, Bangladeshi toy elephants, and a scooter made by children from World War II bomb debris.

The ground-floor cafe is a lovely spot sporting numerous highchairs, but snacks are overpriced. The gift shop is good for pocket-money trinkets. A stroller park with ramps has a lift that allows you to take the stroller with you. You'll want to spend about a half-day taking in the sights here. *Note:* The Museum is closed until October 2006 for renovations.

Cambridge Heath Rd., E2. ℂ 020/8980-2415. www.vam.ac.uk/moc. Free admission. Sat–Thurs 10am–5:50pm. Tube: Bethnal Green.

Natural History Museum ★★★ **Ages 3 and up.** Britain's mighty three-building "storehouse" of plants, minerals, and fossils is best known for its Dinosaurs Gallery; but though the fearsome animatronic dinosaurs have now gone, March 2005 saw the arrival of a new "super-sensing" Tyrannosaurus rex that detects motion—*your* motion, so that it follows your course around the room with its head. And there's another 68 million items to delight budding natural historians here, on everything from evolution and human biology to ecology, bugs, and meteorites—check out the touchscreen guides in the impressive Central Hall presided over by a 26m (85-ft.) diplodocus skeleton to find out exactly what's where. Above all, don't let older kids miss the Darwin Centre (dedicated to naturalist Charles Darwin), where you get an insider's look at the museum's research activities, laboratories, and storage facilities (large enough to accommodate a staggering 22 million preserved specimens). You may want to join one of the 14 daily free behind-the-scenes tours (for ages 10 and up), or fire questions at the museum's researchers and curators during a program of free special events; if so, book when you get to the museum.

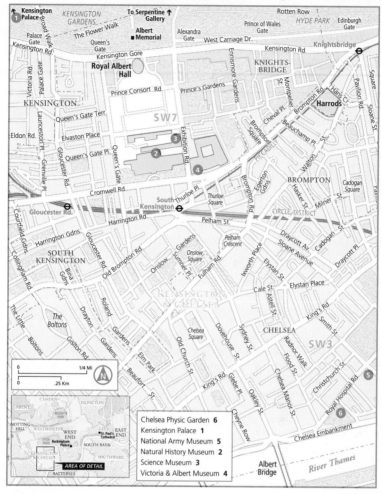

Chelsea Physic Garden **6**
Kensington Palace **1**
National Army Museum **5**
Natural History Museum **2**
Science Museum **3**
Victoria & Albert Museum **4**

Other highlights are the life-size model of a blue whale (the length of three buses) in the Mammal Hall, the simulated earthquake in "The Power Within"—a guaranteed hit with tots—and the live ant colony in "Creepy Crawlies." Catering especially to 7- to 14-year-olds is "Investigate," a hands-on science center with microscopes and other equipment with which they can explore a huge range of specimens, both inside the center and in a courtyard garden with a pond. Periodic special events include animation workshops, music sessions, Easter trails, storytelling, craft workshops, and trolleys loaded with nature-related crafts and activities. Those with under-7s can pick up Explorer backpacks with drawing materials and themed activities from the information desks (free, but a £25/$48 deposit is required). Older children might like to chat with one of the "characters," including Darwin and Carl Linnaeus, who roam the galleries. Before your visit, you might want to download the website's Discovery

Guides with activity sheets for various galleries and exhibitions, tailored for children ages 3 to 18.

Most galleries are stroller-accessible, and baby-changing and -feeding facilities are available. All three eateries have highchairs; the most family-friendly is the self-service Life Galleries Restaurant with its children's menu and heating facilities for baby food. If these options are too hectic, try the snack bar or bring your own sandwiches and eat in the picnic area. Another little-known and peaceful oasis during busy times is the Wildlife Garden with its wildflowers, birds, and dragonflies. The garden is open daily from noon to 5pm April to October, except in bad weather. Allow yourself a half-day to a day here. *Insider tip:* During the busy school vacations, it's usually easier to enter the museum via the Earth Galleries entrance on Exhibition Road.

Cromwell Rd., SW7. © 020/7942-5011. www.nhm.ac.uk. Free admission (except special exhibitions). Mon–Sat 10am–5:50pm; Sun 11am–5:50pm. Tube: S. Kensington.

Riverboat Cruise to Greenwich ★★ **All ages.** Getting to historic Greenwich the way Henry VIII did is half the fun, if you don't mind sharing your trip with circling seagulls—a reminder of how close to the ocean London is. These days, the 6.5km (4-mile) journey takes 50 to 75 minutes each way, depending on the tides and the ferry company you choose. Along the way, you pass beneath the ultra-modern Millennium Footbridge and the historic London and Tower bridges, and enjoy unparalleled views of the BA London Eye, the Tate Modern, St. Paul's Cathedral, the Tower of London, and more. You'll disembark near the historical *Cutty Sark* (p. 159), beside which is the Greenwich Tourist Information Centre. City Cruises and Thames River Services depart from Westminster Millennium Pier, and Catamaran Cruisers depart from Embankment and Waterloo. Note that Travelcard holders get a discount on fares, that City Cruises offers a River Red Rover ticket for unlimited hop-on hop-off travel, and that Thames River Services has a round-trip family ticket for two adults and two kids for £22 ($42). Allow about a day for the tour and Greenwich sightseeing.

Catamaran Cruises: © 020/7987-1185. www.catamarancruisers.co.uk. City Cruises: © 020/7740-0400. www.city cruises.com. Thames River Services: © 020/7930-4097. www.westminsterpier.co.uk. Admission £8–£8.20 ($15–$16) round-trip for adults, £4–£4.10 ($7.60–$7.80) round-trip for children 5–15. Tube: Embankment, Westminster, or Waterloo.

Science Museum ★★★ **Ages 2 and up.** I defy anyone, of any age, to come away disappointed from this gargantuan five-floor museum of science and industry. Before you start, get your bearings at one of the touchscreen information terminals placed throughout the museum, which give directions (this is not the easiest place to find your way around) and suggest itineraries for families, teens, and those with special interests, such as transport or medicine. Hands-on hits include the flight simulator; the virtual ride to Mars; the Launch Pad science exploration playground for ages 5 and up; and "On Air," where children 12 and up can produce their own radio show. Eight- to eleven-year-olds can even enjoy themed sleepover Science Nights (p. 152). Tots are not forgotten, either. They can use the futuristic Pattern Pod interactive space as well as the Garden, a basement section where 3- to 6-year-olds encounter simple scientific ideas through dressing up, water- and softplay, and building.

In addition to hosting temporary exhibitions, the museum holds such world-altering inventions as Stephenson's Rocket, Bell's telephone, Whittle's jet engine, the *Apollo 10* command module, and the computer used by Tim Berners-Lee to design the Internet. The Welcome Wing explores genetics, digital technology, and artificial intelligence, and

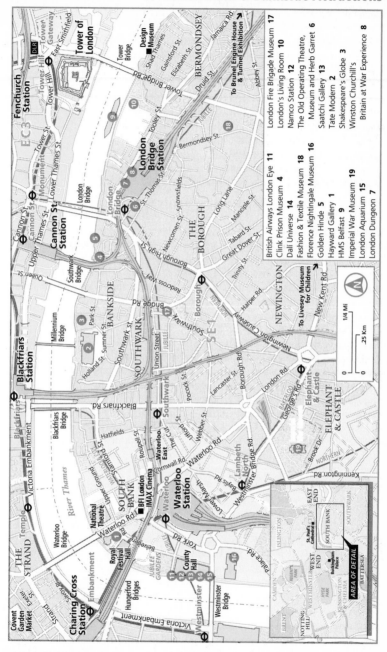

British Airways London Eye **11**
Clink Prison Museum **4**
Dalí Universe **14**
Fashion & Textile Museum **18**
Florence Nightingale Museum **16**
Golden Hinde **5**
Hayward Gallery **1**
HMS Belfast **9**
Imperial War Museum **19**
London Aquarium **15**
London Dungeon **7**

London Fire Brigade Museum **17**
London's Living Room **10**
Namco Station **12**
The Old Operating Theatre, Museum and Herb Garret **6**
Saatchi Gallery **13**
Tate Modern **2**
Shakespeare's Globe **3**
Winston Churchill's Britain at War Experience **8**

has a 450-seat IMAX theater showing spectacular 2D and 3D films on screens as tall as four double-decker buses. School vacation events for ages 6 and up include quizzes, storytelling, and workshops, but every day there's a program of tours, shows, demonstrations, and drama presentations. The bookshop and sales desks sell children's trail guides for £1 ($1.90) each.

Practically speaking, staff members are attentive to wandering children, there are stroller parks near the relevant exhibits, and almost every floor has baby-changing facilities. Pit stops include the Deep Blue Cafe in the Welcome Wing, offering a children's meal package for £3.99 ($7.60), or a "family share" meal of a whole roast chicken with double fries, salad, and sauces for £13 ($25). There are even picnic spaces if you bring your own food.

Exhibition Rd., SW7. ℭ 0870/870-4868. www.sciencemuseum.org.uk. Free admission (except some exhibitions, rides, and IMAX cinema, with family discounts). Daily 10am–6pm. Tube: S. Kensington.

Tower of London 🅐 ★ **Ages 5 and up.** The best-preserved medieval castle of any European capital, this former royal mini city oozes with history and heraldry, though it's most famous as the site of the beheadings of three queens (Anne Boleyn, Catherine Howard, and Lady Jane Grey), the murder of two little princes (the sons of Edward IV, killed by Richard III in order to remain king), and the prison of Sir Walter Raleigh. It is also the home of the **Crown Jewels.** The oldest part is the **White Tower,** begun by William the Conqueror in 1066–67 to keep London's native Saxons in check. Here you'll find royal armor from the reign of Henry VIII, as well as instruments of torture and execution. After William, subsequent rulers added towers, more walls, and fortified gates, and Henry III started a royal menagerie (the basis for London Zoo, housing the first elephant ever seen in the country).

Older kids won't begrudge the longish wait (now reduced by moving walkways and redesigned—and bulletproof—cabinets) to admire the prize exhibit, kept in the **Jewel House**—the Imperial State Crown, made for Queen Victoria in 1837 and now worn by Elizabeth II when she opens Parliament. And all children love the six **ravens** (plus two spares) registered as official residents—according to a legend, the Tower will stand as long as those ominous birds remain, so they all have their wings clipped. They're not the best-tempered critters, however, so don't let the little ones get too close.

Popular new features include permanent interactive displays on the theme of prisoners in the **Bloody Tower** and **Beauchamp Tower,** which try to dispel popular myth and allow visitors to experience at least some of the reality of imprisonment here. Another feature is a rolling program of temporary exhibitions on aspects of the Tower's history. If you're short on time, try a **1-hour guided tour** of the compound given by the 39 rather hammy Yeoman Warders or "Beefeaters" (Tudor-outfitted ex-servicemen) every half-hour. They also give short free talks and preside over the nightly ancient **Ceremony of the Keys,** the 9:30pm locking-up of the Tower. (Free tickets are available by writing to the Ceremony of the Keys, HM Tower of London, London EC3N 4AB, at least 2 months in advance; you must specify several possible dates and enclose a stamped, self-addressed envelope with British stamps or two International Reply Coupons.)

Special **family activities** include trails, seasonal workshops, fun days with minstrels and storytellers, and reconstructions of medieval tournaments in the Tower's ancient moat, featuring expert horsemen and fighters. The New Armouries **restaurant** offers

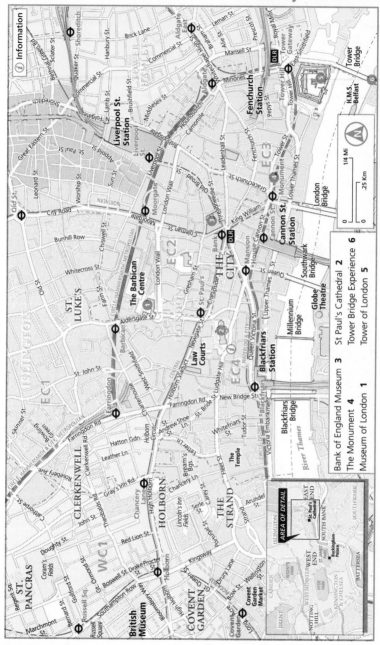

Bank of England Museum **3**   St Paul's Cathedral **2**   Tower Bridge Experience **6**

The Monument **4**   Tower of London **5**

Museum of London **1**

Bedtime Fun

Having trouble dragging 'em away? Well, the fun doesn't have to stop at the Science Museum, British Museum, *Golden Hinde,* or other London museums, all of which run special sleepover nights for kids and accompanying adults.

The **Science Museum**'s program of themed Science Nights involve hands-on workshops, lively demonstrations, and trails for 8- to 11-year-olds based on its galleries and exhibitions. You'll need to form a group of five to nine children, accompanied by at least one person over 18; prices are £30 ($57) per child and £25 ($48) per adult. Don't forget your sleeping bag, wash bag, evening snack, and maybe a pillow and favorite cuddly toys; breakfast is provided. For information and booking, call ℭ **020/7942–4747** or e-mail science.night@nmsi.ac.uk.

For themed sleepovers at the **British Museum** (p. 158), kids (8–15) must join the Young Friends (£20/$38 per year), which includes free entry to exhibitions, a thrice-yearly magazine, special events, behind-the-scenes visits, Sunday Clubs, competitions, and the use of a Friends Room. The events, during which kids and their caregivers bed down among ancient Egyptian sculptures, then cost an additional £28 ($52) per person. Call ℭ **020/7323-8566** or e-mail youngfriends@thebritishmuseum.ac.uk.

The *Golden Hinde* (p. 158) hosts "Living History" overnight stays allowing kids to experience an imaginary voyage with Sir Francis Drake. Dressed in period clothes, they are taken back in time by actors playing colorful crew members and learn skills that were needed in 16th-century seafaring life. Tudor meals are provided, and guests sleep on the lower decks, under simple

---

kids' lunchboxes, traditional English afternoon teas, and more. A cafe sells cakes, sandwiches, and hot and cold drinks. Note that many parts of the Tower are far from stroller-friendly. Last admission is an hour before closing time, and all internal buildings close 30 minutes after last admission. *Insider tip:* Tickets can be bought up to 7 days in advance, either online or at any Tube station, allowing you to circumvent the long queues. Online tickets are also £1 cheaper.

Tower Hill, EC3. ℭ **0870/756-6060.** www.hrp.org.uk. Admission £14 ($26) adults, £11 ($20) students and seniors, £9 ($17) children 5–16, £38 ($71) family ticket for up to 2 adults and 3 children. Mar–Oct: Sun and Mon 10am–6pm, Tues–Sat 9am–6pm. Nov–Feb: Sun and Mon 10am–5pm, Tues–Sat 9am–5pm. Tube: Tower Hill.

WWT Wetland Centre 🏵🏵   **Ages 2 and up.** At this pioneering and award-winning wetland project—the world's only such center in a capital city—you can see more than 130 bird species (some threatened), as well as other rare wildlife at a beautiful 42-hectare (105-acre) site just a short way south of central London. Wetland areas are second only to rainforests in the diversity of life forms they support, and are thus crucial to the world's ecology. On a daily basis, visitors can enjoy free daily 90-minute guided tours (11am and 2pm) and bird-feeding rounds with wardens (noon and 3 or 3:30pm depending on the season). At the Visitor Center you can pick up trail sheets and maps, and hire binoculars (or buy kids' pairs). Then you're ready to explore the hands-on Discovery Centre; a glass observatory; numerous hides (concealed places from which

warm covers (you might want to bring a pillow). Tickets cost £40 ($76) per person (one adult can accompany several kids), and early booking is recommended (© 08700/118700 for a booking form).

The **WWT Wetland Centre** (p. 152) does summer sleepovers for kids aged 8 to 14, costing £45 ($86), where they can spend the night watching the bats and bugs that live by the center.

In summer 2005, the **Cabinet War Rooms** (p. 160) launched their take on the sleepover, in the form of "Evacuee Nights" in which kids 8 to 11, accompanied by an adult, can experience a night in a re-created underground shelter. After tucking into a supper of "ration food" (no cookies or candy!) that they bring along with them, they are taken on an exploration of the museum by an actor dressed as a warden, and get to make their own gas masks before bedding down in their sleeping bags. A rationed breakfast of cornflakes without sugar is provided the next morning. The events are scheduled to take place four times yearly, during school half-terms, with kids and adults both paying £30 ($57), except for locals, who pay just £5 ($9.50). For a booking form, call © 020/7766-0150.

Lastly, if you can get together a group of 15 kids ages 8 and up, you can book a "Kip on a Ship" night (or up to 3 nights) aboard the **HMS** *Belfast* (p. 158). Participants sleep in real sailors' bunks, with adults in separate cabins. There must be at least one adult per 10 children. Accommodations cost £23 ($43) per person, including a continental breakfast. Call © 020/7940-6323 or e-mail hms-edu@iwm.org.uk.

to observe wildlife), including the three-story Peacock Tower with panoramic views of both the reserve and the London skyline (a lift enables you to take strollers up); a children's farmyard; and an "airport" lake where birds come in to land. All of the 14 types of wetland habitat, which range from Asian rice paddies to Siberian tundra, are dotted with interactive displays, and the paths are wide and accessible by stroller, though there's a park where you can leave them if you prefer. The truly wild areas of the reserve can be observed via CCTV live footage.

For maximum enjoyment, bring kids during weekends, when special activities are on offer: Arts and crafts; pond safaris; bat walks; guided "adventures"; science workshops exploring, for instance, the ways in which certain species adapt to survive; and introductory bird-watching workshops for ages 11 and up. These are followed by full English breakfasts in the cafe—book early, because the activities are incredibly popular. Keep a special lookout, too, for the World Wetland Day celebrations each January, when the center throws open its gates for free and hosts events such as the "Great Pondskater Experiment" (an attempt to walk on water). Special activities are offered at Easter as well, such as an "Egg Watch" (seeing duck eggs hatch) and pond-dipping for newts, frogs, and snails. Late-night summer openings include sunset barbecues to the strains of bird song. In term-time, stressed mums enjoy "Wetland Workout" yoga, walking, and toning sessions.

The Water's Edge Room restaurant offers three-course Sunday roasts, including kids' portions. There's also a cafe with outdoor seating, and picnic tables by the Visitor Center. See the website for details on how to adopt swans, flamingoes, and more; or check out how you can become a member of the worthy World Wetlands Trust charity.

Queen Elizabeth's Walk, SW13. ⓒ 020/8409-4400. www.wwt.org.uk/visit/wetlandcentre. Admission £6.75 ($13) adult; £5.50 ($10) senior; £4 ($7.60) child 4–16, £18 ($33) family ticket. Summer, 9:30am–6pm; winter, 9:30am–5pm (check website for late-night openings). Tube: Hammersmith, then "Duck Bus" (no. 283).

2 Best Views

Some of the best views of London can be had during a ride on the **BA London Eye;** see p. 142.

London's Living Room   Ages 2 and up. City Hall, an egg-shaped steel-and-glass building on the south bank of the Thames, is home to the mayor of London and his local government. The public can normally access the second floor and below, where there are exhibition spaces, including the London Photomat, an impressive aerial view of the whole of London, and a cafe. Try to attend one of the special weekend openings of London's Living Room, a rooftop gallery with an external walkway affording stunning panoramic views over London, from neighboring Tower Bridge and the Tower of London to farther afield. Don't miss the ramp that winds down from the top floor to the second story. *Insider tip:* The Living Room is open during Open House weekend (p. 22).

City Hall, The Queen's Walk, SE1. ⓒ 020/7983-4000. www.london.gov.uk/gla/city_hall. Free admission. Occasional weekends (other areas Mon–Fri 8am–8pm). Tube: London Bridge.

The Monument   Ages 4 and up. The 61.5m (202-ft.) height of this classical Doric column, built to commemorate the Great Fire of 1666, is no fluke—it corresponds with the distance from the structure's base to the spot where the blaze started, in a Pudding Lane bakery. The world's tallest isolated stone tower, the Monument was dreamt up by architect Sir Christopher Wren (he of St. Paul's Cathedral fame). Its 311 twisting, steep stone steps can be ascended by the fairly robust and the non-claustrophobic. (A handrail can help you get up there in half an hour.) You're rewarded with a close look at the flaming copper urn at the column's tip, fabulous 360-degree views of London, and a certificate when you make it back down. (Not everyone did—in 1842, iron railings had to be erected around the viewing platform to halt the suicides occurring here.)

Monument St, EC3. ⓒ 020/7626-2717. www.cityoflondon.gov.uk. Admission £2 ($3.80) adults, £1.50 ($2.85) children 5–15. Daily 10am–6pm. Tube: Monument.

St. Paul's Cathedral   Ages 5 and up. It's a steep 378-step climb to the **Stone Gallery** of this Christopher Wren–designed structure, and another 152 steps to the **Golden Gallery,** but both of them amply reward you with panoramic views of the Thames and London at your feet. These amazing galleries are accessed via the disorienting gap between the outside dome and the one viewed from the interior, as is the famous interior Whispering Gallery, where an acoustic anomaly allows you to hear someone whisper at the walls way across the other side.

St. Paul's was built to replace a Norman cathedral that burned down in the Great Fire, which was itself believed to have occupied the site of two previous Saxon cathedrals and a Christian church, all of which were also destroyed by fire. Before that, a Roman temple is thought to have stood here. It's a wonder that this "new" building remains, given that it was directly hit by bombs on more than one occasion in World War II. Highlights include the crypt, with the tombs of Lord Nelson, Christopher Wren, and the Duke of Wellington; and "Great Paul," the biggest bell in England (hear it daily at 1pm). Note that a £40-million restoration project in honor of the cathedral's 300th birthday in 2008 means some areas may be temporarily off limits.

Guided and audiotours are available at a small cost, and the **Explorers' Guide** (£1.99/ $1), available from the shop or online, contains pictures to color in, puzzles, and fun facts for all ages. There's a cafe in the crypt, a restaurant, and space to picnic in the gardens, which are full of roses in the spring.

St. Paul's Churchyard, EC4. © 020/7236-4128. www.stpauls.co.uk. Cathedral and galleries £8 ($15) adults, £7 ($13) seniors and students, £3.50 ($6.65) children 6–16, £20 ($37) family ticket. Mon–Sat 8:30am–4pm. Tube: St. Paul's.

Thames Flood Barrier   **Ages 3 and up.** Thames Barrier Park, a 9-hectare (22-acre) stretch of arresting modern landscaping—constituting London's first new major public park for more than 50 years—is situated on the north bank of the Thames River and affords unparalleled views of the gleaming stainless-steel **Thames Flood Barrier,** part of the flood-defense system protecting London against tidal surges and rising water levels. In addition to admiring the structure from the park, you can watch working vessels ply the waters (when they want to pass through the barrier they have to radio ahead for permission) and observe the park's birdlife. At low tide, you might see gray herons feeding and cormorants drying themselves along the shore, as well as rare wading birds such as oystercatchers. The Visitor Pavilion, with its views of the barrier, as well as wildflower meadows and manicured lawns, has a coffee shop. The park also contains a sunken garden, sculptures, a riverside promenade, a playground, and fountains that kids love to play in during hot weather. Best of all, the park is still not well known and thus is rarely crowded.

Thames Barrier Information & Learning Centre on the opposite side of the river at Woolwich has a working model of the barrier, a video about its construction and importance, display boards on the Thames and its wildlife, a wetlands area with pond-dipping, and a wildlife garden. As this book went to press, staff members were hoping that new riverfront walks, a playground, and a picnic area would be completed within a year or so. Note that by far the most enjoyable and stress-free way to get here is by ferry from Westminster Millennium Pier, which also picks up passengers at Greenwich en route (© **020/7930-4097;** www.westminsterpier.co.uk).

Tip: Once a month, you can see the barrier's 10 moveable gates (four of them each as tall as a five-story building when raised) in action during maintenance work; check the park or information center websites for dates.

Park: Barrier Point Rd., E16. © 020/7511-4111. www.thamesbarrierpark.org.uk. Free admission. Daily dawn–dusk (pavilion Fri–Sun 10am–4pm). Tube or DLR: Canning Town. **Information & Learning Centre:** 1 Unity Way, SE18. © 08708/506506. www.environment-agency.gov.uk/regions/thames. Admission £1.50 ($2.85) adults, £1 ($1.90) seniors, £0.75 ($1.40) children. Daily, Apr–Sept 10:30am–4pm, Oct–Mar 11am–3:30pm. Tube: North Greenwich (then 40-min. walk).

Tower Bridge Experience   **Ages 2 and up.** Pay to see the exhibition inside one of the world's greatest and most photographed landmarks, built in 1894, and you can enjoy spectacular views of St. Paul's, the Tower of London, and the Houses of Parliament from high-level enclosed walkways reaching between the bridge's north and south towers. Accessed by lift, the walkways are fitted with special windows that allow you to take photos without being obscured by glass. Exhibits inside the bridge employ animatronic characters, videos, and touchscreens; in the Victorian engine room you can see the boilers and steam engines that raised and lowered the bridge for passing ships. If you're here when the bridge is lifted to allow a large river vessel through (which happens about 900 times a year), imagine that, as late as 1952, London buses were forced to make the leap from one bascule (drawbridge) to the other when the bridge began to rise!

You'll need to pre-book a 2-hour **Behind the Scenes Tour** if you want to see the current machinery and control cabins, and to descend into the vast bascule chambers that reach below the riverbed. (Note that this option is only available Oct–Mar, involves steep stairs and confined spaces, and costs £20/$38 per person.) Year-round **family events** include costumed shows and seasonally themed talks. The shop offers a Children's Activity Pack (£1.70/$3.25), with games and pictures to color. All parts of the exhibition are stroller-accessible. Last entry is an hour before closing.

Tower Bridge, SE1. ✆ 020/7403-3761. www.towerbridge.org.uk. Admission £5.50 ($10) adults; £4.25 ($8) students and seniors; £3 ($5.70) children 5–15; £14 ($27) family ticket (2 adults and 2 kids). Daily, Apr–Sept 10am–6:30pm, Oct–Mar 9:30am–6pm. Tube: Tower Hill or London Bridge.

Wellington Arch   **Ages 2 and up.** This splendid neoclassical arch was built in 1826, initially to form a royal gateway to Buckingham Palace (it was moved from its original site). It boasts wide, stroller-accessible balconies offering views across the royal parks, the Houses of Parliament, and the London Eye. It's best to come here in wintertime, since foliage can obscure sightlines. The statue of the angel of peace resting on top of the arch replaced a statue of the Duke of Wellington, and is Britain's largest bronze sculpture. Exhibitions within trace the arch's history and highlight some of London's best-known statues and memorials.

Joint entry is possible with Apsley House across the street, including family tickets. The arch is the site of free costumed talks for the whole family during the museum's Waterloo Weekend. Wellington Arch is also the starting point for 2-hour walks around the city's royal sites (£5/$9.50 adults and children).

The Queen's Guards

There are two places where you can see the **Changing of the Guard** (properly known as "guard mounting"), with all the attendant pomp and pageantry. The most famous is Buckingham Palace (p. 180), where new **Foot Guards** in their familiar black bearskin hats and scarlet tunics take over from the old watch at 11:30am every morning in spring and summer, and on alternate days in fall and winter. The ceremony (which is not carried out in very wet weather) takes about 45 minutes and is accompanied by a band playing anything from traditional military marches to pop tunes.

More enjoyable (because it's less mobbed by tourists) is the mounting of the **Horse Guards** by the arch of the Horse Guards Building (the British Army's HQ) in Whitehall, which is the official entrance to the royal palaces. This mounted regiment dressed in red or blue tunics with white or red plumes changes shift daily at 11am (10am Sun); the ceremony lasts about 30 minutes.

Insider tip: Animal-loving kids and fans of pageantry will enjoy seeing the mounted Horse Guards pass between the arch's columns every day at 10:40 and 11:40am (an hour earlier on Sun).

Hyde Park Corner, W1. © 020/7930-2726. www.english-heritage.org.uk. Admission £3 ($5.70) adults, £2.30 ($4.35) seniors and students, £1.50 ($2.85) children 5–16. Open Wed–Sun, Apr–Oct 10am–5pm, Nov–Mar 10am–4pm. Tube: Hyde Park Corner.

Westminster Cathedral **Ages 5 and up.** The Roman Catholic Church's eccentric but lovely British headquarters, built in 1903 and based, in part, on Santa Sofia in Istanbul and St. Mark's in Venice, has a viewing platform at the top of its 82m (269-ft.) campanile (accessible by lift), allowing wonderful views of Buckingham Palace, Westminster Abbey, the Houses of Parliament, the London Eye, and St. Paul's Cathedral. Inside the massive structure, you'll find marble aplenty, and some fine mosaics. Prime Minister Tony Blair, though not a Catholic, sometimes comes here to pray. Children's tours can be arranged for ages 6 and up. The cafe, serving light snacks, is open 9am to 5pm.

Cathedral Piazza, Victoria St., SW1. © 020/7798-9055. www.westminstercathedral.org.uk. Cathedral free; lift tower £3 ($5.70), £1.50 ($2.85) children 5–15, family ticket £7 ($13). Mon–Fri 7am–7pm, Sat 8am–7pm, Sun 8am–7:30pm; campanile lift 9am–5pm daily Apr–Nov, Thurs–Sun Dec–Mar. Tube: Victoria.

3 More London Museums

For the **Wimbledon Lawn Tennis Museum** and **Museum of Rugby,** see p. 258 and 258.

Bank of England Museum **Ages 5 and up.** This museum manages to make the history of money fun, with a reconstructed banking hall peopled with costumed dummies, examples of the forger's art, Roman and modern-day gold bars, and weapons once used to defend the bank. Visitors learn, for instance, that the £ sign evolved from the letter "L" (the initial letter of the Latin word *libra,* meaning a pound of money); and that the Queen's portrait did not appear on Bank of England notes until as late as 1960. You'll also find out how banknotes are made, and get the chance to lift a genuine gold bar. The information desk provides activity sheets for kids ages 5 to 8, ages 9 to 12, and ages 13 to 15. Free, easy-to-follow presentations for children are given during special-event days, including calligraphy, craft sessions, and egg trails. Stroller access can be tricky in parts and there's no cafe, but there are baby-changing facilities and a shop with pocket-money items.

Bartholomew Lane, EC3. © 020/7601-5545. www.bankofengland.co.uk. Free admission. Open Mon–Fri 10am–5pm. Tube: Bank.

British Library ★★ **All ages.** The world's greatest collection of books, manuscripts, newspapers, maps, music, and stamps, as well as a mighty research center and reading facility, the British Library is home to some of the world's most fabulous literary treasures. It shouldn't, by its nature, be child-friendly, but among the 18 million items in its collections are such gems as the original version of the children's classic, *Alice's Adventures in Wonderland,* handwritten and illustrated by its author Charles Dodgson (Lewis Carroll); and original sheet music by John Lennon and Paul McCartney. Temporary exhibitions trace the lives and careers of favorite authors; in 2005 the Hans Christian Andersen exhibition used puppets, pulleys, and projections to bring the fairy-tale author's characters to life.

Planes, Trains & Automobiles (& Not Forgetting Boats)

With five airports (including Heathrow, the world's busiest) and six railway stations, London is a global transport hub—a fact that is well illustrated in many of its museums and sights. The **Science Museum** (p. 148) is a good place to start, especially for techno-geeks. Over to the east, train buffs should make the pilgrimage to the **North Woolwich Old Station Museum** (Pier Rd., E16; ✆ 020/7474-7244; free admission; Jan–Nov Sat and Sun 1–5pm, daily during school vacations), a Victorian station with a 1920s ticket office, old engines, carriages, models, posters, and memorabilia, and lots of hands-on action for kids. The best times to come are Steam Days on the first Sunday of each summer month, when a pair of steam engines are brought back to life.

It's a 30-minute walk or so from this former flower market building across the river and along the South Bank to the *Golden Hinde* ✪ (St. Mary Overie Dock, Cathedral St., SE1; ✆ 0870/011-8700; www.goldenhinde.co.uk; admission £3.50/$6.65 adults, £2.50/$4.75 children, £10 ($19) family ticket for 2 adults and 3 kids; hours vary according to scheduled events and pre-booked tours). This ship is a replica of the tiny 14-cannon vessel in which Sir Francis Drake circumnavigated the globe in the 16th century. A former floating museum that has itself sailed round the world, it host tours by costumed guides, pirate events, storytelling for 6- to 12-year-olds, seasonal plays, drama and fancy dress workshops, and overnight stays (p. 152).

Another 10 minutes' walk along the riverfront is the 11,500-ton **HMS Belfast,** a World War II cruiser with an exhibition about sailors' lives in war (it played a leading role in the Normandy landings) and in peacetime, and nine decks to explore, including the engine room. Free activities include

A program of free workshops, activities, tours, and storytelling for 5- to 11-year-olds heats up during school vacations. Year-round, parents can make use of a creative guide to the Treasures Gallery, with a make-your-own treasure chest and mini-books with activity ideas; free creative guides and/or activities for each major exhibition; and a "Looking at Art" activity sheet highlighting contemporary artworks around the building (you download this from the website before your visit). Bookworms will delight in "Turning the Pages" technology allowing you to view priceless texts by moving your hands on a computer screen, and there's a world-class permanent collection of stamps for budding philatelists.

The library has a restaurant and several cafes. Exhibition galleries are stroller-accessible, and there are baby-changing facilities.

96 Euston Rd., NW1. ✆ 020/7412-7639. www.bl.uk. Free admission. Open Mon and Wed–Fri 9:30am–6pm; Tues 9:30am–8pm; Sat 9:30am–5pm; Sun and bank holidays 11am–5pm. Tube: King's Cross/St. Pancras or Euston.

British Museum ✪✪ **Ages 4 and up.** This almost absurdly huge museum, which grew from a "cabinet of curiosities" given to the nation by a private collector in 1753 and now has 4km (2½ miles) of galleries, is best tackled cautiously and over the course of several days. The 90-minute **Highlights** tours are handy for novices, allowing you medal-making workshops and science shows, and the last weekend of the month sees free drop-in family events. From London Bridge City Pier nearby, hop on a ferry to Greenwich (p. 148), where another historical vessel can be found in permanent dry dock—the 1869 *Cutty Sark,* a clipper that carried tea from China and wool from Australia and was the fastest sailing ship of its day. Onboard are restored decks and crew's quarters complete with dummies, plus interactive displays about life at sea.

Nearby, the vast **National Maritime Museum** (Romney Rd., SE10; ℂ **020/ 8312-6608;** www.nmm.ac.uk; free admission; daily 10am–5pm) traces the history of seafaring, from early explorers to modern technology. Head for interactive galleries All Hands and The Bridge, which are based on the lives of seafarers and allow kids to hoist flags, steer boats, send distress signals, and more. Family events include interactive drama, art-making, and discovery sessions for 2- to 5-year-olds; Family Sundays involving workshops, storytelling, and music; "Magical Journeys" interactive tours for those with under-6s; and boat-making and other craft workshops. Trail guides and backpacks are available, and there's a play area next to the Regatta Cafe.

For a city-specific overview, don't miss the **London Transport Museum** ★★★ (Covent Garden Piazza, WC2; ℂ 020/7379-6344; www.lt museum.co.uk), which demonstrates the evolution of the British capital's transport system and the way it's shaped Londoners' lives. *Note*: This museum is closed for refurbishments at the moment, but promises to be spiffier than ever upon reopening in early 2007.

an overview of the masterpieces of ancient civilizations. Free 30-minute **Family Eye-opener** tours on the first weekend of every month explore different galleries. Alternatively, pick up one of the family activity sheets or themed **trails** from the information desk, which send you in search of games and ancient toys from around the world; or hire a **Family Audio Tour** £3.50 ($1.80), which takes you on three different trails: "Bodies," "Boardgames," and "Beasts." **Half-term holidays** are a particularly fun time to visit, when a week of free activities—workshops, toys, stories, and trails—is based around particular exhibitions. For details on children's sleepovers, see p. 152.

Star attractions include the **Rosetta Stone,** in the Egyptian Room, the discovery of which led to the deciphering of hieroglyphics; the **Egyptian royal tombs** (with its mummies); and **Lindow Man,** a body superbly well preserved in peat, in the Celtic Europe gallery. If your heart is set on seeing a specific item, though, call to make sure it's on display, as exhibits change throughout the year. The famous domed **Reading Room,** once part of the British Library and the place where figures as eminent as Karl Marx came to work, now houses a library and touchscreens detailing the museum's collections. It's enclosed within the magnificent glass-roofed **Great Court,** an airy central plaza where you can enjoy snacks or full meals, or browse in the bookshop.

Great Russell St., WC1. © 020/7636-1555. www.thebritishmuseum.ac.uk. Free admission. Highlights tour (daily at 10:30am, 1pm, and 3pm) £8 ($15), £5 ($9.50) for students and children under 11. Sat–Wed 10am–5:30pm; Thurs and Fri 10am–8:30pm. (Great Court open Sun–Wed 9am–6pm; Thurs–Sat 9am–11pm.) Tube: Holborn, Tottenham Court Rd., or Russell Sq.

Brunel Engine House & Tunnel Exhibition   Ages 5 and up. This museum celebrating the world's first tunnel built under a river, the Thames Tunnel in 1843, was designed by Marc Brunel and his son Isambard Kingdom Brunel. It was dubbed by Victorians "The Eighth Wonder of the World." The focal point of the exhibition, which describes the hardships undergone by the miners who carried out this great engineering feat, is an old steam engine used to drain the tunnel. Kids are given quiz sheets and activities to help them get a handle on the subject. Among other facts, they'll learn that society ladies and other spectators paid a shilling each to be lowered down for a glimpse of the dangerous work in action.

Entry sometimes includes a guided tour through the tunnel by Tube train; see the website for details. It's astonishing to think that before trains ran here, this was the site of 64 shops selling the likes of garters, silk handkerchiefs, and lovers' tokens, and that a Fancy Fair held in the tunnel saw visitors entertained by novelty acts, sword swallowers, and acrobats. Today an annual Fancy Fair held above the water includes samba, percussion, and lanterns. Events such as family tea parties are held at a new riverside garden, including drawing competitions.

Railway Ave., SE16. © 020/7231-3840. www.brunelenginehouse.org.uk. Admission £2 ($3.80) adults; £1 ($1.90) seniors, students, and kids 5–16; £5 ($9.50) family tickets. Open Thurs–Sun 1–5pm. Tube: Rotherhithe.

Cabinet War Rooms/Churchill Museum ★ **Ages 5 and up.** These are the actual secret bombproof bunkers in which Winston Churchill and his War Cabinet hid out during air raids on the city, maintained just as they were when hostilities ended. As well as the Map Room with its huge wall maps and compasses, and the tiny Transatlantic Telephone Room housing a special scrambler phone on which Churchill conferred with President Roosevelt, you can see Churchill's bedroom-cum-office, with two BBC microphones via which he made his nation-stirring speeches, and his chamber pot (there were no flush toilets). Children's versions of the free audioguides in English are available. Occasional free drop-in workshops for the family teach topics such as "how to make do and mend," and provide computer games and quizzes as well.

A good time to come is Saturday, when between 10:30am and 5pm families can visit the Clore Learning Centre to pick up museum activity sheets, watch film clips, look up information in the digital suite, and test your knowledge of wartime Britain with new computer games and quizzes. In summer, drop-in Family History workshops teach you what life was like for your family in World War II using a new "Your History" website, along with interactive "debriefing" sessions by costumed actors re-creating daily life in the HQ. In 2005 the museum introduced sleepover events (p. 152).

In early 2005, to mark the 40th anniversary of Churchill's death, the War Rooms completed an expansion program with the opening of the **Churchill Museum,** exploring his roles not only as a statesman, politician, and soldier, but as a husband, father, and son. Exhibits include his ivory baby rattle, copies of his school reports, photos of his pets, and soft toys (pick up one of the toys to hear a recording of an animal quote by Churchill).

Strollers are manageable inside the museum, baby-changing facilities are available in male and female restrooms, and there's a cafe with kids' lunchboxes.

Clive Steps, King Charles St., SW1. ℂ 020/7930-6961. www.iwm.org.uk. Admission £7.50 ($14) adults, £6 ($11) seniors and students, free for children 16 and under. Daily 9:30am–6pm. Tube: Westminster or St. James's Park.

Church Farmhouse Museum

All ages. This old hay and dairy farm, built circa 1660, is worth visiting if you're journeying to the nearby RAF Museum (p. 162). Each year it mounts one exhibition especially for kids—past exhibits have been devoted to teddy bears, construction toys, jigsaws, and puppets. Very young children get toys and games to play with, and for older ones there's a drawing competition. During summer vacations, kids' events are held in the museum's garden, including traditional Punch & Judy shows and clown performances. Another good time to come is December, when the museum's three furnished 19th-century rooms are decorated as they would have been for a Victorian Christmas.

Greyhound Hill, Hendon, NW4. ℂ 020/8203-0130. www.churchfarmhousemuseum.co.uk. Admission free. Open Mon–Thurs 10am–1pm and 2pm–5pm, Saturday 10am–1pm and 2–5.30pm, Sun 2–5:30pm. Tube: Hendon Central.

Clink Prison Museum

Ages 8 and up. A schlocky re-creation of a medieval prison in which both adults and children were locked up, not just for murder and theft but for "crimes" like having the wrong faith, or falling into debt. Although the reconstructed cells with their shackled waxwork figures are looking a little threadbare these days, and the sound effects are a bit overdramatic, ghoulish kids will love the torture and restraining devices the same way they love the Chamber of Horrors at Madame Tussaud's (p. 167). The shop sells historical trinkets such as "lucky charms" in the form of severed heads and skeletal feet. Note that the Clink, which stood on this site, held many prostitutes (this was the city's red-light district), and exhibits on the area's colorful past include displays on the history of prostitution.

Clink St., SE1. ℂ 020/7403-0900. www.clink.co.uk. Admission £6 ($11) adults, £3.50 ($6.65) children 5–15; £15 ($29) family ticket. Daily 10am–6pm. Tube: London Bridge.

Design Museum

Ages 6 and up. This fascinating modern-design museum explains how mass-produced objects function and why they look the way they do, from chairs and telephones to cars and fashion items. All kids are given a free Design Action Pack containing treasure trails of exhibits in the permanent and temporary collections, creativity exercises, and a "Spot The Building" game involving landmarks visible from the museum's riverfront terrace, including the futuristic Lloyds Building in the City. Justifiably popular are the weekend design workshops suitable for 6- to 12-year-olds; booking is necessary.

Shad Thames, SE1. ℂ 0870/833-9955. www.designmuseum.org. Admission £6 ($11) adults, £4 ($7.60) children, £16 ($30) family ticket (2 adults, 2 children). Daily 10am–5:45pm. Tube: Tower Hill or London Bridge.

Discover ★★★

Ages up to 8. Discover is a wonderfully original space where younger kids come to "story build" through play, performances, and storytelling. Basically, children pick up a "storybook" bag at the door and draw and write their ideas as they follow the **Story Trail,** crossing Sparkly River on the Spider Trolley to reach Secret Cave. Along the way, they collect postcards, tickets, finger puppets, menus, and invitations to keep in their books. Story builders are on hand to help kids get their best out of the experience. A bank of TVs with cameras lets the kids watch themselves "enter" stories on screen.

On a sunny day, the **Story Garden,** with its spaceship, monster's-tongue slide, tunnels, weird mirrors, water features, and more is an oasis in this relatively deprived area of east London. It has stroller access, a stroller park with lockers, and baby-changing.

More Planes, Trains & Automobiles (& Not Forgetting Boats)

Air travel junkies need to head further afield, to Hendon north of the city, where the superb **Royal Airforce Museum London** ♠ (Grahame Park Way, NW9; ✆ **020/8205-2266;** www.rafmuseum.com; free admission; daily 10am–6pm) displays more than 200 aircraft, half of them full-size, on the site of the original London Aerodrome, plus photos, memorabilia, and related artifacts. Platforms let you get up close to the planes, which range from classic bombers to state-of-the-art jet fighters. In addition, there are two flight simulators (£2.50/$4.75) per 4-min. ride), a sound-and-light show (hourly 11am–5pm), and an interactive Aeronauts gallery where kids can, for instance, take an RAF aptitude test and control a propeller rotating at 500 revolutions per minute. Family events range from half-term themed activities on the likes of helicopters, to science-based Easter events, to arts and crafts.

Also far out of town but in the opposite direction, **Croydon Airport Visitor Centre** (Airport House, Purley Way; ✆ **020/8669-1196;** www.croydonairport. org.uk; free admission; 1st Sun of month 11am–4pm), traces the history of the airport (London's main airport from 1920 to 1959, and the world's first international airport) in its former control tower, with a re-creation of its radio room. Kids can inspect Amy Johnson's flight bag, dress as 1930s passengers, and use hands-on models to calculate fuel loads, identify aircraft from their silhouettes, and the like.

An impressive 19th-century pumping station, **Kew Bridge Steam Museum** in Brentford (✆ **020/-8568-4757),** is worth a visit to see its five Cornish engines, which pumped west London's water for more than a century. It's best to come on a Sunday between March and October, when you can hitch a ride on steam locomotives Cloister and Wendy (many Victorian waterworks had their own railway). Don't miss the **Water for Life** gallery, which

---

Insider tip: Admission to the Story Trail is half-price from 3 to 5pm, Tuesday to Friday during school sessions.

1 Bridge Terrace, E15. ✆ 020/8536-5555. www.discover.org.uk. Admission £3.50 ($6.65), free for children under 2. Garden free. Tues–Sun 10am–5pm, daily 10am–5pm during school holidays. Tube: Stratford, then 10-min. walk.

Fan Museum   Ages 10 and up. The world's only museum dedicated to fans, and a must for budding fashion designers of either sex, is located out in Greenwich. The 3,500 pieces on display are mainly antiques. A permanent exhibition traces their history and explains production methods, while thrice-yearly temporary displays explore a particular theme, such as ancient myths and legends. Teens can take part in weekend fan-making workshops, but numbers are limited to six, so reserve ahead. The Orangery overlooking a "secret" Japanese-style garden is a civilized place for afternoon tea, served on Tuesday and Sunday; snacks are served the rest of the week.

12 Crooms Hill, SE10. ✆ 020/8305-1441. www.fan-museum.org. Admission £3.50 ($6.75) adults, £2.50 ($4.75) children 7–15. Tues–Sat 11am–5pm, Sun noon–5pm. Tube: Greenwich .

tells the history of water supply and use in London from Roman times to the 19th century, and takes visitors through an actual section of the Thames Water Ring Main tunnel 40m (131 ft.) below ground, and as well as into a mock sewer tunnel. Here, you'll learn about the control of sanitation from medieval England to the present day—fascinating stuff. Kids love taking turns controlling a robot that's sent through pipes too small for human workers. The cost is £5.20 ($9.90) adults, £4.20 ($8) seniors and students, £3 ($5.70) children 5–15, £16 ($30) family ticket. Hours are daily 11am to 5pm. (Tube: Gunnersbury or Kew Gardens, then 10-min. walk.)

An intriguing little canalside museum tracing the history of the city's artificial waterways, the **London Canal Museum** (✆ **020/7713-0836**) is set in a 19th-century ice warehouse built for renowned ice cream maker Carlo Gatti. (The museum also tells the story of the ice and ice cream trades.) Kids love peering down into the massive Victorian ice well used to store ice imported from Norway (for restaurants, fishmongers, and so on); on rare occasions, and under carefully controlled conditions, adults and older kids can even descend into it. Special activities include the likes of Science Saturdays, with free bridge-building, boat trips, and science-based activities; and summer activity days for 6- to 12-year-olds (£2/$3.80), involving crafts, boat trips, and treasure hunts. There are also towpath walks and, if you visit in summer, atmospheric evening canal theater performances. The museum is largely stroller-accessible, and has baby-changing facilities. There's no cafe, but the shop sells cold drinks and ice cream. Museum entry costs £3 ($5.70) adults, £2 ($3.80) seniors and students, £1.50 ($2.85) children 8 to 15, and £16 ($30) family ticket. Hours are Tuesday to Saturday 10am to 4:30pm, plus bank holiday Mondays.

Fashion & Textile Museum   **Ages 6 and up.** Britain's first contemporary Fashion & Textile Museum was opened by posh-punk designer Zandra Rhodes in 2003, in a suitably exuberant pink and orange former warehouse. The British and international designers showcased here include Biba, Christian Dior, and Rhodes herself. Generally, there are two or three temporary exhibitions a year. The shop is every fashion princess's dream, stocking unique fashion items (the proceeds from some of which go to charity), hair flowers, contemporary dolls, paper dress-up dolls, jewelry and accessories, postcards, books, and magazines.

83 Bermondsey St., SE1. ✆ **020/7403-0222.** www.ftmlondon.org. Admission £5 ($9.50) adults; £3 ($5.70) seniors, students, and children 5–15; £13 ($25) family ticket (2 adults, 2 children). Tues–Sun 10am–5:45pm. Tube: London Bridge.

Firepower, the Royal Artillery Museum   **Ages 7 and up.** Not for the faint of heart, this museum tracing the history of the Army's Royal Artillery shakes, rattles, and hums with gunfire and other sound effects—all part of its simulations of modern warfare. Children love the military equipment and vehicles on display, including some monster tanks, but they tend, unsurprisingly, to congregate in the hands-on Real Weapon Gallery. (Don't fear—they can do little harm firing a jet of water from a small cannon.) Vacation events include paintballing and rides in military vehicles, but the best time to visit with kids is the summer season opening weekend in March or April (free for children), featuring a motorcycle display team, a hot-air balloon, a climbing wall, a paintball range, and a Rapier missile. Stroller access isn't a problem, and there's baby-changing, a cafe, and a popular shop with military paraphernalia.

Royal Arsenal, SE18. (C) 020/8855-7755. www.firepower.org.uk. £5 ($9.50) adult, £4.50 ($8.50) seniors and students, £2.50 ($4.75) children 5–15, £12 ($23) family ticket (2 adults, 2 children, or 1 adult, 3 children). Summer 10:30am–5pm Wed–Sun. Train: Woolwich Arsenal.

Florence Nightingale Museum **Ages 8 and up.** This small museum is dedicated to the life and work of Britain's most famous nurse, the "Lady with the Lamp," best known for her role in the Crimean War of 1854–57, when she won the hearts of her patients through her kindness (this at a time when nursing was considered a profession unfit for well-educated women such as her). On display are medical artifacts, battlefield relics, travel souvenirs, a snakeskin, flyswatters, personal effects, domestic objects, and even Florence's stuffed pet owl, which she used to carry in her pocket. Temporary exhibitions allow younger visitors to gain a sense of the time by, for instance, touching and smelling objects from Nightingale's dispensary. Half-term family events include trails, sculpture and lamp-making workshops, and competitions.

St. Thomas's Hospital, 2 Lambeth Palace Rd., SE1. (C) 020/7620-0374. www.florence-nightingale.co.uk. Admission £5.80 ($11) adults; £4.20 ($8) seniors, students, and children 5–15; £13 ($25) family ticket (2 adults, 2 children). Mon–Fri 10am–5pm; Sat and Sun 10am–4:30pm. Tube: Westminster or Waterloo.

Foundling Museum ★★★ **Ages 3 and up.** Kids love this wonderful, touching museum telling the story of the Foundling Hospital, London's first home for abandoned children, and its founder, philanthropic sea captain Thomas Coram. The hospital, demolished in 1926, housed some of the 1,000 babies that were abandoned every year in early-18th-century London. Displays include fascinating photos and objects associated with their lives, such as poems written by the mothers, and lists of "renamed" children—at one point, a William Shakespeare and a Julius Caesar lived here. The hospital also became home to the country's first public art gallery when William Hogarth, one of its governors, persuaded other leading artists to donate works, and you can still see paintings by Gainsborough, Reynolds, Hogarth himself, and others in the 18th-century interior. *Messiah* composer George Handel was also a governor, and you'll see a collection of manuscripts, musical scores, and more. Art tours with drawing activities are customized to a child's age and interests; the receptionist will chat with them first. The museum offers free kids' activity packs, storybooks, audioguides with poems by kids' book authors, guidebooks, and occasional themed family days for all ages.

The original hospital building was largely demolished in 1926, but you can still see its colonnades in the adjacent Coram's Fields children's park (p. 207). The museum's Clore Gallery & Walker Vaults display bright works by local children and young people. You'll find stroller access, an airy cafe, and changing facilities.

40 Brunswick Sq., WC1. (C) 020/7841-3600. www.foundlingmuseum.org.uk. Admission £5 ($9.50) adults, £3 ($5.70) seniors and students, under-16s free. Tues–Sat 10am–6pm; Sun noon–6pm. Tube: Russell Sq.

Geffrye Museum ★ **Ages 3 and up.** This fascinating look at British middle-class interiors from the past 400 years is well worth the trek into the relative wilds of east

London. Free family events include Saturday specials the first weekend of the month, with workshops (cushion making, marquetry, carving), quizzes, and other activities. Summer Sundays feature live music, creative activities, and storytelling. Holiday activities are extremely popular: For 13- to 15-year-olds these might include box-making or T-shirt design, while for 5-and-overs it's mini-throne making, and for 3-pluses chair modeling. The lovely walled herb garden is open in the warmer months. There's an attractive restaurant, stroller access, and baby-changing facilities.

Kingsland Rd., E2. ℂ 020/7739-9893. www.geffrye-museum.org.uk. Free admission. Tues–Sat 10am–5pm; Sun and bank holiday Mon noon–5pm. Tube: Old St. (then 15-min. walk).

Hackney Museum ⭐ *(Finds* **All ages.** This museum, set up to preserve the history of east London and the waves of immigrants who have come to make up its population from Saxon times on, is worth traveling out of the center for its child-oriented interactive displays—kids can load a Saxon boat, dress in historical garb, and tour a virtual Victorian home. Temporary exhibits touch on themes as diverse as Gainsborough studios, where Alfred Hitchcock began his career, and the history of local buildings. Free weekend family workshops (1st Sat of month) and vacation activities may include explorations of the history of Cockney rhyming slang or of the Creole language, Chinese calligraphy, drawing workshops, Indian dance, African drumming, and Caribbean storytelling. A free explorer pad full of children's activities, relating to the themes of immigration and settlement, is available at the front desk.

Technology & Learning Centre, 1 Reading Lane, E8. ℂ 020/8356-3500. www.hackney.gov.uk. Free admission free. Tues, Wed, Fri 9:30am–5:30pm; Thurs 9:30am–8pm; Sat 10am–5pm. Train: Hackney Central.

Imperial War Museum ⭐⭐ **Ages 4 and up.** This museum of modern war— fittingly situated in the former Bethlehem Royal Hospital for the insane—isn't as bloodthirsty as you might expect. Amidst the wide range of weapons and equipment on display, you'll find a huge clock hand reminding visitors that the cost of warfare currently stands at more than 100 million lives. The Trench and the Blitz are vivid re-creations of life during wartime from two different perspectives, while the extraordinarily humbling Holocaust exhibition includes the letters of an 8-year-old French Jewish boy who hid in an orphanage before being sent to Auschwitz. The popular 1940s House, a reconstruction of a wartime home, has reopened as part of **The Children's War Exhibition,** where it is the centerpiece of a new hands-on gallery about everyday life on the home front. The gallery and exhibition will be open until March 2008.

Also be sure to check out the Battle of Britain Spitfire, a German one-man submarine, and a rifle carried by Lawrence of Arabia. James Bond buffs will love the "Secret War" exhibition exploring the worlds of espionage and clandestine warfare. Family events include "Do Touch the Exhibits," which gives kids the chance to handle objects from both World Wars; "Voices," an opportunity to meet and talk to war veterans about their experiences; drop-in art activities; National Science Week activities; and Easter egg hunts. The cafe has a wholesome kid's menu and highchairs. Strollers are easily maneuvered throughout most of the museum, and baby-changing facilities are available.

Lambeth Rd., SE1. ℂ 020/7416-5000. www.iwm.org.uk. Free admission except special exhibitions. Daily 10am–6pm. Tube: Lambeth N. or Elephant and Castle.

Jewish Museum ⭐ **Ages 4 and up.** Jewish history comes to life for younger visitors at this museum, which offers a vivid account of Jewish life in Britain from the

Normans' arrival to the present day. The centerpiece is the fabulous ceremonial art collection, which includes an astonishing 16th-century Venetian ark. Monthly creative activities, from family workshops, puppet shows, and storytelling afternoons, to craft sessions exploring Jewish life, such as mask-making for Purim, add to the appeal. At the front desk, ask to look at the family file of free gallery-based activities for children ages 4 to 14, including animal hunts in the Ceremonial Art Gallery and a time trail of historical objects. Some of these activities even garner prizes. There's also a free children's activity for every temporary exhibition, and a "Jewish History in Britain Pack" (£2/$3.80) aimed at encouraging children ages 8 to 12 to discuss their own histories. Another great resource is "Doing Wonders" (£2.50/$4.75), written by and for children ages 6 to 12, which uses the Ceremonial Art Gallery to investigate the symbols and customs of the Jewish year though facts, quizzes, and activities for both the gallery and at home.

The museum's other branch in Finchley (© 020/8349-1143) focuses on immigration and settlement in London, and the Holocaust. It offers a Treasure Trail for ages 7 to 11. Hands-on displays such as a tailor's and a cabinet-maker's workshops allow kids to test the weight of a flat iron and find out how a suit is made.

Raymond Burton House, 129–31 Albert St., NW1. © 020/7284-1997. www.jewishmuseum.org.uk. Admission £3.50 ($6.65) adults, £2.50 ($4.75) seniors, £1.50 ($2.85) students and children, £8 ($15) family ticket. Mon–Thurs 10am–4pm; Sun 10am–5pm. Tube: Camden Town.

Livesey Museum for Children ★ Ages 2 to 12. This stimulating, fully interactive free museum for younger kids hosts temporary annual exhibitions created with the help of local children, artists, and craftspeople. Past shows, all of which were aimed at children up to 12, included "Number Crunching," "Air Aware," "The Great Rubbish Show," and "Energy" (which featured a walk-in forest, an eco-friendly house, and a disco). The emphasis is on encouraging creativity and imagination through investigating displays and objects, many of them from the Livesey's sister institution, the Cuming Museum of local history. There's no cafe, but you will find a pleasant courtyard space for picnics.

682 Old Kent Rd., SE15. © 020/7639-5604. www.liveseymuseum.org.uk. Free admission. Tues–Sat 10am–5pm. Tube: Elephant & Castle, then bus 53, 453, or 172.

London Dungeon Ages 7 and up. This "indoor theme park of historical horror" is definitely not for very young kids or the fainthearted (children over 3 are admitted at their guardian's discretion, but the place really should be avoided by under- 8s). The London Dungeon is filled with genuinely chilling tableaux reproducing medieval conditions, all set to a soundtrack of tolling bells. The dreadful experiences that you witness here include life under the bubonic plague (complete with real—though thankfully caged—rats); the Great Fire of London; a burning at the stake; fingernail extraction in the torture chamber; and a journey through the streets of London in the footsteps of Jack the Ripper. A £1-million ($1.9-million) "Boat Ride to Hell" is designed to play on many basic fears at once—of drowning, of the dark, and of death. The park's newest attraction, "Labyrinth for the Lost," is a spooky, smoky, mirror-filled maze based on the newly discovered catacombs of the church of All Hallows by the Tower (p. 196). Seasonal highlights include a Halloween Vampire Fest and a Christmas Satan's Grotto. The theme is taken to its logical extreme with gory gifts in the Shop of Horrors and refreshments at the Blood & Guts cafe.

28–34 Tooley St., SE1. ⓒ 020/7403-7221. www.thedungeons.com. Admission £16 ($30) adults, £12 ($23) students and seniors, £11 ($21) children 5–15. Daily 10am–5:30pm. Tube: London Bridge.

London Fire Brigade Museum **Ages 5 and up.** This museum offers pre-booked 2-hour guided tours telling the colorful history of firefighting, from the Great Fire of London in 1666 through the Blitz to today, via old firefighting appliances and other equipment, uniforms, and assorted memorabilia. Kids tend to gather into their own tours separate from adults. Ad hoc activities include drawing, coloring, and trying on uniforms. If they're lucky, your kids will glimpse recruits training next door. The shop sells fire-engine jigsaws, model engines, and other paraphernalia to satisfy budding firepersons.

Winchester House, 94a Southwark Bridge Rd., SE1 0EG. ⓒ 020/7587-2894. Admission £3 ($5.70) adult; £2 ($3.80) seniors, students, and children 7–14. Tours 10:30am and 2pm Mon–Fri. Tube: Borough.

Madame Tussaud's & Tussaud's Auditorium (London Planetarium) **Ages 5 and up.** It's cheesy, yes, but kids love Madame Tussaud's wax museum, best-known for its **Chamber of Horrors** with its re-creations of infamous murder scenes. If you can stomach that, proceed on to the more recent **Chamber–Live!,** which features actors posing as serial killers (unsurprisingly, under-12s aren't admitted). But it's not all about cozying up to celebs, infamous or otherwise—interactive exhibits let you in on the action, dancing in scenes from movies, getting your picture taken with the Queen, and addressing the nation from a president's podium. More palatable among the changing exhibitions is **Divas,** where pop princesses get a chance to meet Britney and Beyonce, and perform on stage while being judged by a Divaometer, which measures the audience's reaction to declare if performers are divas or just plain desperate. Boys will probably prefer the **Spiderman** exhibit, which gives them a chance to take a world-exclusive picture of the superhero. The **Spirit of London,** meanwhile, makes a vague concession to education in the form of a "time taxi" ride through 400 years of the city's history, from Shakespeare to the swinging '60s. For budding astronomers, there's **Tussaud's Auditorium** (better known as the **London Planetarium**), which currently screens *Journey to Infinity,* a short celluloid journey from Earth to the edge of the visible universe, during which you witness spectacular cosmic activity, skim the surface of Mars, and see inside a star nursery as new solar systems form.

The ticket-pricing system here is incredibly complex. Prices quoted below are for weekdays and do not include "Chamber–Live!" (add £2/$3.80); you pay more for certain times at weekends, less if you go during the final hour before closing. Note that opening times, auditorium show times, and admission prices may alter during school vacations. *Insider tip:* You can sometimes get reduced-price tickets by booking online. Fast-track tickets allow you to circumvent the off-putting queues, but you pay a premium. You can also buy family tickets when paying in advance.

Strollers aren't permitted, but there's a safe place to leave them, and carriers for babies up to 9 months are available for a small refundable deposit. There's also a cafe and baby-changing facilities.

Marylebone Rd., NW1. ⓒ 0870/400-3000. www.madame-tussauds.co.uk. Admission £20 ($38) adults, £17 ($32) seniors, £16 ($30) children 5–16. Mon–Fri 9:30am–5:30pm; Sat and Sun 9am–6pm (but may alter during school vacations). Auditorium shows Mon–Fri 12:30–5:30pm, Sat and Sun 10:30am–6pm (off peak). Tube: Baker St.

Museum in Docklands ★★★ **All ages.** One of London's most child-friendly attractions, this museum opened in 2003 in a Georgian quayside warehouse and explores 2,000 years of London's history as a river port, from Roman settlement to the modern-day regeneration of this Docklands area. The 12 main galleries have all manner of hands-on exhibits and touchscreens to engage kids' interest. Particularly popular are a 1:50 scale model of the original London Bridge, the first stone structure over the Thames; and Sailortown, a re-creation of riverside streets and gas-lit alleyways complete with the sounds of tigers and cockatoos from a wild animal emporium. But under-12s should make a beeline for the fabulous **Mudlarks** children's gallery, where they can hoist and weigh cargoes in the Dockwork Zone, get a diver's-eye view of undersea work in the Water Zone, search for archaeological finds in the Foreshore Discovery Box, and construct scale versions of Canary Wharf buildings in the Building Zone. For tiny tots, there's an Early Years Zone with superior softplay equipment.

Among the free weekend and school-vacation **family events** are storytelling, drama, dance, film, art workshops, puppet shows, rhyme times, and discussion sessions with people who once lived on the river. Chinese New Year in February is a great time to visit, with its range of celebrations from mahjong lessons and calligraphy to mask-making and lion dances, while Easter sees lots of chocolate-related activities.

The museum has a coffee shop and a bar/restaurant, plus a good lobby shop selling pirate hats, play sets, model boats, and more nautically inspired gifts and souvenirs. The galleries are accessible by stroller, and there's a baby-changing facility.

No. 1 Warehouse, W. India Quay, Hertsmere Rd., E14. Ⓒ **0870/444-3857.** Admission £5 ($9.50) adult, £3 ($5.70) seniors, free for students and under-16s. Daily 10am–6pm. Tube: Canary Wharf.

Museum of London ⭐ **Ages 5 and up.** Appropriately sited overlooking the city's Roman and medieval walls, this newly expanded museum traces the compelling 250,000-year history of London from prehistoric times to the 20th century. The chronologically arranged displays include more than a million items in seven permanent galleries, from archaeological finds to costumes, maps, and models. As this went to press, the Medieval London Gallery was slated to replace the old Saxon, Medieval, and Tudor galleries, where you learn that medieval London was founded twice, in different places, and that the Black Death of 1348–49 killed half the city's population (you can even see the excavations of a Black Death cemetery). Elsewhere, kids flock to see the Lord Mayor's Coach, a 3-ton gilt-and-scarlet fairy-tale contraption dating from 1757, as well as the "Princess of the City," the skeleton of a privileged young Roman woman found in nearby Spitalfields in 1999, together with a clay facial portrait by a medical artist, and her sarcophagus. A dramatic audiovisual presentation re-creates the disastrous Great Fire of 1666. You can view the death mask of Oliver Cromwell as well as cell doors from Newgate Prison, made famous by Dickens. Temporary exhibitions confront themes as diverse as Roman gold and fashion. Sunday and school vacation family events include drama, dance, music, storytelling, art and archeology workshops, craft displays, object handling, fashion shows, and more. **Hint:** The website provides activity sheets that you can download and print out before your visit. There's a cafe providing hot and cold food, including kids' meals, picnic areas, and baby-changing on levels 1 and 2. All galleries are stroller-accessible.

150 London Wall, EC2. Ⓒ **0870/444-3852** within U.K. only; or 020/7600-0807. www.museumoflondon.org.uk. Free admission (except some temporary exhibitions). Mon–Sat 10am–5:50pm; Sun noon–5:50pm. Tube: St. Paul's or Barbican.

Musical Museum **Ages 7 and up.** Young and old music fans will appreciate this quirky little museum in a disused church, where you can come to hear the workings of various instruments dating from the days before electronics and microphones. These include musical boxes; a Steinway DuoArt grand piano, reproducing the performance of pianists such as Gershwin; a Clarabella Orchestrion, which contains all the instruments of a small dance band; and a powerful Wurlitzer cinema organ, designed to accompany silent films. Since the museum is open only on weekends, you can combine a visit with a trip to the Kew Bridge Steam Museum (p. 162) just up the road. Strollers can be accommodated.

368 High St., Brentford, Middlesex, TW8. ℰ 020/8560-8108. www.musicalmuseum.co.uk. Admission £3.20 ($6.10) adults, £2.50 ($4.75) seniors and children 5–15, £10 ($19) family ticket (2 adults and 2 children, or 1 adult and 3 children). Apr–Oct Sat and Sun 2–5pm. Tube: Gunnersbury then 10-min. walk.

National Army Museum **Ages 5 and up.** Here at the British Army's own museum, which traces the British army's history from the Battle of Agincourt in 1415 to present-day peacekeeping activities, the prize possession is Marengo—the skeleton of one of Napoleon's favorite horses. But there's plenty more to keep the kids amused, including an amputation saw, reconstructions of a World War I trench and dugout, and a modern-day Phoenix pilot-less aircraft. Hands-on fun includes trying on a Civil War helmet, assessing the weight of a contemporary cannonball, and measuring military skills through computer challenges. Themed monthly event weekends (usually free) feature actors dressed as soldiers telling visitors of their experiences, lectures by specialists, and children's workshops and activities, including archaeological digs, hobbyhorse cavalry drills, and arts and crafts. There's stroller access and a cafe, The Great Escape.

Royal Hospital Rd., SW3. ℰ 020/7730-0717. www.national-army-museum.ac.uk. Free admission. Daily 10am–5:30pm. Tube: Sloane Sq., then 10-min. walk.

The Old Operating Theatre, Museum & Herb Garret ⭐ *Finds* **Ages 7 and up.** Spellbinding but little-visited, this museum is housed in the country's oldest surviving operating theater, dating to 1822—a time before anesthetics and antiseptic surgery. Long abandoned, the theater has been restored and filled with original furniture, including a 19th-century operating table at the end of which lies a box of sawdust that was used to soak up blood. The stalls surrounding the table used to be occupied by medical students; these days they are used for reconstructions of Victorian surgery (normally free on top of the ticket price) involving real amputation kits. Back then, amputations were undertaken for such minor complaints as ingrown toenails.

Further exhibits reinforce the horrors of medicine before the age of science; you'll view instruments such as biting gags, gigantic forceps, and formaldehyde-preserved specimens. Less gruesome is the adjoining herb garret of old St. Thomas's Hospital (of which this building was a part), with its bundles of herbs stored by the hospital apothecary to use in medicinal compounds, and displays on the history of nursing at St. Thomas's (the first home of Florence Nightingale's nursing school).

Note: The museum is located in the roof space of an old church and can only be accessed via a rickety spiral staircase.

9a St. Thomas St., SE1. ℰ 020/7188-2679. www.thegarret.org.uk. Admission £4.25 ($8.10) adults, £3.25 ($6.20) seniors and students, £2.50 ($4.75) children 5–15, £11 ($21) family. Daily 10:30am–5pm. Tube: London Bridge.

Ragged School Museum **Ages 7 and up.** This unique little museum traces the history of London's East End, in particular the Copperfield Road Ragged School, London's largest charity school for orphans and poverty-stricken children. In a re-created classroom, kids can learn how their Victorian counterparts were taught and can take part in workshops, history talks, treasure hunts, and canal walks. There are also displays on local history, industry, and culture, featuring objects as diverse as a Jewish printer's chests and a Bangladeshi flute.

46–50 Copperfield Rd., E3. © 020/8980-6405. www.raggedschoolmuseum.org.uk. Free admission. Wed and Thurs 10am–5pm; 1st Sun of month 2–5pm. Tube: Mile End, then 10-min walk.

Royal Gunpowder Mills ★★ **Ages 5 and up.** You'll have a blast (pardon the pun) at this attraction in Epping Forest, which illustrates the evolution of explosives and of the 17th-century Royal Gunpowder Mills. Displays, both traditional and interactive, include trying on powder-boat and mill-worker costumes, viewing a private arms collection, and touring an exhibition about the "bobbies on the beat" in this area, featuring a reconstructed 1860s police station. Outside the historic buildings, you'll spot a network of canals that transported explosives around the vast site. Surprisingly, you'll also see an array of wildlife. (The Mills was cut off from its surroundings by its river boundaries and the secrecy of its work, so nature took over.) You might see herons, Muntjac deer, bats, and otters from the boardwalks, bridges, and footpaths, or from the viewing tower at the woodland's edge, where there's also an animal mural.

Ask at the ticket office for kids' I-Spy activity sheets, and make sure you all wear comfy shoes—a lot of walking is involved. Ask, too, about free special events such as "living history" costumed re-enactments of the American Civil War.

Beaulieu Dr., Waltham Abbey, Essex, EN9. © 01992/707370. Admission £5.50 ($10) adults, £4.70 ($9) seniors and students; £3 ($5.70) children 5–16. May to early Oct: Sat, Sun, and bank holidays 11am–5pm. Train: Waltham Cross; then 25-min. walk or short bus ride.

Royal London Hospital Museum **Ages 7 and up.** The star attraction at this museum in a former church crypt is Joseph Merrick—or rather a replica of a hat and veil worn by the "Elephant Man," as well as documents relating to his residence at the Royal London, once the city's largest general hospitals. Visitors can also see a BBC video on Merrick. But other displays have their fascinations, particularly the 19th-century section, which looks at surgery before antiseptics; Florence Nightingale and nursing; and the special section on forensic material, sponsored by crime writer Patricia Cornwell and including material on Jack the Ripper and fellow murderers Dr. Crippen and John Christie. Twentieth-century displays include X-rays, blood transfusions, and a carbon arc lamp used to give UV light treatment to King George V in 1928. If you're making a special trip out here, call ahead, as hours can vary at short notice.

St. Augustine with St. Philip's Church, Newark St., E1. © 020/7377-7608. www.brlcf.org.uk. Free admission. Mon–Fri 10am–4:30pm. Tube: Whitechapel.

Royal Observatory ★ **Ages 4 and up.** Older kids of a scientific bent love this World Heritage Site, the original home of Greenwich Mean Time—which makes it, by international decree, the official starting point for every new day, year, and millennium. Here, you can stand in both the Eastern and Western hemispheres simultaneously by placing your feet on either side of the prime meridian, the center of world time and space. Other galleries explore the mysteries of time, space, and astronomy, and trace the history of timepieces and navigation at sea. A planetarium features "live" shows by an astronomer (temporary, pending the construction of a new one); in London's only public camera obscura, you can see a live image of the city projected on a viewing table; and this is the location of the world's biggest refracting telescope. Child-friendly events include Science Week activities such as clock-building, and sunspot- and star-spotting. Stroller access is available throughout the observatory, except to the dome.

Greenwich Union (56 Royal Hill, SE10; *©* **020/8692-6258**), a little off the tourist track yet handy for the Royal Observatory and the National Maritime Museum, is a wonderfully kid-friendly pub with a large beer garden. Parents flock here on Sundays, when the whole family can enjoy a superb traditional roast, and they can sample the products of the local microbrewery that owns the place, including chocolate stout and raspberry beer (staff are happy to provide tasters if you're not sure which to brave).

Greenwich Park, SE10. *©* **020/83120-6565.** www.rog.nmm.ac.uk. Free admission; planetarium £3 ($5.70). Daily 10am–6pm summer, 10am–5pm winter; planetarium show times vary. Tube: Greenwich DLR.

Shakespeare's Globe ⭐ **Ages 7 and up.** This faithful re-creation of Shakespeare's open-air playhouse stands nearby, where many of his works had their debut. Inside, an exhibition tells the story of its construction using the materials (including goat hair in the plaster, and a thatched roof) and skills available 400 years ago. You'll see costumes, props, and models used by this and other local theaters. Kids are especially interested in the displays about the production of special effects in the Bard's time, the sword-fighting demonstrations, and the technology allowing them to add their voices to scenes played by Globe actors.

Year-round actor-led backstage **tours** take place every 15 to 30 minutes. Summer brings staged **performances** of plays by Shakespeare and his contemporaries, as well as modern authors. Audiences either stand or sit on hard seating as in Elizabethan times, and heckling is encouraged, so performances aren't suitable for younger kids. On Saturday, those 7 to 11 can attend workshops—while you watch the play, they enjoy drama, storytelling, and art activities. During performances, guided tours are diverted to the nearby excavated **Rose Theater,** the first on Bankside, where Christopher Marlowe and Ben Johnson wrote their greatest plays and Shakespeare learned his trade. The Globe has a cafe, coffee shop, restaurant, baby-changing facilities, and stroller access.

21 New Globe Walk, SE1. *©* **020/7902-1400.** www.shakespeares-globe.org. Admission £8.50 ($16) adults, £7 ($13) seniors and students, £6 ($11) children 5–15, £25 ($48) family ticket (up to 2 adults and 3 children). Oct–Apr daily 10am–5pm; May–Sept daily 9am–noon and 12:30–5pm. Tube: Mansion House or London Bridge.

Sherlock Holmes Museum *Overrated* **Ages 7 and up.** Confused? You should be—Sir Arthur Conan Doyle's famous sleuth is said to have lived at 221B Baker St.; this museum is at no. 239 but has a sign on the door saying 221B. Inside, the flat appears as if the detective actually existed, with his deerstalker cap, his magnifying glass, and other "personal effects," including letters Holmes "wrote" to his equally fictional assistant, Dr. Watson. Still, if you're a fan, you'll probably be willing to swallow the whole charade and enjoy the waxwork tableaux of scenes from the books, as well as the re-created Victorian interiors. Note that there's no stroller access.

221B Baker St., NW1. *©* **020/7935-8866.** www.sherlock-holmes.co.uk. Admission £6 ($11) adults, £4 ($7.60) children 5–16. Daily 9:30am–6pm. Tube: Baker St.

Sir John Soane's Museum **Ages 12 and up.** Although unwelcoming to younger kids, this delightful museum will appeal to older kids with artistic leanings, with its distorting mirrors, rooms within rooms, secret staircases, picture gallery filled with three times too many paintings (achieved through the use of folding hidden panels); spooky crypt centered around the superbly preserved sarcophagus of Pharaoh Seti I; Gothic "monk's parlor" with a human skull; and mummified cats and fossils. Every nook and cranny of this labyrinthine building is filled with a sculpture, a plaster cast, or other objects amassed by Soane, an eminent 19th-century architect who lived here. *Insider tip:* Avoid Saturday mornings, when queues can be very long. Whenever you come, leave a donation, as the museum has restored the neighboring house and plans to extend the collection into it.

13 Lincoln's Inn Fields, WC2. © 020/7405-2107. www.soane.org. Free admission. Tues–Sat 10am–5pm; 1st Tues of each month 6–9pm. Tube: Holborn.

Theatre Museum (National Museum of the Performing Arts) ★★ **Ages 3 and up.** This performing-arts branch of the V&A, in the heart of Theaterland, is a hive of creative activity, with a daily program of (mostly free) workshops, demos, storytelling sessions, and guided interactive tours for 4- to 12-year-olds. Kids can dress up in costumes or make their own; get up on stage; play at puppet master; meet and talk to real performers; and design models and props. There's also a Saturday morning theater club for 8- to 12-year-olds (£5/$2.60; advance booking required), centering on current West End shows such as *The Lion King* and *Chitty Chitty Bang Bang.* The information desk provides free trail sheets and discovery bags for age ranges relating to the temporary exhibitions, which involve not just theater but related arts such as ballet, opera, music hall, circus, pantomime, puppetry, rock, and pop; sometimes a competition is involved. All levels and galleries are accessible by stroller, and baby-changing facilities are available. A great shop sells toy theaters, face-painting kits, and more.

Russell St., WC2. © 020/7943-4700. www.theatremuseum.org. Free admission. Tues–Sun 10am–6pm. Tube: Covent Garden.

Vestry House Museum **Ages 5 and up.** This fun local-history museum merits an hour or two of your time if you're in the neighborhood for its Toys and Games Gallery. These toys were played with or made in the 19th and 20th centuries, before PlayStation took over the universe. Replicas of some of these toys are available in the shop. Kids might also like the Bremer Car, one of the oldest British-built petrol-driven cars, built in 1892; the re-constructed Victorian parlor; the Costume Gallery; and the original police cell with its bench and toilet (the building once housed a police station). Visitors can see a tableau of a scene from 1861, and may even get locked in the cells themselves. Note that only the ground floor and gardens are stroller accessible.

Vestry Rd., E17. © 020/8509-1917. www.lbwf.gov.uk. Free admission. Mon–Fri 10am–1pm and 2–5:30pm; Sat 10am–1pm and 2–5pm. Tube: Walthamstow Central.

Victoria and Albert Museum ★★★ **Ages 3 and up.** The world's greatest decorative-arts museum, known as the V&A, is the perfect place to bring fashion-addict teens to see its stunning Dress Collection; art fiends, who marvel at its quirky Fakes & Forgeries gallery with its authentic-looking copies of Old Masters; and budding musicians, who are fascinated by the remarkable array of instruments. Much thought has been put into making these wonderful collections accessible and interesting to kids, who have lots of opportunities to handle objects, draw, listen to stories, and create designs using computers.

Most of the **hands-on displays** are in the three "discovery areas," where you can try on a corset and crinoline, make a bookplate, build a model of the Crystal Palace, construct a chair, guess a mystery object, design a picture frame; weave tapestry; try on an armor gauntlet; and much more. On Sunday between 10:30am and 5pm, and during some school holidays, an **Activity Cart** helps 3- to 12-year-olds explore the collections through drawing and activities in various galleries, from making a samurai helmet or a kimono in the Japanese gallery to creating an elephant headdress in the South East Asian gallery.

The program of (mainly free, drop-in) **family art and design activities** ranges from drawing and creative sessions, to storytelling, performance, and digital photography; most activities are aimed at 5- to 12-year-olds. The information desks have free **themed trails** for 7- to 12-year-olds. Otherwise, on Saturday during certain school holidays, you can borrow one of seven **themed backpacks** (for 5- to 12-year-olds; ID required), including Murder Mystery and Chinese Treasures, which contain jigsaws, handling objects, puzzles, and games. (A few Fancy Furnishings backpacks are available daily from the British Galleries, as well as an under-5s pack with color activities.) *Insider tip:* One of the best times to visit is the third weekend in October, when the museum takes part in the national **Big Draw** event, hosting a free program of drawing activities.

The museum has several interesting craft and souvenir shops (Shop 3 is best for kids); a range of eateries, including the lunch room for bring-your-own meals; and baby-changing facilities. All galleries are stroller-accessible.

Cromwell Rd., SW7. (✆) 020/7942-2000. www.vam.ac.uk. Free admission (charges for some exhibitions and events). Thurs–Tues 10am–5:45pm, Wed and last Fri of month 10am–10pm. Tube: S. Kensington.

Wallace Collection ★★   **Ages 5 and up.** Boasting the finest private collection of art ever assembled by one family, this national museum contains one of the world's best collections of French 18th-century pictures, porcelain, and furniture; a remarkable array of 17th-century paintings; and an armory that includes superb inlaid suits of armor and magnificent Persian scimitars. Free **family trails** help guide those with youngsters around the temporary exhibitions and, for kids 5 and up, there are all-day and half-day **family events** (£6/$3.15 and £12/$6.30 per child respectively; advance booking required). These include the likes of supervised weapon handling; mobile making, drawing and painting workshops; puppet shows and workshops; Halloween mask-making; Passover, Hanukkah, harvest, and Divali celebrations; and Christmas ornament making. There are also occasional drop-in creative workshops, and in October the museum hosts free drop-in drawing workshops.

The atmospheric glass-roofed Sculpture Garden contains **Café Bagatelle,** an excellent, peaceful spot for morning coffee, lunch, or afternoon tea; or you can enjoy a picnic lunch on the lawns fronting the elegant building. There is full stroller access, and baby-changing facilities are available.

Hertford House, Manchester Sq., W1. (✆) 020/7563-9500. www.the-wallace-collection.org.uk. Free admission (charges for some exhibitions and events). Daily 10am–5pm. Tube: Bond St. or Baker St.

Wimbledon Windmill Museum *Finds*   **Ages 5 and up.** Located in the weirdly shaped but picturesque mill on Wimbledon Common, this museum about windmills contains machinery, tools, and working windmill models, including early Greek and Persian incarnations. It's a place where kids can really get involved, trying their hands at grinding wheat using a saddle stone, a pestle and mortar, or a hand mill; lifting sacks using a block and tackle; and even changing the cloth on the mill's sails. One room has been kept as it was in 1870, when the by-then defunct mill was made into living quarters for a handful of local families. The shop sells the obligatory cut-out model windmills and windmills on sticks, as well as toy Wombles and honey made by bees on the common. A tearoom serving huge breakfasts (till noon) has attracted the likes of Mick Jagger. You can walk off your meal on the stroller-friendly circular

Windmill Nature Trail over Wimbledon Common and Putney Heath (trail guides are available at the Ranger's Office).

Wimbledon Common, SW19. ⓒ 020/8947-2825. www.wimbledonwindmillmuseum.org.uk. Admission £1 ($1.90) adults; 50p (85¢) seniors, students, and children. Apr–Oct: Sat 2–5pm; Sun and bank holidays 11am–5pm. Tube: Wimbledon, then 10-min walk.

Winston Churchill's Britain at War Experience   *Ages 7 and up.* Come here to see what life was like during the London Blitz. There's plenty of hands-on fun: Kids can huddle in a reconstructed London Underground air-raid shelter and hear sirens wail and bombers pass overhead; watch wartime news broadcasts in an underground cinema; and listen to messages from Churchill, Roosevelt, and others in a mock-up BBC radio studio. As well as all the interactive features, there are re-creations of a GIs' club and a local street, and lots of static displays featuring real bombs, ration books, rare documents, and photos. During school holidays, kids get a quiz to fill out while walking around, which they can enter into a prize drawing. *Tip:* Look on the website for discounts on the rather hefty admission prices.

64–66 Tooley St., SE1. ⓒ 020/7403-3171. Admission £8.50 ($16) adults, £5.50 ($10) seniors and students, £4.50 ($8.50) children 5–15, £18 ($34) family ticket (2 adults and 2 children). Daily Apr–Sept 10am–5:30pm, Oct–Mar 10am–4:30pm. Tube: London Bridge.

4 Art Galleries

Camden Arts Centre ⚐   *Ages 7 and up.* This ultra-hip gallery of avant-garde art shows by the likes of Sophie Calle and Runa Islam doesn't appear child-friendly at first sight, but closer inspection reveals a lively program of (mainly free) artist-led family days and kids' art days, plus school-vacation clay and mixed media courses for infants and juniors. Some events involve a special family menu in the excellent cafe (p. 129). In terms of the displays themselves, the installation pieces tend to go down well with younger visitors, though be warned that some of the exhibitions can contain risqué material. On your way out, don't miss the lovely lobby bookshop with its outstanding children's section.

Arkwright Rd., NW3. ⓒ 020/7472-5500. www.camdenartscentre.org. Free admission. Tues, Thurs–Sun 10am–6pm; Wed 10am–9pm. Tube: Finchley Rd.

Dalí Universe   *Ages 7 and up.* This riverside attraction finds itself constrained to put up warning signs for parents, since much of the Spanish surrealist's work is erotic in nature. Steer clear of the nudes and bestiality, though, and much of Dalí's work— his lobster phones, spider-legged elephants, melting clocks, and lip-shaped sofas, for instance—is great fun for kids. Watch out for half-price family deals, which include an activity pack with souvenirs, stickers, and more. There's also a children's audioguide with a trail and interactive quiz.

County Hall Gallery, Riverside Building, SE1. ⓒ 0870/744-7485. www.daliuniverse.com. Admission £9 ($17) adults, £5.50 ($10) children 8–16, £3.50 ($6.65) children 4–7, £24 ($46) family ticket for 2 adults and 2 children. Daily 10am–6:30pm. Tube: Waterloo.

Dulwich Picture Gallery ⚐⚐ *Finds*   *Ages 7 and up.* This little-visited gem in deepest south London boasts one of the world's most important collections of European Old Masters from the 17th and 18th centuries, including works by Rembrandt, Rubens, and Canaletto. Given the weightiness of its subject matter, this is a surprisingly fun place for kids—especially in summer, when an outdoor Architecture Family Day celebrates Architecture Week (£2/$3.80 ages 2 and up, family ticket for two adults and four kids

£10/$19). During this week, children of all ages can help build anything from a ginger-bread house to a mechanical TV remote control, as well as take part in storytelling and detective trails. Six weeks of drop-in creative workshops are held in the beautiful gallery gardens on Wednesdays for £2 ($3.80) per child—visitors are welcome to bring a picnic to enjoy on the lawns. On the first Sunday of the month from April to August, drop-in family arts play workshops are held for kids 4 and up (free with a gallery ticket).

Gallery Rd., SE21. ℭ 020/8693-5254. Admission £4 ($7.60) adults, £3 ($5.70) seniors, free for students and children. Tues–Fri 10am–5pm; Sat and Sun 11am–5pm. Train: W. Dulwich.

Hayward Gallery   Ages 4 and up. Part of the South Bank Centre arts complex (p. 243), the newly revamped Hayward offers up an eclectic mix of historical and contemporary shows. The emphasis is on the latter, and there's a strong international flavor to the programming. The interactive foyer space has touchscreen monitors where you can see cartoons, artists' videos, and other new media pieces. Family events include the likes of puppet sessions followed by live performances and storytelling, for which booking is essential. Kids love checking out the landmark Neon Tower at the top of the building's lift, with colored strips activated by changes in the strength and direction of the wind.

Belvedere Rd., SE1. ℭ 020/7960-5226. www.hayward.org.uk. Admission varies. During exhibitions open Mon, Thurs, Sat, Sun 10am–6pm; Tues and Wed 10am–8pm; Fri 10am–9pm. Tube: Waterloo.

National Gallery ⭐ Ages 3 and up. This majestic institution covers every great European school from the late 13th to the early 20th century, including 18th-century British masterpieces by Hogarth, Gainsborough, Reynolds, Constable, and Turner, and lots of French Impressionist and post-Impressionist works by Manet, Monet, Degas, Renoir, and Cézanne. A handy computer information center allows you to access background notes on the paintings and design your own tour map of 10 paintings you would like to view. Free family activities include storytelling for under-5s; themed family talks and drawing events for 5s to 11s; and holiday painting and craft workshops for 5s to 11s and 12s to 16s. (*Tip:* Workshops can't be booked, so get here early.)

Trafalgar Sq., WC2. ℭ 020/7747-2885. www.nationalgallery.org.uk. Free admission. Thurs–Tues 10am–6pm; Wed 10am–9pm. Tube: Charing Cross.

National Portrait Gallery   Ages 5 and up. Right next door to the National Gallery, this museum is a bit like an upmarket Madame Tussaud's, in that you come to see famous faces—in this case, portraits of those deemed significant to British national life over the centuries. Historical figures include Sir Walter Raleigh, Henry VIII, Shakespeare, the Brontë sisters, Virginia Woolf, and Princess Di; among contemporary luminaries are Liz Taylor, Mick Jagger, Margaret Thatcher, and David Beckham. The painters represented range from total unknowns to luminaries as diverse as Hans Holbein and Andy Warhol. Family events for those with kids ages 5-plus include self-portrait sessions, and mask- and puppet-making. *Insider tip:* The shop is a great stopping-off place for postcards.

St. Martin's Place, WC2. ℭ 020/7312-2463. www.npg.org.uk. Free admission. Mon–Wed, Sat and Sun 10am–6pm; Thurs and Fri 10am–9pm; Sat and Sun 10am–6pm. Tube: Leicester Sq.

Pump House Gallery ⭐ Ages 7 and up. This exciting contemporary gallery in a lovely lakeside setting in Battersea Park runs exhibitions embracing film, photography, sculpture, painting, and sound, all of which explore big themes like the relationships between animal instincts and social conditioning. It all sounds a bit heavy for kids, but there are exciting monthly drop-in family workshops on Sunday afternoons, during which artists help kids 3 and up develop creative ideas inspired by works in the current exhibitions—you might make animal headpieces or a family photo album. Events are free, but small donations are appreciated.

Battersea Park, SW11. © 020/7350-0523. www.wandsworth.gov.uk. Free admission. Open Wed, Thurs, and Sun 11am–4pm; Fri and Sat 11am–5pm. Train: Battersea Park.

Royal Academy of Arts ☆ **Ages 5 and up.** This venerable establishment holds a permanent collection built up from members' donated works, but it also hosts popular temporary exhibitions, including a famous annual Summer Exhibition. Its family workshops (£2/$3.80 with exhibition ticket) comprise introductory slide talks, exhibition visits, and hands-on sessions. A fun worksheet for young visitors, *The Art Detective's Guide,* is available at reception and at the exhibition entrance; it features picture trails, questions, fascinating facts, poem writing, and drawing.

Burlington House, Piccadilly, W1. © 020/7300-8000. www.royalacademy.org.uk. Admission varies according to exhibition and includes audioguide; free for children under 7. Sat–Thurs 10am–6pm; Fri 10am–10pm. Tube: Green Park.

Saatchi Gallery **Ages 12 and up.** In the same building as the Dalí Universe, this modern gallery became infamous as the bastion of the controversial Brit art movement in the 1990s and contains many icons of contemporary art, including Damien Hirst's pickled shark. It still sees itself as a springboard to launching the career of young artists, so work tends to be provocative and suitable only for older kids (it's very popular with school groups). During summertime, the gallery hosts daily free drop-in arts workshops for kids aged 6 to 14, and there's an interactive family art trail.

County Hall Gallery, Riverside Building, SE1. © 020/7823-2363. www.saatchi-gallery.co.uk. Admission £9 ($17) adults, £6.75 ($13) children 5–15, £25 ($48) family ticket. Sun–Thurs 10am–8pm; Fri and Sat 10am–10pm. Tube: Waterloo.

Somerset House ☆☆ **All ages.** This place is most popular among kids for its glorious fountain court, which has water jets through which they love to run in hot weather, and a glittering ice rink at Christmas (p. 212). Inside, it holds a trio of excellent galleries: **Courtauld Institute of Art,** focusing on Impressionist and post-Impressionist paintings, including masterpieces by Monet, Manet, Van Gogh, and Matisse; the **Gilbert Collection,** with a world-class collection of decorative arts, including snuffboxes and mosaics; and the **Hermitage Rooms,** which contain rotating exhibitions of Czarist treasures from St. Petersburg's State Hermitage Museum. Free family events for those with 6- to 12-year-olds begin in the Learning Centre, after a visit to one of the collections, and consist of craft-making inspired by objects that the children have seen. Kids 10 and over can be left here while their parents listen to a talk in the Courtauld. Other activities include storytelling for 3- to 10-year-olds, and creative sessions for under-5s. There's a lovely river terrace where you can bring sandwiches and cakes from the cafe.

The Strand, WC2. © 020/7848-2777. www.somerset-house.org.uk. Admission to each collection £5 ($9.50) adults, free for children under 18. Daily 10am–6pm. Tube: Embankment.

Tate Britain ☆☆ **Ages 5 and up.** *The* place to view Britain's national art dating from the 16th to the 19th centuries, the Tate includes works by Turner and Francis Bacon. Kids are tempted through its hallowed portals by an audiotour for those ages 8 to 12, and trail and activity bags for those ages 5 and up. There are also artist-led workshops for families and young people, with storytelling, audio resources and photography; poetry tours and workshops; creative sessions; and dance sessions in association with the English National Ballet. Most events are for kids 5 and over, though there's the occasional activity suitable for all ages.

Insider tip: The polka-dotted **Tate to Tate** boat (£3.40/$6.50 adults, £1.70/$3.25 children 5–15) is a fun way of getting to the gallery's sister institution, the Tate Modern; the trip takes 18 minutes.

Millbank, SW1. © 020/7887-8000. www.tate.org.uk. Free admission. Daily 10am–5:50pm. Tube: Pimlico.

Tate Modern ★★★ **Ages 5 and up.** Boasting Britain's foremost collection of international modern art, displayed in an impressive former power station, the Tate is a truly great venue for children because it shows paintings thematically, rather than chronologically, so they can see how various themes and objects have been represented at different epochs and by different schools of art, from still lifes to sunsets. Of particular interest is the Subversive Objects room with its playful curiosities made by the Surrealists and Dadaists and those they inspired, including Man Ray's metronome. To help you navigate, there's an award-winning audiotour for 8- to 12-year-olds (£2/$3.80; ID required), with two 30-minute discovery trails, and free activity sheets for ages 5 and up. There are also drop-in and ticketed weekend and school holiday activities for the same age group (with soft games for their younger siblings), most of them free (IDs are needed to borrow games).

Bankside, SE1. © 020/7887-8008. www.tate.org.uk. Free admission. Sun–Thurs 10am–6pm; Fri and Sat 10am–10pm. Tube: Southwark.

5 Best Rides

It doesn't get any better than the London Eye (p. 142), but you also won't want to miss the **Docklands Light Railway (DLR),** a driverless overland train linking Greenwich and the Isle of Dogs with the Tube at Tower Hill and Bank stations. Kids love to sit at the front and pretend to steer the train as it winds between buildings and climbs and descends like a genteel version of a roller coaster. Other great London rides take you along the Thames (see "Take Me to the River," box below); along **Regent's Canal** between Little Venice and Camden Town; to **Regent's Park** (p. 202); and to **London Zoo** with its dramatic Snowdon Aviary (p. 143). See www.tfl.gov.uk for suggested sightseeing itineraries using the DLR, including a "Kids Day Out" taking in the Museum in Docklands (p. 167), Greenwich Park (p. 201), and Discover (p. 161). You can use any London Tube ticket or pass on the DLR providing it covers the correct zone (the DLR travels through zones 1–3).

Jason's (Jason's Wharf, opposite 60 Blomfield Rd., W9 (© 020/7286-3428; www.jasons.co.uk), offers round-trips on out-of-service narrow boats between April and early November, accompanied by live historical commentary. Round-trips take about 90 minutes and cost £7 ($13) for adults, £5.50 ($10) for children 4 to 14, or £22 ($42) for a family ticket for 2 adults and 2 kids. It also has a canalside restaurant offering modern European dishes, including seafood. Setting off from the other end of the route, *Jenny Wren* (Walker's Quay, 250 Camden High St., NW1; © 020/7485-4433; www.walkersquay.com) plies the waters daily from March to October, and on weekends during winter (weather permitting). Round-trips cost £7 ($13) for adults, £3.50 ($6.65) for children 3 to 15; a family ticket for 2 adults and 2 kids costs £18

Take Me to the River

For a different perspective on London than the one you get from land, take a **boat trip along the Thames.** You'll see how many of the city's landmarks turn their faces toward the water, proof that the city grew along and around its link with the sea. For a long time, this tidal river was London's chief commercial thoroughfare and royal highway—monarchs traveled along it on fairy-tale gilded barges (which you can still see at the National Maritime Museum in Greenwich; p. 159)—as well as the route via which state prisoners were delivered to the Tower of London, eliminating the chance of an ambush in one of the narrow alleys surrounding it.

Numerous companies run trips to and from various destinations along the river. Commuter services are the cheapest, while tourist-oriented cruises with live or taped commentary, refreshment services, and sometimes even live music or a cabaret are the most expensive. A laid-back if quite expensive family option is the **Sunday Lunch Jazz Cruise** (© 020/7925-2215; www.bateauxlondon.com), offering a three-course set menu and fruit punch for 5- to 12-year-olds; its cost is £22 ($42) kids, £39 ($73) adults. The cruise leaves from Embankment and Waterloo piers and lasts about 2½ hours, passing the London Eye, Tate Modern, Millennium Bridge, St. Paul's Cathedral, and Tower Bridge.

For details on trips to Greenwich, see p. 148; otherwise, **Transport for London** publishes a comprehensive river services leaflet, available at Tube stations or online at www.tfl.gov.uk/river. (Travel information is also available 24 hr. at © 020/7222-1234.)

($34). This firm also has a cruising restaurant and a panoramic waterside restaurant where you can enjoy breakfast, morning coffee, or dinner. Best of all, perhaps, is **London Waterbus Company** (58 Camden Lock Place, NW1; © 020 7482 2660; www.londonwaterbus.com), which gives you the option of one-way trips, and allows you to stop off at the London Zoo—it has its own canal gate entrance, allowing you to circumvent the queues, and offers lower-priced tickets. The narrow boats operate daily from April to October, and weekends only from November to March, with one-way trips costing £5.20 ($9.90) for adults, £3.40 ($6.45) for children 3 to 15; a family ticket for two adults and two kids costs £18 ($34). Note that credit cards are not accepted. Strollers can only be carried if small and folded.

If all this boat touring makes you yearn for something a little more adventurous, the London Waterbus Company offers a variety of **all-day cruises** in the summer months. These explore the architecture and industrial history of some of London's less-known waterways. Destinations include Limehouse to the east—a journey during which the vessel descends through 12 locks—Hillingdon to the west, taking in the ultra-modern Paddington Basin; and Horsenden Hill, from which you can see seven counties, and where there's an adventure playground, a visitor center, and a canoe club. Advance booking is essential, with tickets costing around £10 to £14 ($19–$27) for adults.

If it's white-knuckle action you seek, there are two theme parks within easy reach of London. (For **Legoland,** see p. 262.)

Chessington World of Adventures ✪ **Ages 2 and up.** It doesn't make for a cheap day out, but periodic special offers for kids can slash the cost of visiting this theme park catering to all age groups, be they mini-adventurers, junior adventurers, family adventurers (all the family, though height/size restrictions may apply), or experienced adventurers. Opened in 2005, Land of the Dragons is a £6-million ($11.4-million) themed area for 2- to 8-year-olds, with 10 rides and attractions, including a puppet theater, treetop adventure scrambles, softplay areas, and two dragonboat rides for toddlers. Other areas include Animal Land, where you can get up close and personal with a West Lowland gorilla family; the Forbidden Kingdom, with its hard-core spinning Rameses Revenge ride; and Pirate's Cove, caught up in its high-seas adventure, Seastorm.

Chessington is 18km (12 miles) from London, and has free car parking. Trains from Waterloo take about 30 minutes, and the park is 10 minutes from the station. When you arrive, it's a good idea to ask at admissions about child wristbands with contact details in the event that you become separated. Those with small kids should also ask at Guest Services about the Parent Swap facility. Inside the park, kid-friendly eating options run the gamut from hot dogs and nachos in the Fizz & Burp Café to traditional fish and chips in Chips Ahoy. The medical center sells baby milk and food should you forget either, and there are numerous nursing and baby-changing facilities where you can also buy diapers. There are even family-sized toilet stalls in case a parent needs to tend to two toddlers at the same time.

Insider tip: To avoid high-season queues, pre-book a Day Planner ticket with pre-allocated time slots on the top five rides—the Dragon's family coaster, Vampire, Dragon's Falls, Tomb Blaster, and Professor Burp's Bubbleworks. Alternatively, online booking gives you fast-track entry. The website also has downloadable day guides with advice on the rides and attractions suitable for each age range, and details of family facilities.

Leatherhead Rd., Chessington, Surrey, KT9. ✆ **0870/444-7777.** www.chessington.com. Admission £28 ($53) adults and children 12 and over, children 4–11 free with each full-paying visitor (£18/$34 each child thereafter). Family tickets vary according to number and ages of visitors but average £60 ($114). Mid-Mar to Oct 10am–6pm (with variations for special events). Strollers £10 ($19) with £30 ($57) refundable deposit. Train: Chessington S.

Thorpe Park ✪ **Ages 2 and up.** While Chessington trumpets itself as a family park, Thorpe Park makes no bones about appealing to adrenaline junkies (they're both owned by the Tussaud's group, so they're not in competition)—if you're in any doubt, check out the picture of the scowling Hell's Angel on the website. In 2005 this thrill-seekers' paradise opened the Slammer giant freefall ride, which catapults riders 360 degrees; older favorites include the Vortex, a giant metal structure that twists its victims around like a huge egg whisk. That said, there are concessions to younger kids, in the form of Thorpe Farm, with its animal petting area (there's a gentle waterbus to take you there), and the Octopus Garden and Neptune's Kingdom, hosting gentler rides such as "Sea Snakes & Ladders" and "Up Periscope," which get a meager Fear Factor rating of 1/5. At the opposite end of the spectrum are periodic Fright Nites, offering rides in the dark, Circus of Horrors performances, and Horror Mazes.

Thorpe Park is 30km (20 miles) from central London, and car parking is free. Direct trains run from Waterloo to Staines (taking 35 min.), from where there's a shuttle to the park. It's essential to call before you set out, as there's a hard-to-fathom system of closures throughout the season. Purchasing tickets online can save you a few pounds, or you can spend more and get tickets with allocated time-slots to popular rides.

Staines Rd., Chertsey, Surrey, KT16. © 0870/444-4466. www.thorpepark.com. Admission £27 ($51) adults and children 12 and over, £20 ($38) children 4–11, £75 ($143) family of 4, £95 ($181) family of 5. Mid-Mar to Oct 9, 10am–5pm or 6pm; later on Fright Nites. Strollers £10 ($19) with £30 ($57) refundable deposit. Train: Staines.

6 Royal Residences

In addition to the listings below, see **Kew Palace** (p. 188).

Buckingham Palace, Queen's Gallery, & Royal Mews ✤ **Ages 5 and up.** Love 'em or hate 'em, Liz and her gang are one of the city's great tourist attractions and a perennial source of fascination for Brits and visitors alike. There's no better way to get a glimpse into their soap-opera existences than a visit to one of their not-so-humble abodes—starting, of course, with this one-time country house, which became the official royal residence under Queen Victoria. It has 600 rooms, 19 of which you can visit during the "Annual Summer Opening" when the Royal Family has usually decamped to one of their country homes, safely out of reach of commoners. (If the Queen *is* here, you'll see the Royal Standard flying from the mast outside.) These are the State Rooms, which are used by the Royals to receive and entertain guests on state, ceremonial, and official occasions, and which contain masterpieces by Rembrandt, Rubens, and others; sculpture; and fine furniture. The interactive family audiotour uses quizzes, music, and an activity trail to help 5- to 11-year-olds explore the place. In August, a Family Activity Room hosts creative activities. There's also an activity trail corresponding to the 16-hectare (39-acre) garden with its 19th-century lake and its wildlife.

The palace's most famous but overrated spectacle is the **Changing of the Guard** (daily 11:30am Apr–July, alternate days 11am rest of year, but it's frequently canceled due to bad weather, state events, and so on), when the new guard, marching behind a band, takes over from the old one in the palace forecourt. Arrive up to an hour in advance to stake out a space. Visits to the palace can be combined with tours of the adjoining **Queen's Gallery** (© 020/7766-7301; £7.50/$14 adults, £4/$7.60 children 5–16, £19/$36 family ticket for 2 adults and 3 kids; daily 10am–5:30pm), a former chapel where Her Royal Majesty, bless her, holds a wide-ranging collection of art and treasures "in trust for the Nation" (which means British citizens have to pay for the privilege of seeing what actually belongs to them—go figure). A free family program for 5- to 11-year-olds includes photography workshops, and self-directed activity packs encourage kids to find out about objects collected by kings and queens. Plus there's an E-Gallery where you can see high-resolution, magnified images of paintings and objects in the Royal Collection.

From March to October, the **Royal Mews** (Buckingham Palace Rd., SW1; © 020/7766-7302; admission £6/$11 adults, £3.50/$6.65 children 5–16, £16/ $30 family of 2 adults and 3 kids; Mar–Oct Mon–Thurs, Sat and Sun 11am–4pm, and summer daily 10am–5pm) can be visited in conjunction with the palace and gallery; ask about combined tickets. These are the Queen's working stables, where you can see carriage horses and state vehicles, including—looking like it came straight from a scene in *Cinderella*—the Gold State Coach used for coronations. Among the special activities devised for 5- to 11-year-olds are weekend tours, craft sessions, object handling and quizzes, and self-directed activity packs. Families can also use the Education Room for their own art activities.

The Mall. © 020/7766-7300. www.royal.gov.uk. Admission £14 ($26) adults, £7 ($13) children 5–16, £34 ($65) family ticket for 2 adults and 3 kids. Late July or early Aug to late Sept, daily 9:30am–6:30pm, with last admission at 4:15pm. Tube: St. James's Park.

Clarence House   Ages 10 and up. The Prince of Wales's official London residence, and the home of his sons William and Harry, was previously occupied by his grandmother the Queen Mother, and before that by the Queen, Prince Philip, and Charles as a very young boy. It's only open to visitors in late summer, for guided tours of five ground-floor rooms where official engagements are held and VIPs are received. The rooms are filled with artworks and antiques from the Royal Collection and Charles's own collection. Note that tickets are only available with advance booking.

Stableyard Rd., SW1. © **020/7766-7324.** www.royal.gov.uk. Admission £6 ($11) adults, £3.50 ($6.65) children 5–17. Early Aug to mid-Oct daily 9:30am–6pm. Tube: Green Park.

Hampton Court Palace ★★★ **All ages.** No longer a royal residence but still the most majestic palace of all, this Tudor confection is 21km (13 miles) west of London on the north side of the Thames. Given (reluctantly) to Henry VIII by Cardinal Wolsey around 1526, its subsequent royal residents included Mary I, Elizabeth I, Charles I, William III, and Mary II, and it still contains many furnishings and artifacts from their times, as well as important artworks and furnishings from the Royal Collection. Highlights are the Tudor Kitchens and the costumed guided tours of Henry VIII's apartments. There are kids' trails and audioguides, plus drop-in family craft workshops on certain weekends, but young 'uns tend to flock to the famous maze in the riverside gardens, where you can see the world's oldest vine, planted in 1768 and still going strong, and the royal tennis court. Those with under-5s can take a break (from the awkward stairs, cobblestones, and precious objects) in the Family Room, which has a Lego table, an activity cube, and softplay shapes. Music lovers might prefer to come in June, when the Hampton Court Palace Festival puts on open-air performances by top musicians, from Nigel Kennedy to Van Morrison, plus fireworks.

Note: One of the most laid-back ways to get to Hampton Court from central London is by river (© **020/7930-2062;** www.wpsa.co.uk; one-way £14/$26 adult, £6.75/$13 children 5–15, £34/$64 family ticket), but the 7- to 8-hour return trip, which runs between April and October, may not be suitable for restless kids, and doesn't give you much time at the palace. A better option is to sail there and return by train (half-hourly trains travel from Hampton Court to Waterloo, taking 35 min.). Along the way you see Syon House (p. 187); The London Apprentice, a famous inn where Henry VIII did some of his courting; Old Isleworth Parish Church, where victims of the Great Plague were buried; and Ham House (p. 183). Alternatively, you can stay here a few nights, at one of two Landmark Trust holiday apartments at the palace (p. 84).

E. Molesey, Surrey, KT8. © **0870/752-7777.** www.hrp.org.uk. Admission £12 ($23) adults, £9 ($17) seniors and students, £7.80 ($15) children 5–15, £35 ($67) family of 2 adults and up to 3 kids. Apr–Oct daily 10am–6pm; Nov–Feb Mon 10:15am–4:30pm, Tues–Sun 9:30am–4:15pm; Mar daily 10am–4:30pm. Train: Hampton Court.

Kensington Palace   Ages 7 and up. Though it hasn't been the official home of reigning kings since George II, this is a working royal residence housing the offices and apartments of various members of the Royal Family, including the Prince and Princess Michael of Kent. The birthplace and childhood home of Queen Victoria, it's furnished with items of Victoriana and paintings from the Royal Collection, which can be seen during tours of its State Apartments. Little princesses will be most taken by the Royal Ceremonial Dress Collection, containing royal togs from the 18th century on, including evening gowns worn by Diana, Princess of Wales. Sadly, you don't get to see the apartments where Di lived with princes Harry and William until her death.

Kensington Gardens, W8. ℂ 0870/751-5170. www.hrp.org.uk. Admission £11 ($21) adults, £8.30 ($16) seniors and students, £7.20 ($14) children 5–15, £32 ($61) family ticket (up to 2 adults and 3 children). Mar–Oct daily 10am–6pm; Nov–Feb daily 10am–5pm. Tube: High St. Kensington.

7 Historic Buildings

For **Kenwood House,** see Hampstead Heath, p. 142; for **Syon House,** see London Butterfly House, p. 187.

Apsley House   **Ages 5 and up.** This one-time mansion of the great British general the Duke of Wellington is informally known as No. 1 London because it was the first building after the Knightsbridge tollgates. The scene of glitzy banquets during which the general celebrates his victory over Napoleon at Waterloo, the house (which has private rooms still inhabited by the duke's descendants) is crammed with art treasures, including three Velázquez paintings, military mementos such as the duke's medals and battlefield orders, and historical curiosities such as a Sèvres Egyptian porcelain service intended as a divorce present from Napoleon to Josephine (she refused it). The best time to bring kids is Waterloo Weekend each June, when there's a re-creation in miniature of the famous battle and a range of family activities. Joint tickets are available with the Wellington Arch opposite (p. 156).

149 Piccadilly, Hyde Park Corner, SW1. ℂ 020/7499-5676. www.english-heritage.org.uk. Admission £4.50 ($8.50) adults, £3 ($5.70) seniors and students, £2.30 ($4.40) children 5–15, £15 ($29) family ticket. Tues–Sun: Apr–Oct 10am–5pm, Nov–Mar 10am–4pm. Tube: Hyde Park Corner.

Dickens House ✦   **Ages 7 and up.** The only survivor of Charles Dickens's numerous London homes (he lived here from 1837 to 1839, and it was here that he wrote *Oliver Twist*) is now a museum full of manuscripts, rare editions, paintings, original furniture, and other items relating to the Victorian novelist. It all makes for an atmospheric setting for special events, including guided tours, readings from the novels, and handling sessions, during which visitors can write with a quill pen used by the great author and touch other objects he owned. The museum also runs various walks through Dickensian London. The very best time to visit, though, is Christmas, when there's an exhibition, "Christmas with Dickens," a charity reading of *A Christmas Carol,* and Sunday family workshops centered around a traditionally decorated tree. You can even come on Christmas Day—perfect if you're far from home but want to celebrate (and Dickens *is* the author most people associate with the festive season). As well as entry to the exhibition, admission includes a glass of mulled wine made according to Dickens's own recipe, Christmas cake or a minced pie, and a gift pack.

48 Doughty St., WC1. ℂ 020/7405-2127. www.dickensmuseum.com. Admission £5 ($9.50) adults, £4 ($7.60) seniors and students, £3 ($5.70) children, £14 ($27) families (2 adults and up to 5 children). Mon–Sat 10am–5pm; Sun 11am–5pm. Tube: Russell Sq.

Eltham Palace ✦✦✦   **Ages 5 and up.** A truly unique spot, combining the remains of a medieval royal palace with Art Deco glamour, Eltham Palace was purchased by industrialist and art patron Stephen Courtauld and his wife in the 1930s, who proceeded to build their dream home from the surviving structures. Of greatest interest to younger visitors are the centrally heated quarters belonging to Mah-Jongg, the Courtaulds' pet ring-tailed lemur, with a bamboo ladder that lets him descend to the entrance hall below. Kids also love the gadgetry that was revolutionary for the 1930s and still seems Utopian today—including sockets in every room that sucked dirt down to a central vacuum cleaner in the basement. At the other extreme, there's the impressive Tudor Great Hall, where kings and queens of England entertained as many as 2,000 people; and there's tunnels to explore (these were built as a waste system under Henry VIII). The 7.6-hectare (19-acre) gardens with their panoramic views of London are fantastic, but make sure you keep the kids away from the moat.

Try to plan your visit to coincide with one of the plentiful **special events,** which range from Tudor Days and open-air performances of Shakespeare to teddy bear picnics and 1930s and '40s fashion shows. Before your visit, download the "Making Your Visit Fun" sheets from the website. At the house itself, you can pick up trail sheets for young children, one of which follows Mah-Jongg. Older kids enjoy the Venetian Room, with its touching panel designed (paradoxically) to help them understand why adults often say, "Don't touch." Teenagers appreciate the lively audiotour explaining how the house and interiors were restored. Strollers aren't allowed in the house because of its delicate surfaces, but staff will store them and provide hip seats with which to carry older babies and toddlers. There are changing facilities and a tearoom in the former kitchen. Trains to Eltham from Charing Cross and London Bridge take about 20 minutes.

Court Yard, SE9. 𝄐 **020/8294-2548.** www.elthampalace.org.uk. £7 ($13) adults, £5.30 ($10) seniors and students, £3.50 ($6.65) children, £17 ($33) family ticket. Mon–Wed and Sun, April–Oct 10am–5pm, Nov–Mar 10am–4pm. Train: Eltham.

Ham House 🟊 **Ages 3 and up.** This outstanding Thameside Stuart house was once home to the scheming Duchess of Lauderdale, whose ghost is said to roam the corridors (along with those of other former inhabitants, as you'll discover if you sign up for a family ghost tour). The lavish original interiors embrace furniture, textiles, and paintings, but it's the lovely grounds that kids will want to roam, with its mazelike wilderness of garden rooms; walnut and chestnut trees—home to a large flock of green parakeets; water meadows; an ice house (later used as an air-raid shelter); a still house (where the herbalist duchess distilled potions and medicines); and a dairy, with marble slabs supported by cast-iron cows' legs. Ham House offers a kids' guide and quiz/trail, school-vacation family events (usually for a small extra fee), musical afternoons in the Orangery garden, and open-air theater (see www.english-heritage.org.uk for details of tours and events). The Orangery tearoom and terrace offers historically inspired fare made from home-grown produce, including a kids' menu. Baby-changing facilities are available, and you can borrow baby slings and hip seats. *Insider tip:* If you and your kin are really into historic houses, there's a seasonal foot/bike ferry across the Thames close to **Marble Hill House,** a Palladian villa built for George II's mistress and set in parkland. Note that Ham House's grounds can be visited out of season, when the house is closed up.

Ham St., Ham, Richmond-upon-Thames, TW10. 𝄐 **020/8940-1950.** www.nationaltrust.org.uk. Admission £7.50 ($14) adults, £3.75 ($7.10) children, £19 ($36) family. Mid-Mar to Oct Sat–Wed 1–5pm (garden all year Sat–Wed 11am–6pm). Tube: Richmond, then 2km (1-mile) walk on towpath. Drivers take road 3km (2 miles).

Handel House Museum 🟊 **Ages 3 and up.** Here, in the restored Georgian town house of baroque composer George Frederic Handel (who resided here from 1723 until his death in 1759), some of the world's greatest music was composed, including

Messiah. As well as prized musical artifacts such as Mozart's handwritten arrangement of a Handel fugue, you can see portraits and prints of Handel and his contemporaries, and—most importantly—hear live music. If that inspires you, come along and join in a rousing chorus from *Messiah* (original or Gospel version) at a singing workshop—kids are welcome. Every Saturday sees drop-in family events, with trails, quizzes, and activity bags for those 6 and over, and arts and crafts for 3-year-olds and up. Teenagers should be most keen on occasional tours of ill-fated musician Jimmy Hendrix's one-time flat, on the top two stories of 23 Brook St. (£8/$15; pre-booking is essential).

25 Brook St., W1. © 020/7495-1685. www.handelhouse.org. Admission £5 ($9.50) adults, £4.50 ($8.50) seniors and students, £2 ($3.80) children. Tues, Wed, Fri, Sat 10am–6pm; Thurs 10am–8pm; Sun noon–6pm. Tube: Bond St.

Houses of Parliament & Big Ben ★ Ages 12 and up.

The Houses of Parliament, the ultimate symbols of London and strongholds of Britain's democracy, contain more than 1,000 rooms and 3km (2 miles) of corridors. But what kids most want to see is visible only from the outside—the clock tower housing the world's most famous time-piece, **Big Ben,** though the name actually refers to the largest bell in the chime, weighing close to 14 tons. (There *are* tours of the clock tower, but they're not open to overseas visitors or kids under 11.) If your offspring are set on observing a debate in the House of Commons or House of Lords (which are both in the former Palace of Westminster, the king's residence until Henry VIII moved to Whitehall), there's no lower age limit, but they have to be old enough to sign the visitors' book. The best time to visit is "Prime Minister's Question Time" (Wed 12–12:30pm), when Tony Blair has to hold his own against opposition MPs, but you're unlikely to get in without a ticket, for which you have to apply from your native embassy or high commission in advance. Alternatively, there are guided tours for overseas visitors during the summer recess (late July/early Aug to early Oct). Across the street, you can visit **Jewel Tower** (© 020/7222-2219), one of two surviving buildings from the medieval palace; inside is an exhibition on the history of Parliament and a touchscreen tour of both houses of Parliament.

St. Margaret St., SW1. © 020/7219-3000. www.parliament.uk. Free admission; guided tours £7 ($13) adults; £5 ($9.50) seniors, students, and children 5–16; £22 ($42) family. Hours are complicated; see website for details. Tube: Westminster.

Osterley House ★★ (Finds) Ages 3 and up.

This is a real hidden gem—an elegant neoclassical villa out west towards Heathrow Airport, with spectacular interiors surrounded by a magnificent estate boasting 16th-century stables (still in use), extensive park- and farmland, pleasure grounds, woods, meadows, and lakes. There's also a contemporary art gallery (Apr–Oct). Special events include a behind-the-scenes tour of the house as it wakes from its winter sleep; guided dawn walks with a warm drink en route, followed by breakfast; walks through the bluebell woods, complete with story-telling about trees and plants along the way; live interpretations of life at Osterley 200 years ago by costumed actors; and Easter egg hunts, trails, and craft activities. A 3km (2-mile) trail around the park is detailed in the estate guide, a children's guide, and family activity packs. The Stables tearoom has a kids' menu, baby-changing facilities are available, and strollers are allowed, although baby slings and hip seats can be loaned. *Insider tip:* You get reduced-price entry if you show your Travelcard.

Jersey Rd., Isleworth, TW7. © 020/8232-5050. Park and pleasure grounds free. House £4.90 ($9.30) adult, £2.40 ($4.60) child, £12 ($23) family. Park and pleasure grounds open daily 9am–7:30pm, house open 1–4:30pm early Mar to mid–Mar Sat and Sun, mid-Mar to Oct Wed–Sun. Tube: Osterley, then 10-min walk.

Brassed Off?

The crypt of St. Martin-in-the-Fields in Trafalgar Square once held the remains of Charles II (he's in Westminster Abbey now), who was christened here. His mistress, Nell Gwynne, and highwayman Jack Sheppard are both interred here (the floors of the crypt are actually gravestones). Today it's a popular family destination for its **London Brass Rubbing Centre** 🛝 (*☎* 020/7930-9306; £2.90–£15/ $5.50–$29 per rubbing, depending on size; Mon–Wed 10am–7pm, Thurs–Sat 10am–10pm, Sun noon–7pm), where kids can make rubbings using 88 exact copies of bronze portraits, including kings and queens, and a life-size Crusader knight. There's classical music to enjoy as they proceed. If they get the bug, the gift shop sells kids' brass-rubbing kits, plus model knights, Celtic jewelry, and more. Make sure you call ahead, as at press time the church had begun a huge building project that should run until 2007.

St. Martin also hosts free **lunchtime concerts** on Monday, Tuesday, and Friday at 1pm, and has the decent **Cafe in the Crypt**. There's a daily **crafts market** at the back of the church.

Sutton House 🛝🛝 **All ages.** This National Trust–owned Tudor house in the East End, home to merchants, Huguenot silk-weavers, Victorian schoolmistresses, and Edwardian clergymen over the centuries, now has some great free family-activity days on the last Sunday of every month (Sept–Nov). Kids of all ages can meet costumed characters, explore different types of art with support from artists and storytellers, and take part in crafts and games. On the second Sunday of the month, kids and adults can grasp the house's fascinating history with help from a professional artist and free art materials, while on Fridays in August, free arts and crafts activities take place in the courtyard, again assisted by an artist. Another good time to come is December, when there's a craft fair selling unusual Christmas gifts and hosting kids' activities; a wonderful costumed Victorian carol evening is featured as well.

On ordinary days, for which there is an admission fee, you can explore the oak-paneled rooms with their carved fireplaces, follow an exhibition on the history of the house and its former occupants, and peek into the contemporary art gallery—kids get quizzes, trails, and activity packs to bring it all to life. Look out, too, for the program of concerts, plus talks and walks on everything from black jazz history to the evolution of the Spitalfields area and local Jewish settlement. Older kids love the occasional evening Ghost Tours (£6.50/$12 adults, £3.50/$6.70 kids). The Brick Place Cafe has a kids' menu, and there are baby-changing facilities and stroller access.

2 & 4 Homerton High St., E9. *☎* 020/8986-2264. www.nationaltrust.org.uk. Admission £2.50 ($4.75) adults, 50p (95¢) kids, £5.50 ($10) family. Mid-Jan to mid-Dec: art gallery Wed–Sun 11:30am–5pm, historic rooms Fri and Sat 1–5pm and Sun 11:30am–5pm. Train: Hackney Central.

Westminster Abbey   Ages 7 and up. Just about every major figure in English history has left his or her mark on this remarkable place. Edward the Confessor founded the Benedictine abbey in 1065 on this spot, and in January 1066 Harold may have become the first English king crowned here. The man who defeated him at the Battle of Hastings later that year, William the Conqueror, had the first recorded coronation in the abbey, and the tradition has continued to the present day. On a darker note, the many tombs here include those of Elizabeth I, Mary Queen of Scots, Henry V, Geoffrey Chaucer, Samuel Johnson, and Charles Dickens. The latter three are in Poet's Corner, where there's a statue of Shakespeare and memorials to many other writers, including Henry Wadsworth Longfellow, T. S. Eliot, and Dylan Thomas. Various statesmen and men of science, including Sir Isaac Newton and Charles Darwin, are also interred in the abbey or honored by monuments, while the tomb of the Unknown Warrior commemorates the British dead of World War I. Bringing this up to the present day, 10 modern martyrs drawn from every continent and religious denomination are memorialized in statues above the West Front door, including Martin Luther King, Jr. If it's all a bit daunting, families can book **90-minute verger-led tours** (£4/$7.60 per person) that take in the shrine of Edward the Confessor, the royal tombs, Poet's Corner, the cloisters, and the nave.

The **Abbey Treasure Museum** in the crypt (admission free with abbey tickets) holds some creepy royal effigies used for lying-in-state ceremonies (because they smelled better than the corpses), plus other oddities, including Henry V's funeral armor and a corset from Elizabeth I's effigy.

Broad Sanctuary, SW1. ℂ 020/7654-4900. www.westminster-abbey.org. Admission £8 ($15) adults; £6 ($11) seniors, students, and children 11–16; £18 ($34) family ticket. Abbey hours: Mon, Tues, Thurs, Fri 9:30am–3:45pm; Wed 9:30am–7pm; Sat 9am–1:45pm. Museum hours: daily 10:30am–4:30pm. Tube: Westminster or St. James's Park.

8 Zoos & Aquariums

For **London Zoo,** see p. 143. There are also small petting zoos on Hampstead Heath (p. 142) and at Brent Lodge Park (p. 204).

Battersea Park Children's Zoo ★★   **All ages.** A well-kept little secret in the park stretching along the Thames opposite Chelsea, this zoo almost closed down in 2003, after half a century of introducing city children to farmyard and more exotic animals. Luckily, local support bought it some time, and in 2004 it was refurbished and reopened by the Chestnut Centre, an otter and owl sanctuary based in north England. Along with otters and owls, its residents include monkeys, lemurs, meerkats, wallabies, emus, and talking mynah birds. In addition, there are some great new areas—the Mouse House, Farm Yard Encounter, and Butterfly Banquets—among the old favorites. The new Lemon Tree Cafe has indoor and outdoor tables where you can dine to the sounds of exotic birds. The zoo also has a kids' playground, indoor toddlers' toys, a wildlife gift shop, and a Pooh Bear baby-changing room. Note that the surrounding park is a haven for wildlife, including ducks, herons, and butterflies; see p. 205 for more info.

Battersea Park, SW11. ℂ 020/7924-5826. Admission £4.95 ($9.40) adults, £3.75 ($7.10) seniors and children, £16 ($30) family ticket (2 adults, 2 kids). Daily 10am–5pm. Train: Battersea Park.

London Aquarium   **All ages.** This isn't one of the world's great aquariums by any stretch of the imagination, but it is one of the largest in Europe, and it has enough toothy beasties to keep the kids goggle-eyed. Among the 350 species here are sharks, piranhas, jellyfish, and clownfish (you know, Nemos). The ray touchpool is one of the most popular spots, while the very young can explore a seashore area with starfish and crabs, open every day at selected times (there's an activities screen at the ticket desk). Regular events include feeds (rays, piranhas, sharks), talks (rainforests, coral reefs), and diving displays. Unless you're a family of marine biologists, arm yourselves with a copy

Hyde Park Pet Cemetery ★★

If you enter or leave Hyde Park by Victoria Gate on its north side, from the Bayswater Road, you may catch a glimpse of an unusual—and poignant—sight: hundreds of tiny gravestones in an inner garden behind the old gatekeeper's cottage. These date from a pet cemetery established here in 1880, after the Duke of Cambridge's pet dog was run over in the road nearby. Dogs, cats, monkeys, and birds were subsequently buried here by their upper-class owners. The cemetery was full by 1915, at which time it closed. It can be viewed by appointment only, at a cost of £16 ($30) for one to six people, then an additional £1.50 ($2.85) per person (✆ 020-7298-2112).

---

of the 30-page *Aqua Safari* from the ticket office (£3.75/$7.10 with free poster) to help you navigate through the aquatic habitats; it also contains tasks and activities for ages 7 and up.

Note that the prices quoted below are for peak times; it's £1 ($1.90) cheaper per person the rest of the year (mid-Jan to mid-Feb, 1st 3 weeks of Mar, early Sept to mid-Oct, and early Nov to mid-Dec). The aquarium is stroller accessible, and there are various eating options in the County Hall building, as well as the **Namco Station** entertainment center.

County Hall, Westminster Bridge Rd., SE1. ✆ 020/7967-8000. www.londonaquarium.co.uk. Admission £9.75 ($19) adults, £7.50 ($14) students and seniors, £6.25 ($12) children 3–14, £29 ($55) family ticket. Daily 10am–6pm. Tube: Waterloo.

London Butterfly House & Tropical Forest (Syon House) ★★★   **All ages.** You'll

find two up-close-and-personal animal attractions situated on the lovely grounds of historic Syon House, the Duke of Northumberland's London residence way west of the city center. The **Butterfly House** gives you the chance to walk among hundreds of free-flying tropical butterflies in a glass-house environment, and also has a tropical aviary and tropical Mini-Beasts Gallery with birds and insects from around the world. The **Tropical Forest** (formerly known as the Aquatic Experience) displays rescued and endangered species that live in or near water, especially in rainforest areas, including piranhas, snakes, crocodiles, iguanas, huge marine toads, poison arrow frogs, and terrapins. The critters here are housed in a tropical environment complete with waterfalls, and some of the friendlier ones can be handled and fed.

As if all that weren't enough, **Syon House in Syon Park** (✆ 020/8560-0881; www.syonpark.co.uk) itself can be toured, with its wonderful interiors, and runs special events such as historical reenactments combined with children's trails. The 16-hectare (40-acre) gardens host miniature steam train rides on selected days, including midsummer Sundays. Also in the gardens are an ice house, a rose house, and an indoor adventure playground (✆ 020/8847-0946; www.snakes-and-ladders.co.uk) suitable for ages 6 months to 12 years. All in all, a well-nigh perfect day out.

Syon Park, Brentford, Middlesex, TW8. Butterfly House: ✆ 020/8560-7272. www.londonbutterflyhouse.com. Daily summer 10am–5pm, winter 10am–3:30pm. £5.25 ($10) adults, £4.25 ($8.10) seniors and students, £3.95 ($7.50) children 3–16, £16 ($30) family ticket (2 adults, 2 kids). Tropical Forest: ✆ 020/8847-4730. www.aquatic-experience.org. Admission £5 ($9.50) adults; £3.75 ($7.10) seniors, students, and kids 3–15; £15 ($29) family ticket (2 adults, 3 kids). Daily summer 10am–6pm, winter 10am–5pm. Tube: Gunnersbury, then bus 237 or 267.

9 Gardens & Conservatories

Lovers of green spaces should look out for the annual **Open Squares weekend** (www.opensquares.org.uk), during which many of London's private garden squares and community gardens are open to the public. Some run family activities during the event.

Chelsea Physic Garden   **Ages 7 and up.** A botanical garden set up by a king's doctor (George II's) to grow plants for medicinal study may sound tame, but not when you consider that among the 7,000 or so species residing here are numerous carnivorous specimens, including Venus flytraps. Unless your kids are truly plant mad, though, it's best to come during spring or summer vacations, when **family activities** for 7- to 11-year-olds take place. (You can even leave kids 9 and up with the staff, though you must accompany them during lunch.) Hits include science workshops exploring the pond and compost heap; safaris in search of creepy-crawlies; plant-dye workshops; and art sessions, including paper-stick sculpture. All activities cost £4.50 ($8.50), and pre-booking is essential. The teashop whips up some superior cakes.

66 Royal Hospital Rd. (entrance on Swan Walk), SW3. © 020/7376-3910. www.chelseaphysicgarden.co.uk. Admission £5 ($9.50) adults, £3 ($5.70) students and children 5–15. Early Apr to –Oct, Wed noon–5pm, Sun 2–6pm (plus special open days). Tube: Sloane Sq.

Royal Botanic Gardens, Kew ★★★   **Ages 3 and up.** The world-famous botanical gardens are an even better place to visit with kids now that **Climbers & Creepers,** billed as "the U.K.'s first interactive botanical play zone," has opened its doors. Set in the former cycad house, Climbers & Creepers is designed to teach 3- to 9-year-olds the importance of plant/animal relationships through play: They can climb into a plant to pollinate it, get "eaten" by a giant pitcher plant, and crawl through a bramble tangle. The gardens also boast an outdoor space for fine weather, and an observation area with refreshments (although the historic **Orangery** with its panoramic views has better food, including traditional afternoon teas, and serves kids' portions). Many of Kew Gardens' family vacation activities, such as shadow puppet and rain-stick making, crafting with plant materials, and Indian dance and culture workshops, are based in the Climbers & Creepers play zone. Other events in the gardens include guided walks and feeding and petting animals from a visiting farm.

All of this barely scratches the surface of the rest of the beautiful 120-hectare (300-acre) gardens, which actually constitute a vast scientific research center, with thousands of plant varieties, plus lakes, hothouses, walks, pavilions, museums, and an architectural heritage. To get an overview or ease your way in area by area, especially with kids in tow, make use of the hop-on hop-off **Kew Explorer** bus (£3.50/$6.65 adults, £1.50/$2.85 children 5–16). A **Kids' Kew** self-guided, 2-hour trail is aimed at 7- to 11-year-olds, introducing some of the garden's amazing plants and the people involved in creating them. Note that the grounds are also home to **Kew Palace,** which was George III's family home. It's been closed for major restoration work since 1996, but Queen Charlotte's Cottage nearby, used by the king and his family as a summerhouse, is open for special events (© **0870/751-5179**). When the palace reopens in Easter 2006, the new exhibition will include displays on George's boyhood and royal education as well as those of his sons. A family events program will embrace live interpretation, music, and other activities.

Richmond, Surrey, K9. © 020/8940-1171. www.rbgkew.org.uk. Admission £10 ($19) adults, £7 ($13) students and seniors, free for children 16 and under. Early Feb to late Mar daily 9:30am–5:30pm; late Mar to early Sept Mon–Fri

9:30am–6:30pm, Sat, Sun and bank holidays 9:30am–7:30pm; early Sept to Oct 30 daily 9:30am–6pm; Nov to early Feb 9:30am–4:15pm. Tube: Kew Gardens.

10 Nature Centers

For a full-on, back-to-nature experience in the city, **WWT Wetland Centre** (p. 152) is the place to head. Smaller in scale are London's many **city farms,** which were set up to offer inner-city kids the opportunity to experience a little bit of the countryside on their doorsteps. While these are not tourist attractions and are generally located in less privileged areas, they're worth visiting if you happen to be with animal-loving kids—most offer animal-petting and -feeding sessions, rare breeds, and more, and some sell their own produce. For details on locations of city farms, as well as **community gardens** (which offer handy oases in the metropolitan jungle), see www.farmgarden.co.uk, or call 🕻 **0117/923-1800.** One particularly good community garden, the **Calthorpe Project** on Gray's Inn Road, WC2 (🕻 **020/7837-8019**), offers "Little Green Fingers" gardening sessions for kids under 5.

There are plenty of other natural sanctuaries if you are prepared to seek them out. One of the most atmospheric is **Abney Park Cemetery & Nature Reserve** (Stoke Newington Church St., N16; 🕻 **020/7275-7557;** www.abney-park.org.uk), a 13-hectare (32-acre) Victorian burial ground and conservation area in north London, with a children's garden and a visitor center hosting events and workshops, including woodland crafts, kite-making, and wildlife walks. (Local residents include grey squirrels, bats, and foxes.)

London Wildlife Trust (🕻 **020/7261-0447;** www.wildlondon.org.uk) has lots of sites in and around the city. The most central is **Camley Street Natural Park** (12 Camley St., NW1; 🕻 **020/7883-2311**) on the banks of the Regent's Canal near King's Cross, with birds, bees, butterflies, and amphibians, plus a Wildlife Watch Club and other activities, such as Frog Days with pond dipping. The Trust also runs the **Centre for Wildlife Gardening** (28 Marsden Rd., SE15; 🕻 **020/7252-9186**), which teaches kids how to attract wildlife to their own gardens. Similarly, and also south of the river, **The Environment Centre** (Dorlcote Rd., SE18; 🕻 **020/8773 0632**) gives advice on caring for and encouraging wildlife in your garden. It opens to the public on Sunday, offering displays on wildlife and environmental matters, hosting kids' discovery projects and creative activities such as mask- and model-making, and selling wildlife gifts and bird-care products. In the East End, the dynamic **Lea Rivers Trust Discovery Team** (a waterway charity; 🕻 **020/8981-0040;** www.leariverstrust.co.uk) offers a family program that includes free summer Sunday craft workshops with environmental themes. You can also drop by this heritage area; leaflets are available.

11 Kid-Friendly Tours
DRIVING TOURS

Open-top bus tours are a real thrill for kids. For parents in the city, they're also the quickest and cheapest way to get a handle on London, allowing you to cherry-pick sights to return to at a later date. Buses depart from lots of convenient points, and you can hop on and off when the mood takes you—to see a specific sight in detail, or just for a restroom or snack break. There's usually live English commentary, or recorded commentaries in a range of languages. The following companies offer online ticket discounts, plus fast-track entry to busy attractions such as Madame Tussaud's and the Tower of London.

The leader of the pack when it comes to taking a bus tour with kids is **The Original London Sightseeing Tour** (Baker St. Station; ℂ **020/8877-1722;** www.theoriginal tour.com), since it's the only operator offering—at least on its Red Route, which takes in all the major sights—special children's commentaries, together with a free Kids' Pack with an activity/quiz book and competitions, and a "passport" to London that gets stamped when they climb aboard. Tickets cost £16 ($30) for adults, £10 ($19) for children 5 to 15 inclusive, or £60 ($114) for a family ticket for two adults and three children, and include a free river cruise. A similar option is the **Big Bus Company** (48 Buckingham Palace Rd., SW1; ℂ **020/7233 9533;** www.bigbustours.com). In addition to another free river cruise, you get a 90-minute walking tour (themes include The Beatles, James Bond, Royal London, and Ghosts by Gaslight) thrown in with your ticket, plus money off certain West End shows. Tickets cost £18 ($34) for adults, £8 ($15) for children 5 to 15.

For a more personal road trip around London, you can spring for a black cab to take you to see the sights. The advantage of this is that you choose your own itinerary if you wish, and can stop off whenever and for however long you like. **London Black Cabs** (ℂ **07957/696673;** www.londonblackcabs.co.uk) offers 1-hour to 1-day tours costing from £35 ($67) an hour; or try **London Taxi Tours** for kid-friendly themed tours (p. 191). For something completely off-the-wall, **Karma Kabs** (ℂ **020/ 8964-0700;** www.karmakab.com) has a fleet of four kitschy Indian cars for hire (including the Bollywood Kar, and the bright-pink Ab Fab Kab), with prices starting at around £40 ($76) an hour. Options include tarot card readings.

Equally original are the **rickshaw rides** run by the **London Bicycle Tour Company** (1a Gabriels Wharf, SE1; ℂ **020/7928-6838;** www.londonbicycle.com). The company uses modern rather than traditional vehicles (so they have gears for the uphill bits, and can accommodate up to one adult and two kids), and the drivers have a great knowledge of London (though they aren't official tour guides). Their fee is £40 ($76) per hour. The same firm, as the name implies, leads 3-hour **bike tours** of London along the capital's cycle routes, side streets, and alleyways. Kids must be ages 8 and up (with younger kids you can hire equipment and go solo). Tours run on weekends from 2pm in summer and from 10:30am in winter, costing £17 ($32) for adults and £12 ($23) for kids up to 16. Alternatively, you can form a small group and pre-book a trip for anytime.

WALKING TOURS

The Original London Walks (ℂ **020/7624-3978;** www.walks.com) is London's oldest walking-tour company, with a repertory of more than 300 walks. Though the walks are pitched at adults rather than kids, some can be and are enjoyed by older kids (6 and up), including weekly costumed ghost walks, treasure hunts, and occasional Thames beachcombing walks. Kids will love "A Walk on the River Bed," guided by a former Museum of London marine archaeologist (who's great with kids). During the walk, you learn all about the river's wildlife and investigate detritus on the shore, some of which you can take home (bring along a carrier bag). Another surefire hit is the costumed Mary Poppins walk ("Supercalifragilisticexpialidoceous London"), with sing alongs encouraged. If you want to take your kids on one of the pub walks, the company recommends "Along the Thames," which passes attractions of interest to kids, such as the *Golden Hinde* (p. 158) and Shakespeare's Globe (p. 171), and visits pubs

Fair's Fair

Funfairs can be tacky, noisy, overbearing affairs for kids. Not so **Carters Steam Fair,** a traditional and very family-friendly event that tours various London parks (including Clissold Park and Ravenscourt Park; see p. 206 and 204) throughout the summer months. Here the garish rides typical of modern funfairs are replaced by lovingly restored vintage rides, including 1960s rock 'n' roll bumper cars and the "new" Dive Bomber, a restored 1946 thrill ride. Nearly all the side stalls, which include hooplas and a fishing game, are pre–World War II, and this is also virtually the only remaining funfair with old-style living vans (similar to caravans). Visit www.carters-steam-fair.co.uk for more information.

with outdoor spaces. For older teens, the company's "Jack the Ripper" walks are far ahead of the competition (of which there is plenty).

Staff members are incredibly helpful when it comes to which walks (and which *guides*) are best for kids, so call or e-mail in advance. Walks last an average of 2 hours and cost about £5.50 ($10) for adults, with kids under 15 free when accompanied by an adult, which makes them an amazing value. Note that you can organize private group walks, and that the company also runs "Explorer Days outside London," including Richmond and Hampton Court, Windsor and Eton (p. 260), Oxford, and Cambridge.

WATER TOURS

London Duck Tours (Chicheley St., SE1; © **020/7928 3132;** www.londonduck tours.co.uk) offers a quirkier tour that children enjoy, which uses DUKWS amphibious vehicles (employed in the D-Day landings) to take in various landmarks (including Big Ben and Buckingham Palace) before launching out of a slipway into the Thames for a water cruise. Tours last 75 minutes and cost £17 ($31) for adults, £13 ($25) children 13 to 15, £11 ($21) children 12 and under; a family ticket for two adults and two children under 12 is £49 ($93).

SPECIALIST TOURS

Harry Potter fans rejoice! **London Taxi Tours** ★★★ (© **07957/272-1791;** www. londontaxitour.com) can currently incorporate **Harry Potter movie location sites** into a regular tour of London, or concentrate on all things Potter in a 3½-hour London tour (£129/$244 per taxi). An 8-hour Potter London tour or a 10-hour Potter Oxford tour costs £295 ($560) and £385 ($732) per taxi respectively. For the latter, cars pick up parties from their residence or hotel and head first for Oxford and its world-famous university, where some Hogwarts school scenes where filmed, including those set in the Great Hall and the library. There's then an optional excursion to Lacock Abbey, to see the corridors, classrooms, and grounds used for filming. You'll end up back in London, where further movie locations include Platform 91/4, Leadenhall Market (p. 197), the outside of the Leaky Cauldron, and Gringott's Bank. Guides are well versed in the books, and all are excellent with kids. The same company offers fixed-priced general sightseeing tours lasting 2 to 8 hours, as well as other themed tours, including a **James Bond tour,** which you can combine with a Harry Potter tour, and a **Monopoly Board tour.** Taxis can hold up to five adults and have integral child seats, with booster seats available by request.

Lovers of the small screen, meanwhile, will be pleased to hear that the popular **tours of BBC Television Centre** (Wood Lane, W12; ✆ **0870/603-0304;** www.bbc.co.uk/tours), now include a special kids' tour of the CBBC children's channel for ages 7 and up. They vary according to shooting schedules, but last up to 2 hours and include visits to some of the presenters' studios and to an interactive studio. Standard tours, which include visits to the newsroom and sessions in an interactive newsroom, are open only to those over 9. Pre-booking is essential for both. Tickets cost £8.95 ($17) for adults, £6.50 ($12) for children, and £25 ($48) for a family (two adults and two children, or one adult and three children).

7

Neighborhood Strolls

London is a great city for walking—it's largely flat in the center, with stunning juxtapositions of old and new, of urban vistas and more bucolic scenes. Pay the city close enough attention, and you'll see that layers of history are just begging to unfurl around you.

The following walks are designed to provide glimpses into some of London's lesser-known and more offbeat treasures, which I didn't have space to squeeze into Chapter 6, "Exploring London with your Kids."

1 A Bloomsbury Jaunt

Beneath the sedate facade of academic Bloomsbury, within the University of London, ghoulish-minded kids will find some sights that will keep them talking for the rest of their trip. Coming out of Euston Square Tube, walk down Gower Street to **University College;** visitors are free to stroll into its **South Cloister** daily between 8am and 5:30pm (except Sun) to meet **Jeremy Bentham,** the philosopher and University co-founder—or at least, his preserved body, clad in his clothes and posed in a glass-fronted wooden case in the hallway. You might almost mistake it for a waxwork; except for the head (which *is* made of wax; the skull has been kept in a safe since some students stole it as a prank), this is the real McCoy, stuffed with a mixture of lavender, cotton, wool, straw, and hay. Nearby displays hold photos (not for the squeamish) documenting the preservation, plus items tracing his career. Most weirdly of all, you'll discover that the body sat in on University governors' meetings for years after Bentham's death in 1832, once attended a beer festival in Germany, and is still wheeled out to preside over pre-dinner drinks at the annual Bentham dinner.

Further grisly sights are on offer right next door, at the University's **Petrie Museum of Egyptian Archaeology** (© 020/7679-2884; Tues–Fri 1–5pm, Sat 10am–1pm; free admission), in the form of mummified heads, some complete with eyebrows and eyelashes. This museum boasts one of the world's best collections of Egyptian and Sudanese antiquities, and contains an astonishing 80,000 objects. Among the fascinating artifacts on display here are the world's "oldest dress" (a piece of Egyptian linen dating from around 5000 B.C.), a suit of armor from the palace of Memphis, socks and sandals from the Roman period, and lots of jewelry.

If you need cheering up after the macabre sights at the University, wander a couple of blocks to **Tavistock Square** (© 020/7974-1693; 7:30am–dusk), an unofficial peace garden centered around a statue of Mahatma Gandhi, who lectured nearby. People congregate around this statue to burn incense, light candles, and practice tai chi. Other peace memorials here include a cherry tree in memory of the victims of the atomic bombs dropped on Hiroshima and Nagasaki (every Aug 6, flowers are placed at the bottom of the tree, and origami birds are hung from its branches), and a 450-million-year-old slate in honor of conscientious objectors.

If you're hungry, it's a short walk to the popular **North Sea Fish Restaurant** (7–8 Leigh St., at the end of Burton Street (© **020/7387-5892**), a good-value favorite among London cabbies. You can either eat in or get takeout, but be aware that portions are enormous. The best way to get here is up Woburn Place and along **Woburn Walk**, a charming, tree-lined alley with quirky bow-windowed stores and cafes. The Irish poet W. B. Yeats lived at no. 5 between 1895 and 1919.

From here it's a 10-minute walk via Marchmont Street to the intensely moving **Foundling Museum** (p. 164), which traces the lives of the orphaned or abandoned children taken in at the Foundling Hospital, built in 1742 on the site of **Coram's Fields** (p. 207)—now one of the city's best playgrounds. After playing on the equipment and meeting the resident animals, older kids might want to make a detour to the atmospheric **Dickens House** (p. 182), home of the Victorian novelist, on nearby Doughty Street. Or you can wander along Great Ormond Street until you come upon a **statue of Peter Pan,** placed outside the entrance to Great Ormond Street Hospital for Sick Children in memory of J. M. Barrie, who bequeathed to the hospital the royalties from his best-known book. See below for more on the generous J. M. Barrie.

A lovely nearby dinner option on Lamb's Conduit Street is **Cígala** (no. 54; © **020/ 7405-1717**), a trendy but unpretentious Spanish restaurant that welcomes babies and children (for whom the extensive tapas menu is a good option).

2 In the Footsteps of Peter Pan

"You must see for yourselves that it will be difficult to follow Peter Pan's adventures unless you are familiar with the Kensington Gardens," begins J. M. Barrie's little-known but magical *Peter Pan in Kensington Gardens,* published in 1906. Indeed, you'll want to familiarize yourself with the wonderful **Diana Memorial Playground** in Kensington Gardens (p. 207), which rests where an older playground funded by Barrie once stood. Here in the gardens, Barrie befriended the Llewelyn Davies boys. While Barrie told them the tale that would become *Peter Pan,* the five boys dressed up and acted out stories. The character himself was inspired in part by Barrie's brother, who died at age 13, and in part by the boys themselves.

Peter Pan in Kensington Gardens, originally titled *The Little White Bird,* is the first appearance of Peter, the little boy who refuses to grow up; we meet him as a baby, living a wild life with birds and fairies in the middle of London. Today, the park has a suitably Peter Pannish theme (the centerpiece is a pirate ship, a stone crocodile resides here, and images from 1930s illustrations of Peter Pan are etched into the glass in The Home Under The Ground—named after the Lost Boys' dwelling—which houses the restrooms and playground attendant's office).

The house where Barrie lived, and where he wrote *Peter Pan,* is not far from Queensway Tube, at **100 Bayswater Rd.** Here you can see a blue heritage plaque attesting to the fact. Crossing the road, you can enter the park at Inverness Terrace Gate, and turn right to reach Diana Memorial Playground. When you and your kids have had your fill of the playground's many delights, you can refuel at the new **Cafe Boardwalk,** unless there's an ornithophobe (someone with a fear of birds) in the family—our last visit resembled a scene from Hitchcock's *The Birds,* with creatures dive-bombing onto our trays and even trying to peck a piece of muffin from my young one's hand!

Now stroll up **Broad Walk,** where the hero of *Peter Pan,* David, takes his little brother on walks. Before long you'll come to **Round Pond,** which David describes as "the wheel that keeps all the gardens going." Like David, you may want to stop and sail your toy yacht here—or perhaps even better, create your own stick-boat as described in the stories.

From the Round Pond you have a choice of paths, from relatively straight ones to the more higgledy-piggledy "Paths that Have Made Themselves." (David concludes that such paths must materialize at night, since he never sees them spring into life.) Take the one leading due east; at the next meeting of paths, carry on down towards the **Long Water** and turn left. Soon you'll reach the bronze **Peter Pan Statue,** decorated with fairies and woodland creatures. It was placed here in 1912; Barrie arranged for it to be installed in the middle of the night so that it retained its aura of enchantment, but he hadn't obtained permission from the authorities, and questions were asked in the House of Commons about an author's right to promote his own work in a public park. Luckily, it was allowed to stay (and was even bestowed with a plaque unveiled by Princess Margaret). Later given its own little fenced-off plot, it's now one of the city's best-loved statues. Despite this, Peter's pipes have been stolen several times by pranksters (the pipes have always been recovered or quickly replaced).

Walking back to the Bayswater Road, past the sparkling Italian fountains on your right and the little statue of the hugging bears on your left, you may be surprised by how little has changed here in a century. Barrie once remarked on the never-ending line of omnibuses here, and today those buses still chug up and down; this at least makes it easy to catch a ride back into central London.

3 Into the City & Back Through Time

It's not London's most family-friendly area, granted, but London's financial heart is where the British capital took seed. Alongside the glass and steel office blocks, you'll sight a fascinating patchwork of Roman remains, winding medieval alleys, centuries-old churches, and charming Victorian ale houses. You'll miss out if you don't dedicate a day or two to exploring the area's riches.

Approach the City from the Strand, along **Fleet Street,** famous as the erstwhile home of the British newspaper industry (now based mainly in Docklands). If you're of a literary bent, you might like to peek into the restored **Dr. Johnson's House** at 17 Gough Sq. (© 020/7353-3745), where the writer compiled the first comprehensive English dictionary. It's situated amidst a maze of courtyards and passages just off Fleet Street, bringing to mind Johnson's own words:

"If you wish to have a just notion of the magnitude of this city, you must not be satisfied with seeing its great streets and squares, but must survey the innumerable little lanes and courts."

Leading back from Gough Square to Fleet Street, **Ye Olde Cheshire Cheese** (© 020/7353-6170) in Wine Court Lane was a favorite not only with Johnson but with fellow writers Dickens and Thackeray. It also happens to be one of London's most child-friendly pubs, with two dining rooms where you can enjoy proper British grub such as roast beef and Yorkshire pudding, and steak-and-kidney pie. Take a look at the leather-bound visitors' books above the bar: They contain the names of prime ministers, lords, and ambassadors who supped here.

Carry on along Fleet Street, turning right after a couple of minutes down Bride Lane. **St. Bride's Church** (© 020/7427-0133) is said to have been the inspiration

---

Blink & You'll Miss It

Many people rush by one of London's oldest landmarks without realizing it. The **London Stone,** embedded into a wall opposite Cannon Street Tube station (in a building that was a Chinese bank at press time but was scheduled to be turned into offices), is believed by many historians to have marked the center of the Roman province of Britain. At that time, it would have stood on the grounds of the governor's palace, the remains of which were found beneath Bush Lane next to the Tube station.

Take a peek at the London Stone on your way down Cannon Street between St. Paul's and the Monument—it's at no. 111, set behind an iron grille. This small piece of limestone is a mere fragment of the original stone, which could have been up to 2.5m (8 ft.) high and was probably used as a marker to provide a reference point for travelers. What happened to the rest of it is a mystery that will probably remain unsolved.

---

behind the tiered wedding cake. The church was one of 51 city churches ravaged by the Great Fire of London but rebuilt by Sir Christopher Wren, the architect of St. Paul's Cathedral. Descend to its crypt to see some Roman and Saxon remains, including Roman pavement dated to A.D. 180.

Back onto Fleet Street, take a left after Ludgate Circus. Here you'll find the **Old Bailey** (© **020/7248-3277**), Britain's Central Criminal Court, which has seen the trials of criminals as notorious as Dr. Crippen and the Yorkshire Ripper. Kids 14 and over can watch trials from the public galleries if accompanied by an adult. The court occupies the site of Newgate Prison where, until 1868, crowds, including kids, gathered to watch public hangings. Many local children used to spend all day on these streets, enjoying the constant music and entertainment, including organ grinders, acrobats, and jugglers.

Back on Ludgate Hill, it's a short walk to Wren's masterpiece, **St. Paul's Cathedral** (p. 154), which Wren was commissioned to build after the Great Fire of London. To see where the mighty conflagration broke out, walk down Cannon Street for about 10 minutes to reach **The Monument** (p. 154), a column the height of which corresponds to the distance from its base to the king's bakery on **Pudding Lane.** This narrow street, then lined with timbered buildings, many of them housing cooking shops, was where the Great Fire took hold; it lasted 3 days and destroyed 80% of medieval London. The silver lining on this particular cloud, though, was that the fire killed off the rat population that carried the Plague (that had claimed the lives of 100,000 Londoners the previous year).

Continue east, along Eastcheap and then Great Tower Street, to visit **All Hallows by the Tower** (© **020/7481-2928**), the church from which famous London diarist Samuel Pepys watched the Great Fire. As well as containing one of London's two brass rubbing centers (the other is in St. Martin-in-the-Fields; see p. 185), it has a museum in its undercroft containing a perfectly preserved portion of Roman pavement (the floor of a late-2nd-century domestic house) beneath an arch dating from an original church on the site, founded in A.D. 675. Because it is located next to the **Tower of London** (p. 150), the church has dealt with its fair share of beheaded bodies, including those of Thomas More and Archbishop Laud. William Penn, founder of Pennsylvania, was baptized here and educated in the schoolroom (now the Parish Room), while John Quincy Adams, sixth president of the U.S., was married here in 1797.

Follow the wonderfully named Seething Lane northwards; more Roman walls and pavements were unearthed along here. This was also where Pepys lived—there's a bust of him in Seething Gardens. He's buried in St. Olave Hart Street (© **020/748-4318**), which Dickens renamed Saint Ghastly Grim because of the three skulls on its gateway. You might notice that the graveyard is nearly a meter higher than the floor of the church—this is partly a result of the number of Plague victims buried here in 1665.

In total contrast, just 5 minutes' walk northwest from here on Lime Street, you'll find the high-tech **Lloyd's Building.** Like the Pompidou Center in Paris, this building was designed by Sir Richard Roger and distinctly puts its services (lifts, power conduits, and water pipes) on the outside to leave the inside uncluttered. Though opened in 1984, it looks shockingly modern.

To go back in time again, make a detour to neighboring **Leadenhall Market,** a covered arcade dating from the 14th century and still full of traditional cheese mongers, fishmongers, and butchers, as well as restaurants and cafes. The entrance to the Leaky Cauldron in the first Harry Potter movie was filmed here. Alternatively, to stay in the hyper-modern world, continue up Lime Street and into St. Mary Axe to see Sir Norman Foster's jaw-dropping **Swiss Re Building,** nicknamed "The Gherkin" for its peculiar shape. It's a working building, but 45-minute tours of the common areas can be booked (£250/$475 per group of eight; © **020/7071-5023**).

Unless you refueled in Leadenhall Market, you're probably dropping with hunger by now, in which case you can combine a look around the country's oldest surviving synagogue, **Bevis Marks,** with lunch in its adjoining restaurant (© **020/7283-2220**). From the dining room you can see into the old Spanish and Portuguese house of worship with its chandeliers. The menu combines traditional Jewish fare such as chicken soup and matzo balls with inventive combos such as roast sea bass with mango salsa. When you leave, walk along the parallel street, **Houndsditch;** once the city's eastern boundary, it got its name in the days it was a furrow into which locals tossed their dead animals.

Liverpool Street Station rises to your right, but you'll want to head behind it, to a very unusual public space by the name of **Broadgate.** In pre-Roman and Roman times, this was a large marshland outside the city wall; it froze in winter, and local people skated here until the 12th century (a fact commemorated in its open-air winter ice rink; see p. 212). It's now full of sculptures that people are invited to touch and interact with, so it's a great place to bring kids. Pieces include Richard Serra's textured *Fulcrum* (into which you can step in order to look up at the sky); Stephen Cox's *Ganapath & Devi,* two stone figures based on the Hindu goddess Devi and the elephant god Ganesh; and Xavier Corbero's *The Broad Family,* consisting of three separate figures, a dog, and a ball. The space also plays host to free lunchtime entertainments and to City of London Festival events (p. 20) during the summer.

Make your way down Blomfield Street to **London Wall** which, as the name implies, follows the course of the wall built nearly 20 centuries ago to enclose the Roman city. It's now a modern thoroughfare, but you can still see part of the wall, while also catching a glimpse of **St. Alphage Garden** about 5 minutes' walk away. (The gates are sometimes locked but you can see them from the street.) Adjoining **Fore Street** was the first place where German bombs were dropped during World War II.

Round off your thoroughly historical day with a tour of the **Museum of London** (p. 168), built on the site of a Roman fort at the end of the London Wall; or relax in the tiny hidden gem of **Postman's Park** just south of it, with its beautiful tiled wall. The wall commemorates ordinary people who died while carrying out acts of courage in the 19th century, including children who were killed while trying to save their siblings or friends.

If you choose to stay in the area to dine, a branch of **Pizza Express** (℃ 020/7600-8880) actually straddles London Wall (the street), so that you can watch cars race by beneath you. You're also near the trendy restaurants of Smithfield Market, including **Smiths of Smithfield** (p. 132).

4 A Refreshing Thames Meander

Die-hard river fans might like to tackle the Thames in its entirety by walking the 350km (215-mile) Thames Path (p. 214), but mere mortals—particularly those with kids—must aim for more bite-size encounters with London's main waterway. There are few better places to do this than lovely, leafy **Chiswick,** another of London's "villages" popular with young families, not least because its historic pubs and gourmet restaurants are some of the most welcoming in the city for those with children.

Arriving in the neighborhood at Hammersmith Tube or bus station, head south along Hammersmith Bridge Road. Turn left at the river to reach **Riverside Studios** where, if it's Sunday morning, you can catch a family movie screening (p. 256). If you turn right at the river onto the Lower Mall, you'll soon pass through the refurbished **Furnival Gardens,** a popular patch of green from which to watch the annual **Oxford and Cambridge Boat Race** (p. 18). The path now becomes the Upper Mall, where you might stop at ivy-clad **Old Ship Inn** (no. 25; ℃ 020/8748-2593) to appreciate views of the river and of the jets swooping down into Heathrow to the west. If the weather's fine, you can sit out on the spacious terrace or first-floor balcony for excellent breakfasts (9am–noon) such as cinnamon French toast with cream and maple syrup, or for a wide-ranging and well-priced all-day menu featuring standard kids' dishes for just £3.50 ($6.70).

If the inn is too full, which it often is on summer weekends, a nearby child-friendly option is the colorful **Black Lion** on the site of a former piggery at South Black Lion Lane (℃ 020/8748-2639). Serving good food (including Sunday roasts) and real ales, it has a lovely courtyard with an ancient gnarled chestnut tree, and a rumored ghost. While waiting for this "resident ghost," an officer mistakenly shot a local bricklayer. Further up the street, on Black Lion Lane itself, **Cross Keys** (℃ 020/8748-3541) is another relaxing place to stop. It features original Victorian tiles and etched glass, a patio garden, board games, and good-value, simple cooking.

When you've replenished yourselves sufficiently, continue westward along the river, which has now become **Chiswick Mall,** a particularly scenic stretch with 17th- to 19th-century town houses complete with wrought-iron verandas. At the end, follow the road round into Church Street, halting perhaps at the partly 15th-century **church of St. Nicholas,** where you'll find tombstones (but not the graves) of local artistic giants J. M. Whistler and William Hogarth. **Hogarth's House** (℃ 020/8994-6757; Tues–Fri 1–5pm, Sat and Sun 1–6pm), at the top of Church Street, is now a gallery with some of his famous engravings and displays about his life. The wonderful walled garden surrounding it still boasts the painter's mulberry tree, and there are occasional kids' activities relating to the exhibitions.

Just a few minutes' walk west again, along Burlington Lane, is **Chiswick House** (℃ 020/8994-6757; Apr–Oct Wed–Fri and Sun 10am–5pm, Sat 10am–2pm), a fine

Palladian villa with amazing interiors (it was built in the 18th century to host parties for the London elite). The beautiful old park surrounding it, with a lake, a temple, classical statues, Italianate gardens, and a newly restored water cascade, has plenty of space for kids to run around in.

From here you're spoilt for choices. You could walk 20 minutes west to reach the little-visited **Kew Bridge Steam Museum** (p. 162) and neighboring **Musical Museum** (p. 168). By the time you've looked around those, you'll probably be hungry again. If so, you're in luck. There are a couple more historic riverside pubs on Thames Road: **Bell & Crown** (✆ 020/8994-4164), an old smuggler's haunt with excellent food, a bright conservatory, and outdoor seating; and **Bull's Head** (✆ 020/8994-1204), with its creaking floorboards, worn flagstones, and leaded windows. On weekends families jostle for space at the picnic benches on the towpath. Oliver Cromwell made this inn his HQ during the Civil War, and supposedly took refuge on the island you see opposite, hence its name—**Oliver's Island.** Alternatively, Chiswick High Road looping up from Kew Bridge has branches of the child-friendly chains **Est Est Est** (p. 111), where kids can wear chefs' hats and help cook their own pizza, **Giraffe** (p. 99)., and **Zizzi** (p. 111).

Another option is to head north from Chiswick House to shop at **Turnham Green Terrace** with its mass of kid-oriented stores: **Tots** (✆ 020/8995-0520) for smart clothes and accessories; **Something Nice** (✆ 020/8742-7135) for toys, gifts, and cards, plus Rift Kids shoes at the back; and **Snap Dragon** (✆ 020/8995-6618) for toys. There's also a branch of the excellent **Fishworks** seafood cafe (✆ 020/8994-0086; see p. 99), and **Theobroma Cacao** (✆ 020/8996-0431) chocolate shop, where you can drink hot chocolate and sample truffles. To the north, on The Avenue, is the **Little Trading Company** (✆ 020/8742-3152), selling kids' clothes and dress-up wardrobes, toys, books, videos, bikes, new and secondhand strollers, and secondhand furniture. A kids' hairdresser is on hand during certain days, usually Wednesday and Friday afternoons and Saturday mornings. Just to the south, on this northern stretch of Chiswick High Road, there's a branch of **Petit Bateau** (✆ 020/8987-0288; see p. 230), and on Devonshire Road leading back down to Hogarth's House is **Chiswick Shoes** (✆ 020/8987-0525). Farther along Chiswick High Road, by Turnham Green itself, there's a branch of Art 4 Fun (✆ 020/8994-4100; see p. 217), where you can get creative while enjoying drinks and snacks.

If shopping's not your bag, head back towards Hammersmith Tube. **Ravenscourt Park** (p. 204) has an adventure playground and a teahouse serving children's meals. Not far away, on Hammersmith Grove, you can round off your day with delicious food at the ultra-child-friendly **Chez Kristof** (p. 121).

8

For the Active Family

London may seem like one vast urban sprawl, but lovers of the great outdoors don't have to pine for open spaces. On the contrary, the city's parks make up one of the most advanced green lung systems found in a large urban space. Unlike the more pruned gardens of, say, Paris, London's parks are charmingly informal in style, though well maintained and lovingly nursed. And for the adventurous there are some pretty wild areas, too, in the form of windblown heaths and dense woods and forests.

Award-winning and innovative playgrounds also abound here, both outdoors and indoors. Workshop-based activities provide a calmer alternative for those who want to get active in London.

London already has world-class sports venues, many of which will be used to host Olympic Games events in 2012—from archery at Lord's cricket ground to tennis at Wimbledon. The Dome Arena, scheduled to open in 2007 (p. 257), will host Olympic gymnastics and basketball events. But most events will take place at a brand-new Olympic village, which will be built in lower Lee Valley, spurring regeneration of part of the city's largely deprived East End.

See www.sportengland.org for sports-related information and a searchable database of facilities.

1 Green London: The Top Parks

For **Hampstead Heath,** see p. 142. For **Thames Barrier Park,** see p. 155.

ROYAL PARKS

London is blessed with eight superb royal parks totaling about 2,023 hectares (5,000 acres), all of them free for visitors. Come to stroll, jog, play sports, splash about in the water, watch open-air theater or a pop concert, romp in the playgrounds, get friendly with wildlife, admire architecture and memorials, kick back, sunbathe, or enjoy a sedate picnic. All eight parks have fascinating histories, often as royal hunting grounds. See www.royalparks.gov.uk for full information.

Bushy Park It's hard to imagine that you can exhaust London's central parks, but this little-known space north of the river by Hampton Court Palace (p. 181) is worth venturing out of town for, not least for its interesting history. Its artificial waterway, the Longford River, was created by Charles I to supply the Tudor palace, and it later served as a center for planning Operation Overlord (the D-Day landings) under Eisenhower. This is the second largest royal park, providing a great spot for informal games, cycling, in-line skating, and skateboarding (allowed on all its roads—other parks are much more restrictive). There's also a playground, tennis courts (p. 213), an open-air pool and, on Chestnut Sunday in May, family entertainment that includes carousels, swing bands, face painting, and a parade. Hampton, Middlesex, TW12. ℭ 020/ 8979-1586. Train: Hampton Court.

Green Park   This one-time hunting and dueling ground is a short walk under the dramatic Wellington Arch (p. 156) from Hyde Park, which rather dwarfs it. Games aren't permitted here, but it's still a great place for sunbathing, picnicking, and strolling or jogging on its fine walkways. It's said that if you stand in the middle of the park on a quiet day, you can hear the gurgle of the subterranean Tyburn River that flows into the Thames. The park's main monument is the Queen Victoria Memorial, in honor of the monarch who survived three attempts on her life near this spot, in 1840, 1842, and 1849. Between Bayswater Rd., Park Lane, Knightsbridge, and West Carriage Dr., SW1. ℭ 020/7930-1793. Tube: Green Park.

Greenwich Park   This oldest enclosed royal park offers impressive views over the Thames towards the City from its hilltop location. As well as the historic Royal Observatory (p. 170) and some Roman remains, it contains a large deer, fox, and bird sanctuary known as The Wilderness; a tennis center (p. 213); space for informal games; a playground and boating pool; two cafes with gardens; and the Secret Garden Wildlife Center, hosting activities such as owl prowls. In summer, little ones can enjoy puppet shows and workshops. Between Crooms Hill, Romney Rd., Maze Hill, and Shooters Hill, SE10. ℭ 020/ 8858-2608. Tube: Greenwich DLR.

Hyde Park ★★★   The city's biggest central park—once Henry VIII's deer and wild boar hunting estate, and a dueling ground in the 18th century—is focused around The Serpentine, where you can hire a paddle boat or rowboat, or even swim in high summer (p. 214). That's just scratching the surface of Hyde Park, though—you can also horseback-ride (p. 211); in-line skate (p. 212); watch the famous soapbox ranters at Speakers' Corner (be aware that language can get fruity here, and hecklers aggressive); bounce around in the playgrounds (on the south side and by W. Carriage Dr.); visit the nature and wildlife education center, The Lookout, in the old police observation post; play everything from football to Frisbee on the informal sports field; enjoy a game of tennis on the "pay and play" courts (p. 213); and take a look at Diana, Princess of Wales Memorial Fountain, which opened in 2004 and has proven wildly popular—perhaps too much so, since paddling here is now forbidden after some visitors paddled a bit too vigorously.

You may also be lucky enough to catch a concert in the park by an international act such as REM or Pavarotti, though these sell out well in advance and you'll want to check the website before your visit. "Proms in the Park," relayed from inside Albert Hall onto giant screens, is another rousing experience (p. 249). The best dining option here is probably **The Dell** (ℭ 020/7706-0464), with its large terrace overlooking the Serpentine, but you can also choose among cafes, hot dog stands, and ice cream stands galore. If you come in or out by Victoria Gate, sneak a peek at the curious pet cemetery (p. 187). Between Bayswater Rd., Park Lane, Knightsbridge, and W. Carriage Dr., W2. ℭ 020/ 7298-7210. Tube: Hyde Park Corner, Lancaster Gate, or Marble Arch.

Kensington Gardens ★★★   Blending in with Hyde Park (of which it used to be a part), Kensington Gardens is home to Kensington Palace (p. 181), which was Princess Diana's last home. The princess is remembered both in the 11km (7-mile) Diana Memorial Walk, which begins here and winds through Hyde Park, Green Park, and St. James's Park; and in the Diana Memorial Playground on the north side of the

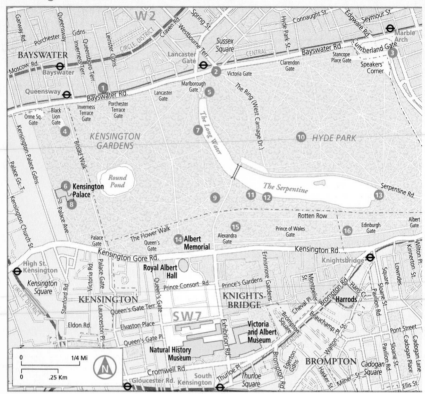

Gardens (p. 207). Games aren't encouraged outside the play park itself, but there's plenty else to keep Junior amused, including the Round Pond with its swooping bird life and its fish and eels (you can also bring model boats to sail); kids' entertainment during the summer; and magical Elfin Oak, a gnarled tree stump brought here from Richmond Park, carved with elves, fairies, and small creatures (it's by the entrance to the Diana playground). Also worth seeking out is the bronze statue of Peter Pan ; it was paid for by author J. M. Barrie, who lived nearby and often walked in the gardens. (See p. 194 for a Peter Pan walk.) Make time for afternoon tea at Kensington Palace's stunning Orangery restaurant; or visit the Serpentine Gallery, which hosts kids' art workshops (p. 217). Between Bayswater Rd., W. Carriage Dr., Kensington Rd., and Palace Green, W2. ℭ 020/7298-7210. Tube: Queensway or High St. Kensington.

Regent's Park ★★ This hunting ground and farming area under Henry VIII was transformed into an ornate park by 18th-century architect John Nash and is still surrounded by his glorious white-stuccoed terraces, giving it a very refined feel. Aside from the lovely formal gardens, the park contains an open-air theater (p. 248); the London Zoo (p. 143); three playgrounds; open-to-the-public tennis courts (p. 213); a huge new outdoor sports facility called The Hub that includes 16 mini-football pitches for

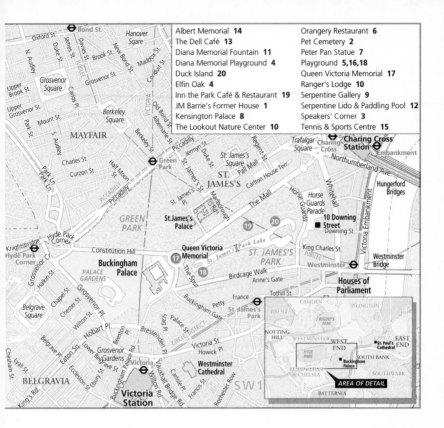

Albert Memorial **14**	Orangery Restaurant **6**
The Dell Café **13**	Pet Cemetery **2**
Diana Memorial Fountain **11**	Peter Pan Statue **7**
Diana Memorial Playground **4**	Playground **5,16,18**
Duck Island **20**	Queen Victoria Memorial **17**
Elfin Oak **4**	Ranger's Lodge **10**
Inn the Park Café & Restaurant **19**	Serpentine Gallery **9**
JM Barrie's Former House **1**	Serpentine Lido & Paddling Pool **12**
Kensington Palace **8**	Speakers' Corner **3**
The Lookout Nature Center **10**	Tennis & Sports Centre **15**

children; and large (for adults) and small (for kids) lakes for summer boating. Children flock here for summer puppet shows and for a popular "Wildlife for All" trailer (near Clarence Gate), which hosts events such as heron-watching. Cafes include The Honest Sausage, with lots of free-range and organic fare. For wonderful views of the London skyline, head for the park's summit, **Primrose Hill.** Between Marylebone Rd., Park Rd., Prince Albert Rd., and Albany St., NW1. ℂ 020/7486-7905. Tube: Regent's Park, Baker St., or Camden Town.

Richmond Park ⚱ London's biggest open space, situated south of the river, is famous for its fallow and red deer (remnants of its history as a deer park under Charles I), its ring-necked parakeets, and its vast array of wildlife, including swans, pike, and more than 1,000 beetle species (you can even adopt an endangered stag beetle!). Because of these unique inhabitants, the park has been designated a National Nature Reserve. Locals flock here to use the playground, play informal games of football and French cricket, cycle on the designated paths (bike rentals are available in summer from the car park near Roehampton Gate), or fish on Pen Ponds (p. 210). Adventurous types use the wooded areas and hill climbs for cross-country running and orienteering. The lovely Georgian Pembroke House with its garden is a fine place for a drink or a snack. Surrey, TW10. ℂ 020/8948-3209. Train: Richmond, then bus 371.

St. James's Park ⊛⊛   Once a marshland near a leper hospital, before it was converted into a deer nursery by Henry VIII, this wonderful park is dramatically set at the center of three palaces: Westminster (now the Houses of Parliament), St. James's, and Buckingham. In the middle of the park is romantic Duck Island, which is also home to some pelicans (the descendants of a pair presented to Charles II by the Russian ambassador in 1662) and more than 30 other bird species. You can come and watch the pelicans being fed daily at 3pm, and in summer there are guided tours of the island. The Inn the Park cafe and restaurant (p. 113) is excellent. The small but imaginative playground has unusual features, like giant wooden snails. Between Buckingham Palace, The Mall, Horse Guards Rd., and Birdcage Walk, W1. ℂ 020/7930-1793. Tube: St James's Park.

WEST LONDON
Lovely **Holland Park** ⊛ (ℂ 020/7471-9813; www.rbkc.gov.uk) is about a 20-minute stroll west of Kensington Gardens, in the chi-chi neighborhood between Notting Hill Gate and Shepherd's Bush. This is the one-time estate of Holland House, a Jacobean mansion now home to a scenic youth hostel, a posh restaurant, and an open-air opera venue in summer. Kids love both the forested areas with their wild rabbits and the more formal Kyoto Zen garden with its koi (carp), waterfalls, and bridges. The park also features free-roaming peacocks. An ecology center in Old Stable Yard sponsors vacation activities such as pond dipping, leaf painting, bug hunts, orienteering, and magpie walks for 5- to 10-year-olds (£3/$5.70); advance booking is required (ℂ 020/ 7471-9802). Other park amenities include an adventure playground, an under-8s sandpit play area, sports facilities (including tennis courts; p. 213), Whippersnappers music and movement classes (p. 218), and a cafe with plenty of outdoor seating, though a local hobo contingent sometimes gathers under the arches.

A little farther afield but popular with kids for its summer paddling pool and its children's farm with goats, rabbits, and ducks, **Queen's Park** (ℂ 020/8969-5661; www. cityoflondon.gov.uk) is the focal point of a hip family enclave north of Notting Hill. Other attractions include a playground, a sandpit play area for under-6s, a woodland walk, a sensory garden, pitch and putt, tennis courts, and a *pétanque* rink for boules. In summer you can enjoy the paddling pool, as well as bouncing castles, performances, and an annual event featuring stalls and entertainment such as clowns and jugglers. The child-friendly cafe (p. 113) is worth the trip in itself, but try to come before the students rush in at 3:30pm.

Back down alongside the Thames, bordered by Fulham Palace and Fulham Football Club, **Bishop's Park** (SW6; ℂ 020/8748-3020) has a pets' corner, aviaries, a paddling pool, a playground, riverside walks (where a scene from *The Omen* was filmed), sports amenities, and an ornamental lake. A similarly family-friendly space is **Ravenscourt Park** (W6; ℂ 020/8748-3020) in Hammersmith to the west, with a large paddling pool, a wooden adventure playground, an under-5s club, tennis courts, and basketball nets. The best time to come is summer, when the annual Play Day takes place, with arts and crafts, storytelling, pony rides, face painting, bouncy castles, clowns, and more. Or come on Bonfire Night, when there's a superb fireworks display created with kids in mind. The Tea House is a relaxing spot for breakfast, lunch, or snacks, and offers a children's menu.

Far to the west, just north of Osterley House (p. 184), **Brent Lodge Park** (W7; ℂ 020/8566-1929) has a maze, an animal center, and next to that an animal-themed playground for 2- to 10-year-olds, with monkey bars, treetop huts, and crocodile benches. Nearby is the largest flight of canal locks in London, **Hanwell Locks;** you can walk up or down the flight, which is very rural in feel, and admire the Three Bridges, where a railway runs beneath a canal which runs beneath a road, built by famous railway engineer Isambard Kingdom Brunel.

SOUTH LONDON

On the south bank of the Thames, Victorian **Battersea Park** (SW11; © 020/8871-7530) is a large area of woodland, lakes, and lawns set on an old dueling ground. It underwent a huge renovation starting in 2003, so now is a great time to come. The high point for kids is the children's zoo (p. 186), but there's also a boating lake, a deer and bird enclosure, a nature reserve with trails, a riverside promenade, an adventure playground, sports fields and tennis courts, bicycle rentals, a Japanese peace pagoda, impressive fountains, and the Pump House modern art gallery. Bonfire Night sees a massive fireworks display set to music and lights—one of the best in London.

East along the river, in the area properly called the South Bank, **Jubilee Gardens** by the BA London Eye is due to be transformed into a world-class £5-million to £6-million ($9.5-million to $11.5-million) public park to rival those in Paris and Barcelona by 2006 or 2007. Promised are a superb children's playground and a wide range of open-air entertainment and public events.

Much farther south but worth the trek, **Crystal Palace Park** (SE20; © 020/8778-9496) is most famous for its newly refurbished Dinosaur Park, built in 1854 (it was the world's first) and containing 30 life-size models of prehistoric creatures, plus a geological time trail. Though some of the models have been discredited by subsequent scientific discoveries (for instance, the iguanadons are shown on all fours, rather than upright), they're still fascinating. The park was also the site of the original Crystal Palace, built for the Great Exhibition of 1851, and a few remains of the structure can be seen, including the terrace arches and the sphinx. Elsewhere, you'll find the National Sports Centre (p. 208); a concert bowl by a lily-covered pond, a maze, a boating lake, and a play area.

Further west, **Wimbledon Common** (SW19; © 020/8778-7655; www.wpcc.org.uk), best known for its fictional Womble inhabitants (from a TV show about recycling critters living on the Common), is a much wilder space with woods, ponds, horse-riding tracks (p. 211), and the Windmill Museum and nature trail (p. 173). Together with adjoining **Putney Heath,** it hosts lots of events throughout the year, including funfairs, walks, bat watches, pond dipping, and fungi forays. To the west of this, beside Kew Gardens, the **Old Deer Park** (© 020/8831-6115) got its name from a hunting park created by James I in 1604. As well as a swimming complex called "Pools on the Park" (p. 214) and sports facilities, there are brilliant play areas here for tots and teens, plus circus big tops and funfairs during vacations.

EAST LONDON

London's East End isn't best known for its green or child-friendly spaces, which makes the family-oriented **Mile End Park** (© 020/7364-4147; www.mileendpark.co.uk) all the more a surprise. Subject to an ongoing multi-million-pound makeover, it now boasts an ecology park with a lake complex, a wind turbine, and wildlife habitats; an adventure park with a 21st-century metal spaceship tree house and more; a children's center with indoor and outdoor play (including under-5s drop-in sessions); an arts park with a gallery; a sports park with tennis courts and other amenities (a pool is scheduled to be ready by Feb 2006); a go-cart track; cycle tracks; a climbing wall (p. 209); and tree-lined Green Bridge (with restaurants beneath it). As if that weren't enough, there's also a healthy program of family events, including an annual carnival parade and Halloween celebration. A skateboarding, in-line skating, and BMX facility (complete with half-pipes) should be in place by the end of 2005.

A little more sedate, but worth a visit if you're in the area, is **Victoria Park** (© 020/ 7638-8891; www.towerhamlets.gov.uk), an appealing 19th-century canal-side park dubbed "the Regent's Park of the East End." Here you'll find deer and goats, play areas, a paddling pool, lakes, ponds, fountains, ornamental gardens, a Chinese summerhouse, tennis courts, and tearooms. Frequent festivals include fêtes, circuses, and open-air concerts. **Royal Inn on the Park** pub (© 020/8985-3321) by the main entrance has a beer garden and a good Sunday lunch, though service can be lousy.

Stretching 42km (26 miles) from the Thames at East India Dock Basin out of London into Hertfordshire, **Lee Valley Park** ⚘ (© 01992/702200; www.leevalleypark. org.uk) is an astonishing 4,047-hectare (10,000-acre) network of countryside areas and parks, urban green spaces, heritage sites, nature reserves, farms, lake and riverside trails, and sports and recreation centers, soon to be one of the Olympic 2012 sites. The vast array of activities on offer here include bird- and wildlife-watching, boating, cycling, walking, horseback riding (p. 211), and fishing. There's also an ice rink (p. 212), a swimming complex (p. 213), and a cart track. In fact, the park is so vast that you'll find it worthwhile to call in advance for advice on how to get the most out of your visit.

NORTH LONDON

North London's most central park is Islington's **Highbury Fields** (N5; © 020/7527-4971), with its acclaimed under-12s adventure playground, tennis courts, soccer pitches, picnic area, and cafe, but there are several very good green spaces farther north. **Clissold Park** (N16; © 020/8800-1021) is a true family park, with a small zoo featuring an aviary and a deer enclosure; a playground and a paddling pool; tennis and kids' mini-tennis courts; and pitching grounds. The cute cafe has lawn tables overlooking a river chock-full of ducks and swans. Combine a visit here with a trip to **Abney Park Cemetery & Nature Reserve** (p. 189) along the same street, then explore the quirky little shops, restaurants, and cafes of bohemian but family-friendly Stoke Newington, known affectionately as "Stokey" by locals.

Over to the west, not far from Hampstead, **Waterlow Park** ⚘ (N6; © 020/7974-1693; www.camden.gov.uk) is quite secluded and has remained a bit of a hidden gem. It's gorgeous, though, with its green slopes, three lakes, wonderful views of the City and south London, and tennis courts. Kids head here for its toddlers' playground, its aviary (used as a recovery center for injured birds), and most of all for Lauderdale House, with its vastly popular workshops and shows (p. 253), as well as its cafe terrace.

Farthest north of all is **Alexandra Park** (© 020/8365-2121; www.alexandrapalace. com), a 79-hectare (196-acre) hilltop park best known for its panoramic views over London. Surrounding the reconstructed Victorian Alexandra Palace (from which the BBC made the first public TV transmissions in 1936), the park has a boating lake, a pitch-and-putt golf course, a conservation area, an animal enclosure with deer and donkeys, a playground, a skateboarding park, and a cafe. Come for one of the vacation family funfairs, or for the superb Bonfire Night fireworks display, when there are indoor and outdoor funfairs and a food festival. There's also a year-round ice rink inside Alexandra Palace.

Real Wild London

Halfway between Alexandra Park and Hampstead Heath, **Highgate Wood** (✆ **020/8444-6129;** www.cityoflondon.gov.uk) was declared "an open space for ever" by London's Lord Mayor in 1886 and, astonishingly for space located in such an urban area, it's blossomed over the years into a dense, ancient forest with an array of wildlife. This is one of the best places in the city for a lung-expanding walk, even—or perhaps especially—on a downright chilling morning, when its winding, leaf-strewn pathways are at their most romantic. If you want something more structured, there are nature trails, sporting grounds, and two award-winning playgrounds, one for older kids and one for tots, with plenty of features for youngsters with disabilities. An imaginative program of events takes place year-round: readings at the Story Telling Tree, bird-of-prey displays, beetle safaris, and bat watches. Afterwards, repair to the delightful Pavilion Cafe for a warming mug of chocolate inside or outside on its terrace. (The cafe hosts live jazz on Thurs evenings in summer.) Then visit nearby Ripping Yarns bookshop for its secondhand kids' classics (p. 224).

If Highgate Woods haven't made you feel all Blair Witch, you might want to venture out to **Epping Forest** (✆ **020/8508-0028;** www.eppingforest.co.uk), on the far northeastern outskirts of the city. London's largest public space, this ancient woodland covers almost 2,428 hectares (6,000 acres) of grassland, heath, rivers, bogs, and ponds, and is a fantastic place to bike and horseback-ride (p. 211). It's a good idea to get your bearings at the Conservation Centre at High Beech, Loughton, at the end of the road next to the Kings Oak pub (✆ **020 8508 0028**), where you can get information and advice, books, and maps.

2 Playgrounds

Most of the parks described above have playgrounds, usually separate ones for toddlers and older children. **Highgate Wood**'s playgrounds are particularly good, while **Phoenix Gardens** is a handy central spot. For many of London's 80-plus adventure playgrounds, see **www.londonplay.org.uk/adventure-playgrounds.html**; for information on adventure playgrounds designed with children with disabilities in mind, see **www.kidsactive.org.uk**. Also keep an eye out for notice boards near these playgrounds, which often advertise children's events not publicized elsewhere.

Coram's Fields ★★   This wonderful 2.8-hectare (7-acre) playground is located on the site of the 18th-century Foundling Hospital for abandoned children. (See p. 164 for the Foundling Museum.) This is a proper kids' sanctuary in a rather deprived area of Bloomsbury, with adults allowed in only if accompanied by a child—safety is paramount here. Inside the charming space are an excellent adventure playground, an under-5s sandy play area, a toddlers' club, a summer paddling pool, a fountain, an animal-petting enclosure with goats, sheep, and ducks, all-weather sports pitches, and an outdoor cafe to which parents can retreat when things get too hectic. Guilford St., WC1. ✆ 020/7837 6138. Tube: Russell Sq.

Diana Memorial Playground ★★★   London's truly innovative play park has a loose Peter Pan theme—a previous playground on the site was funded by the book's author, J. M. Barrie. (See p. 194 for more information.) Designed for kids up to 12, it is based around an almost life-size pirate ship with a mast that older kids can climb, and has teepees, a beach cove with fossil imprints for paddling, "tree phones" allowing kids to communicate across the playground, a tree house encampment suitable for wheelchair users, and more. On summer weekends, locals and visitors battle it out for lawn space on which to spread their picnic blankets, and the cafe becomes a scene of terrifying chaos. Try to come during the week or out of season. Kensington Gardens, W8. ℂ 020/7298-2141. www.royalparks.gov.uk. Tube: Queensway.

3 Sports & Games

If you're staying at an expensive hotel or in a serviced apartment, you'll likely have access to a swimming pool (see p. 63 for hotels with pools) and health club, either directly or through temporary membership to a nearby facility, though gym equipment is usually out of bounds for under-16s. For comprehensive listings of municipal centers across the capital, as well as private health clubs, see www.health-club.net.

One of London's best general sports venues is **Westway Sports Centre** (1 Crowthorne Rd., W10; ℂ 020/8969/0992; www.westway.org/sports/wsc), which has Britain's biggest indoor climbing center, outdoor climbing (inside a road roundabout!), eight indoor tennis courts, four public clay tennis courts, four Eton Fives (handball) courts, six football pitches, a gym accessible to those with disabilities, a basketball court and hoops, and a cafe and sports bar. Farther to the south, **Crystal Palace National Sports Centre** (Ledrington Rd., SE19; ℂ 020-8778-0131; www.bromley.gov.uk) is a world-class stadium used for national and international competitions. Facilities include four swimming pools, a diving pool with springboards and platforms, a climbing wall, a dance studio, and an indoor playground (p. 216). In summer, "Camp Energy" holiday courses are offered for kids of various ages for a whole range of sports, from basketball to trampolining to snorkeling. The **Central YMCA** (112 Great Russell St, WC1; ℂ 020/7343-1700; www.ymcaclub.co.uk) is another option--a well-located, good-value, and well-equipped sports club.

If you're here for a while and want to stay fit, one of the best options is to become a member of **Esporta Swiss Cottage** (02 Centre, 255 Finchley Rd.; ℂ 020/7644-2400; www.esporta.com/swisscottage), which has a Zone Junior Club for 6- to 12-year-olds, with children's fitness classes and activities, games, painting, drawing, and cooking, plus a day nursery for kids ages 6 weeks to 6 years (£3.50/$6.70 per hour on top of membership). While the kids are otherwise detained, parents can make use of a 25m (82-ft.) swimming pool, fitness studios (one with holistic classes), saunas, steam rooms, sun beds, beauty salons and treatment rooms, and a bar and brasserie. A separate toddlers' pool offers swimming lessons for kids 3 and up. This is such a family-oriented club that it even holds an annual picnic in Golders Hill Park, with games and activities.

BIKING

Traffic-frenzied London, let it be said, is not a great place for cyclists—dedicated lanes are scarce, even in many of the major parks, which allow you to cut through but not take a leisurely tour. If your heart's set on a two-wheeler tour of the capital, arm yourself with a copy of the extremely informative **Haynes' London Cycle Guide** (£8.99/$7.60 from www.haynes.com), which points out the best areas for cycling, from touristed sites to lesser-known areas such as waterways, many of them traffic-free. Alternatively, the **London Cycle Network** has a series of 19 free local guides with routes and useful contacts such as cycle stores—see www.tfl.gov.uk or call **020/ 7222-1234** to order one. The same website has details on a variety of leisure routes, including the royal parks, the Thames path, and an "ice cream route." For organized trips by the **London Bicycle Tour Company,** see p. 190.

One very gentle, civilized option for parents with young children are the free **PPP (Parks, Playgrounds, and Pubs) rides** ⚐ run on the last Sunday of each month from Wimbledon Tube station forecourt. Rides start at 10:30am, cover about 16 to 24km (10–15 miles), and take in plenty of kid-friendly stops along quiet, mainly traffic-free streets. Kids are transported in bike seats or trailers, or on their own bikes, depending on age. There's no need to book, but information is available at ✆ **020/8672-3990.** For a list of recommended cycle-hire shops in London, visit www.lcc.org.uk; the closest to Wimbledon station is **Smith Brothers** (14 Church Rd., SW19; ✆ **020/8946-2270**).

Great fun is also to be had with **London Recumbents** ⚐⚐ (✆ **020/8299-6636;** www.londonrecumbents.com), which hires out low-slung, horizontal bikes, family tandems, and bikes with trailers that you can take for a spin around Dulwich Park (usually daily) or Battersea Park (weekends and holidays; see p. 205), both in south London. Other attractive places to cycle are tranquil **Lee Valley Park** (p. 206) and **Epping Forest** (p. 207).

BOWLING

The most central addresses for this good, cheap, rainy-day standby are **First Bowl,** at 17 Queensway just off Kensington Gardens (W2; ✆ **020/7229-0172**), with 12 full-size bowling lanes, plus a modern ice rink, video games, and a burger bar; **Funland** in the Trocadero Center in Piccadilly Circus (p. 259), with 10 lanes; and **Namco Station** in Country Hall on the South Bank (p. 259), with 12 ultraviolet lanes and a special floor that makes shoe hire unnecessary. Out of the center, **Streatham Megabowl** (142 Streatham Hill, SW2; ✆ **0871/550-1010;** www.megabowl.co.uk) has 36 lanes and offers "Cosmic Nights" with music, lights, and fluorescent bowling balls. It also has American pool tables, a space-age laser-gun zone, and a games zone.

CLIMBING

London is basically devoid of hills and mountains, so your best option for a spot of climbing is the fairly central **Westway Sports Centre** (p. 208), which contains Britain's largest indoor climbing complex. Facilities here include indoor bouldering, a vertigo-inducing high-ropes adventure course with rope ladders, balance beams, caving areas, and a totem pole; there are outdoor walls as well. Junior taster sessions for kids 5 and over take place on Saturday from 3 to 5pm and cost £8 ($15) each, but sessions are limited to six participants, so book well ahead. Otherwise, it costs £5 ($9.50) per casual climbing session, £7.50 ($14) for adults (these are peak prices for weekends and for after 5pm on weekdays).

Castle Climbing Centre (✆ **020/8211-7000;** www.castle-climbing.co.uk) is another excellent facility a little farther out of town in an old pumping station in Manor House, north London. Children of any age can climb here under the supervision of a registered adult climber, and 8- to 16-year-olds can sign up for Geckos, a kids' climbing school providing supervision and instruction, including 3-day beginners' and intermediate courses. French- and Spanish-speaking instructors are available. Occasional trips are made to outdoor climbing venues, such as the Southern Sandstone in Kent and beautiful Peak District National Park. Prices are £9 ($17) for adults after a one-time registration fee of £4 ($7.60), and £4.50 ($8.50) for under-16s.

Also a ways out of town, the East End's **Mile End Climbing Wall** (© **020/8980-0289;** www.mileendwall.org.uk) is an established center that has trained some of the country's top climbers and mountaineers but welcomes total novices. Its popular Kids' Club "fun-level" sessions for children 8 to 18 cost £6.50 ($12) and last 90 minutes. There's also a climbing wall at **Crystal Palace National Sports Centre** (p. 208).

For something a little more offbeat, visit Ellis Brigham's winter sports shop at 3–11 Southampton St. in Covent Garden, WC2, to experience the **Vertical Chill,** an 8m (26-ft.) concave real ice-climbing wall running up through its two stories. Lessons cost £40 ($76). A 1-hour Climb & Hire with equipment, for experienced climbers, is £30 ($57). There's a lower age limit of 12, but those parents with under-16s should discuss their kids' fitness, strength, and experience at the time of booking (© **020/7395-1010;** www.verticalchill.com).

DANCE

Danceworks ☆ (16 Balderton St., W1; © **020/7629-6183;** www.danceworks.co.uk) offers Europe's biggest selection of dance, fitness, and yoga classes (168, to be precise) in a listed Victorian building. The Xpress Yo'Self Kids' Club is a 90-minute street-dance class (£3/$5.70) for 10- to 16-year-olds involving jazz styles such as hip-hop, jiving, and lindy hop. For younger kids, a fantastic, extremely central facility is **Drill Hall** ☆☆ (16 Chenies St., WC1; © **020/7307-5063;** www.drillhall.co.uk). It offers Saturday-morning drop-in creative dance classes for children 6 months to 3 years, 3 to 5 years, and 5 to 11 years. Saturday-afternoon Little Latin Rhythms classes are for 5 to 8s and 8 to 11s. Both classes are excellent value at £2.50 a pop; caregivers get in free. However, you must sign up for the Latin American classes 4 weeks in advance.

There are also highly popular dance and drama workshops at **The Tricycle** ☆☆ theater and cinema in Kilburn (p. 253). *Note:* This is a generally run-down and scruffy neighborhood, clustered around a hellishly busy main road out of London, although it's up-and-coming.

FISHING

London, need it be said, is not fishing central. However, attractive places at which to while away a few hours with a rod and line include **Lee Valley Park** (p. 206), **Syon Park** (p. 187), **Clapham Common,** and **Pen Ponds** in lovely Richmond Park (p. 203). The latter are open July to February and offer special rates of £8 ($15) per permit for children 10 to 17. Note that anyone over 12 who fishes in fresh water in England or Wales must have an Environment Agency rod license, which is available from post offices and costs from £3.25 ($6.20) for 1 day to £64 ($121) for a season, depending on age and the type of fish caught. The fine, if you get caught without a license, is huge.

See www.londonanglers.net for a list of waters in and around London, mainly canal towpaths, that can be fished on one of the good-value **day tickets** (£ 3.50/$6.60) for adults, £ 1.50/$2.85 for children).

FLYING

For an uplifting experience, **Adventure Balloons** (© **0125/284-4222;** www.adventure balloons.co.uk) offer 1-hour early-morning or evening flights from Hampshire over London and its surrounds, with no lower age limit, though there's no point in bringing along kids who aren't tall enough to see over the basket sides (about 1.1m or 42 in.). Allow 3 to 4 hours for the experience, including preparation of the balloon, deflation and packing of the balloon, and return to the launch site in a retrieval vehicle. (Balloons cover 3–32km/2–20 miles, with the direction determined by the wind.) Flights cost £165 ($314) per person and take place shortly after dawn on weekday mornings from May to mid-August.

Alternatively, try a 30-minute **helicopter sightseeing tour** from Elstree Aerodrome in north London, available on Sunday and selected Saturdays (*✆* **020/8953-4411; www.cabairhelicopters.com/sightseeing**). Flights (£149/$283 per person) follow the route of the Thames as far east as the Thames Flood Barrier, while the captain gives a full commentary.

GOLF

Little legs tend to do better with **pitch-and-putt** short golf courses than full-sized versions; two of the most convenient are at **Queen's Park** in west London (p. 204) and at **Alexandra Park** to the north of the city (p. 206). There are also putting facilities in royal **Hyde Park** and **Greenwich Park** (p. 201). For larger-scale golfing action, there's either central **Regent's Park** (p. 202), offering coaching, membership, and ad-hoc "turn up and play" (*✆* **020/7724-0643**); or **Richmond Park** (p. 203), which has two public 18-hole courses used for pay and play, a 16-bay driving range, a large pro shop, and group lessons for kids on Saturday mornings (*✆* **020/8876-3205**).

HORSEBACK RIDING

London may not seem like the most obvious place for horseback riding, but the sport has a long tradition in the city—all those lovely mews houses you see were originally built for horses and carriages—and there are wonderfully atmospheric places to ride here. The best riding spot of all, perhaps, and certainly the most central, is **Hyde Park** ★★★, which has two riding arenas, or *maneges,* plus two designated bridleways, the North Ride and the South Ride. Trotting along the park's sandy tracks between modern and classic buildings and frolicking park-goers is a quintessential London experience, especially on a beautiful summer evening. **Hyde Park Stables** (63 Bathurst Mews, W2; *✆* **020/7723-2813;** www.hydeparkstables.com) welcomes beginners, and its horses and ponies are extremely docile beasts. Group rides start at £40 ($76) per person, boots and hats included.

Another fine royal park for equestrian excursions is **Richmond Park** (p. 203), which has five stables nearby (*✆* **020/8948-3209** for details). Prices are a little lower than in Hyde Park, and some ponies can be ridden by kids as young as 1½. One of the firms, **Wimbledon Village Stables** (24a/b High St., SW9; *✆* **020/8946-8579;** www. wvstables.com), also offers rides on **Wimbledon Common** (p. 205). Family rides or lessons are an option, and there are 3-day holiday courses (£120/$228) involving riding instruction, pony feeding and grooming, tack cleaning, and gymkhana (obstacle-riding) games.

In a more unlikely setting beneath west London's main flyover, **Westway Stables** (*✆* **020/8964-2140;** www.westwaystables.co.uk) has been refurbished and boasts a shiny new arena. Riding takes place either on the large outdoor sand area or on the nearby open space of Wormwood Scrubs, which is where folks used to come to hone their skills before exposing themselves to high society on Rotten Row. Prices are keen. For really horse-mad kids, Pony Days feature grooming and other aspects of horsemanship, riding tuition, gymkhana games, quizzes, and other fun activities (half-day £28/$53, full day £50/$95).

On the other side of London, **Lee Valley Riding Centre** in Lee Valley Park (*✆* **020/ 8556-2629**) has indoor and outdoor arenas and cross-country trails. Pretty far east but specializing (not exclusively) in riding for adults and kids with disabilities is **Docklands Equestrian Centre** (2 Claps Gate Lane, Beckton, E6; C 020/7511-3917). Finally, Epping Forest (p. 207) is another good spot for riding.

ICE SKATING

London's loveliest rink, in the splendid 18th-century courtyard of **Somerset House** ★★★ (p. 176), is open for a lamentably short period each year, from late November to the end of January. This means tickets and space are difficult to obtain, so it's often necessary to book ahead. Skating generally takes place from 10am to 10pm, with occasional late skates to 11:15pm. They cost £9.50 ($18) per hour for adults (or £11/$21 in the evening); £6 ($11) for kids, and £27 ($51) for a family ticket (all including skate hire). The venue is superb whenever you come, but in the evening, flaming torches and architectural lights illuminate the building's classical facades. Don't forget a post-skate hot chocolate at the cafe overlooking the rink.

Another outdoor rink, **Broadgate Ice Arena,** is open for a longer period between November and April. It's in the City, close to Liverpool Street station (3 Broadgate, EC2; C 020-7505-4068). There's also one at **Marble Arch** (C 0870/534-4444; www. marblearchonice.co.uk) over the Christmas period. This gets less crowded than Somerset House because it's a whole lot less atmospheric, but it is handily situated for a skate before or after a spot of Christmas shopping, and you get to enjoy the slightly surreal sight of local Middle Eastern women skating in full traditional chador. There's talk of the rink shifting slightly to Speakers' Corner in Hyde Park (p. 201) in future years. You might find other festive open-air rinks at **Greenwich, Kew Gardens,** and **Hampton Court Park,** since new ones seem to materialize each year; see www.londonskaters.com for up-to-date information.

Current year-round indoor facilities include **First Bowl** (p. 209) near Hyde Park, which used to be huge but got scaled down to fit in the bowling lanes and gaming facilities; **Lee Valley Ice Centre** (Lee Bridge Rd., Leyton; C 020/8533-3154) in Lee Valley Park (p. 206), which offers family sessions and a club night with a music-and-light show; **Alexandra Palace** (p. 206), where you can also ice cart; and **Streatham Ice Arena** (386 Streatham High St., SW16; C 020/8769-7771; www.streathamicearena.co.uk).

IN-LINE SKATING

There aren't many places to in-line skate in the capital, since most parks ban the sport. Your best bets are **Hyde Park** and **Kensington Gardens** (p. 201), especially alongside the Serpentine, but keep to the marked areas or you might get fined. Informal **mass sunset skates** through London set out from here Wednesday evenings from April to the end of September (and on occasional other days, starting from the bandstand opposite Serpentine Rd.). You'll need to be able to keep up with the skaters; otherwise, a marshal will ask you to drop out.

If you've never skated before, **SkateFresh** (www.londonskate.com) offers free lessons in Hyde Park; see the website for details. In summer 2005 they also introduced drop-in inline hockey classes for kids ages about 6 to 11. **Bananablade** rents skates 7:15 to 8pm from the Hyde Park end of Grosvenor Crescent, SW1, but you must pay in advance via www.bananablades.com. There are also free 8pm **Friday-night skates** from the Wellington Arch at Hyde Park Corner, covering 16 to 19km (10–12 miles) along a variety of routes and taking about 2 hours. These are organized by **Citiskate** (see www.thefns.com, or call C 020/7731-4999). Citiskate also offers lessons and skate rentals, and runs the new **Easy Peasy Skate** in **Battersea Park** ★★ (p. 205) on

Saturdays at 10:30am; it's a slow skate that avoids roads and hills, and is therefore particularly great for kids.

Other places to rent skates are **Slick Willies** (12 Gloucester Rd., SW7; ✆ 020/ 7225-0004); and **Club Blue Room,** Marble Arch Tower (12–14 Edgware Rd., W2; ✆ 020/7724-4884). It costs about £10 to £15 ($19–$29) per day. Those who want to go it alone might like to try **Bushy Park** (p. 200), where you can skate wherever you like.

MOTOR SPORTS

Petrolheads keen to experience the thrill of driving real racing carts can head for south London's **Streatham Kart Raceway** (390 Streatham High St., SW16; ✆ 020/8677- 8677; www.playscape.co.uk), which offers practice sessions for kids ages 8 to 16 on weekdays. There are also 4-hour summer schools. Practice sessions cost £20 ($38) for 30 minutes, £30 ($57) for an hour. **F1 City Racing Circuit** out in the East End (Gate 119, Connaught Bridge, Royal Victoria Dock, E16; ✆ 020/7476 5678; www.f1city. co.uk) also offers junior racing in 72kmph (45mph) single-engine carts on their new 500m (1,640-ft.) Monaco outdoor circuit, costing £20 ($38) for 15 minutes, £30 ($57) for 30 minutes, and £45 ($86) for 45 minutes.

SKATEBOARDING

London's unofficial skateboarding hot spots are under the Royal Festival Hall at **South Bank Centre** (p. 243) and at **Shell Centre** just along the road; for insider tips, see www. knowhere.co.uk. You can also unofficially skate under the **Westway** flyover in west London, although at Acklam Road, W10, you'll find the **Playstation Skate Park** ★★ (✆ 020/8969-4669), with a great layout, a huge variety of ramps, occasional visits from pro skaters, and a shop. It's not cheap, at £6 ($11) for a 4-hour session, and you should avoid Saturdays, when it's very busy.

SWIMMING

Britain's capital is a surprisingly great place to swim, with some atmospheric venues, both indoor and out (for the latter, see the "Alfresco Swimming at London's Lidos" box below). One of the best is **Ironmonger Row Baths** near Old Street (Ironmonger Row, EC1; ✆ 020-7253-4011), a 1930s pool with original features and Turkish baths (steam room, massage slabs, and an icy plunge pool) where parents can take turns relaxing. At the other end of the extreme, **Crystal Palace National Sports Centre** (p. 208) is far from cozy but has world-class swimming and diving facilities.

If you're more interested in swooshing down slides than swimming laps, the following pools have extras, which may include wave machines, beach areas, rapids, and flumes: **Archway Leisure Centre,** N19 (✆ 020/7281-4105), **Janet Adegoke Leisure Centre,** W12 (✆ 020/8743-3401), **Latchmere Leisure Centre,** SW11 (✆ 020/ 7207-8004), **Leyton Leisure Lagoon,** E10 (✆ 020/8558-4860), **Tottenham Green Leisure Centre,** N15 (✆ 020/8365-0322), and **Waterfront Leisure Centre,** SE18 (✆ 020/8317-5000). Despite its name, vast **Broxbourne Lido** (✆ 01992/702200) is an indoor pool in Lee Valley Park (p. 206), with a wave machine and a learner pool, as well as a softplay area.

TENNIS

Visitors keen to get a tennis fix should check out a trio of moderate and inexpensive hotels in Bloomsbury's Cartwright Gardens. These offer free use of four communal

Alfresco Swimming at London's Lidos

Given the generally perilous state of Britain's weather, there's an amazing number of outdoor pools in London, and many of them are quite stunning reminders of architecturally more glamorous times, as well as family life-savers on long, hot summer days. One of the best-known is the 1930s **Brockwell Lido** ⚐⚐ (Brockwell Park, Dulwich Rd., SE24; ✆ 020/7274-3088; www.thelido.co.uk), rescued from oblivion after being sponsored by water bottler Evian, and boasting paddling pools and Whippersnappers activity sessions (music classes) for kids (p. 218).

Another 1930s Art Deco venue is **Charlton Lido** (Hornfair Park, SE7; ✆ 020/8317-5000; www.greenwich.gov.uk), set in a landscaped park and consisting of an unheated 50m (164-ft.) pool, a children's splash pool, sunbathing areas, and a cafe. South of the river, **Tooting Bec Lido** ⚐ (Tooting Bec Rd., SW16; ✆ 020/8871-7198; www.wandsworth.gov.uk) was London's first purpose-built (1906) open-air pool, and is one of Europe's biggest. As well as a Jacuzzi and saunas, added in the last few years, it has a paddling pool with toy animals.

Richmond's **Pools on the Park** complex (Twickenham Rd., TW9; ✆ 020/8940-0561) consists of a 33m (108-ft.) outdoor swimming pool with a sun-bathing area, plus an indoor and a learners' pool. Not too far away on the north bank of the river, **Hampton Heated Open Air Pool** ⚐ (✆ 020/8255-1116; www.hamptonpool.co.uk) on the western boundary of Bushy Park (p. 200) is an excellent lido built in 1922, with a springboard and two small slides, as well as a smaller teaching pool.

One of London's most famous outdoor venues is in the heart of the city, in Hyde Park (p.201), in the form of a marked-off area of the **Serpentine** ⚐⚐⚐

tennis courts, as well as free racket and ball loan (p. 69). The Four Seasons hotel in Canary Wharf (p. 92) also allows access to an indoor court.

Otherwise, most larger London parks have courts, with some of the best in the royal parks (p. 200), which encourage visitors to turn up and play (you can book ahead, too). Prices tend to be £8 to £10 ($15–$19) per hour. Some offer coaching; among these are **Hyde Park** (✆ 020/7262-3474), **Greenwich Park** (✆ 020/8858-2608), and **Bushy Park** (✆ 020/8831-6132). **Holland Park** (p. 204) also has some smart central courts (✆ 020/7471-9813). **Westway Sports Centre** (p. 208) has London's only public clay courts, plus eight indoor courts. **Regent's Park** (✆ 020/7486-4216) also offers coaching, and includes two kids' half-size courts that can be booked for up to 30 minutes at a time.

WALKING & ORIENTEERING

London is a great city for strolling, whether through its parks, round its street markets, or along its canal banks. If you're feeling more energetic, there's a **Green Chain** (www.greenchain.com) network of walks from three points along the Thames to Crystal Palace in south London, threading its way through 27km (17 miles) of open space, boating lake (℡ 020/7706-3422; www.serpentinelido.com). It's open June to September, but some hardy members of its swimming club take the plunge on Christmas morning. It has a paddling pool, a sandpit, swings, and a slide, and on summer afternoons a kids' entertainer. Another central option is the outdoor pool at **Oasis Sports Centre** (32 Endell St., WC2H; ℡ 020/7831-1804; www.camden.gov.uk), on the site of a *bagnio* (Turkish bath) used by Queen Anne and now surrounded by office blocks, making it peculiarly urban in feel. Even on a chilly winter's day, it's more popular than the center's indoor pool, though it's more of a lap pool than somewhere to splash around.

North of here, there has long been a tradition of free open-air swimming in the single-sex (nude) and mixed **ponds on Hampstead Heath** ★★, NW3 (℡ 020/7482-7073; www.cityoflondon.gov.uk). The men's pool is a particularly fascinating clublike environment with a cast of chess-players, weight lifters, and readers, as well as swimmers and sunbathers. The ponds are fed by natural springs, so they're pretty clean, but they are closed for treatment if algae levels get out of control. Under-16s need to be accompanied, and under-8s are not allowed. Also on the heath, the unheated **Parliament Hill Lido/Hampstead Heath Lido** ★★, NW5 (℡ 020/7485-3873), dates back to 1938 but has just been refurbished. Farther north, **Park Road Pools** (Hornsey, N8; ℡ 020/8341-3567) are pleasant warmed pools with grassy banks for sunbathing and enjoying ice creams and cold drinks from the cafe. Toddlers love both the children's pool and the fountain.

For fascinating background on London's lidos, with lots of historical photos, see www.lidos.org.uk.

which takes in wildlife, ruins, farms, playgrounds, and the model dinosaurs of Crystal Palace Park (p. 205). The website has an excellent page on walking with kids and keeping them amused along the way, plus details of all the routes. You can buy an official Routes Pack (£3.50/$6.60 via the website) with detailed color maps.

If you're interested in orienteering in the city (orienteering is a walk—or run—during which you use a map to find your own way to checkpoints or "control sites"), there's a course of varying difficulties on **Hampstead Heath** (p. 142), with maps and compasses available from the Information Center next to the Lido.

WATERSPORTS

There are few finer ways of spending a steamy city afternoon than taking a boat out on the lakes in **Hyde Park** ★★ (p. 201) or **Regent's Park** ★★ (p. 202). For something altogether more structured and windblown, you can try **Surrey Docks Watersports Centre** (Rope St., off Plough Way, Greenland Dock, Rotherhithe, SE16; ℡ 020/7237-4009; www.fusion-lifestyle.com). The center offers canoeing, windsurfing, and sailing for kids, on both inland and tidal waters, plus spectator events such as regattas and dragonboat racing. Or try **Docklands Sailing & Watersports Centre** (35a West-ferry Rd., Millwall Dock, E14; ℂ 020/7537/2626; www.dswc.org), which has access to both a large sheltered dock area and the River Thames. In west London, **Canalside Activity Centre** (Canal Close, W10; ℂ 020/8968-4500; www.rbkc.gov.uk) offers canal-based watersports such as kayaking, together with special kids' activities that include trampolining and martial arts.

YOGA

Yoga of all forms has seen a massive revival over the last few years, and that includes yoga for kids. As well as teaching kids to control their emotions and relieve anxiety, yoga can increase their concentration levels and their physical strength. The **Special Yoga Centre** in Queen's Park (Pember House, Pember Rd., NW10 5LP; ℂ 020/8933-5475; www.specialyoga.org.uk) runs classes for kids ages 2 to teens, including Saturday-morning family sessions and yoga for boys, though you generally must book for a term. Classes cost £5 ($9.50) per child. **Triyoga** in hip Primrose Hill (6 Erskine Rd., NW3; ℂ 020/7483-3344; www.triyoga.co.uk) runs various classes for 5- to 8-year-olds, 6- to 11-year-olds, and 9- to 11-year-olds, with prices averaging £10 ($19) per hour. There are also mum-and-baby sessions, and baby massage. Lastly, **Yogabugs** (ℂ 020/8772-1800; www.yogabugs.com) integrate yoga postures into adventures and creative stories for kids 2½ to 7; their 350 teachers work at health clubs and yoga centers throughout London.

4 Indoor Playgrounds

One of the best indoor playgrounds in London is the superb new plant-themed **Climbers & Creepers** area at Kew Gardens (p. 188). Syon Park also has a **Snakes & Ladders** indoor playground (p. 187), and Crystal Palace National Sports Centre (p. 208) has **Spike's Madhouse.** Both **Waterfront Leisure Centre** in south London (p. 213) and **Broxbourne Lido** in east London (p. 213) have good softplay areas. All charge a nominal fee, and most are suitable for kids up to about 12.

Other reasonably central indoor playgrounds are **The Playhouse** (Old Gym, High-bury Grove, N5; ℂ 020/7704-9424), and **Bramley's Big Adventure** ★★ (136 Bram-ley Rd., W10; ℂ 020/8960-1515; www.bramleysbig.co.uk). Farther afield, there's the excellent **Zoomaround** in Stoke Newington (46 Milton Grove, N16; ℂ 020/7254-2220; www.zoomaround.co.uk); and **Discovery Planet** in Rotherhithe's Surrey Quays Shopping Centre (Redriff Rd., SE16; ℂ 020/7123-2388; www.discovery-planet.co.uk).

Gymboree Play & Music (ℂ 020/7258-1415; www.gymboreeplay.uk.com) runs interactive activity sessions for babies and children up to 5. In theory, you sign up for a term's worth of classes, but you can get coupons for trial classes, and branches may allow visitors in on a one-time basis. There are relatively central branches in the O2 Centre (p. 255), Whiteleys shopping mall (p. 238), and the Business Design Centre in Islington, NW1. For a less upmarket option, where you're more likely to meet local mums with their tots rather than nannies, London has a wide network of (usually free) **One O'Clock clubs,** often in parks such as Hampstead Heath (p. 142), Holland Park (p. 204), Highbury Fields (p. 206), Battersea Park (p. 205), and Coram's Fields (p. 207), generally offering painting, crafts, and softplay areas. For details on these and other parent-and-baby groups by area, see www.childcare.gov.uk.

5 Classes & Workshops

Most of the museums and historic houses listed in chapter 6, "Exploring London with Your Kids" host family workshops on weekends and during school vacations, as do many theaters.

ART & CRAFTS

For activities at the major **art galleries,** see p. 174.

Art 4 Fun/Colour Me Mine ✫ This "creative cafe" allows budding artists of all ages to come together to paint on ceramic, wood, glass, paper, silk, or fabric, or to create a mosaic. A studio session, which can last all day, costs £5.95 ($11); then from £1 ($1.90) per item. Kids can enjoy soft drinks and muffins while they work; parents can enjoy a coffee or even bring a bottle of wine. There are other branches in Chiswick, W4, and Muswell Hill, N10. Similar activities are offered by the three-branch **Ceramics Cafe** (✆ 020/8741-4140; www.ceramicscafe.com) and the two-branch **Pottery Cafe** (✆ 020/7736-2157; www.pottery-cafe.com). 172 W. End Lane, NW6. ✆ 020/7794-0800. www.art4fun.com. Tube: W. Hampstead.

London Film Festival Workshops ✫ This major film festival, screening around 280 films from 60 countries from mid-October to early November, includes a 3-day film and TV school for 13- to 19-year-olds, including scriptwriting, filming, animation, and—a big favorite—horror makeup workshops. Added treats are free film screenings and seminars for kids 14-plus. The program is run by the British Film Institute, so it tends to be arty. Various venues include the National Film Theatres, SE. ✆ 020/7815-1392. www.lff.org.uk. Tube: Waterloo.

London International Gallery of Children's Art ✫ A unique venue in a family-friendly entertainment mall, this center hosts a free exhibition of artworks by children from around the world. Visiting kids can use the art materials provided to produce something in response to what they have seen. Call for details of Saturday workshops held during school vacations. O2 Centre, 255 Finchley Rd., NW3. ✆ 020/7435-0903. www.ligca.org. Tube: Finchley Rd.

The Making Place This space runs informal school-vacation sessions, giving families the chance to explore scientific principles by designing products to take away with them. These could be ice candles, magnet toys, jack-in-the-boxes, shadow puppets, soap, or lemonade (activities are designed for kids ages 3–10). You can also buy kits to design torches, make dancing bears, and more. 3 Exmoor St., W10. ✆ 020/8964-2684. www.the-making-place.co.uk. Tube: Ladbroke Grove.

Orleans House Gallery This contemporary art showcase sits in a baroque mansion to the southwest of the city near Marble Hill House (p. 183). Here you'll find the Octagon Art Club, which offers art sessions for 5- to 9-year-olds. Activities include sculpture, photography, printmaking, collage and poster creation, and mask making. Riverside, Twickenham, TW1. ✆ 020/8831-6000. www.richmond.gov.uk. Train: Twickenham.

Serpentine Gallery ✫✫ A contemporary gallery beautifully set in an old tea pavilion in Kensington Gardens, the Serpentine provides an atmospheric spot for free creative family days relating to its exhibitions. The Art Packs, with suggestions for visitors of all ages on producing art, are a great value at £1 ($1.90). Kensington Gardens, W2. ✆ 020/7298-1516. www.serpentinegallery.org. Tube: Lancaster Gate.

MUSIC

For family opera workshops run by the **English National Opera,** see p. 254.

The Music House for Children ★★   This superb option for aspiring musicians, inside west London's Bush Hall venue, offers classes in music appreciation and various instruments, plus drop-in music and movement classes for babies and kids up to 3 (£5/$9.50).A drop-in Saturday Club of dance, drama, and art for 6- to 12-year-olds costs £12 ($23) for the morning. An adjoining shop sells musical supplies and arts and crafts. There is also a coffee shop. 310 Uxbridge Rd., W12. © 020/8932-2652. www.musichouse forchildren.co.uk. Tube: Shepherd's Bush.

Wigmore Hall ★★★   Young band members should check out this hall, which hosts some brilliant kids' workshops, including Chamber Tots music and movement sessions for 2- to 5-year-olds (£5/$9.50), with a short concert in the auditorium followed by singing with musicians. Family days for those ages 5 and up are also on offer at £10 ($19) per adult, £8 ($15) per child, letting kids try out an array of instruments, work with musicians to make their own pieces, and have a go at drawing and animation with a BBC animator. Those with musical experience can get involved in Young Fiddlers' Day Workshops for ages 12 to 18 (£8/$15), which culminate in a play that parents can attend. Unfortunately, all these workshops get booked up months in advance, so check them out well ahead of your visit. 36 Wigmore St., W1. © 020/7935-2141. www.wigmore-hall.co.uk. Tube: Bond St.

Whippersnappers ★★★   Kids have the chance to get funky at these excellent drop-in workshops for 0- to 5-year-olds at Brockwell Lido open-air pool (p. 214), with African drumming, shadow puppets, and singing. The company's trademark is Pickny Beat, a mix of Jamaican and English music using reggae and dance overlaid by children's songs. Tickets cost £6.50 ($12) for the first child, £9 ($17) for two siblings. The same venue hosts an indoor and outdoor sports club for 8- to 16-year-olds, and acrobatics for 4- to 7-year-olds and 7- to 11-year-olds. Whippersnapper classes are also held in Holland Park (p. 204). Brockwell Lido, Dulwich Rd., SE24. © 020/7738-6633. www. whippersnappers.org. Train: Herne Hill.

9

Shopping

London can be shopping heaven or shopping hell. The range of shops and goods here is huge, but so are the crowds, and some areas that used to be fun have become touristy and overpriced—such as Covent Garden. Conversely, areas that went into decline, including Carnaby Street, have been given a new lease on life in the last couple of years.

Of course, you'll find all the multinationals here, at generally higher prices than elsewhere. Gap Kids and the Disney Store are familiar sights—you can't miss them. My advice is to investigate the best of the city's homegrown goods in London's charming, small-scale complexes and unique boutiques.

1 The Shopping Scene

SHOPPING HOURS

Smaller London shops tend to open at about 9:30 or 10am and close at 5:30 or 6pm Monday to Saturday; larger shops and department stores often stay open at least an hour or two later, with Thursday for traditional late-night shopping, especially in the weeks leading up to Christmas. Some stores in shopping districts such as Chelsea and Covent Garden also keep slightly later hours. On Sunday, shops are generally now open for up to 6 hours, usually 11am to 5pm.

SALES TAX & SHIPPING

Value-added tax (VAT), British sales tax, is 17.5% on most goods (children's clothes are exempt), but it's included in the price, so what you see on the price tag is what you pay at the register. Non-E.U. residents can get back much of the tax by applying for a refund from participating retailers (who charge a small administration fee); you show them your passport to prove you are eligible, and they give you a refund form to complete. The minimum expenditure required differs from store to store. You then present your goods and form to U.K. Customs at the airport, and claim your money from the refund booth. The **National Advice Service (© 0845/010-9000)** will answer any VAT-related queries.

VAT is not charged on goods shipped out of the country, and many London shops will help you beat the VAT by **shipping** for you. But watch out—this may be even more expensive than the VAT, and you might also have to pay U.S. duties when the goods reach you at home. You can ship your purchases on your flight home by paying for excess baggage (rates vary by airline), or have your packages shipped independently, which is generally less expensive—try **CargoBookers (© 0800/731-1747).** By either of these means, you still have to pay the VAT upfront and apply for a refund.

SHOPPING DISTRICTS

THE WEST END   Central London is home to most of the city's world-class department stores; **Oxford Street,** running east–west through the heart of the capital, also has the flagship stores of most of the city's or country's high-street chain stores. It's a bit tacky these days, though, and madly busy any day of the week—if you've got little kids in tow, you might want to give it a wide berth. **Regent Street,** curving south from Oxford Circus to Piccadilly, is a little more upmarket; it's here that you'll find the toy store giant Hamleys and a branch of its rival The Disney Store. There are some real gems to be found in smaller West End streets, including **Carnaby Street** running parallel with Regent Street through Soho; this, a key locale in the Swinging '60s, lost its cred for a while but has been revitalized and should be high on any fashion-conscious teen's "place-to-shop" list. Farther west, running north off Oxford Street up into villagey Marylebone, **Marylebone High Street** has a civilized feel, charming independent shops, lots of child-friendly eating options, and a great Sunday farmers' market.

At the eastern end of Oxford Street, **Covent Garden** is focused around the piazza, the former site of London's biggest fruit and vegetable market. It's scenic but touristy, and prices are hiked up accordingly. Fashion mavens, however, will find much to tempt them along **Neal Street** and the streets radiating off **Seven Dials,** with their hip boutiques and New Agey stores.

KNIGHTSBRIDGE, CHELSEA & KENSINGTON   Knightsbridge, home of Harrods and Harvey Nichols, is London's most luxurious shopping district—Sloane Street in particular is chock-a-block with designer clothing emporia. At the end of it, Sloane Square is the starting point for the **King's Road,** synonymous with the Swinging '60s. These days it's far less alternative and cutting-edge, but as the number of mums and strollers testifies, it's one of the best places in town for kids' shopping. Toy stores and clothing boutiques abound. It's not the place for a bargain, but it's a great way to spend a day (avoid weekends if you can). Don't forget the major museums in nearby **South Kensington**—all have good gift shops. From there it's a short walk to **Kensington High Street,** a fertile hunting ground for teen-friendly street chic.

NOTTING HILL & PORTOBELLO   From Kensington High Street, it's a pleasant stroll up Kensington Church Street past posh antiques shops to ridiculously trendy Notting Hill, dotted with fashionable boutique stores frequented by the hippest celebs. Make sure you check out the western end of **Westbourne Grove** and intersecting **Ledbury Road** and **Portobello Road,** famous for their antiques market but boasting superb clothes stores and stalls, too.

NORTH LONDON   There are a couple of areas farther out of the center worth a visit. **Upper Street Islington** has plenty of quirky little stores (and lots of family eating options), but as this is a main road out of London, it can feel a bit hectic. Farther afield, both **Hampstead** and **Highgate** have laid-back, villagey high streets with interesting shops in which to poke around. **Stoke Newington Church Street** is a little more bohemian, and correspondingly cheaper.

DEPARTMENT STORES

London's wonderful array of department stores, many of them historic, provide something for all members of the family, from toy sections to superb food halls to designer clothing. On-site cafes or restaurants suit all tastes and pocketbooks, and good restroom and parenting facilities are available. You can easily lose yourself for the day in the following. Note that they are superb wet-weather standbys.

Also-rans that don't merit a review in their own right but that do have children's departments of one kind or another, parents' facilities and, in most cases, kids' menus, include: **Bhs** (252–8 Oxford St., W1; ℭ **020/7629-2011;** www.bhs.co.uk), **House of Fraser** (318 Oxford St., W1; ℭ **0870/160-7258;** www.houseoffraser.co.uk) and its sister store **Dickens & Jones,** 224–4 Regent St., W1; ℭ **0870/160-7262**), **Fenwick** (63 New Bond St., W1; ℭ **020/7629-9161;** www.fenwick.co.uk), **Harvey Nichols** (109–25 Knightsbridge, SW1; ℭ **020/7235-5000;** www.harveynichols.com), which has a **Buckle My Shoe** concession (p. 222), and **Marks & Spencer** (458 Oxford St., W1; ℭ **020/7935-7954;** www.marksandspencer.com). Most have branches elsewhere as well. The lovely and rather decadent **Liberty** (Regent St., W1; ℭ **020/7734-1234;** www.liberty.co.uk) doesn't sell kids' stuff, but teenage girls swoon at its exquisite jewelry and accessories and love its hyper-trendy (and rather forbidding) beauty hall.

Debenhams   For those in the know, Debenhams, though lacking the character of the city's older department stores, is a great spot for specially commissioned fashion by international names such as Jasper Conran, Matthew Williamson, and John Rocha. And that's just the kids- and babywear! Prices, relatively speaking, aren't bad, though there's an in-house clothing line at still-keener prices. Toys run the gamut from the educational and the electronic to more eccentric, crafty items such as Butterfly Garden and Paint Your Own Gnome kits, as well as traditional board games. A branch of the excellent Early Learning Centre (p. 240) is located here. *Insider tip:* If you're heading for one of the nearby royal parks (p. 200), this is a great place to stop off for well-priced outdoor game equipment such as Frisbees (£3/$5.70) and bats (£5/$9.50). There's also a well-respected nursery and kids' furnishings department, and The Restaurant has a VIP Baby Service (kids' meals, low-cost jars of baby food, food- and bottle-warming facilities, highchairs, wipes, and baby-changing facilities). Note that there are other branches in London's suburbs. 334–8 Oxford St., W1. ℭ **0844/561-6161.** www.debenhams.com. Tube: Oxford Circus.

Fortnum & Mason ⭐   Most famous for the sumptuous hampers dispatched from its magnificent food hall, Fortnum & Mason has been going strong as a provider of traditional nursery toys, books, and games since 1707. One look at its restrooms, called "powder rooms" and "cloak rooms" respectively, says it all—you don't get much more upper-class English than this. **The Fountain** restaurant on the ground floor is known for its ice-cream sundaes (£5.25/$10) served during afternoon tea, but you might be equally happy with an original shake (flavors include toffee, praline, and black cherry), divine hot chocolate, or a dishful of bread-and-butter pudding. Just make sure you book a dental visit for your return home! 181 Piccadilly, W1. ℭ **020/7734-8040.** www.fortnumandmason.com. Tube: Piccadilly Circus.

Harrods ⭐   The "Palace in Knightsbridge," with its 330-plus departments, attracts love and hate in equal measure. It doesn't come without its quota of snobbery, yet staff is as friendly and helpful as can be. Kids will want to head straight for the fourth floor, with its vast Toy Kingdom. Here, again, you may find your head spinning at the prospect that anyone, no matter how fat his or her wallet, would contemplate spending £40,000 ($76,000) on a kids' Lamborghini Countache! Still, there are "real" toys and books here, even if the prices aren't on a par with Woolworths. It was in Harrods that writer A. A. Milne bought the original Winnie the Pooh bear for his son Christopher. There's also designer kidswear aplenty, some very chi-chi nursery furniture, a children's theater, and a hair salon. If you're here during Christmas season, don't miss a visit to London's best Santa's grotto; queues can be up to 2 hours long, but it's well worth the wait, and the singing elves keep even the most fidgety kids happy with free cookies and lollipops.

All that, yet a trip to London is still not complete without a visit to its breathtaking food hall. Among the 26 (count 'em!) food bars, cafes, and restaurants are the frenetic, family-oriented Planet Harrods with its blaring cartoons and kids' menu (£5.75/$11); and the Max Brenner Chocolate Bar, with its gloriously thick chocolate drinks and fondues. On your way back down to reality, stop in at the second-floor pet shop, where you can buy cats and birds or order all manner of exotic beasties. (In 1967 an Albanian prince bought a baby Indian elephant here for Ronald Reagan.) 87–135 Brompton Rd., SW1. © 020/7730-1234. www.harrods.com. Tube: Knightsbridge.

John Lewis ★★ Value   We rate this above all other London department stores in terms of value (their motto is that if you find the same goods cheaper within a certain radius, they'll refund the difference) and in terms of how well they treat customers. (Just witness the parents' space on the fourth floor, with its comfy breast-feeding room, bottle-warming area, and baby-changing facilities.) Expectant parents flock here for nursery furniture, backed up by expert advice from staff. Practical but attractive kidswear fits a range of budgets. The toys and books department is well-stocked with excellent goods. The store is a little unglamorous compared to, say, Selfridges, but it's a rock-solid option. There are other branches in the giant north London shopping center, Brent Cross, and in Sloane Square—the last, confusingly, is called **Peter Jones.** Oxford St., W1. © 020/7629-7711. www.johnlewis.com. Tube: Oxford St.

Selfridges ★★   Stylish Selfridges excels in so many departments, you scarcely know where to begin—the great food hall with its frequent free tastings, the mouthwatering candy and chocolate department, the superlative, cutting-edge men's and women's fashions, or the unrivalled beauty hall. The small but perfectly formed kids' department fuses fashion and toys in a trendy space-age setting. The clothes, by the likes of DKNY, Ralph Lauren, and Caramel, aren't cheap, but keep an eye out for periodic sales. If you hate the tyranny of blue boys' and pink girls' wear, or the predominance of pastels in many shops, this is the place to come. Toys range from the cultish (Hello Kitty) to the prosaic (Bob the Builder). Check the website for occasional children's events, such as makeovers. This is also the place to come for the **Buckle My Shoe** store, purveyor of more than 250 styles (including Diesel, Prada, and Puma) to the offspring of, among others, Madonna, Jude Law, and Uma Thurman. (There's another branch in Harvey Nichols; see p. 221.) Of Selfridges' 19 restaurants, bars, and cafes, the most family-friendly are Café 400 in the basement, with its handmade pizzas and decent pasta dishes, and the Food Garden Café on the fourth floor. 400 Oxford St, W1. © 08708/377377. www.selfridges.com. Tube: Bond St.

2 Shopping A to Z

ARTS, CRAFTS & STATIONERY

There are kids' drawing and arts-based workshops at some of the art galleries mentioned on p. 217 and 174, including the National Gallery and Somerset House.

London Graphic Centre   Central London's biggest art shop is an Aladdin's cave of supplies, catering to Damien Hirsts in the making and little princesses looking for temporary body tattoos. For those who wish to record their London trip *à la Monet*, the range of pads, sketchbooks, and notebooks includes the famous Moleskin brand;

some of them have handy little pouches in which you can store precious souvenirs, such as theater tickets. You'll find branches in Tottenham Street, W1; and Upper Richmond Street, SW15. 16–18 Shelton St., WC2. ✆ 020/7240-0095. www.londongraphics.co.uk. Tube: Covent Garden.

Paperchase ★★★   With its three floors of art supplies, gorgeous handmade papers, pens and pencils, sketch- and notebooks, wrapping paper, ribbons, bows, picture frames, and storage solutions, Paperchase is irresistible. The ground floor has an outstanding choice of greeting cards and pocket-money gifts—it's worth letting the kids loose here to stock up for boring flights or car trips. On the first floor there's a cafe where you can refuel while writing home. Smaller branches include Covent Garden Piazza, WC2; and King's Road, SW3. 213–5 Tottenham Court Rd., W1. ✆ 020/7467-6200. www.paperchase.co.uk. Tube: Goodge St.

Smythson of Bond Street ★   With its luxury leather-clad notebooks and its personalized writing paper and envelopes, this is the Rolls Royce of the stationery world. Young travelers go wild over the baby pink and blue leather passport covers (from £65/$124), the Places to Remember notebooks (from £125/$238), and the diaries and wee books with their silver embossed slogans. There's another branch in Sloane Street, SW1, plus concessions in Selfridges (p. 222) and Harvey Nichols (p. 221). 40 New Bond St., W1. ✆ 020-7629-8558. www.smythson.com. Tube: Bond St.

BOOKS, COMICS & MAGAZINES

There are so many great independent kids' bookstores outside the city center that there simply isn't space here to list them all, including the Lion & Unicorn in Richmond and Tales on Moon Lane in Herne Hill. See **www.booktrusted.co.uk** for a full list of bookstores and contact details, as well as kids' literature events, theatrical productions, and exhibitions.

Bookworm   An independent little kids' bookstore, Bookworm is worth a visit if you happen to be around Hampstead Heath, especially on Tuesday or Thursday at 2pm, when free costumed storytelling sessions are presented for 2- to 5-year-olds. 1177 Finchley Rd., NW11. ✆ 020/8201-9811. Tube: Golders Green.

Children's Book Centre   This kids' bookstore contains about 15,000 titles, plus videos, tapes, multimedia products, audiobooks, and selected toys. The best thing about coming to a specialized store like this is that the staff members really know their stuff and dole out useful insider advice. Special activities include author readings and charity days. 237 Kensington High St., W8. ✆ 020/7937-7497. www.childrensbookcentre.co.uk. Tube: High St. Kensington.

Daunt Books ★★★   This is one of the world's loveliest bookstores. It's best known for its travel books, which are uniquely grouped with novels and nonfiction from the same country. Its kids' room is a doozy, too, containing a whole host of quirky titles that get overlooked by the more commercial stores (you won't find any movie or TV tie-ins here). The section is not huge, let it be said, but there's room for junior bookworms to get down on their hands and knees and spread out their selections for further investigation. Flanked by childcare, interior design, and cookery sections for sneaky parental browsing, it's a great place to while away a couple of hours. There are two branches near Belsize Park in north London. 83 Marylebone High St., W1. ✆ 020/7224-2295. www.dauntbooks. co.uk. Tube: Bond St.

Forbidden Planet   The monster of all sci-fi, fantasy, and cult entertainment stores, now in much bigger, jazzier premises (it moved from New Oxford St. in 2004), has something to please both avid collectors and pocket-money browsers, whether it's a Chewbacca mask, a Buffy key ring, or a pack of Lord of the Rings playing cards. Come here to find a mind-boggling array of action figures, comics, graphic novels, manga, anime, cult movies, TV merchandise (from *Star Trek* to X-*Men*), books (science, fantasy, and horror), DVDs, videos, and video-game merchandise. Popular signing events allow you to get up close and personal with the likes of Christopher Lee, Neil Gaiman, and Leonard Nimoy. 179 Shaftesbury Ave., WC2. ✆ 020/7420-3666. www.forbiddenplanet.com. Tube: Covent Garden.

Foyles   The hallmark of this famous five-story general bookstore is its enthusiastic and knowledgeable staff. The sizeable kids' department hosts frequent talks and appearances by top writers (free, but bookable in advance). The quirky annual Open House event is a blast, with children's storytelling sessions, piranha-feeding, and stilt walkers. Don't miss the gift department's new line of retro Foyles memorabilia, including a vintage delivery van. 113–9 Charing Cross Rd., WC2. ✆ 020/7434-1580. www.foyles.co.uk. Tube: Tottenham Court Rd.

The Golden Treasury Fulham ⭐⭐   London's biggest independent kids' bookstore, the Fulham is spread over two floors. It includes American and French titles and a new Maisy Mouse corner stocked with books, toys, clothes, and small gifts. Staff members, who are mines of information, organize regular signings by authors as renowned as Jacqueline Wilson, and events such as World Book Day parties. There's a smaller branch farther south, at 27 Replingham Rd., SW18. Both stores have weekly story times on Friday afternoon. 95–97 Wandsworth Bridge Rd., SW6. ✆ 020/7384-1821. www.thegoldentreasury.co.uk/home. Tube: Southfields.

Marchpane Children's Books ⭐⭐   This lovely antiquarian specialist in rare children's and illustrated books sits in a quaint Victorian thoroughfare full of bookstores with traditional facades and signs. Stock ranges from 18th-century to modern works such as first editions of Harry Potter books, with the works of Lewis Carroll being of particular interest. Although it's not necessarily the best place to *bring* kids, Marchpane is a great place to browse for special presents. 16 Cecil Court, off Charing Cross Rd., WC2. ✆ 020/7836 8661. www.marchpane.com. Tube: Leicester Sq.

Ottokars ⭐   It's a shame this little chain doesn't have more central branches, since in addition to kids' book events, competitions, and promotions, venues are generally very welcoming to little ones, with rocking horses and reading areas. There's a small branch in the Science Museum (p. 148); otherwise, the most easily accessible options are in Clapham (which hosts a story time and sing along every Friday at 11am, plus an annual literary festival for adults and kids) and Greenwich (which runs a reading group for young kids on Wednesdays at 10:45am). If you happen to be out in the sticks of south London, its award-winning Bromley branch has a dedicated children's floor with a Tin Tin rocket to clamber on. The store hosts launch parties and arts and crafts events. 70. St John's Rd., SW11. ✆ 020/7978-5844. www.ottakars.co.uk. Train: Clapham Junction.

Ripping Yarns ⭐   This chaotic but charming secondhand bookstore boasts a large section devoted to collectible children's classics, including adventure stories and annuals, and out-of-print modern kids' fiction. Staff can be a little unfocused, but otherwise this is an excellent spot for a browse on your way out of Highgate Woods (p. 207). 355 Archway Rd., N6. ✆ 020/8341-6111. www.rippingyarns.co.uk. Tube: Highgate.

Waterstone's   This large chain features a well-stocked kids' department, hosting regular free events at the flagship Piccadilly store (Europe's biggest bookshop) and the new Oxford Street branch (© **020/7499-6100**). Recent activities have included Spot's Birthday Party, with story sessions and party-hat decorating; and Meet Poppy Cat, with mask-making and coloring. 203–6 Piccadilly, W1. © **020/7851-2400**. www.waterstones.co.uk. Tube. Piccadilly Circus.

CDS, DVDS & GAMES

For small-scale **specialist music stores,** head for Soho, especially Berwick Street.

HMV   A range of music, DVDs, and games is stocked at this megastore, which has three branches on Oxford Street alone (one is in Selfridges; see p. 222). Its clearance sales are worth looking out for. The store's new range of board games, perfect for chilling out in your hotel room, include Simpsons Monopoly and Lord of the Rings Risk. 150 Oxford St., W1. © **020/7631-3423**. www.hmv.co.uk. Tube: Oxford Circus.

Virgin Megastore   Another media emporium, Virgin is really not that distinguishable from HMV, except that one branch now occupies the coveted Piccadilly Circus spot formerly held by Tower Records. The Oxford Street branch (© **020/7631-1234**), however, is the place to go for live performances and signings by international acts such as Moby. 1 Piccadilly, W1. © **020/7439-2500**. www.virginmegastores.co.uk. Tube: Piccadilly.

DRESSING UP

Angels 🌟   You'll pay a bit more at this glitzy store in the heart of Theaterland, but the choice and quality really are inspiring—ranging from Dorothy in the *Wizard of Oz* to the Incredible Hulk. Among the superior accessories are wigs, masks, make-up, and tiaras. 119 Shaftesbury Ave. © **020/7836-5678**. www.fancydress.com. Tube: Leicester Sq.

Escapade 🌟🌟   This long-established store comes with keen prices and an impressive client list (the BBC, Disney, Nickelodeon). The thousands of costumes to hire or buy include a vast range of highly original, well-made kids' outfits, including Alice in Wonderland. Or become a Beefeater for that traditional London look. Accessorize to your heart's content with masks, wigs, makeup, jewelry, and novelty products. 150 Camden High St., NW1. © **020/7485-7384**. www.escapade.co.uk. Tube: Camden.

EQUIPMENT & NURSERY ITEMS

John Lewis (p. 222), **Debenhams** (p. 221), and **Daisy & Tom** (p. 239) have good nursery and stroller departments.

Anna French   A contemporary fabrics, lace, and wallpaper showroom, Anna French is renowned for its stunning children's collection, which ranges from the ultra-girly (fairy-stripe fabric and angel-wing wallpaper) to patterns that even boys will love: whale-print voile and bee cut-outs. 43 King's Rd., SW3. © **020/7351-1126**. www.annafrench.co.uk. Tube: Sloane Sq.

Blooming Marvellous   This well-respected and competitively priced mail-order outfit has one London store (and another in Bluewater; p. 238) stocking most of its nursery equipment, from contemporary and travel cots to hip seats and great products for journeys and flights. 725 Fulham Rd., SW6. © **020/7371-0500**. www.bloomingmarvellous.co.uk. Tube: Parsons Green.

Designers Guild 🌟   One of the most influential names in modern interior design, Designers Guild eschews minimalism in favor of bright bursts of color that suit kids' products perfectly, from Cats' Chorus fabric and wallpaper to polka-dotted blankets to cute little notebooks, bags, and other accessories. 267 King's Rd., SW3. ℭ 020/7351-5775. www.designersguild.com. Tube: Sloane Sq.

Dragons of Walton Street This long-standing Knightsbridge firm will hand-paint any design of your choice onto its traditional English hand-crafted children's furniture. Favorite designs are Beatrix Potter characters and flower fairies, but kids can even bring in photos of pets to be copied onto items. There's also an exclusive range of kids' fabrics. 23 Walton St., SW3. ℭ 020/7589 3795. www.dragonsofwaltonstreet.com. Tube: Knightsbridge.

Ikea ⭐ The crowds and store layout will drive you nuts, but there's no arguing with Ikea's prices——where else can you get a sturdy and stylish highchair for as little as £12 ($22)? For such mass-produced stuff, this is imaginative design that sets kids aglow, especially the play furniture, which includes frog cushions, bee chairs, and teddy bear armchairs. There's a nursery for 3- to 7-year-olds, and vacation activities such as face painting and puppet shows, although you'll probably find that kids are more than happy trying out the goods in the showroom. 2 Drury Way, N. Circular Rd., NW10. ℭ 0845/355-1141. www.ikea.co.uk. Tube: Neasden.

Lilliput This store promises that it either stocks or can source "virtually everything that is suitable for your baby or child." I haven't been able to test the claim, but there certainly is a huge range of strollers (including the pull-not-push Tug), car seats, carriers, furniture, books, toys, and accessories. Staff members provide excellent service, too. There's another branch in Wimbledon, and a stroller-repair service as well, should yours come unstuck. 255–9 Queenstown Rd., SW8. ℭ 020/7720-5554. www.lilliput.com. Train: Battersea Park.

The Little White Company ⭐⭐ Lovers of The Little White Company's minimalist yet homely collections of predominantly white and gray housewares and clothing will be thrilled to hear that there's now a dedicated kids' store with expanded ranges of its chic and simple bed linen, nursery furniture, clothes, nightwear, accessories, and gifts. Bright colors even creep in here, in the form of gingham PJs and striped hoodies for boys and girls. 261 Pavilion Rd., SW1. ℭ 020/7881-0783. www.thewhitecompany.com. Tube: Sloane Sq.

Mothercare Glam it's not, and the staff can be downright incompetent, but this is a handy central store for nursery furniture, strollers, fashion (including a Clarks shoes concession), toys, and gifts, and prices are good. (Look out for sales and other seasonal offers.) Recent developments include a new Kid's First furniture and bedding range to match adult styles from minimalist to French Provençal. There are plenty of suburban branches. 461 Oxford St, W1. ℭ 020/7629-6621. www.mothercare.com. Tube: Marble Arch.

Natural Mat Company ⭐⭐⭐ *Finds* A specialist in natural baby and kid's products, the store sells everything from natural-fiber crib mattresses to soft, chemical-free bed linen and stylish furniture. The superb clothes range features fun T-shirts, jerseys, hooded tops, and bibs. Brilliant gifts include chicken wall hooks, bunny hangers, and sea lion mobiles. 99 Talbot Rd., W11. ℭ 020/7985-0474. www.naturalmat.com. Tube: Westbourne Park.

Nursery Window Come to this dependable place for old-fashioned, expensive nursery and children's furniture; bedding (from plain waffle to racing cars); and luxury accessories, including cashmere and/or lambs wool throws, rabbit-eared towels, and the fluffiest of dressing gowns. 83 Walton St., SW3. ✆ **020/7581-3358**. www.nurserywindow. co.uk. Tube: S. Kensington.

Simon Horn   This classic designer has acquired a reputation around the globe for his fine wooden beds and "metamorphic" nursery furniture, which include cots that can become beds and then sofas, and changing-tables/chests of drawers. Prices are high, but these pieces are investments (not to mention collectors' items). 117–21 Wandsworth Bridge Rd., SW6. ✆ **020/7736-1754**. www.simonhorn.com. Tube: Parson's Green.

FASHION
CLOTHING

There are countless specialist kids' boutiques all over London. Here are some of my personal favorites, and some of the most accessible (many are in out-of-the-way neighborhoods). For **surfing- and skating-**inspired fashion, see p. 238. Many **department stores** (p. 220) have good designer kidswear sections. At press time, a **Baby Dior** store was in the pipeline, but the date and location were as yet undecided.

Also Caramel   This hip boutique, with a good choice of jeans and with footwear by Converse, Puma, and others, caters to older kids. Wednesday and Saturday afternoons they can get haircuts here; it's advisable to book in advance, but sometimes there are last-minute openings. There's also a **Caramel Baby & Child** store for kids ages 0 to 6 on Brompton Road, stocking shearling baby carriers, baby oils, postcards, and chocolates. Or try the concession in Selfridges (p. 222). 259 Pavilion Rd., SW1. ✆ **020/7730-2564**. Tube: Knightsbridge.

ArmyKid ✪   This is a trendy yet practically minded Notting Hill store selling fashionwear and hardwearing army surplus for kids up to 13, plus army surplus for ages 14 and up. 49 Pembridge Rd., W11. ✆ **020/7221-7117**. www.armykid.co.uk. Tube: Notting Hill Gate.

Ben's   Your kids might think they're too cool for a shop uniquely for teens (10- to 16-year-olds, to be precise), but chances are they'll change their minds when they see the stock at this new store, which includes Monkeywear, Diesel, Prada, and Bomb Boogie. There's also a range of occasion wear, such as satin and organza dresses and Armani suits. On the same street, sister shop **Tiddlywinks** sells pre-teen clothes and shoes. 5 St. John's Wood High St., NW8. ✆ **020/7722-5599**. www.tiddlywinks.co.uk. Tube: St John's Wood.

Burberry   Kids who want to look like grownups shop at this classic designer store, whose wares include beige macs and quirkier little pink checked wellies. If your wallet's not screaming for mercy after that, a Burberry stroller comes fitted with its classic beige check fabric. 165 Regent St., W1. ✆ **020/7734-4060**. www.burberry.com. Tube: Piccadilly.

Cath Kidston ✪✪   These six little stores (Marylebone, Covent Garden, Holland Park, Chelsea, Fulham, and Wimbledon) are renowned for their floral wallpapers and fabrics but also offer a delightful range of imaginative kids' items, whether it be football-themed oilcloth aprons, printed kaftans, sarongs in a bag, halter sundresses, or sleeping bags. 51 Marylebone High St., W1. ✆ **020/7935-6555**. www.cathkidston.co.uk. Tube: Baker St.

Catimini   Come here for colorful clothes, shoes, bed- and bath-linen, sunglasses, cutlery, and dishes made in France but with a distinctly ethnic feel. There's another branch on the King's Road (✆ **020/7824-8897**). 52 S. Molton St., W1. ✆ **020/7629-8099**. www.catimini.com. Tube: Bond St.

Chrysaliss ✪   Bewildered by choice? This exclusive little boutique just north of Hyde Park offers 1-hour appointments with a stylist who will guide you through its stock of contemporary classics from Britain, France, Belgium, and Italy for kids up to 8. Or you can opt to have clothes tailor-made for your little boy or girl, who can play on the rugs or watch the DVD wall projection as you peruse the latest collections. 31 Connaught St., W2. © 020/7402-7109. www.chrysaliss.co.uk. Tube: Marble Arch.

Couverture ★★★   Filled with quirky kids' gifts, housewares, and fashion, including knitwear and knitted toys, this is the type of place magazine stylists come to look for inspiration. Items that caught my eye on a recent visit included chocolate-colored lambs-wool pompom mittens with a matching poncho; squirrel cardigans; Fair Isle socks; and a toy coffee set based on a 1964 design, in its own nifty carrying case. 310 King's Rd., SW3. © 020/7795-1200. www.coverture.co.uk. Tube: Sloane Sq.

The Cross ★★   An achingly trendy lifestyle boutique, this place boasts beautiful clothes, accessories, and housewares. Teenage girls come to swoon over the brocade bags, embroidered chinoiserie, and butterfly jewelry by Jade Jagger, while Holland Park mommies stock up on chic babies' and kidswear by the likes of Clements & Ribeiro and Little Badger, as well as kitschy gifts. It's frustratingly stroller-unfriendly, though. 141 Portland Rd., W11. © 020/7727-6760. Tube: Holland Park.

Fatface ★   This superb activewear and outdoor clothing chain has a kids' range for ages 6 months to 11 years, embracing covetable printed T-shirts, cropped jeans, crew pants, fleeces, swimwear, and accessories, all at reasonable prices. London branches include Covent Garden, Hampstead, and Brent Cross. 126 King's Rd., SW3. © 020/7581-9380. www.fatface.co.uk. Tube: Sloane Sq.

French Connection Kids   This stylish, mid-priced casualwear company, known for its provocative T-shirt slogans, sells trendy kidswear in various branches but only stocks its full range at its Kensington High Street (© **020/7937-4665**) and Chelsea branches. 140–4 King's Rd., SW3. © 020/7399-7200. www.frenchconnection.co.uk. Tube: Sloane Sq.

H&M   Hot-off-the-catwalk looks at throwaway prices translate into funky and highly desirable children's and teenagers' clothes here. The garb won't last too long, but neither will the fashions, and happy shoppers in 21 countries and 1,068 stores worldwide can't be wrong. Of the central branches, Regent Street sells teens' gear, and Oxford Street sells babies' and younger children's wear. 174 Oxford St. © 020/7612-1820. www.hm.com. Tube: Oxford Circus.

Humla   This traditional affair, located on an atmospheric cobbled lane in chic Hampstead, sells well-made, colorful clothes and accessories, including lovely embroidered dresses and soft-toy backpacks. The two shops of yore have merged into one, but there's still space for a pleasing array of wooden toys and cute furnishings. 13 Flask Walk, NW3. © 020/7794-8499. Tube: Hampstead.

Jakes ★★★   Hands-down the worthiest fashion store in town, Jakes stocks a kids' and adults label that donates a percentage of its profits to a charity for cerebral palsy (the illness that affects the eponymous 5-year-old Jake). The famous hand-printed Lucky 7 T-shirts (£10/$19 for kids; £25/$47 for adults) have been seen on fashion icon David Beckham and a variety of pop stars. There's also kids' Aran knitwear, cargo pants, tracksuits, and trucker caps. 79 Berwick St, W1. © 020/7734 0812. www.jakeskids.com. Tube: Oxford Circus.

Jigsaw ★   This is a smart, mid-price fashion chain with six branches, selling almost unfeasibly cute clothes for girls up to 13. (There are two in Chelsea, one on Westbourne Grove, one in Hampstead, one in Richmond, and one on New Bond Street, selling junior clothes, too.) Sequins, frills, and flowers abound at all locations, and sparkly accessories complete the look. 6 Duke of York Sq., King's Rd., SW3. *C* 020/7730-4404. www.jigsaw-online.com. Tube: Sloane Sq.

JoJo Maman Bébé   Though best known as a mail-order operation, JoJo Maman Bébé has four London stores (Clapham, Golders Green, Croydon, and Chiswick), all selling its comprehensive range of babies' and children's wear, toys, nursery equipment, and maternity wear. The child-friendly stores have play tables to keep little ones out of mischief, and a personal-shopper service can be booked. 68 Northcote Rd., SW11. *C* 020/7228-0322. www.jojomamanbebe.co.uk. Tube: Clapham Junction.

Kent & Carey   Come here for good-quality, classic English styles for kids up to 6, including popular pajamas and nightdresses. Staff members are friendly, and videos keep the little ones entertained while you shop. A second branch is located farther south in Wandsworth. 154 Wandsworth Bridge Rd., SW6. *C* 020/7736-5554. www.kentandcarey. co.uk. Tube: Parsons Green.

Mimmo ✹   Mimmo's exciting shop sells ultra-hip togs for kids up to 12, with designers including Nolita Pocket, Juicy Couture, Christian Lacroix Junior, and Miss Blumarine, plus footwear for the most discerning young feet, from denim flip-flops to wedge sandals. 602 Fulham Rd., SW6. *C* 020/7731 4706. www.mimmo.co.uk. Tube: Parson's Green.

Monsoon Children ✹✹✹   Known foremost for its sequin-embellished and embroidered clothes for women, Monsoon produces divine girls' clothes—we know young ladies who'd sell their souls for the Swan Lake ballerina print with a fitted satin-trimmed bodice, a pair of butterfly-embroidered mules, or a pink Stetson. Surprisingly, there's also boys' clothes, taking in attractive daywear, imaginative formal pieces such as embroidered *kurtas* (Indian collarless shirts), and funky beanie hats and other accessories. Stock varies across the numerous Monsoon stores throughout London, but there's another dedicated kidswear store at Brent Cross. 25 Covent Garden Market, WC2. *C* 020/7497-9325. www.monsoon.co.uk. Tube: Covent Garden.

Mystical Fairies   A riot of pink, this outrageous little store on a historic lane shimmers with anything fairy, whether it be sparkly tutus or everyday wear (such as pink fleeces and matching trousers), ballet tights or books, luggage or collectable toys. For the truly smitten, there's even an Enchanted Garden party venue on-site. 12 Flask Walk, NW3. *C* 020/7431-1888. www.mysticalfairies.co.uk. Tube: Hampstead.

Notsobig   This cool local kids' boutique sells expensive clothes (including Maharashi and Organics for Kids), shoes (such as UGG boots and Birkenstocks), dress-up clothes, jewelry, gifts, and a small selection of toys. 31a Highgate High St., N6. *C* 020/8340-4455. Tube: Highgate.

Oilily ✹✹   Winner of the European Kids Fashion Label of the Year award in 2004, Oilily knows its stuff when it comes to eye-catching babies' and children's wear. Your wallet might not thank you for coming here, but if your kids like bright colors and fun prints, stripes, and checks, they will. 9 Sloane St., SW1. *C* 020/7823-2505. www.oilily-world.com. Tube: Knightsbridge.

Patrizia Wigan   Strictly for traditionalists, this posh boutique places such a high value on exclusivity, it manufactures its kids' outfits in small quantities and rotates its stock every 4 to 6 weeks. Clothes are of the timeless, quintessentially English ilk, made from luxurious fabrics such as velvet, moleskin, light wools, linen, and silk, in warm countryside and seaside shades, and are apparently beloved by royals and celebs such as Liz Hurley. 19 Walton St., SW3. ℭ 020/7823-7080. www.patriziawigan.com. Tube: Knightsbridge.

Paul Smith   Of Paul Smith's three London stores, Westbourne House near Portobello is the place to come for his gorgeous, pricey boys' and girls' T-shirts (£30/$57) with original, witty prints such as singing butterflies. Also sold are upmarket toys such as mounted model Mini cars and posh stationery. Westbourne House, 122 Kensington Park Rd., W11. ℭ 020/7727-3553. www.paulsmith.co.uk. Tube: Notting Hill Gate.

Petit Bateau ⭐   Live out your Gallic fantasies at this established French name set up in 1893 and now boasting more than 100 boutiques in its own country, not to mention stores in Japan, Morocco, and Brazil. This most central branch is strongest in girlswear, but it does have items for both boys and girls up to 18, whereas in other stores there's nothing for boys over 12. Strong marine colors are a focal point, overlaid with polka dots for girls and sailor stripes for boys. Special wool and cotton knits are ideal for winter sports. Prices may be a little on the high side, but this is quality, long-lasting gear that can be boiled in the wash without losing its color (crucial for babywear), so see it as an investment. The branches include S. Molton St., W1; Hampstead, NW3; and the King's Road, SW3. 171 Regent St., W1. ℭ 020/7734-0878. www.petit-bateau.com. Tube: Piccadilly Circus.

Rachel Riley   Classic styles for kids up to 12, in natural fibers such as silk, wool, cashmere, and leather, can be found here. All clothes are made in workshops by the Loire, and while they might look dainty and delicate, the emphasis in on ease of laundering. Bridesmaid and pageboy outfits are a specialty, as are handmade slippers, and there's a fitting service for Start-Rite shoes. You'll find a second shop at 14 Pont St. in Knightsbridge. 82 Marylebone High St., W1. ℭ 020/7935-7007. www.rachelriley.com. Tube: Baker St.

Ralph Lauren Children's Store ⭐⭐   This was the U.S. designer's first free-standing kids' store, set up in 2000 and selling classic and vintage clothes and accessories for babies, girls, and boys, plus luxury gifts and bedding. Prices are what you'd expect for its Oxford cloth shirts and cable sweaters, but there are free seasonal events such as Easter parties and Halloween celebrations, with face-painting, live magic, and a lucky dip in which you can win a cashmere teddy, books, or Ralph Lauren vouchers. 143 New Bond St., W1. ℭ 020/7535-4600. http://global.polo.com. Tube: Green Park.

Sasti ⭐⭐   Come to Sasti for an injection of fun and originality: The categories—including Cowboys & Prairie Girls, Young Punks, Bees 'n' Bugs, and Angels & Yetis—say it all. Highlights among the playful but hard-wearing designs for ages up to 10 are the bright tops emblazoned with Pow! and Zapp! and fleeces with spider-web imprints. The store has a spacious play area to keep junior shoppers entertained. 8 Portobello Green Arcade, 281 Portobello Rd., W10. ℭ 020/8960-1125. www.sasti.co.uk. Tube: Ladbroke Grove.

Semmalina ⭐   A charming and eclectic little shop, Semmalina lures kids in with its fairy castle, and parents with its constantly changing stock. It caters to children up to 6, with clothes, funky toys, accessories, baby items, fancy dress-up gear, and gorgeous made-to-order party bags, fans of which include none other than designer Diane von Furstenberg. Those who fear the chain-store look should check out the inspired one-offs made from vintage fabrics. 225 Ebury St., SW1. ℭ **020/7730-9333.** www.semmalina.com. Tube: Sloane Sq.

The Girl Can't Help It ⭐   This pair of zany little shops within the creatively chaotic Alfie's Antiques Market sells retro clothing and accessories from the '30s, '40s, and '50s for both guys and dolls. Owners Sparkle Moore and Cad van Swankster, a pair of true

London eccentrics, really dress the part—you'll never catch them in clothes that aren't glam. Teenage girls just love the trashy jewelry (Bakelite and hand-blown fruit; poodle, cat and exotica brooches; and Mexican silver). All stock is in good condition (many items still have their original tags attached), so prices aren't low, but if you're looking for a slice of Hollywood (or Hawaiian) glamour, this is your place—as style mavens Kylie Minogue and Stella McCartney know. Shops G100, G90, and G80 (ground floor next to fishpond), Alfie's Antique Market, 13–25 Church St., NW8. © 020/7724-8984. www.sparklemoore.com. Tube: Marylebone.

Their Nibs ★★   Opened in 2003 and already voted one of London's three best kids' shops by Japanese *Vogue*, this trendy area boutique is celebrity-magnet central. You may very well bump into Kate Moss shopping for Lila here. The focus is on stunning original prints, whether they be retro cars and vintage fairies for babies, or cowboys and Japanese floral motifs for boys and girls up to 12. Kids can get haircuts here on Tuesdays. 214 Kensington Park Rd., W11. © 020/7221-4263. www.theirnibs.co.uk. Tube: Ladbroke Grove.

Tomboy Kids   Guaranteed to put a smile on any little style warrior's face, this bright and local boutique is the setting for seriously fun and funky kids' clothes, footwear, and accessories from the likes of Antik Batik, Pink Pig, Little Badger, Birkenstock, and Handed By. There's lots of urban cowboy gear from Authentic Western Wear, plus some desirable baby bed and bath products. 176 Northcote Rd., SW11. © 020/7223-8030. www.tomboykids.com. Tube: Clapham Junction.

Top Shop ★★★   This high-street chain with its vast Oxford Circus flagship store has gone from strong to stronger in recent years. By offering an enormous choice of the latest catwalk looks at rock-bottom prices, it is now a prime hunting ground for teens. The buzzing atmosphere helps too, with its video screens and DJ beats. On your way in, take note of the leggy beauties trying to look nonchalant outside—this is

---

Market Value

Rebellious teens into body piercings, blue hair, and grungy clothing head straight for **Camden Market** (Tube: Camden Town), which is open daily but really comes to life, in its inimitably tacky way, on weekends. Another hippy paradise is **Jubilee Market** (Tube: Covert Garden) alongside Covent Garden Market, selling cheap clothes and accessories from Tuesday to Sunday (on Mon it's an antiques market). The world-famous **Covent Garden** hosts several markets daily, including **Apple Market** in the courtyard, selling handcrafted toys, clothes, hats, and jewelry.

Perhaps London's most famous market, **Portobello Market** ★★★ (Tube: Notting Hill Gate) is best known for its antiques stalls and shops but also sells fruit and vegetables and—best of all--some truly innovative fashion. Get there bright and early on a Friday morning to see Stella McCartney or other top young British designers shopping for inspiration. The best area for fashion is under the Westway, where creative young things set up their stalls, but the street is also lined with vintage clothes stalls where you're guaranteed to find something original. Make sure you stop at the north end of the market, where it peters out into junk stalls, and enjoy a custard pastry at one of the Portuguese bakeries along trendy Golborne Road.

---

prime territory for model-agency scouts looking for the next top model. 36–38 Great Castle St., W1. © 020/7636-7700. www.topshop.co.uk. Tube: Oxford Circus.

Trotters ★★★ This was London's first store dedicated to kids, and it remains a good all-rounder for top brands such as Tommy Hilfiger Junior, Oilily, Quiksilver, and more, backed up by an excellent choice of accessories and dressing-up items. The Trotters Express Train takes the boredom out of shoe-fitting, and there's an in-store spaceship-themed hairdresser with an aquarium to keep kids entertained (they get a bravery certificate at the end of their first cut). The staff is clearly fond of kids, and the atmosphere is lively. Aside from fashion, you can stock up on traditional toys and on baby, kids, and parenting books. There's another branch on Kensington High Street, and a big new outlet in the Brent Cross shopping center. 34 King's Rd., SW3. © 020/7259-9620. www.trotters. co.uk. Tube: Sloane Sq.

JEWELRY & ACCESSORIES

Many of the clothing stores reviewed above also stock jewelry and accessories.

Accessorize ★ This treasure trove is a few steps upmarket from Claire's, but it's still a good value considering how well it keeps pace with the latest trends, and wherever you are in London, you're not far from a branch. The kids' collection is basically the same as what you'll find at sister company Monsoon (p. 229), but once your little one spots what's on offer in the rest of the store, there'll be no keeping her away. 293 Oxford St., W1. © 020/7629-0038. www.accessorize.co.uk. Tube: Oxford Circus.

Claire's Accessories The word "trashy" might come to mind when describing this global chain, but its range of cheap, disposable jewelry, makeup, hair accessories, and dressing-up products is perfect for pop princesses looking for an instant glamour fix. Among must-haves on a recent visit to one of the countless London branches were butterfly and flower hairclips, cherry nose studs, body glitter sets, and Hello Kitty makeup bags. 108 Oxford St., W1. © 020/7580-5504. www.claires.co.uk. Tube: Tottenham Court Rd.

Halcyon Days A supplier of "objets d'art" to the Queen and company, this Mayfair store is known for its enamel boxes, which include a Winnie the Pooh edition. Its new jewelry collection is worth checking out, too; its kids' line features very pretty Twinkle, Twinkle heart and star bracelets, Teddy earrings, and related gifts, such as cups and photo frames. 14 Brook St., W1. © 020/7629-8811. www.halcyon-days.co.uk. Tube: Bond St.

Octopus ★ It may be a chain, but walking into one of Octopus's bright little stores always feels like a discovery, and brings a smile to your face on the gloomiest of days. Among the fun accessories, gifts, and housewares (80% of which are exclusive to Octopus), you'll find animal-shaped handbags and cufflinks, rubber jewelry, themed watches, and bright luggage. If your eco-conscience needs salving, know that lots of items are made from recycled materials. There are branches on Carnaby Street, Coventry Street, and the King's Road. 54 Neal St., WC2. © 020/7836-2911. Tube: Covent Garden.

FOOD

A highlight of any trip to London is browsing some of its wonderful **food halls,** of which Harrods' and Fortnum & Mason's are delightfully over-the-top in a very upper-crust English way, and Harvey Nichols' and Selfridges' more modern (and modest) in feel. (See p. 220 for full department-store listings.) A street version of a food-hall browse involves wandering around one of London's 10 **farmers' markets,** where local food producers come to sell their (often organic) wares. There's really no better experience than a stroll in the sunshine helping yourself to the free samples of breads, cheeses, jams, and other goodies as you fill your basket with top-quality produce to cook back home. The most central markets take place weekly in Islington, Marylebone, and Notting Hill; for full details on all, see www.lfm.org.uk. In a similar vein, **Borough Market** ★★★ (© 020/7407-1002; www.boroughmarket.org.uk) on the South Bank is a historic and atmospheric fruit-and-vegetable market that in recent years has been transformed into a gourmet food market on Friday and Saturday, when you can taste and buy excellent meats, cheeses, breads, coffees, patisseries, and more.

For **organic specialists,** see p. 235.

CAKES

The Hummingbird Bakery ★ *Finds*   An unexpected little oasis of American home baking in the heart of Portobello, this bakery specializes in cute cupcakes—works of art in their own right, and a must-have at Notting Hill birthday parties. It also offers chocolate Devil's Food cake, Brooklyn Blackout cake, North Carolina pecan pie, brownies, cookies, coffee, and more, which can be sampled in its little cafe. 133 Portobello Rd., W11. © 020/7229-6446. www.hummingbirdbakery.com. Tube: Notting Hill Gate.

Patisserie Valerie ★   This divine little patisserie has branches in Soho, Covent Garden, Kensington, Knightsbridge, Piccadilly, and Belgravia. It offers a shabby-chic setting in which to linger over superior sandwiches and treats such as Belgian white hot chocolate, but the candies and specialty cakes are the main draw, including vertiginous chocolate constructions, superb fruit tarts, and the sweetest little marzipan animals. The owners also run the Left Wing Cafe and Gelateria Valerie on Duke of York Square (p. 134), on the King's Road. 105 Marylebone High St., W1. © 020/7935-6240. www.patisserie-valerie.co.uk. Tube: Bond St.

CANDY

Charbonnel et Walker   A long-standing favorite patronized by the Royal Family, this shop is famous for its hot chocolate, its seasonal chocolate-covered strawberries, and its classic English violet creams—go on, it would be rude not to indulge. You can also get your paws on C&W chocolates at Selfridges (p. 222) and Harrods (p. 221). 1 The Royal Arcade, 28 Old Bond St., W1. © 020/7491-0939. www.charbonnel.co.uk. Tube: Green Park.

Cybercandy ★★ *Finds*   Every dentist's nightmare, this place is serious about its sweet stuff, whether you want American classics, British favorites, limited editions, or even candy-flavored cosmetics, from Reese's Peanut Butter Lip Balms to S'mores Soaps. For homesick American visitors or expats, Hostess Twinkies are sometimes flown in direct from the States (numbers are limited, so hurry), and Shirley Temple Soda has just made it onto the stock list. 11 Shelton St., WC2. © 020/7240-5505. www.cybercandy.co.uk. Tube: Covent Garden.

Hope & Greenwood ★★   Candy stores don't get much more old-fashioned or English than this gorgeous 1955 sweet shop with an original marble counter and vintage-clad staff. Specializing in the "great and glorious confections of this land," this place is well worth the trip out of the center (it's handy for the Dulwich Picture Gallery; see p. 174) if you hanker for such nostalgic treats as flying saucers, sherbet lemons, and cola cubes, stored in 175 glass jars. More grown-up treats include handmade chocolates with such flavors as "damson in distress" and "voluptuous violet." 20 N. Cross Rd., SE22. © 020/8813-1777. www.hopeandgreenwood.co.uk. Train: E. Dulwich.

HAIRDRESSING

In addition to the listings below, places kids can get shorn are **Harrods** (p. 221), **Daisy & Tom** (p. 239), **Trotters** (p. 232), **Also Caramel** (p. 227), and **Their Nibs** (p. 231).

Junko Moriyama ★★   This laid-back Japanese salon caters to a happy band of locals and their kids. The youthful staff is adept at keeping children entertained, or you can book a double appointment so your offspring can be shorn at the same time as you— great if your kids are not too confident about the whole experience. I've even had my hair cut while breast-feeding here, without anyone batting an eyelid! Parents get free cups of green tea and an addictive 10-minute shiatsu head, neck, and shoulder massage at the end of their competitively priced treatment. There's a second branch at the other end of Marylebone, more convenient for those coming from Oxford Street. 58 Upper Montagu St., W1. ⓒ 020 7724 8860. www.jmoriyama.co.uk. Tube: Baker St.

Little Willie's ★   This is the kids' version of Willie Smart's hairdresser a few doors away, specializing in kids' cuts (about £15/$29). It also stocks trendy children's clothes, shoes, accessories, and gifts by upmarket labels such as Diesel Baby and Prada. The adult shop is now an Aveda salon offering relaxation treatments and a massage chair, with friendly staff who are happy if you bring babies and children along (book a lunchtime appointment when it's less busy). There's even a kids' play area. 16 The Pavement, SW4. ⓒ 020/7498-7899. www.williesmarts.com. Tube: Clapham Common.

HEALTH & BEAUTY

For eco-friendly products, see p. 235.

Boots the Chemist   This national chain provides life's little necessities, from medicine to mascara. All outlets stock diapers, wipes, and baby food; larger branches have kids' departments with clothes, nursery equipment, and toys. There are branches everywhere, but this one just north of Hyde Park is open till 10pm daily. 75 Queensway, W2. ⓒ 020/7229-9266. www.boots.com. Tube: Bayswater.

Lush   I defy anyone to walk past one of Lush's divine-smelling stores without being tempted inside for a closer inspection of its fresh, handmade cosmetics and bath-time products, all based on essential oils and non-animal synthetics (ingredients are listed on the packaging). Choose from among slices of colorful soap, bath ballistics, massage bars, and much, much more. London branches include King's Road, South Molton Street, and Covent Garden. 40 Carnaby St., W1. ⓒ 020/7287-5874. www.lush.com. Tube: Oxford Circus.

MUSIC

Chappell of Bond Street   Not many music stores can count Beethoven, Richard Strauss, and Charles Dickens among its clientele, but Chappell, set up in 1811, certainly can. Customer service is second to none, whether your kids are budding Vanessa Maes or enthusiastic beginners who just want to mess about on an inexpensive plastic recorder (most staff have music degrees). The selection of instruments and sheet music (both classical and pop) is unparalleled. 50 New Bond St., W1. ⓒ 020/7491-2777. ww.chappellofbondstreet.co.uk. Tube: Bond St.

Dot's   This welcoming north London music store stocks a range of secondhand instruments; a good choice of chord books and play alongs, from Bob Marley to Henry Mancini; and a wide pop and classical CD selection. There's always a pot of coffee brewing, and staff members are a mine of information, particularly if you're looking for a tutor. 132 St. Pancras, NW1. © 020/7482-5424. www.dotsonline.co.uk. Tube: Camden Town.

ORGANIC

On Sunday, pick up organic fruits and vegetables, breads, meat, fresh tofu, chocolate, and more at **Old Spitalfields Organic Market** at 65 Brushfield St., E1 (Tube: Liverpool St.). A hippyish treat, it also hosts craft stalls, secondhand goods, and an East Asian–style food mart.

Fresh & Wild   A hip "real foods" chain with branches in Soho, Notting Hill, Camden, Stoke Newington, the City, and Clapham, Fresh & Wild was bought by the U.S. company Whole Foods Market in 2004. Baby food and products are well represented, but just try to resist the smell from the bakery with its fresh breads made from unbleached flour. Most stores have their own cafes where you can tuck into soups, cakes, and fresh juices, and some branches have minicarts for tots to push. 69–75 Brewer St., W1. © 020/7434-3179. www.freshandwild.com. Tube: Piccadilly Circus.

Green Baby ⭐   London's most environmentally dedicated kids' store sells plain, unpretentious clothes and accessories for babies and toddlers, much of it made from organic cotton produced by community projects in India. It's also the place to come for glass and nickel- and PVC-free feeding items, eco-friendly wooden or cotton toys, award-winning (if pricey) bath and health products, and household products. The Canadian founder is a champion of washable nappies, but you'll find eco-friendly disposables such as Tushies or the compact Mother Earth diapers—great for those on the move. The tiny Islington branch (345 Upper St., N1) doesn't stock the full product range. 5 Elgin Crescent, W11. © 020/7792-8140. www.greenbaby.co.uk. Tube: Notting Hill Gate.

Planet Organic ⭐⭐   Don't come to this organic supermarket at lunchtime, when the aisles, cafe, and excellent takeout/juice bar get packed out with office workers hunting for delicious healthy fare. The rest of the day, the supermarket is a joy to wander around, with its fab cosmetics and natural remedies; a superb array of produce that buries any notion that organic fare is inferior (looks-wise, that is); and a good choice of kids' and babies' items, be it snack food or earth-friendly diapers. There are less-central outlets in Fulham and Westbourne Grove. 22 Torrington Place, WC1. © 020/7436-1929. www.planet organic.com. Tube: Goodge St.

SHOES

For **Buckle My Shoe,** which was Britain's first footwear store just for kids, see Selfridges (p. 222). **Ecco,** at 445 Oxford St. (© 020/7629-8820) and at **102 Kensington High St.** (© 020/7938-2583) also has an excellent range of kids' sporty shoes, while some of the clothing stores reviewed above stock shoes and offer fitting services.

Adidas Performance Centre   Sports don't come much more fashion-conscious than here, where Stella McCartney's daring collection runs to babies' and infants' wear. You'll also find serious outfits for young football players, swimmers, and tennis players; footwear from babies' trainers to sandals; and everyday clothes such as hooded jackets, tracksuits, and even skirts. There's an Adidas Originals store in Covent Garden. 4159 Oxford St., W1. © 020/7493-1866. www.adidas.co.uk. Tube: Oxford Circus.

Feet First ⭐   This dedicated shoe store is part of the long-standing, upmarket British shoe company Russell & Bromley. Its shoe stocks are so fashionable but hardwearing, and its fitting service is so expert, that you won't mind the relatively high prices. As well as its own brand, Feet First sells practical StartRites and Clarks, plus trendy labels such as Diesel and DKNY. There's a second kids' store, Feet Two, at Bluewater (p. 238). Some of the regular Russell & Bromley stores have a children's department. Upper Mall, Brent Cross Shopping Centre, NW4. ℂ 020/8203-4161. www.russelland bromley.co.uk. Tube: Brent Cross.

Geox Respira   If fetid bedroom odors are the bane of your life, especially after a hot and sticky day of sightseeing, take a deep breath—the U.K. has received its first branch of the revolutionary "shoes that breathe," which have airflow holes in the footbeds to keep feet cool and minimize sweating. This is an especially useful feature when it comes to kids' trainers, but all styles of kids' shoes are sold here as well. There's a fitting service for children, too. 5 S. Molton St., W1. ℂ 020/7493-5628. www.magicgeox.it. Tube: Bond St.

Instep 🔾   At this long-established, nationwide kids' shoes chain, fashionable looks don't mean poor quality. As well as brand names such as Kickers, Nike, Start-rite, Rhino, and Babybotte, there's a brilliant Italian brand, plus football boots, ballet shoes, wellies, and socks. The staff are more than helpful, and the fitting service is second to none. There are four south London branches, plus an outlet in Harrods (p. 221). 45 St. John's Wood, High St., NW8. ℂ 020/7722-7634. www.instepshoes.co.uk. Tube: St. John's Wood.

One Small Step, One Giant Leap 🔾🔾🔾   Set up in 2003, this store's rapid expansion is testament to its success in its mission to bring parents expert shoe-fitting (for which advance booking is advised), great brands, and value for money. Labels for babies through teenagers include Adidas, Ralph Lauren, and Roberto Cavalli Angels. The bright, contemporary outlets (there are branches in Clapham, Putney, and Sheen) are single-story to cut the hassle for those laden with shopping bags and strollers. 3 Blenheim Crescent, W11. ℂ 020/7243-0535. www.onesmallsteponegiantleap.com. Tube: Ladbroke Grove.

Office   Come to this great chain to find up-to-the-minute fashion footwear at a fraction of what you'd pay for the designer versions. The trainers section, which includes Converse All-Stars, is particularly fine. 55 S. Molton St., W1. ℂ 020/7491-8027. www.officeholdings.co.uk. Tube: Bond St.

SHOWER & BABY PRESENTS

Many of the stores listed under "Clothing," "Equipment & Nursery Items," and "Toy Stores" also sell baby toys and accessories.

Blossom Mother & Child 🔾   This super-stylish boutique focuses on expectant moms and newborns, with luxury baby clothing, hand-embroidered bed linens and gifts, books, and soothing CDs such as *Vivaldi for Babies* (or *Elvis for Babies* if you prefer!). It's also the only place in London where you can get the Netto Collection of modern nursery furniture. 164 Walton St., SW3. ℂ 020/7589-7500. www.blossommotherand child.com. Tube: Knightsbridge.

Brora   This is the place to splurge on special-occasion blankets, teddies, baby booties, bonnets, and mittens in the finest cashmere, as well adults' and kids' clothes made from the same luxurious wool. The winter sale is always a good time to snap up bargains. There are branches on the King's Road, Ledbury Road in Notting Hill, Islington, and Wimbledon. 81 Marylebone High St., W1. ℂ 020/7224-5040. www.brora.co.uk. Tube: Baker St.

The Farmyard 🔾   This cozy outfit specializes in lovingly crafted and hand-painted toys and furniture, many of which can be personalized with a name or date. Among the tactile traditional toys on offer are wooden Noah's arks, farms, dollhouses, and London buses; there's also a selection of nursery gifts such as personalized wooden rattles and baby blankets. Items for the home include treasure and keepsake boxes, and traditional but colorful wall clocks. For exclusive hand-painted toy boxes with Groovy Cow and other vibrant designs, brightly painted chairs and beds, and other larger items, there's a bigger branch in Richmond Hill, Surrey. 63 High St., Barnes, SW13. © 020/8878-7338. www.thefarmyard.co.uk. Train: Barnes Bridge.

Monogrammed Linen Shop   Amidst its classical and contemporary linens, laces, embroideries, cottons, and silks, this jolly store offers exquisite christening presents that can be monogrammed to order (in about 10 working days), including pillowcases decorated with boats, butterflies, or even London buses, and hand-smocked cotton nightdresses (which can be hand-embroidered with rosebuds for newborns). A great gift idea is the pillowcase embroidered with a beloved kid's drawing. You can also get personalized bathrobes for ages 1 to 14. 168–70 Walton St., SW3. © 020/7589-4033. www.monogrammedlinenshop.com. Tube: Knightsbridge.

Peter Rabbit & Friends   Touristy but still appealing, this little shop sells all kinds of merchandise relating to the 1901 bestseller *The Tale of Peter Rabbit* by Beatrix Potter and its 22 follow-ups. Everything is thought of, from christening gifts, soft toys, and dolls, to games, clothing, books, and videos, to tableware and soft furnishings. Older kids will undoubtedly find it a bit overly cute, but it's a brilliant place for presents for new babies and for nursery items such as musical watering cans. Note that the same firm runs a Paddington Bear stall in—wouldn't you know it—Paddington Station. 42 The Market, Covent Garden, WC2. © 020/7497-1777. www.charactergifts.com. Tube: Covent Garden.

SPORTS & SPORTSWEAR

Decathlon   It's worth the schlep out of the center to this, the city's biggest sports store (part of a global chain). As well as selling clothing and equipment relating to 65 sports, it has repair/maintenance workshops for in-line skates, bikes, racquets, and more, plus a golf simulator, a putting green, and a cafe. Look out for the orange arrows flagging reduced items. Surrey Quays Rd., SE16. © 020/7394-2000. www.decathlon.co.uk. Tube: Canada Water.

JD Sports   This sports footwear specialist is hard to avoid, with no less than four Oxford Street branches and more than 300 in the country. Competitively priced brands for juniors include Phat Farm and Puma, while for tots there are Adidas Piccolo, Nike Nursery, Reebok Infant, and more. 268–9 Oxford St., W1. © 020/7491-7677. www.jdsports.co.uk. Tube: Oxford Circus.

Lillywhites ★★   This vast, famous sports store (now part of the Sports Soccer chain), boasts floor after floor of clothing, equipment, and footwear catering to every sport, from football to snowboarding. You can count on finding all major brands, and there's a dedicated Junior section. Prices aren't so keen, but you're paying for a wide choice and a handy central location. 24–36 Lower Regent St., SW1. © 0870/333-9600. www.lillywhites.com. Tube: Piccadilly Circus.

O'Neill ★★   Budding beach bums would be mad to look elsewhere—O'Neill's range of shorts, plain or in funky prints and bright colors such as egg yolk yellow and Spanish red, is unbeatable. For boys there are also sweats, fleeces, headgear, and warmer-weather gear such as jackets and pullovers. Girls aren't left out, with a surprisingly pretty range that includes striped shirts in ice-cream hues, curved color block skirts, printed dresses, and cute bags. 9–15 Neal St., WC2. © 020/7836-7686. www.oneill europe.com. Tube: Covent Garden.

Quiksilver   This Australian surf- and snow-wear brand has definitely gone global, though you'll still hear chirpy Oz accents ringing out from its three central London stores—in addition to Carnaby Street, there are two in Covent Garden (one in the Thomas Neal Centre on Earlham St., and one in the North Piazza). The youth and boys' range includes good-quality, road-tested fleeces, snow jackets, and knits. A Kid's Essentials line offers beanies, belts, underwear, snow gloves, and wallets. 11–12 Carnaby St., W1. © 020/7439-0049. www.quiksilver.com. Tube: Oxford Circus.

Mall-to-Mall Shopping

Fast-food, Muzak, artificial light . . . they can be a adult's nightmare, but many kids seem genetically programmed to love malls. And, as with department stores (p. 220), there's a lot to be said for having everything under one roof, including superior parents' facilities.

London's biggest mall is way on its northwest outskirts but has its own Tube station for ease of access. **Brent Cross** (www.brentcross.co.uk) boasts 110 stores and cafes, including John Lewis, Mothercare, Baby Gap, Gap Kids, H&M Kids, Monsoon Kids, Feet First, Early Learning Centre, and Fun Learning. As well as special family parking spaces, it offers free stroller loans and Boobaloo toddlers' car hire—great for keeping the kids entertained and under control at the same time. During some vacations, a funfair is set up in the parking lot.

Smaller but more central (it's just north of Hyde Park), **Whiteleys** (www. whiteleys.com; Tube: Bayswater) has more than 70 shops (including Accessorize, Gap Kids, and JD Sports), plus weekend face painting, bungee trampolining every couple of months or so, permanent kids' rides, and a branch of the Gymboree kids' activity center (p. 216). There's also an eight-screen cinema and family-friendly restaurants such as Ask Pizza and Yo! Sushi.

When size matters, though, you'll need to head about 24km (15 miles) out of London, to **Bluewater** in Kent (www.bluewater.co.uk; Train: Greenhithe), where you'll find more than 330 stores; 40 restaurants, cafes, and bars; and a 13-screen cinema. Kids' outlets here include Petit Bateau (p. 230), H&M Kids (p. 228), a **Lego Store** with demonstrations and competitions (© 01322/427272; www.lego.com), and the Disney Store, but if you'd rather browse for yourself or have a treatment at the Molton Brown Day Spa, there's a nursery where you can leave 3- to 8-year-olds. There's also a dizzying array of non-shopping activities, including a climbing wall for ages 6 and up, an active zone with games and puzzles, fishing lakes, a golf-putting course, and a discovery trail through the surrounding landscaped park, through which you can also cycle (bikes, unicycles, tandems, family fourwheelers, and kids' pedal-powered go-karts are available for hire). You'll build up quite an appetite, which you can sate at the likes of Carluccio's (p. 103), Ed's Easy Diner (p. 137), or Pizza Express (p. 110).

Skate of Mind   Staffed by fanatics and frequented by pros, this skateboarding shop has just about every board on the market, plus the requisite clothes and accessories. Unit 26, Thomas Neal's Centre, Earlham St., WC2. ℂ 020/7836-9060. Tube: Covent Garden.

Slam City Skates   Here's another Covent Garden skateboarding specialist, well known for its sales. There's a £5 ($9.50) refund for the correct performance of a kick flip in any pair of Nikes bought in the store. You can also get snowboarding kits and streetwear here. 16 Neal's Yard, WC2. ℂ 020/7240-0928. www.slamcity.com. Tube: Covent Garden.

Soccer Scene   This soccer-fan's heaven sells team replica kits, boots, trainers, and soccer memorabilia and accessories, from toddler sizes up. There's a Rugby Scene store on the same street, at no. 46. 56–7 Carnaby St. ℂ 020/7439-0778. www.soccerscene.co.uk. Tube: Oxford Circus.

TOYS & GAMES

The gift shop at the **Rainforest Café** (p. 109) is excellent for animal-themed toys. If you just want to pick up a few toys and games for your hotel room or apartment, **Argos** (150 Edgware Rd., W1, and other locations; www.argos.co.uk) and **Woolworths** (168–76 Edgware Rd., W1; www.woolworths.co.uk) both have lots of choices and unbeatable prices. Before you return to your home country, you can donate them to a local community toy library (ℂ 020/7255-4604; www.natll.org.uk) or take them to a thrift store. If you're heading for Bluewater Mall, there's a dedicated **Lego Store** (p. 238) there for construction junkies. Opposite Brent Cross Mall you'll find a branch of the global giant **Toys R Us** (ℂ 0800/038-8889; www.toysrus.co.uk).

Benjamin Pollock's Toy Store   This old-fashioned, family-run shop still sells the cardboard toy theaters for which it was set up in the 1880s, as well as traditional toys for kids and collectors, including Czech marionettes, jack-in-the-boxes, Russian nesting dolls, and music boxes. Toy theater kits range from a simple Cinderella theater suitable for kids ages 6 and up, with no cutting required, to an authentic and detailed model of Shakespeare's Globe Theater (p. 171) for experienced modelers. 44 The Market, Covent Garden, WC2. ℂ 020/7379-7866. www.pollocks-coventgarden.co.uk. Tube: Covent Garden.

Cheeky Monkeys ★★   Distinguishable by its bright yellow frontages, this superb mini-chain also stands out because of its exciting stock. Four branches are located in south London (Clapham, Dulwich, Parsons Green, and Wandsworth), and one in Islington in north London. When I last visited, the flagship Notting Hill branch had just had a new lick of paint and more goodies than ever before, including a pink 1950s Murray Comet pedal car for little girls who fancy themselves '50s movie stars, a shoe-painting kit for aspiring footwear designers, and an Antquarium (developed using NASA technology) where kids can watch ants burrow and feed. 202 Kensington Park Rd., W11. ℂ 020/7792-9022. www.cheekymonkeys.com. Tube: Ladbroke Grove.

The Conran Shop   This stylish housewares emporium stocks pricey but original toys that won't look out of place in the chicest of households, including a giant inflatable world globe with detachable Velcro landmarks and animals (£229/$435), and an Orient Express train set (£210/$399). There are other stores at Conduit Street, W1; and at Fulham Road, SW3. 55 Marylebone High St., W1. ℂ 020/7723 2223. www.conran.com. Tube: Regent's Park.

Daisy & Tom ★★★   This is more of an experience than a store, with a traditional carousel that kids can ride at set times of the day; a puppet theater hosting shows featuring antique marionettes; storytelling sessions; special events; and a kids' hair salon.

But, you're looking for toys? Well, amidst the flurry of activity, you can find every-thing from baby's first toys to science kits, from traditional rocking horses to Technic Cool Movers, with plenty set out for kids to try for themselves. You'll also find excel-lent nursery and equipment sections, a huge selection of clothing and shoes, gifts galore, and a lovely book hall with titles for both kids and parents. (You can read them together in the cozy nooks.) 181 King's Rd., SW3. ☎ 020/7352-5000. www.daisyandtom.com. Tube: Sloane Sq.

Early Learning Centre ⭐⭐ ELC's range of sturdy learning toys for kids from birth to about 4 years are living proof that education needn't be dull. With their great prices, you're bound to end up coming out with a few treats for your little ones. Look out for offers on seasonal products, particularly outdoor toys and equipment. Every Tuesday between 9:30am and 11am, time is devoted to kids who want to test new toys, join organized activities, or give feedback. (At the Debenhams concession this takes place all day every day except Tues.) That said, the relaxed staff seem happy to let kids play with the stock at any time, although this Chelsea branch doesn't have too much room to maneuver. There are branches in Putney, Lewisham, and Hammer-smith; in Debenhams department store (p. 221); and at the Brent Cross and Bluewa-ter malls (p. 238). You can find ELC toys in some branches of Sainsbury's supermarket and Boots chemists (p. 234) too, as well as in Daisy & Tom (see above). 36 King's Rd., SW3. ☎ 020/7581-5764. www.elc.co.uk. Tube: Sloane Sq.

Fun Learning ⭐ The store is aimed at "graduates" of the Early Learning Centre (see above), which means that it, too, eschews movie and TV merchandise in favor of innovative and inspiring educational products (many from the U.S.)—this time for kids 4 years old and up. The shop is chock-a-block with toys, games, books, puzzles, craft kits, posters, science kits, CD-ROMs, and software. The stationery is great—gift bags, wrapping paper, invitations, and thank-you cards. The friendly staff encourages kids to play, and if you don't see what you want, they'll order it for you. *Insider tip:* This is a great place to source easily packed items for car journeys and flights, includ-ing miniature playing cards, magnetic travel games, and miniature 3D animal and vehicle puzzles. There's a second branch in Kingston-upon-Thames in Surrey. Upper Mall, Brent Cross, NW2. ☎ 020 8203 1473. Tube: Brent Cross.

Hamleys *Overrated* This wouldn't be a kids' guide without a mention of Hamleys, but the world's biggest toy store—a tourist attraction in its own right—is a peculiarly charm-less place these days, with its apathetic staff (many of whom seem barely able to speak English); its rip-off cafe serving some of the worst food I've ever had; and its single, grubby changing facility. And forget English tradition; Hamleys was bought out by an Icelandic investor in 2002. That said, kids will be so in awe of the 35,000 or so toys and games arranged over its seven floors that they won't notice the cynicism behind it all. Occasional promotions are dressed up as special events, but don't go out of your way to visit Santa here at Christmas—go to Harrods instead (p. 221). Hamleys has two mini-branches at Heathrow airport. 188–196 Regent St., W1. ☎ 0870/333-2455. Tube: Oxford Circus.

The Kite Store ⭐ If you plan to go up to Hampstead Heath or spend a sunny afternoon in the park, this long-established specialist is the best place in town to stop off for everything from power kites to flying toys such as boomerangs, discs, rockets, and Nerfs. There's also a range of funky clockwork robots (up to 16cm/6.3 in. high) and other tin toys, including cars and boats. 48 Neal St., WC2. ☎ 020/7836-1666. www.kite store.uk.com. Tube: Covent Garden.

Patrick's Toys   This is one of London's biggest traditional toy and model shops, set up more than 50 years ago and still family run. Model makers flock here for the excellent choice of rockets, plane, cars, military vehicles, and sci-fi craft; while transport fiends come here for the Hornby and Scalextric. Also available are dolls, soft toys, traditional wooden toys, games, puzzles, outdoor equipment, and all the latest fads. 107–11 Lillie Rd., SW6. (©) 020/7385-9864. www.patrickstoys.co.uk. Tube: Fulham Broadway.

Puppet Planet ★★★ (Finds)   An enchanting store, Puppet Planet is full of vintage and new puppets, from the Thunderbirds and Punch and Judy to traditional Czech marionettes and Balinese shadow puppets. There's something to please both lovers of kitsch and serious collectors here, plus related toys, gifts, and books, as well as puppet theaters at pocket-money prices. The customized look-alike puppets (around £150/$285) make fabulous gifts. Storytelling and puppet-making workshops are held most Sundays at 3pm, costing £7.50 ($14) per child; accompanying adult and siblings on lap ride free. Organic refreshments are served to all. 787 Wandsworth Rd., SW8. (©) 020/7627-0111. www. puppetplanet.co.uk. Tube: Parsons Green.

Route 73 Kids   This local shop, named for the bus that goes by it (the area is not well endowed with Tube lines), sells lovely old favorites next to the latest crazes. The focus is on stimulation, whether it be in the form of lullaby mobiles, instruments for budding Beethovens, paints and crayons, science experiments, sticky insects, fairy costumes, wands, tiaras, origami, or silk paintings. And that's just to mention a few of the goodies—it's a wonder they fit it all in the minuscule shop and still have room for a play area. 92 Church St., Stoke Newington, N16. (©) 020/7923-7873. www.route73kids.com. Bus: 73.

Tridias   This old family-run toy store makes for a handy stop on the way back from the big museums, with beautifully crafted toys, science kits, arts and crafts, games and puzzles, dressing-up gear, dollhouses, bedroom items, outdoor games and equipment, and books and tapes, including story cassettes handy for long journeys. There's a bigger branch in Richmond. 25 Bute St., SW3. (©) 0870/420 8633. www.tridias.co.uk. Tube: S. Kensington.

10

Entertainment for the Whole Family

London's vast array of entertainment options is centered on the **West End,** where most of its theaters and multiplexes lie. This area is also full of great eating options (as well as its fair share of tourist traps), so you can really make an evening, or an afternoon, of it. Just across the river, the South Bank is the city's cultural hothouse, with an array of world-class performance venues that don't forget children when it comes to scheduling anything from classical music to poetry.

Don't let all this stop you from venturing farther afield, though, or you'll miss out on some offbeat jewels that only a city of London's size and ethnic diversity can spawn. Enjoy those blockbuster musicals, sure, but don't forget the countless innovative kids' companies and community centers that rely on your patronage for their survival. Similarly,

catching a big Hollywood movie at a West End multiplex is all well and good, but not unique to London. Instead, seek out atmospheric and historic little picture houses with creative kids' clubs.

FINDING OUT WHAT'S ON For comprehensive weekly theater, cinema, and events listings and for lively reviews of them, see *Time Out* magazine (p. 40), which has Theatre, Film, Dance, and Sports sections, as well as a dedicated "Kids' London" section.

An excellent source of information for plays and shows is www.officiallondon theatre.co.uk, which has a very useful search facility allowing you to browse current shows by age suitability. It features a well-produced fortnightly family bulletin, together with an online kids' club with quizzes and fun theater facts.

1 The Big Venues

For theatrical performances suitable for older kids, check out **Shakespeare's Globe** (p. 171).

Barbican Centre ★★★ Europe's biggest multi-arts center, with its world-class concert hall, theaters, cinemas, and art galleries, is a wonderful space for families, hosting regular events where parents and kids can get creative together. Budding musicians ages 7 to 11 will be thrilled by the **London Symphony Orchestra's family concerts** (✆ **020/7588-1116;** www.lso.co.uk), to which they can bring along instruments. (Call ahead for schedules, because performances are sometimes suspended.) Screens show close-ups of the players (whom the kids can meet during the intermission) as well as short animations. There's even a free nursery for younger siblings ages 6 months and up, who are entertained by LSO musicians. The concerts are preceded by free foyer events with chamber music, interactive workshops, and face-painting, and before that by creative music workshops at LSO St. Luke's on Old Street, EC1, where kids and adults can create and perform their own music (no musical experience is required).

Another jewel in the Barbican's crown is its Saturday-morning **Family Film Club** ✦✦✦, where for £4.50 ($8.50) each, kids 5 to 11 and their families can engage in creative activities from the Movie Trolley, based on the week's film (activities start at 10:30am, films start at 11am). On the last Saturday of the month, longer themed workshops are offered by guest artists, such as nature model making; you'll need to book ahead, as these are justifiably popular. Older kids might like to catch a winter performance here by the globally renowned **Royal Shakespeare Company.** Further ticketed activities for those 6 and over include poetry and story readings by prominent authors, accompanied by songs and drumming, or followed by dance workshops.

After your cultural fix, there's plenty of opportunity to let off steam in the massive building with its newly improved public spaces full of cafes and free art displays. Check out the fountain-studded courtyard lake and giant fishpond. *Note:* At presstime, Barbican announced that it will be the main venue for a citywide 1st annual London Children's Film Festival, starting in November 2005. Call the Barbican box office for details. Silk St., EC2Y. ✆ 0845/120-7528. www.barbican.org.uk. Tube: Barbican.

National Theatre   Adjoining the South Bank Centre, the world-class National Theatre houses three theaters that among them host eclectic works ranging from Shakespearean classics to radical pieces from artists' collectives. You won't always find a kids' show here, but when you do, you can guarantee it will be worth the wait—the 2003–2004 adaptation of Philip Pullman's *His Dark Materials* trilogy is a case in point. It's especially worth trotting here between late June and early September, for the "Watch This Space" series of more than 100 free riverside performances on the Theatre Square lawn. Otherwise, you can always find free live music and exhibitions in the foyer spaces. South Bank, SE1. ✆ 020/7452-3000. www.nt-online.org. Tickets £16 ($30) for under 18s; adult prices vary according to show. Tube: Waterloo.

South Bank Centre ✦✦   This series of concrete bunkers stretched along the riverbank is another outstanding venue for classical and contemporary music, dance and performance, and literary events. It's currently undergoing large-scale renovation work, though, so disruption to activities is inevitable for the foreseeable future. This includes events at the **Royal Festival Hall** (one of the center's three concert halls), which hosts performances by young local musicians. Regular family concerts are featured by the resident London Philharmonic Orchestra on themes such as "Disappearing Habitats," for which audience members are encouraged to come dressed as favorite animals. You won't be able to enjoy one until at least January 2007, however, as the auditorium is being entirely reworked over the next year and a half. The excellent **Poetry Library,** with its activity trail, cassettes, CDs, videos, and more, is also closed for refurbishment until 2007, but free weekend children's poetry readings continue at 12:45pm in the Voice Box next to the Poetry Library, and the foyers continually buzz with free live music and exhibitions. **Queen Elizabeth Hall,** meanwhile, hosts chamber music, but also performances by the likes of the subversive Circus Oz. Challenging work is available for those 10 and up as part of the New Art Club, which hosts avant-garde dance/theater events.

For activities at **Hayward Gallery,** see p. 175; for the **National Film Theatre,** see p. 256. Belvedere Rd., SE1. ✆ 020/7921-0600. www.sbc.org.uk. Tickets from £16 ($30) vary according to show. Tube: Waterloo.

Royal Albert Hall   This world-famous circular building of gargantuan proportions (it has a mind-boggling seating capacity of 5,200) is best known for its summer Proms

Central London Entertainment

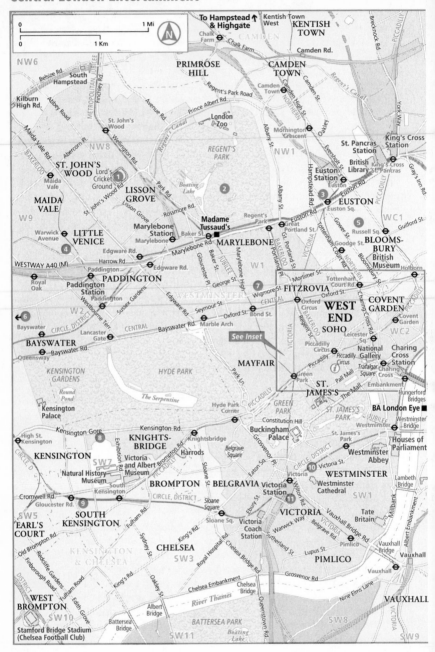

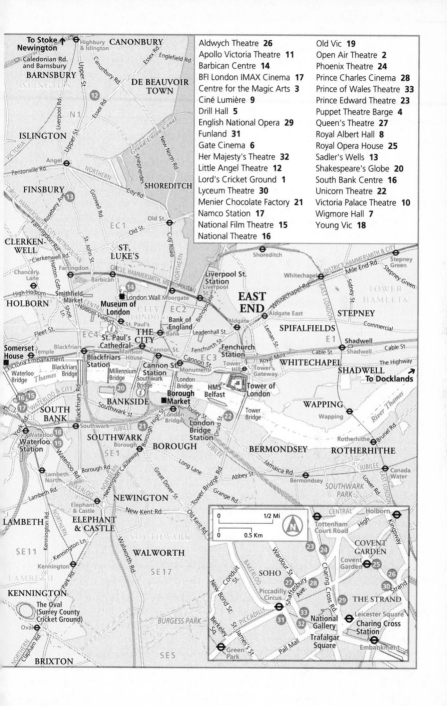

Aldwych Theatre **26**
Apollo Victoria Theatre **11**
Barbican Centre **14**
BFI London IMAX Cinema **17**
Centre for the Magic Arts **3**
Ciné Lumière **9**
Drill Hall **5**
English National Opera **29**
Funland **31**
Gate Cinema **6**
Her Majesty's Theatre **32**
Little Angel Theatre **12**
Lord's Cricket Ground **1**
Lyceum Theatre **30**
Menier Chocolate Factory **21**
Namco Station **17**
National Film Theatre **15**
National Theatre **16**

Old Vic **19**
Open Air Theatre **2**
Phoenix Theatre **24**
Prince Charles Cinema **28**
Prince of Wales Theatre **33**
Prince Edward Theatre **23**
Puppet Theatre Barge **4**
Queen's Theatre **27**
Royal Albert Hall **8**
Royal Opera House **25**
Sadler's Wells **13**
Shakespeare's Globe **20**
South Bank Centre **16**
Unicorn Theatre **22**
Victoria Palace Theatre **10**
Wigmore Hall **7**
Young Vic **18**

Show Time: Where to Get Tickets

You'll probably want to catch a show while you're here, and why not? In my opinion, this is *the* theater capital of the world. But with kids in tow, you're not going to be able to and/or be willing to book seats far in advance, so you may want to go to the opposite extreme and snap up last-minute bargains (usually half-price tickets, with a £2.50 or $4.75 service charge) for top West End shows at the two official **TKTS** ticket booths in Leicester Square and at Canary Wharf DLR Station. (Note that cash is not accepted at TKTS Canary Wharf.) Notice boards detail what's available in front of the booths; or check the daily listings on www.officiallondontheatre.co.uk (which also sells advance tickets).

If tickets for the show you want to see are not available at TKTS, try the theater directly; some release limited numbers of tickets for same-day performances at noon, but they can only be purchased in person at the box office and may be limited to two per person—so a family of four may end up sitting in two separate groups. You can also buy advance full-price tickets from a theater's box office by phone or via its website, though the latter actually links through **See** (© **0870/264-3333**; www.seetickets.com), **Ticketmaster** (© **0870/154-4040**; www.ticketmaster.co.uk), or **www.londontheatredirect.com**. Ticketmaster also has several outlets, the most central in the basement of the Virgin Megastore at Piccadilly Circus.

However you pay, and wherever you get your tickets, you'll be subject to a **booking fee** of about £1.50 ($2.85) *per ticket,* so factor that into the cost of your night out. Note that **www.londontheatredirect.com** offers theater-dinner deals and discounted hotel rooms.

concerts, which it's hosted since 1941. Incorporating a medley of rousing, mostly British orchestral music, this is great fun for older kids, especially if you buy standing-room tickets in the orchestra pit and get a peek at the musicians on stage. Don't despair if you can't get tickets for the spectacular Last Night: The event is relayed on big screens in Hyde Park opposite (p. 201). Alternatively, wait for the School Proms in November, when children can hear lots of different types of music performed by others their own ages, or the Blue Peter Proms held in Hyde Park (it's also called the BBC Family Proms in the Park), in association with the kids' show *Blue Peter*. More events held here include opera and the astonishing acrobatics and aerial acts of the flamboyant Cirque du Soleil, a sure-fire family winner. Kensington Gore, SW7. © 020/7589-8212. www.royalalberthall.com. Tickets £20–£50 ($38–$95) for operas; £2.50–£10 ($4.75–$19) for the Proms. Tube: S. Kensington.

Young Vic   This groundbreaking theater—set up in the 1970s to bring to kids ages 9 to 15 the classics and occasional new plays by younger writers, directors, actors, musicians, and technicians at low ticket prices—is falling apart, and in the meantime it's on "walkabout," or changing venue spots, so check its website for details of performances at other venues. Over the last few years, shows have included *Doctor Faustus* with Jude Law and *As You Like It* with Sienna Miller. Each year there's a theatrical event embracing kids, young people, and adults alike. © 020/7928-6363. www.youngvic.org. Tickets start at £15 ($29) adults and £10 ($19) under 10s; prices vary according to show.

2 Seasonal Events

One of the best times to visit London if you have theatrically minded kids is **Kids' Week** ✦✦✦ (www.officiallondontheatre.co.uk/kids/week), during which you can get free tickets for 5- to 19-year-olds to more than 30 top West End shows throughout the second half of August. (Booking opens mid-July; you get one free ticket with every adult full-price ticket, plus the option of a further two kids' tickets at half price.) In addition, more than 50 special family-friendly events are offered, including backstage visits (to discover the secrets of the shows and to meet the stars), dance, stage-fighting, and make-up workshops. A Theater Bus is parked up in Covent Garden Piazza; the nearby **Theatre Museum** (p. 172) runs activities for under-5s and free daily drop-in events; and many restaurants let kids eat for free. See the website for travel and accommodations discounts, too.

As winter begins to bite, along come Christmas **pantomimes** ✦ (or *pantos*) to cheer you up. A British institution based on popular kids' stories and fairy tales such as *Cinderella,* these demand plenty of audience participation. A recent highlight was Sir Ian McKellen playing Widow Twankey (it's a tradition that the older woman character or dame is played by a man in drag) in *Aladdin* at the Old Vic. Other regular London venues are the Barbican (p. 242), Victoria Palace Theatre, and Richmond Theatre. Full details are released on **www.thisistheatre.com/panto.html** throughout the year.

3 Theater

A seemingly unstoppable new trend among younger kids is touring shows based on some of the most popular British, U.S., and Australian children's TV shows and characters, such as The Wiggles, High Five, and Bear in the Big Blue House. Such events run for a night or two at large venues such as the ExCel Arena in Docklands and the Wembley Arena, or at small local theaters such as the Richmond and the Wimbledon. To keep up to date, watch your chosen show's website, or log on to www.ticketmaster.co.uk and check forthcoming family events.

CHILDREN'S THEATER COMPANIES

As we went to press, the new £ 13 million building for the award-winning **Unicorn Theatre** (Tooley St, SE1; ✆ 020/7700-0702; www.unicorntheatre.com) was due to open on December 1, 2005. The first purpose-designed professional theater for kids in the UK, it will host challenging works for children aged 4 to 12 plus Family Days (£24/$46) combining workshops with performances followed by meetings with the cast.

artsdepot   This dynamic arts venue in north London, opened since 2004, is worth going out of your way for because of its exciting kids' programming, featuring shows by a wide range of innovative theater companies in its Studio Theatre. Specific shows vary, but the venue generally caters to kids 3 and up. The colorful lobby cafe has a healthy but fun children's menu of homemade goodies, including special meals for tots. 5 Nether Street, N12. ✆ 020/ 8369-5454. www.artsdepot.co.uk. Tube: West Finchley. Tickets £12 ($23) adults, kids £6 ($11).

Chicken Shed Theatre ✦   A delightfully named company (its original home was indeed an old chicken shed), this theater comes with a long-standing reputation for imaginative new works and creative adaptations using ingenious staging. It's a fair schlep out of central London, in the northern suburb of Southgate, but you won't regret the trip. Much of the freshness comes from the fact that this youth theater has

Out In The Open

There's no finer way to appreciate a long summer evening in the City than to take the family to one of its magical outdoor events. Right in the center of town, in lovely Regent's Park, **Open Air Theatre** ★★ (Inner Circle, NW1; © 08700/601811; www.openairtheatre.org) hosts light fare such as two Shakespeare romantic comedies, a Gilbert & Sullivan operetta, and a kids' show suitable for all ages. Tickets are a steep £10 ($19). The grounds open early so you can enjoy a buffet and barbecue, or you can bring your own picnic (see p. 115 for tips on where to buy great picnic fare). The season lasts from late May to mid-September. Don't worry about the weather; if the performance has to be abandoned, you get free tickets to another showing.

Another delightful way to spend a balmy evening is at an English Heritage **Music on a Summer Evening lakeside concert** ★★★ (© 0870/890-0146; www.picnicconcerts.com) at Kenwood House (p. 142) or Marble Hill House (p. 183). Performances range from classical and opera to popular (Elvis Costello, *Grease the Musical,* Katie Melua), and culminate in a spectacular fireworks display. Gates open early, so bring a picnic and a rug (you can also hire deck chairs). Be warned that these events are wildly popular, so book well in advance. Ticket prices average £20 ($38), with only tiny concessions for kids, so it's an expensive night out—but one they won't forget in a hurry. Similar concert, firework, and picnic extravaganzas are held at the 1-week **Summer Swing** at Kew's Royal Botanic Gardens (p. 188), with kids under 5 attending free of charge.

Kenwood House and Marble Hill House now host daytime **Jazz Café Picnics** (www.meanfiddler.com) featuring rather funkier, more left-field artists such as Nitin Sawhney, Lemon Jelly, and Rökysopp. Tickets cost £33 to £40 ($63–$76); again, under-5s get in free.

Few people haven't heard of the Last Night of the Proms, the rabble-rousing climax of the summer season at Royal Albert Hall (p. 243). But many

an all-inclusive policy, allowing anyone ages 5 to 24 to join without audition. Works range from experimental pieces or Shakespeare for older kids to *Tales from the Shed* story performances for under-7s, when the edge of the stage is removed to encourage participation. Chase Side, N14. © 020/8292-9222. www.chickenshed.org.uk. Ticket prices vary; generally £4–£16 ($7.50–$30). Tube: Oakwood.

Half Moon Young People's Theatre An exciting East London venue for shows for kids from birth to age 17, Half Moon produces and tours two shows of its own each year. (One venue is the Menier Chocolate Factory on the South Bank.) From October to April, it also hosts performances by outstanding visiting companies, such as Oily Cart (p. 250), Little Angel Theatre (below), and Quicksilver Theatre (p. 250). The choice is particularly great for those with kids ages 2 to 6. 43 White Horse Rd., E1. © 020/7265-8138. www.halfmoon.org.uk. Tickets £3.50–£5 ($6.50–$9.50). Tube: Stepney Green.

Little Angel Theatre ★★ A magical little marionette theater that seems to have left behind the specter of closure, the Little Angel continues to put on shows that go don't know that the event has spilled over into adjacent Hyde Park to become **Proms in the Park** (www.bbc.co.uk/proms/pitp). The highlight of the night is the relaying of the concert inside Royal Albert Hall onto giant screens watched by an audience sitting outdoors beneath the stars. Events actually begin late in the afternoon with concerts by other performers, who might include tribute bands, swing bands, and the BBC Concert Orchestra playing with some of the world's best musicians. You can buy tickets three ways: by calling © 0870/899-8100; via Royal Albert Hall's website; or at the BBC shops (50 Margaret St., W1, Bush House, The Strand, W1).

Something a little more offbeat is in store for you if you book one of the enchanting promenade performances by the **London Bubble Theatre Company** ★★ (© 020/7237-1663; www.londonbubble.org.uk), during which the audience follows the actors round a London park as they perform works such as *Gulliver's Travels.* Performances are particularly atmospheric because they begin at 8:30pm or 9pm, as the light begins to fall; if that's past your young 'uns' bedtime, inquire about the afternoon workshops for 3- to 6-year-olds and 6- to 9-year-olds. Performance tickets cost £12 ($23) for adults, £8 ($15) for kids, and will be refunded or replaced in cases of bad weather. The company also puts on Christmas pantomimes.

Lastly, and more prosaically, **funfairs** and **circuses** like Carters Steam Fair (p. 191) and Zippos and the Chinese State Circus pitch their tents on London's green spaces throughout the summer season; for information, see *Time Out* magazine. Recent years have brought occasional free outdoor movie screenings in venues such as Battersea Park and Greenwich Park; films have included *The Fifth Element* and *Master & Commander,* with PG ratings. See www.stellascreen.com for details.

on to tour nationally and internationally; it also hosts performances by visiting companies. All types of puppets are used, and themes and stories are drawn from a variety of cultural traditions. The main performances are usually aimed at kids 4 and over, but special adaptations for 2- to 5-year-olds run in tandem. Look, too, for family interactive workshops (£25/$48 for one adult and one child, including show tickets), in which you and Junior can create puppets and play with them together, using the performance you've just seen as inspiration. 14 Dagmar Passage, N1. © 020/7226-1787. www.littleangel theatre.com. Tickets £5–£7.50 ($9.50–$14). Tube: Angel.

Polka Theatre ★★★   This inspiring space manages to be both a beloved local venue and a world-renowned center of young people's theater. Events range from teenage dramas to modern-day literary adaptations. Performances are split between the Main Auditorium for ages 4 and up, and the Adventure Theatre for younger kids. That said, the auditorium does host "Watch with Baby" performances of certain productions so parents with older children can see shows without worrying about child care for the youngest; if your baby gets restless, you can take him or her into the foyer and carry on watching the show on the monitor. Most performances in the Adventure Theatre are aimed at those 3 and up, but it's recently hosted a number of developments in theater for babies (6 months plus), and it holds special babies' and toddlers' performances.

A full program of extras includes discussions of rehearsed readings, vacation courses and workshops (drama, songs, storytelling, puppet making), and free drop-in interactive performances by spoken-word artists (with complimentary ice cream) on Saturday at 10:30am. There are great facilities, too, including a welcoming cafe with a kids' menu (staff are happy to warm up baby food), a baby-changing room, and a stroller park. 240 The Broadway, SW19. ℭ **020/8543-4888**. www.polkatheatre.com. Tickets £5–£12 ($9.50–$23). Tube: Wimbledon.

Puppet Theatre Barge ✦   This unique and atmospheric 50-seat theater presents marionette and rod puppet shows. In winter the vessel is moored in the lovely Little Venice neighborhood of west London (p. 48), in summer (July–Oct) it plies the Thames, giving performances at Henley-on-Thames, Marlow, Cliveden, and Richmond-on-Thames. Shows are only recommended for children 9 or over. At press time, the schedule involved evening performances of Shakespeare's *Macbeth, Bottom's Dream,* and *The Tempest,* all beginning at 8pm. However, occasional family shows are suitable for kids as young as 3, some forming part of the Canalway Cavalcade, a local canal boat festival around the May Day holiday. Blomfield Rd., W9. ℭ **020/7249-6876**. www.puppetbarge.com. Tickets £7.50 ($14) adults, £7 ($13) kids. Tube: Warwick Ave.

TOURING THEATERS

Oily Cart ✦✦ (ℭ **020/8672-6329;** www.oilycart.org.uk) is a national touring company offering hip-hop musicals and other groundbreaking and highly interactive performances for under-5s (as well as kids with severe disabilities). London venues include Half Moon Young People's Theatre (p. 248), Drill Hall (p. 210), Croydon Clocktower (p. 252), and Lyric Hammersmith (p. 253). Keep an eye on the tour schedules of **Pop-Up** (ℭ **020/7609-3339;** www.pop-up.net), an innovative company producing thought-provoking work for 3- to 7-year-olds and 7- to 11-year-olds by outstanding kids' authors such as David Almond. **Quicksilver Theatre** ✦ (ℭ **020/ 7241-2942;** www.quicksilvertheatre.org) has won awards for its boldly visual new plays for 3- to 7-year-olds and older kids, performed at the Polka Theatre (p. 249), Lyric Hammersmith (p. 253), and long-standing **Theatre Centre** (ℭ **020/7377-0379;** www.theatre-centre.co.uk), which presents specially commissioned works on three broad themes ("Rites of Passage," "Contemporary Culture," and "The Releasing of the Authentic Voice") to kids 9 and up. Pioneering **theatre-rites** ✦✦ (ℭ **020/ 8946-2236;** www.theatre-rites.co.uk), presents richly poetic works for kids up to 7, such as the installation piece performed in a disused ward of a real hospital.

LONG-RUNNING SHOWS

At press time, the West End shows listed below indicated they would continue indefinitely. Because some last nearly 3 hours (including an intermission), families with kids ought to consider a midweek or weekend matinee performance. Count on spending between £20 ($38) and £50 ($95) per person, more for the best seats. For advice on booking, see p. 246.

As well as the shows specifically oriented toward kids reviewed below, older children enjoy the following long-runners: **Stomp,** a wordless, highly choreographed piece using found objects such as brooms, garbage cans, and oil drums to make uplifting rhythms inspired by **street theater** (Vaudeville Theatre; ℂ **0870/890-0511;** www. vaudeville-theatre.co.uk/www.stomponline.com); the camp classic **Saturday Night Fever** (Apollo Victoria Theatre; ℂ **0870/161-1977;** www.apollovictoria.co.uk), with its sing-along 1970s disco classics like *Stayin' Alive;* the worldwide Andrew Lloyd Webber smash **Phantom of the Opera** (Her Majesty's Theatre; ℂ **0870/160-2878;** www.her majestys.co.uk), about a beautiful opera singer who falls in love with a deformed young composer living a shadowy existence beneath the Paris Opera; the long-running melo-drama **Blood Brothers** (Phoenix Theatre; ℂ **0870/060-6629;** www.phoenix-theatre. co.uk), about twin brothers separated at birth whose lives become unavoidably linked; and **Mamma Mia!** (ℂ **0870/850-0393;** www.princeofwalestheatre.co.uk), about a hol-idaying single mom and her daughter, who pepper their lives and fantasies with rendi-tions of their favorite ABBA songs, which often gets the audience singing and dancing in the aisles.

Billy Elliot ⭐ This feel-good musical trades on the Oscar-nominated movie of the same name, set in a mining town in northeast England and following a young boy's realization of his dream to become a ballet dancer in spite of his father's wish that he become a boxer. The tunes are by Elton John. Victoria Palace Theatre, Victoria St., SW1. ℂ 020/ 7834-1317. www.victoria-palace-theatre.co.uk. Tickets £23–£55 ($44–$105). Tube: Victoria.

Fame the Musical The well-rehearsed tale of a bunch of star-struck students from New York's School of Performing Arts in their quest to "learn how to fly, high!" pro-vides perfect fodder for aspiring actors. Aldwych Theatre, Aldwych, WC2B. ℂ 0870/400-0805. www.aldwych-theatre.co.uk. Tickets £15–£40 ($29–$76). Tube: Covent Garden.

Les Misérables ⭐⭐ This adaptation of the Victor Hugo novel of 1862, one of the world's most popular musicals, has been around for about 20 years in London. It's melo-dramatic stuff, but the plot—about social justice—can be a little dark for kids, and the music isn't best suited to sing alongs. You can now get them better involved by signing up for one of the thrice-monthly **Les Miz Kids Club workshops** for children ages 8 to 11 and 12 to 15 (ℂ **0870/850-9171**), which last 2½ hours and include a behind-the-scenes tour, the chance to try on costumes, a drama workshop with improvisation games, a lyric-learning session, a sack lunch, and a meeting with a cast member. Prices vary according to whether you attend the subsequent matinee, and the seat you choose. Queen's Theatre, 51 Shaftesbury Ave. ℂ 020/7494-5040. www.lesmis.com. Tickets £13–£48 ($24–$90).Tube: Piccadilly Circus.

The Lion King ⭐⭐ An award-winning Disney blockbuster musical about life and love on the savannah, *The Lion King* uses puppetry and masks to magical visual effect. A limited number of seats for the day's performance are released at the box office at noon, but note that you can only buy two per person, so a whole family may end up not sitting together. Lyceum Theatre, Wellington St., WC2. ℂ 0870/243-9000. www.disney.co.uk. Tickets £18–£40 ($33–$76). Tube: Covent Garden.

Mary Poppins ⭐⭐⭐ Critically and publicly acclaimed, this new musical is based on the 1960s Disney movie about a London chimney sweep and a magical nanny, with many of the songs from the Oscar-winning film score plus new ones thrown in for good measure. A small number of tickets are released at noon for that day's per-formance; they can only be bought at the box office in person. *Mary Poppins* is rec-ommended for ages 7 and over, with under-3s not admitted. As we went to press, there were plans to introduce kids' workshops along the lines of those available for *Les Misérables* (see above). Prince Edward Theatre, Old Compton St., W1V. ℂ **0870/850-9191.** www. marypoppinsthemusical.co.uk. Tickets £15–£50 ($29–$95). Tube: Leicester Sq.

WEEKEND SHOWS

Chats Palace   This gritty East End community arts center hosts top professional children's entertainment on Saturday at 2pm, involving puppets, music, clowns, and more, most aimed at 3-year-olds and up. Tickets are a steal, and there's lots of free entertainment, too, including games and face-painting. You can get the kids fired up for the performance with dance and drama workshops for ages 2 to 6, or bring them down gently with post-show arts-and-crafts workshops for ages 4 to 8. 42–44 Brooksbys Walk, E9. ℂ 020/8533- 0227. www.chatspalace.com. Tickets £2 ($3.80). Train: Homerton.

The Colour House   Far-flung but scenically sited, this little kids' theater in a medieval building (once part of a textile factory) just south of Wimbledon hosts classic family musicals *(Snow White, The Wizard of Oz, Beauty & the Beast)* suitable for anyone ages 4 and up. (Many parents and grandparents seem to enjoy them just as much.) Afterward, you'll want to linger awhile in the eclectic weekend market with its ethnic crafts and Indian head masseuse. Shows kick off at 2pm and 4pm on Saturday and Sunday and run for an hour. In July and August, the Abbeyfest celebration features extra shows by The Colour House, as well as live jazz, blues, and chamber music. No. 3, The Show House, Merton Abbey Mills, SW19. ℂ 020/8640-5111. www.wheelhouse.org.uk. Tickets £7 ($13). Tube: Colliers Wood.

Comedy Club 4 Kids   Britain's first stand-up comedy club for children ages 7 to 13, held on Sunday afternoons at 3pm in a chocolate factory turned trendy arts complex, opened to rave reviews in summer 2005. Billed as "alternative comedy without the swearing," it's hosted by well-known comedian James Campbell, who has toured his non-condescending, surreally silly kids' show around the world, and features regular guest comics. Shows tend to be freeform, with Campbell running with feedback from kids in the audience, but topics might include dead hamsters, boring relatives, or the danger of being hit by flying cows while walking home from school. Kids with comedic aspirations get a 5-minute shot at the mic. (They have to attend a course at the "academy" first—see www.jamescampbell.info for details of classes and workshops.) Shows last 2 hours, including an interval. Menier Chocolate Factory, 51–3 Southwark St., SE1. ℂ 020/ 7907-7060. www.menierchocolatefactory.com. Tickets £10 ($19) adults and kids. Tube: London Bridge.

Croydon Clocktower   This south London arts and cultural center is a parents' oasis on weekends, when it hosts plays for ages 3 and up and Saturday-morning kids' movies in its art house. The Clocktower Exhibition Gallery is closed for redevelopment until summer 2006 but usually hosts eclectic touring exhibitions on such fascinating topics as funfair history, and has a permanent interactive display on local history, with a digital memory room where you can record your own stories. The eclectic program of events includes the likes of drop-in sessions about Chinese food, culminating in the creation of a take away food box. There's also a state-of-the-art public library with storytelling sessions for kids, a cafe, and a tourist information center. Katherine St., Surrey CR9. ℂ 020/8253-1030. www.croydon.gov.uk/clocktower. Tickets £4.50–£5.50 ($8.50–$11). Train: E. Croydon.

Jackson's Lane   A thriving 30-year-old north London community center in a converted church, Jackson's Lane hosts Saturday and/or Sunday shows for a variety of age groups (generally kids 4–12) by companies such as Quicksilver Theatre (p. 250) and

Jactito Puppet Theatre. Shows make for an excellent interlude between a romp in Highgate Woods (p. 207) and a browse in Ripping Yarns (p. 224). The center also hosts creative sessions for tots ages 18 months to 4 years, and performing arts classes for young people 8 to 20. 269a Archway Rd., N6. © 020/8341-4421. www.jacksonslane.org.uk. Tickets £4.75 ($9) per person. Tube: Highgate.

Lauderdale House ★★★   This outstanding cultural center in a lovely 16th-century house built for London's lord mayor, set in secluded Waterlow Park in north London (p. 206), is heaven for parents searching for kids' activities. On Saturday mornings you can catch one of two performances (10am and 11:30am) of a show that may involve puppetry, singing, storytelling, or a musical session, or a combination of those. There are also occasional Sunday family specials, and in mid-May the shows are part of the Hampstead & Highgate Festival, which features special family workshops.

In summertime kids can take courses in art, dance, drama, puppet making, and more, lasting four consecutive mornings or afternoons. Throughout the year there are dance, drama, drawing, and painting workshops for kids ages 18 months to 15 years. On Monday at midday and Friday at 10am toddlers get their own drop-in music classes (ages 3 and up). Refuel in the cafe-restaurant before enjoying the rest of the park. Highgate Hill, Waterlow Park, N6 5HG. © 020/8348-8716. www.lauderdalehouse.co.uk. Tickets £4.50 ($8.50) adults, £3 ($5.70) kids, only available on the door. Tube: Archway.

Lyric Hammersmith   This Victorian theater in west London hosts Saturday kids' shows (11am and 1pm) by the likes of Quicksilver Theatre (p. 250), most lasting just less than an hour. Sometimes there's puppetry, other times live music; the majority of performances encourage little ones (ages 2 and up, depending on the show) to jump out of their seats and get involved. Tickets are pricey, though you can save a few quid by getting a family ticket for four, or by booking online. Lyric Sq., King St., W6. © 08700/500511. www.lyric.co.uk. Tickets £8 ($15) adults and £6 ($12) kids. Tube: Hammersmith.

Tricycle ★★   This lively little north London theater, cinema, and gallery is well worth going out of your way for, especially for its Saturday children's theater (usually 11:30am and 2pm). Each show tends to differ in its age range, but something suitable for kids ages 2 to 12 is regularly featured. It may be a traditional Hans Christian Andersen tale such as *The Princess and the Pea,* or puppet shows, storytelling, and rhythms from Africa, the Caribbean, and South America. Children 7 and older can attend alone, while parents chill out over newspapers in the vibrant cafe/bar. Babies under 18 months are admitted free (you'll have to leave if they cry loudly). If you're in London for a while, your kids might like to sign up for the popular 9-week dance, drama, and/or music workshops for those from 18 months to 16 years old. Similar half-term workshops lasting 1 to 2 hours, including puppet-making and mini-garden creating, tend to get booked up long in advance. Check out the program of Saturday family films (normally 1pm; £4/$7.60). ***Insider tip:*** Tickets for theater performances can be a bit cheaper if they're bought in advance. 269 Kilburn High Rd., NW6. © 020/7328-1000. www.tricycle.co.uk. Tickets £5 ($9.50). Tube: Kilburn.

MAGIC

Centre for the Magic Arts ★ *(Finds)*   The Magic Circle's HQ is open to visitors 14 and over (sometimes younger kids are allowed in by arrangement) for regular special evenings called "Meet The Magic Circle," when you can see tricks close up, listen to a talk on the history of mystery from 4,000 B.C. onwards, and watch a stage show in the theater. You'll hear all about the famous bullet-catching trick that has killed several magicians, and about the exploits of Houdini. While you're here, you get access to the Magic Circle Museum (normally open only to members), which has exhibits on great musicians of the past, posters, and other memorabilia. Aspiring young talents should enquire about the Young Magicians Club for 10- to 18-year-olds. 12 Stephenson Way, NW1. © 020/7387-2222. www.themagiccircle.co.uk. Tickets £26 ($49). Tube: Euston.

4 Classical Music, Dance & Opera

For the **Wigmore Hall** classical venue, see p. 218. For the large multi-arts venues, see p. 242.

English National Opera 🌟   Your best bet for opera-going in London with kids, especially if you're new to the art form, is the London Coliseum, home to the ENO, which performs all works in English, making it far easier for novices to follow the story. Works range from crowd-pleasing classics such as *Carmen* and Gilbert and Sullivan librettos to more experimental modern opera. Sporadic ENO Baylis family days (10am–3:30pm; £3/$5.70; attendance sometimes gets you reduced-price opera tickets) allow kids 7 and up to study the themes of an opera currently being performed. London Coliseum, St. Martin's Lane, WC2. © 020/7632-8300. www.eno.org. Tickets £5–£30 ($9.50–$57). Tube: Leicester Sq.

Royal Opera House 🌟   The city's more grown-up option, the Royal Opera House is home to both the Royal Opera and the Royal Ballet, and hosts regular visits by the Kirov Opera and Ballet. Operas are usually sung in the original language, with super-titles projected. Ask about the occasional family operas or concerts. Daily backstage tours for those 8 and over vary according to what's going on, but may include a glimpse of the Royal Ballet in class, or of the impressive behind-the-scenes technology in action. Bow St., WC2. © 020/7304-4000. www.royalopera.org. Tickets £7–£150 ($13–$285). Tube: Covent Garden.

Sadler's Wells 🌟🌟   This is a top-ranking venue for mainstream and cutting-edge contemporary dance (including tango, tap, and flamenco), opera, and family shows, such as Christmas ballets and adaptations of works by current kids' authors as prominent as Jacqueline Wilson. Try to catch a show by the London Children's Ballet, who transform short stories by the likes of Oscar Wilde into fun performances. Occasional family days involve a simple dance workshop based on the performance you are about to see, followed by another activity (perhaps face-painting, an arts workshop, or a costume demonstration), rounded off by the matinee performance. Rosebery Ave., EC1. © 0870/737-7737. www.sadlers-wells.com. Ticket prices vary; generally £10–£18 ($19–$34). Tube: Angel.

Teen Beat

St Katherine's Dock just east of the Tower of London is home to the classy **Copyright** nightclub (110 Pennignton St., E1; © 0871/332-4435), which, on the last Friday of every month, hosts dance and R&B nights for teens (ages 13–17). The sound system is second to none, there's a vibrating dance floor, and the Indo-Chinese decor boasts modern chandeliers, elephant statues, and sari fabrics—all in all, great fun. Parents might like to wait it all out in the adjoining restaurant, where they can enjoy seafood platters and good mojitos.

5 Movies

London has more than its fair share of multiplex cinemas offering the latest Hollywood blockbusters for consumption with monster buckets of popcorn. For reviews and detailed weekly listings, see *Time Out* magazine, published each Wednesday and available from all newsagents. Most of the big-hitters (Empire, vue, Odeon) are in Leicester Square and adjoining West End streets.

Be aware that cinema-going in the center can empty your wallet in no time, with adult tickets averaging £10 ($19), and kids half that. By contrast, some farther-flung venues offer good family deals, such as **Odeon Swiss Cottage** in north London (© 0871/222-4007; www.odeon.co.uk) with its £20 ($38) ticket for two adults and two kids (or one adult and three kids). Another option a little farther north is **O2 Centre** (Finchley Rd., NW3; © 07000/020002; www.o2centre.co.uk), a mall with an eight-screen **vue cinema** (© 0871/224-0240; www.myvue.com) where Liam Gallagher can sometimes be seen catching a movie with his progeny. The mall also has a bookstore, a branch of Gymboree (p. 216), the London International Gallery of Children's Art (p. 217), tempting eating options including a large branch of Ed's Easy Diner (p. 137) and a Smollensky's (p. 107), a big supermarket, and holiday events such as face painting and entertainers, so you can make a day of it. Perhaps the best deal of all is the **Kids' Club at UCI Whiteleys** (© 0870/010-2030; www.uci.co.uk) in the Whiteleys shopping mall in west London (p. 238), where children pay just £1.95 ($3.70) for the 11am showing (weekends, or daily during school vacations), with accompanying adults free.

London's smaller independent picture-houses are more congenial than the City's blockbuster cinemas and often run special family screenings or film clubs. For Barbican's Family Film Club, see p. 242; for the Tricycle, see p. 253; for David Lean Cinema in Croydon Clocktower, see p. 252. Note that by British law, kids under 5 must be accompanied by an adult in a cinema.

Ciné-Lumière ★★   Here's something a little out of the ordinary for French-speaking visitors or budding Francophiles: the Ciné-Teens & Kids program of French-language films, newly introduced at the cinema inside the Institut Français language and cultural center. Movies (all shown with English subtitles) range from 1940s classics of French cinema by the likes of Truffaut and Cocteau to nature documentaries and animated folk tales, divided in age groups 4-plus, 8-plus, 12-plus, and 15-plus. A library in the building offers books, comics, magazines, and videos for kids ages 6 months to 12 years. A bistro offers regional Gallic dishes and snacks. 17 Queensberry Place, SW7. © 020/7073-1350. www.institut-francais.org.uk/cineteensandkids. Tickets £5 ($9.50) adults, £3 ($5.70) under-18s. Tube: S. Kensington.

Clapham Picture House ★   This eclectic local cinema showing both mainstream and art-house films caters to parents in two ways: with its Saturday-morning Kids Club for 3- to 10-year-olds (11:15am; £3/$5.70 adults and kids), preceded by creative activities and games; and with its Big Scream Parents and Babies Club every Thursday at 10:30am, which allows moms or dads to enjoy one of two full-length features, including current blockbusters, classics, art house films, and foreign-language films, with babes on their laps. The Clapham has a good cafe/bar and an art exhibition area, and hosts bimonthly film quizzes. 76 Venn St., SW4. © 020/7498-3323. www.picturehouses. co.uk. Tickets £3.50–£8 ($7–$15) adults; £4.50 ($8.50) kids. Tube: Brixton.

ElectricCinema ★   This achingly trendy Notting Hill cinema stands out for its comfy and roomy leather seating (including sofas and footstools). It hosts a Kids' Club

Saturday at various times; the cost is £4.50 ($8.50) each for kids and accompanying adults. The cinema features new releases generally suitable for those ages 4 to 9. The original "Electric Scream" parents/caregivers and under-1s screenings are held Monday at 3pm. The bar at the back eschews popcorn in favor of calamari-in-a-cup, rice crackers, brownies, and cappuccino. 191 Portobello Rd., W11. ℂ 020/7908-9696. www. electriccinema.co.uk. Tickets £5–£13 ($9.50–$24) adults; £5–£7.50 ($9.50–$14) kids. Tube: Ladbroke Grove.

Everyman Cinema Club   Here's another chi-chi local cinema with handcrafted leather sofas and armchairs, primarily of interest to parents because of its "Everyman Scream" parents'/caretakers' and babies' showings (advance booking required) in its luxurious new second screening lounge on Thursday at noon. You can bring older kids along, too, providing the film's rating allows it. Afterwards, there's a cafe for cakes and excellent coffee. 5 Holly Bush Vale, NW3. ℂ 0870/066-4777. www.everymancinema.com. Tickets for Scream event on Thurs at noon and separate kid screenings on Thurs at 3pm cost £7.50 ($14) and kids get in free. Tube: Hampstead.

Gate Cinema   This is one of London's most atmospheric cinemas, set in a converted coffee palace boasting Edwardian plasterwork and red velvet armchair seating. Its Saturday morning Kids' Club for 3- to 10-year-olds gets underway with creative activities and games at 11am, followed by a reasonably recent movie at 11:30am. 87 Notting Hill Gate, W11. ℂ 020/7727-4043. www.picturehouses.co.uk. Tickets £3 ($5.70) for both kids and accompanying adults. Tube: Notting Hill Gate.

National Film Theatre   The British Film Institute's "Movie Magic" program of films and related events and workshops for kids has sadly dwindled over the past few years, but arty fare is occasionally shown for older, culturally-minded kids, including Iranian films. Belvedere Rd., South Bank, SE1. ℂ 020/7928-3232. www.bfi.org.uk. Tickets £4.50 ($8.50) adults, £1 ($1.90) kids. Tube: Waterloo.

Ritzy   This restored five-screen Edwardian picture house, which is the biggest and the busiest independent cinema in London, offers kids a choice of two films every Saturday morning, at bargain prices, and hosts another popular weekly "Watch with Baby Club," on Friday at 11am. Tickets for the latter (£4/$7.60, plus £1/$1.90 membership) include tea or coffee in the funky jazz bar, which serves good crepes and pizzas and is a venue for live jazz events. Ask, too, about the good-value family tickets for four or five people. Coldharbour Lane, Brixton, SW2. ℂ 020/7733-2229. www.picturehouses.co.uk. Tickets: Sat morning, 2 movies, £3/$5.70 adults, £1/$1.90 kids. Tube: Brixton.

Riverside Studios ☆   At press time, this center for international contemporary performance and cinema had just introduced an eclectic Family Cinema program on Sunday morning at 11am, with movies ranging from the likes of Senegalese animated folk tales and selections of shorts from around the world to big-hitters such as *Robots*, with age ranges dictated by individual ratings. Its lovely cafe-bar with a river terrace hosts art and photography exhibitions, and an espresso bar sells cakes and sandwiches. Alternatively, enjoy a roast for lunch at one of the quaint pubs further along the riverside). Crisp Rd., W6. ℂ 020-8237-1111. www.riversidestudios.co.uk. Tickets £5.50 ($11) adults, £3.50 ($6.70) kids. Tube: Hammersmith.

Sing-a-Long-a-Sound-of-Music (at the Prince Charles Theatre)   This well-known cheapie cinema just off Leicester Square was the original venue for the Sing-a-Long international phenomenon that allows audiences to burst into song to some of their favorite movies. Although you can now sing along to *Joseph* and *The Wizard of Oz* at locations outside London, here you're still restricted to *The Sound of Music*, which shows approximately once a month (book well ahead). The movie is screened with subtitles, and audience members are encouraged to come dressed as nuns (during intermission there's a Mother Superior fancy dress competition with prizes). It's worth stressing that this is an option for older kids, as the screenings are at 7:30pm and can get a little rowdy. 7 Leicester Place, WC2. ℭ 020/7494-3654. www.princecharlescinema.com. Tickets: Sing along £14 ($26); regular films £3–£4 ($5.70–$7.60); reduced rates for members. Tube: Leicester Sq.

IMAX CINEMAS

London has two "image maximum" cinemas that create the illusion, through huge screens and huge sound systems, that the film you're watching is happening all around the audience. On the South Bank, **BFI London Imax Cinema** (1 Charlie Chaplin Walk, SE1; ℭ **0870/787-2525;** www.bfi.org.uk/showing/imax) houses Britain's biggest cinema screen (the height of five double-decker buses), viewed from 14 tiered rows of seats that allow everyone—kids included—to enjoy unobstructed views. Ongoing, specially made 3D shows include *Aliens of the Deep* and *Space Station,* but new releases also make their way here, including animated films. The Film Café inside the dramatic circular building serves kid-friendly fare.

The second IMAX is at the **Science Museum** (p. 148); it shows the same specially commissioned shows, plus extras such as *Bugs! 3D, The Human Body*, and *SOS Planet.*

6 Spectator Sports

In 2007, the ill-fated Millennium Dome in east London is expected to reopen as the **Dome Arena,** an entertainment and sports destination. Events will include matches by the London Knights ice hockey team.

Football (soccer for Brits) has almost assumed the status of a national religion, but it's not a cheap interest to take up, nor is it easy to get into a top match. The English football season runs from August to May. Within that time span there are a number of major tournaments, including the Football Association Cup. Premiership (top-division) matches (which involved London teams Arsenal, Tottenham Hotspur, Fulham, Chelsea, Charlton Athletic, and Crystal Palace at press time, though the latter was looking likely to drop off the list) last 90 minutes, not including an interval of about 15 minutes. Saturday at 3pm is the best time to catch a game at all stadiums, which thankfully now have special family enclosures. Tickets cost £40 ($76) and upwards (about half that for kids), but most matches are heavily oversubscribed (club members get priority on tickets). If your heart's really set on a match, try west London's Queen's Park Rangers (ℭ **0870/112-1967;** www.qpr.co.uk), who are in the less-prestigious Nationwide League. Also check out www.4thegame.com for team and match details and general soccer news.

If you can't get to a match, you might want to sign up for the **Chelsea Football Club Stadium Tour** (ℭ **0870/603-0005;** www.chelseafc.com), a 75-minute behind-the-scenes look at London's biggest football stadium. Visitors see the changing rooms, the players' tunnel, the press room, and more, and a visitor center offers X-Box computer consoles and a seating area for lunch. Special family tours are accompanied by Stamford the Lion, the club mascot. The stunning national stadium, **Wembley** (www.wembleystadium.com), in north London, will host the Football Association final in May 2006.

For another great London sporting institution—Rugby Union—your best bet is to travel a little south out of the capital to **Twickenham Stadium** (ℭ **0870/405-2001;**

www.rfu.com), where you might be lucky enough to catch an England international match, or at least a club or county game. On non-match days, fans can take a guided tour of the stadium and visit its **Museum of Rugby.** (Combined tickets cost £9/$17 adults, £6/$12 kids, £30/$57 family of two adults and three kids.)

Watching **cricket** is a leisurely summer pastime best enjoyed at the world-famous **Lord's** (St. John's Wood Rd., NW8; ℂ **020/7289-1611;** www.lords.org), which hosts international test matches between Britain and Australia, the West Indies, India, or New Zealand. Daily tours of the ground include the players' dressing room, the indoor school with its 160kmph (100mph) bowling machines, and the MCC Museum with paintings, photos, and artifacts tracing the history of the sport. Kids always seem to be most fascinated by the stuffed sparrow here, which was killed by a shot in 1936 (the ball is displayed, too). The excellent shop has a nice range of kids' clothing.

Undoubtedly, though, the quintessential sporting event of the British summer is **Wimbledon** ★★★ (ℂ **020/8971-2473;** www.wimbledon.com), where some of the world's best tennis players battle it out at the All England Lawn Tennis & Croquet Club from roughly the last week in June to the first week in July, with matches lasting from about 2pm until dark. With unpredictable kids in tow, you probably won't want to bother with applying to enter the public ballot for tickets the previous year; nor will you want to queue for several hours on the day (gates open at 10:30am); instead, make do with standing room, and just enjoy the strawberries and cream on sale and the sense of occasion. If you're not in town at the right time of year, you will have to make do with a visit to the **Wimbledon Lawn Tennis Museum,** which features match videos, contemporary player memorabilia, and interactive exhibits, including a special children's corner. The museum runs daily behind-the-scenes tours of the grounds, including Centre Court and the press interview rooms.

Those with equestrian kids will be glad to learn that a **day at the races** is an affordable treat, with all British racecourses offering free admission for accompanied children under 16 (adults pay an average of £12/$23). Kempton Park, Sandown Park, Epsom Downs (home of the world-famous Derby), Windsor, and Ascot (best known for the exuberant headgear worn at its royal meet, and its superb thoroughbreds) are all within 50km (31 miles) of London. Older kids will love seeing racehorses and jockeys close up and watching the bookies in action, while younger children will be greeted with nurseries at some courses and bouncy castles and the like on weekends and holidays. The comprehensive website www.britishracecourses.org has details on family evenings and family fun days with free kids' entertainment such as face painting, traveling farms, soccer coaching, and competitions.

For an altogether different kind of day at the races, and a real London institution, head east to **Walthamstow Stadium** ★★, a world-famous **greyhound racing** track (ℂ **020/8498-3300;** www.wsgreyhound.co.uk). The atmosphere is always electric, and you can usually spot some real old East Enders dressed up in all their finery. Look, too, for vacation Fun Days, with special kids' entertainment such as bouncy castles and face painting. Children under 16 are admitted free, and all visitors get in free Monday and Friday for the lunchtime races. (It's a measly £1–£3/ $1.90–$5.70 to get into the evening meetings.)

Basketball is not widely played in Britain, but the London Tower (www.londontowers.co.uk) is a highly creditable team, and its home games at the National Sports Centre (p. 208) are lively affairs.

7 Story Hours

For **bookstores** with regular storytelling slots, see p. 223; for events at Puppet Planet, see p. 241. Many of the **museums and galleries** listed in chapter 6, "Exploring London with Your Kids" (p. 157 and 174) have story hours as part of their kids' activities programs.

All **libraries** in the central Westminster area (which includes Marylebone, Mayfair, Paddington, St. James's, and Victoria) offer under-5s story times based around storytelling, singing, and rhymes, and ending in a craft activity that can be taken home or displayed in the library. There are also toys to play with, and refreshments are available. The Pimlico library has recently introduced Spanish storytelling, and Queen's Park offers additional "Baby Bounce" and "Rhyme Time" sessions. Days and times vary from venue to venue and are subject to change; see www.westminster.gov.uk for the latest information. The venerable British Library (p. 157) also has storytelling sessions during summer vacation.

The Crocodile Club   This weekly 90-minute storytelling, puppetry, and singing session for kids aged 2 to 5 is held in a charming antiques shop in the family-friendly enclave of Muswell Hill in north London. Tots get to create their own adventure, whether it be a voyage to the bottom of the sea or a journey into Space. The shop also has a cafe popular for its chocolate cake. It's handy for a visit to Alexandra Park (p. 206) or Highgate Wood (p. 207). Crocodile Antiques. 120-2 Muswell Hill Broadway, N10. ✆ 020/8444-0273. Tube: East Finchley. Open Tues 10–11:30am.

8 Arcades

If the rain won't let up, and all else really has failed (I can scarcely believe it will, but I know what kids can be like), your most central arcade is **Funland** (✆ **020/7439-1914;** www.funland.co.uk) in the Trocadero Mall at Piccadilly Circus. One of the world's biggest indoor entertainment centers, it features state-of-the-art simulator rides, more than 400 of the latest high-tech video games, bumper cars, and a 10-lane bowling alley. Parents can flee the mayhem for a few beers in the American pool hall or Sports Bar. Entry is free: you pay as you play, using cash or tokens.

A bit smaller and a little less central, **Namco Station** (✆ **020/7967-1066;** www.namcoexperience.com), in the same building as the London Aquarium on the South Bank, is a similarly dark and noisy prospect, also with bumper cars, "techno" bowling with ultraviolet lanes, and the latest simulators and video games, including the world's first long-distance indoor laser shooting range. If you feel like you've landed on another planet, you're not far wrong—Namco even has its own currency, the Nam.

If all this sounds a bit too brash, make the effort to get to **Oriental City** in north London (399 Edgware Rd., NW9; ✆ **020/8200-0009;** Tube: Colindale), which has the makings of a really great, off-the-wall family day out. In addition to its futuristic **SegaWorld** arcade, it has a vast Asian food mall with goodies from Japan, China, Vietnam, and Indonesia—both at its cheap stalls and in its stores and supermarkets—to take home. Plus check out the Asian bookstores, housewares stores, salon, and indefinable shops selling Hello Kitty items and such.

11

Side Trips from London

There's so much to do in London, you'd be forgiven for not wanting to venture outside its boundaries. If you have time, however, some of the following attractions (many of them off the tourist trail) may tempt you away from the bright lights.

This is when having a car is a bonus: www.easycar.com offers competitive rental prices. If you're using Britain's woefully inadequate railway network, the **National Rail** number is © **08457/484950;** or check www.nationalrail.co.uk.

1 Windsor Castle, Eton College & Legoland ⌖

30km (19 miles) W of London

The Thames-side town of Windsor packs a triple punch: it's the site of England's greatest castle, of its most famous boys' school (Eton College), and of Legoland theme park. You're unlikely to fit all the fun into one day, so my advice is to stay over rather than travel in and out of the City. Note also that Thorpe Park theme park (p. 179) is not far from Windsor.

It takes 30 minutes to travel from London's Paddington Station to Windsor & Eton Central station, with a change at Slough (www.firstgreatwesternlink.co.uk). Trains from London's Waterloo Station go direct to Windsor & Eton Riverside (www.southwesttrains. co.uk). From both stations, there's a bus service direct to Legoland 3km (2 miles) from the town center. For train times and fares, call © **0845/748-4950.** If you're traveling by car, Windsor is a straightforward journey west along the M4 from London, then south along the A332.

EXPLORING WINDSOR

With a thousand rooms, **Windsor Castle** (Castle Hill; © **020/7766-7304;** www. royalresidences.com) was built on the orders of William the Conqueror. Admission is £13 ($24) adults, £6.50 ($12) children 5 to 16, £32 ($60) family of five; hours are March to October daily 9:45am to 5:15pm; November to February daily 9:45am to 4:15pm. Windsor is the world's largest inhabited castle. It's been a working palace for more than 900 years, and when the Queen and Royal Family are in residence (mid-June), the State Apartments, furnished with treasures from the Royal Collection that include paintings by Rembrandt and Rubens as well as sculpture and armor, are off limits to visitors. (Admission prices to the rest of the castle are reduced.) *Note:* The castle is often used by the Queen for State ceremonies and official entertaining, so it's vital to check opening arrangements before setting out (call © **01753/831118**).

The highlight for kids is undoubtedly **Queen Mary's Doll's House.** This palace in perfect miniature (on a 1-inch to 1-foot scale) was designed by the architect Sir Edwin Lutyens and took 1,500 tradesmen and artists 3 years to complete. Each room is exquisitely furnished, and every item is made exactly to scale. There's even electric lighting, working elevators that stop at every floor, and five bathrooms with running water. From October to March visitors can enjoy George IV's private apartments (**"Semi-State Rooms"**) with their richly decorated interiors. Older kids will appreciate the drawings by Leonardo da Vinci in the **Drawings Gallery.** To make the most of a visit here, ask at the desk for family **audiotours** and **activity trails** (available in English only).

Parents should be aware that only bottled water is available inside; if you need further refreshments, the town's many restaurants, cafes, and pubs (see below, "Where to Dine") are within a few minutes' walk—ask for free re-entry bands at the Middle Ward or Lower Ward Shop. The town itself is charming, with several 17th-century buildings set along its narrow cobbled streets. **Windsor Great Park,** where the Queen sometimes rides and Prince Charles plays polo, contains the Saville Garden, an idyllic 14-hectare (35-acre) patch of woodland, streams, and ponds where you can blow away the cobwebs.

Eton College (✆ **01753/671000;** www.etoncollege.com) is an easy stroll across the Thames Bridge. Founded in 1440 by Henry VI, this boarding school has educated 20 British prime ministers, as well as such diverse literary figures as Percy Shelley, Aldous Huxley, George Orwell, and Ian Fleming. Inside its vaulted undercroft, the **Museum of Eton Life** traces its history, with displays including a turn-of-the-19th-century boy's room, canes used by senior boys to apply punishment to their juniors (and birch sticks used by masters for the same purpose), and letters written home by students describing day-to-day life at the school. Casual admission (to the School Yard, College Chapel, Cloisters, and Museum) costs £3.80 ($7.20) for adults, £3 ($5.70) for children. There are also 1-hour guided tours daily at 2:15 and 3:15pm, costing £4.90 ($9.30) for adults, £4 ($7.60) for children ages 9 to 15. The hours are roughly late March to mid-April and July to early September 10:30am to 4:30pm, mid-April to the end of June and early September to early October 2 to 4:30pm, but it's imperative to call in advance, as dates vary from year to year, and the college closes on special occasions.

There are various appealing ways to explore the environs. **Boat trips** of 35 minutes will take you to Boveney Lock and back, passing the castle and college, Windsor racecourse, and more (✆ **01753/851900;** www.boat-trips.co.uk) for £4.50 ($8.50) adult, £2.25 ($4.30) child, £11 ($22) family of four. Among other cruises run by the same firm are a 45-minute jaunt past historic Runnymede (where King John signed the Magna Carta, now home to memorials to JFK and Air Force personnel who died in World War II) aboard the *Lucy Fisher,* a replica of a Victorian paddle-wheeler built in 1982 for the Tarzan film *Greystoke* and also used in *Chaplin.* It makes a short stop at **Runnymede Pleasure Grounds,** a popular riverbank picnicking spot with a children's paddling pool.

Hop-on hop-off open-top **bus tours** of Windsor, Old Windsor, and Eton (✆ **01789/ 294466;** www.city-sightseeing.com) start from the statue of Queen Victoria outside the castle. They take place daily from mid-March to October, weekends only from early November to mid-December. The cost is £6 ($11) for adults, £2.50 ($4.75) for kids 5 to 15 (who get a free kids' passport and felt-tip pens). Somewhat more elegant tours are available in horse-drawn carriages that travel from opposite the Harte and Garter Hotel on High Street to Park Street and then down the Long Walk into Windsor

Great Park. Trips can last 30 minutes or an hour, and can be taken all year, weather per-mitting. The cost is £19 ($36) per 30 minutes (① **01784/435983;** www.orchardpoyle. co.uk). Lastly, the **Royal Windsor Information Centre** opposite the castle sells leaflets for two **self-guided walking tours** around Windsor (50p/95¢), one lasting 45 min-utes, the other about 2 hours.

VISITING LEGOLAND

This unlikely theme park, based around the famous building bricks, has more than 50 rides and attractions ranging from water slides and a Whirly Birds helicopter ride to carousels and themed mazes. Most rides are designed for the 3- to 12-year-old range; older kids might find it tame, but younger ones will find much to amuse them. New features for 2005 include a Fire Academy with huge LEGO fire engines, a Dino Safari through a prehistoric jungle full of giant animated LEGO dinosaurs, and a space center. It's open March to November from 10am to 5, 6, or 7pm, depending both on the season and on special events (including a fireworks extravaganza in late Oct and on Nov 5); call ① **08705/040404,** or see www.lego.com for details.

Insider tip: Tickets are expensive—a 1-day pass is £24 ($46) for adults, £22 ($42) for kids 3 to 15; a 2-day pass is £47 ($89) for adults, £43 ($82) for kids 3 to 15, but you can get money-saving packages, including rail travel, shuttle bus, and park admis-sion, at most major stations in Britain. Alternatively, if you are staying nearby, check whether your hotel offers Legoland packages (see below).

WHERE TO STAY

Just southeast of Windsor at Egham, **Runnymede Hotel & Spa** (① **01784/220980;** www.runnymedehotel.com), sister to the Athenaeum in central London (p. 73), is a quite luxurious option with both classic- and contemporary-styled guest rooms plus three lovely riverside apartments. The apartments, each comprising a double bed-room, living/dining space with sofa bed, fully equipped kitchen, and private terrace, are perfect for families, though you can't have a cot—for that you need one of the larger hotel rooms, which fit an extra bed/cot at a cost of £10 ($19) and £5 ($9.50) respectively. The apartments also require a minimum 7-night stay, at a rate of about £250 ($475) per night. In July 2005, Runnymede introduced new family rooms com-plete with ingenious sofas that convert into a single or bunk bed as required, plus space for a cot.

The hotel lies nearby tennis courts, ponds, and a meadow that's often the site of family entertainment like the Moscow State Circus. There's also a kids' catalogue full of toys and books for various age ranges on hand, which you can have brought up to your room for a small deposit. The health spa boasts an 18m (59-ft.) pool, as well as a wonderful toddlers' pool. Charlie Bell's restaurant with summer terrace has well-priced, child-pleasing fare such as nachos, cottage pie, and crispy duck pancakes; a play area should be added here in 2006. (Note the "early diner" discount of 30% if you eat between 5:30 and 6:30pm.) Legoland packages can be arranged by the hotel (with 1- or –2-day passes), starting at £220 ($418) per night for a family of four.

For those on a tighter budget, **Clarence Hotel** (① **0175/386-4436;** www.clarence-hotel.co.uk) in Windsor offers en suite family rooms in an attractive building with a patio garden for £70 to £91 ($133–$173). You can ask about Legoland packages as well.

WHERE TO DINE

In Windsor, **Browns Restaurant & Bar** on The Promenade, Barry Avenue (© **01753-831976;** www.browns-restaurants.com), is part of a countrywide chain with distinctive, colonial-style venues. The good kids' menu basically consists of downsized versions of some of the regular dishes, including crispy duck salad, goats' cheese crostini, and meatballs and spaghetti, priced at £4.95 ($9.40). The mezzanine terrace with its Thames view is a buzzing area. A branch of **Pizza Express** (p. 110) is located on Thames Street.

For the gastronomic treat of a lifetime, travel a few kilometers to the picturesque 16th-century village of Bray, where chef Heston Blumenthal owns the legendary **Fat Duck** (© **01628/580333;** www.fatduck.co.uk), holder of three Michelin stars and voted the best restaurant in the world, no less, by an international panel of experts in 2005. (Blumenthal, famous for his groundbreaking scientific gastronomy, has written an award-winning book, *Family Food*, about involving children in the kitchen.) Although the restaurant welcomes kids, I'd advise you to book a table at the more informal (and cheaper) **Riverside Brasserie** (© **01628/780553;** www.riversidebrasseries. co.uk) nearby. Its patrons believe that kids enjoy the same food as their parents if it's presented in the right way, so the children's menu features the same ingredients as the main menu arranged slightly differently, in half-size portions with prices to match. Adult mains, such as poached salmon with lettuce, peas, and bacon, cost about £15 ($29).

2 Roald Dahl Country & Beyond ✶✶✶

33km (20 miles) NW of London.

Unlike Windsor, the Chiltern Hills an hour or so to the northwest of London are firmly not on the tourist track. Yet with the opening of the Roald Dahl Museum & Story Centre in Great Missenden in the middle of 2005 (which supplements the Roald Dahl Children's Gallery in Aylesbury, Whipsnade Wild Animal Park, the little-known Walter Rothschild Zoological Museum in Tring, and the Working Steam Rail Museum at Quainton), this region offers a vast number of kid-pleasing outings. And that's not to mention the fantastic discount shopping at Bicester village.

ESSENTIALS

Great Missenden, Aylesbury, and Bicester are on a train route from London's Marylebone Station (www.chilternrailways.co.uk), with the journey taking about 40 minutes, an hour, and 90 minutes respectively. Silverlink (www.silverlink-trains.com) trains between London Euston station and Birmingham city serve Tring Station about 40 minutes away, though not all their trains stop there. Buses run between the main towns in the area. For local taxis, call © **01494/868699.** Driving from London is relatively straightforward—take the A40 out to Gerrards Cross, then follow the A413.

Whipsnade is about a 30-minute drive north of central London. You can opt to catch a Thameslink (www.thameslink.co.uk) train from London Bridge or King's Cross to Luton Parkway; or take a Silverlink train (www.silverlink-trains.com) from Euston to Hemel Hempstead Boxmoor (both about 25 min.), then a 10-minute shuttle bus ride (© **0870/608-2608** or 0870/608-7261).

ON THE TRAIL OF ROALD DAHL

The Buckinghamshire town of Great Missenden has finally recognized its most illustrious son, one of the greatest children's authors of all time, in the form of the **Roald Dahl Museum & Story Centre** (81–3 High St.; ℭ **01494/892192;** www.roalddahlmuseum. org). Hours are Tuesday to Sunday 10am to 5pm; admission is £4.50 ($8.60) adults, £3.50 ($6.70) kids 3 to 18. Visitors step through doors fashioned as huge chocolate bars and emblazoned with the name "Wonka" into two galleries filled with displays that range from the studious (handwritten research material and early drafts) to the playful (interactive bookcases and an exact replica of the garden shed in which Dahl wrote, famously banning disturbances by real children). Little visitors receive Ideas Books on arrival, which they fill with anything that inspires them. A great shop sells books, games, gifts, and stationery. A cafe is due to open in 2006; for now there's a courtyard where you can eat your own food.

Dahl lived at nearby Gipsy House. You can't go inside, but you can visit his grave in the churchyard of **St. Peter & St. Paul,** which is often decorated with chocolate bars left by fans.

It's about a 10-minute drive along the A43 to Aylesbury, home to the magical **Roald Dahl Children's Gallery** at the Buckinghamshire County Museum (Church St.; ℭ **01296/331441;** www.buckscc.gov.uk/museum/dahl). Admission is £5 ($9.50) for anyone over 3. See website for hours. This is one of a network of community-based discovery centers providing younger kids with imaginative hands-on play facilities. (Others include Discover, p. 161; the Livesey Museum for Children, p. 166; Hands on Base at the Horniman, p. 143; and Pattern Pod and Garden at the Science Museum, p. 148.) Inside, kids can study mini-beasts with a video microscope in the Giant Peach; send themselves into TV like Mike in *Charlie and the Chocolate Factory;* walk through an enormous book into Matilda's Library, full of books where they can discover more about Dahl's life and works; and ride in the Great Glass Elevator up to the Imagination Gallery with its Magic Mirrors, eyeball maze, magic writing wall, and Twits's upside-down room. The gallery is very popular, so book ahead.

ANIMAL MAGIC

The area's best-known attraction is **Whipsnade Wild Animal Park** (ℭ **01582/872171;** www.zsl.org/whipsnade). Admission is £15 ($28) adults; £11 ($21) kids 3 to 15; £46 ($88) for saver tickets for two adults and two kids, or one adult and three kids. Hours are March to October, daily 10am to 7pm; November to March, daily 10am to 4pm; closed during Christmas. The park lies at the northern end of the Chilterns near Dunstable, about 45km (28 miles) from London Zoo's sister establishment and one of Europe's biggest wildlife conservation parks. Whipsnade is home to larger animals such as elephants and rhinos, who appreciate its wider spaces, as well as bears, giraffes, Siberian tigers, hippos, camels, and pandas—around 150 species, in fact, spread over a 243-hectare (600-acre) site. Some of the animals, including prairie marmots, are allowed to roam free. If you've come by car, you can cruise the "Passage Through Asia" area, inhabited by various species of deer (otherwise there's a train ride). Car admission to the park costs an extra £11 ($21); if you leave your car in the external car park, the fee is £3.50 ($6.65). Especially popular with kids are the Discovery Center, with seahorses, dwarf crocodiles, giant centipedes, Egyptian tortoises, and more; and for tiny tots, the children's farm has shire horses, pygmy goats, and alpaca. Regular events include daily sea lion feeding and themed animal weeks, and there's a good play park. *Insider tip:* The park can seem daunting at first, its scale in total contrast to London

Zoo's, so it's a good idea to make use of the free safari tour bus rides. Note that you'll get 10% off the quite hefty admission prices with online booking.

A much more obscure attraction just a few minutes' drive away is the **Walter Rothschild Zoological Museum,** an outpost of London's mighty Natural History Museum set in the town of Tring 53km (33 miles) north of London (Akeman St.; ☎ **020/ 7942-6171;** www.nhm.ac.uk). It's open Monday to Saturday 10am to 5pm, Sunday 2 to 5pm; admission is free. Among the 4,000 preserved animals on permanent display here are a giant salamander, an Indian pangolin, and a 2m-long (6.5-ft.) turtle. The weird and wonderful temporary exhibitions embrace such themes as animal mummies, backed up by bookable activities such as mummy-making with visitors' favorite toys, or finger puppet making. Free activity trails are available during school vacations. An interactive Discovery Centre features feelie boxes, microscopes, and the like to encourage a sense of wonder in kids. The Zebra Café has a play corner for tots.

WEST OF AYLESBURY

Train enthusiasts might like to stop off at Quainton, home to the **Buckinghamshire Steam Centre** (Station Rd.; ☎ **01296/655720;** www.bucksrailcentre.org). Admission is £4 ($7.60) adults, £2 ($3.80) children, £10 ($19) family of 4. See the website for hours. This working steam museum displays, among other items, a carriage in which Winston Churchill and General Eisenhower devised war strategies. On some days (for which admission prices are ramped up) you can ride in vintage carriages or open wagons pulled by restored steam engines. At Christmas, special events involve Santa and Thomas the Tank Engine. Watch out, too, for "children's days" with animals.

Nearby **Bicester Village** (☎ **01869/323200;** www.bicestervillage.com) is open Monday to Friday and Sunday from 10am to 6pm; Saturday from 9:30am to 7pm. It holds pleasures of an altogether different order, in the form of discount designer clothes and housewares outlets, including Ralph Lauren Boys & Girls for fashion-conscious kids.

WHERE TO STAY

The very best place to stay in the area is **The Grove** ★★, an award-winning country estate hotel with a fabulous spa and golf course just east of the Chilterns inside the M25 (Chandler's Cross; ☎ **01923/807807;** www.thegrove.co.uk). In late 2004 it opened Anouska's, a club for kids 10 and below, open Monday to Saturday 9am to 5pm and Sunday 9am to 2pm. The club charges £5 ($9.50) per hour for up to 3 hours at a time. It features an adventure playground, a sandpit, indoor activities such as baking and crafts, a library, and a children's pool—although young guests can also swim in the large outdoor pool in the walled garden in summer, and over-13s can use the indoor pool in the spa. Children's golf clubs and tennis racquets can be provided, and nature trails, treasure hunts, and cycling are arranged around the estate. Exceptional kids' menus are available in the Stables and Glasshouse restaurants, as well as through room service. Older kids who prefer to order from the main menu are given a 50% discount. The onsite Colette's is a good option if you have a sitter and feel decadent, and families can even order organic baby food here.

Accommodations-wise, one child up to 12 can sleep in a parent's deluxe-category room, in a travel cot or a sofa bed, at no extra charge. Those families with two or more children can book interconnecting rooms in the contemporary-styled west wing, with the children's twin room going for 50% the price of the parent's room. All rooms boast a fun, contemporary decor, and prices (doubles start at £240/$456) get you milk and cookies, mini bathrobes, and age-specific toy boxes in the rooms, along with books, crayons, and coloring books, and access to a basement games room with video games. Every room also has a TV with giant plasma screen, and there's a DVD library with movies for all ages. All in all, it's heaven.

A less glamorous but great-value, family-friendly option is **Holiday Inn** in Hemel Hempstead (Breakspear Way; ℂ **0870/400-9041;** www.ichotelgroup.com), where, with 14 days' advance booking, you can get a room with a double bed and a sofa bed that converts into two single beds for just £60 ($114). On-site are an outdoor children's play area (plus an indoor one on weekends) and a health club with a swimming pool. Kids get their own Cartoon Network menu in both the lounge and the restaurant.

WHERE TO DINE

One of the area's loveliest places to eat is the Cock & Rabbit by the village green at Great Missenden, a traditional pub housing a great Italian restaurant, **Cafe Graziemille** (The Lee; ℂ **01494/837540;** www.graziemille.co.uk). The house pasta (penne with a dressing of yogurt, thyme, olive oil, and wild garlic gathered in nearby woods) stands out, but there are lots of meat, fish, and vegetarian choices, plus a good range of daily pasta dishes chalked up on the board. Mains average £9 ($17). Food is served in the garden during summers.

Not far from Aylesbury, in the village of Shabbington near Thames, the **Old Fisherman** (Mill Rd.; ℂ **01844/201247;** www.theoldfisherman.com) has a large riverside garden with play equipment. It serves good English dishes with a Mediterranean slant, including an under-11s menu (£4.50/$8.60) of homemade fishcakes, "golden fishes," sausages, and more (served with chips or mash, and fresh vegetables, peas, or beans). Kids are also welcome to share adult meals, which might feature a risotto of forest mushrooms and Parmesan. Don't miss the specialty ice creams, such as white chocolate with honeycomb, available in adult and children's portions.

3 Leeds Castle, Diggerland & Whitstable ★★★

30km (19 miles) E of London

This is another slightly offbeat tour, this time to the east of London as far at the Thames estuary. Its beauty is that it combines three very different attractions—a fairy-tale castle, a wacky little theme park, and an atmospheric seaside town.

ESSENTIALS

Diggerland and Leeds Castle are best reached by car. The first is off the A228 up from the M26 to Rochester, the second just off the M20 leading from Maidstone to the Channel Tunnel. Whitstable is half an hour farther along the M2; then take the A299 from Diggerland. Direct Southeastern trains (www.setrains.co.uk) run there from London Victoria station, taking about 1 hour, 20 minutes.

VISITING DIGGERLAND

This unique adventure park (one of three in the country) was set up to tap into kids' attraction to mechanical diggers. The park is set in Strood near Rochester (Roman Way, Medway Valley Leisure Park; ℂ **08700/344437;** www.diggerland.com). See the website for hours. Under strict supervision, kids (and adults if they like) can take a ride in, and perhaps even drive, various kinds of construction machinery, including Dump Trucks and Mini Diggers. Fully trained staff members are on hand to instruct and explain the machines' workings. For kids too young to enjoy that, play areas include an indoor ball pond and competitions. The Dig Inn cafe serves burgers, salads, snacks, and so on.

Entry is £2.50 for anyone age 2 and up; a ride on a motorized digger costs from £1 ($1.90), depending on its size. If you think you'll be riding on a lot, get a credit voucher (for example, 20 rides for £19/$36), or a wristband allowing unlimited rides/drives. You can now get Family Tickets if you pre-book online. Keep an eye on the website for events, such as the spectacular Digger Wars.

EXPLORING LEEDS CASTLE

This ravishing, romantic fortress (✆ **01622/765400;** www.leeds-castle.com) is open from late March to October 11am to 5pm; November to late March 10:15am to 3:30pm. It was built by the Normans on two little islands in a lake and transformed into a palace by Henry VIII. Retaining its medieval and cobbled causeways, it is full of charming—and often slightly eccentric—attractions: a maze decorated with mythical beasts, with a secret underground grotto at its core; a moat with black swans; a Duckery with ducks, wild geese, and waterfowl; an aviary housing more then 100 species of endangered exotic birds (some of whom talk); a museum of dog collars dating back to the 15th century (some made of iron and bearing fearsome spikes); and a land train that motors visitors up and down the main drive. Inside the castle you can see some stunning interiors, including a medieval queen's room, Henry VIII's banqueting hall, and the 1920s drawing rooms of Lady Baillie, the castle's last private owner. Guides in all the rooms are happy to elaborate on its history.

Full tickets cost £13 ($25) for adults or £9 ($17) for kids 4 to 15; a family ticket for up to five costs £39 ($74). You can get cheaper tickets allowing admission to the dog collar museum, aviary, and grounds only. A restaurant and a tearoom offer refreshments. Especially good times to visit are during the summer open-air classical or pop concerts with fireworks (especially the new Family Picnic Prom); during the half-term, when kids' activities are offered; during the balloon festival in autumn; and during New Year's, which features a treasure trail.

EXPLORING WHITSTABLE

Situated on the north Kent coast just to the north of Canterbury, Whitstable has been famous since Roman times for its Royal Native oysters. It still hosts a summer festival devoted to the slippery sea creatures every July, which includes a regatta of old working boats and a hilarious costumed "fish slapping dance" accompanied by traditional songs. Whitstable is a great, low-key place to visit if your experience of Britain's often-tawdry seaside has been limited to amusement arcades and cotton candy. The seafront, littered with oyster shells, is lined with cute weatherboard cottages and fishermen's huts and boats. Streets bear such intriguing names as "Squeeze Gut Alley," home to attractive art galleries and craft shops.

Horror movie fans will be interested to learn that actor Peter Cushing (the star of late 1950s horror films) lived here: He gave the town a viewing platform with a bench, and there's a display on him in **Whitstable Museum** (5a Oxford St.; ✆ **01227/ 276998;** www.whitstable-museum.co.uk). Hours are daily from 10am to 4pm, and entrance is free. You can view Cushing's makeup and some film stills. The museum also has an exhibition on oysters, shipping, and diving—kids love the fossils, shells, and seaside wildlife; the model ships; and the life-size diver; as well as the full-size horse-drawn fire engine. The staff hands out drawing materials and clipboards so junior visitors can record their impressions, and some of the results are displayed in the museum.

From Herne Bay just up the road, you can embark on a variety of open-yacht trips from April to October (© **01227/366712;** www.wildlifesailing.com). A yacht trip out to the Thames Estuary includes a 5-hour seal watch, roughly £14–£17 ($26–$32) each, or a more manageable 45-minute bird watch, which costs £4.50 ($8.60) per adult, £4 ($7.60) for kids under 14.

WHERE TO STAY

The place to stay in this neck of the woods is Whitstable's **Hotel Continental** (29 Beach Walk; © **01227/280280;** www.hotelcontinental.co.uk), which has six guest rooms in old fishermen's huts right on the shore. Four are for families—they have a double bed on the first floor and two twins on the ground floor, plus a bathroom, color TV, beverage maker, and private parking. For more space, ask for the Anderson Shed, a newly converted boat builders' shed overhanging the sea wall, with a sea-facing lounge, two double bedrooms, and a fully outfitted kitchen. Family huts start at £115 ($219) per night, including a full English breakfast in the hotel, while the Anderson Shed costs £300 ($570). Note that on weekends (Fri and Sat), a 2-night stay is required.

If you want to stay close to Diggerland, **Holiday Inn Rochester-Chatham** (Maidstone Rd., Chatham; © **0870/400-9069;** www.ichotelsgroup.com) offers reduced rates to those visiting the theme park. A 14-day advance booking will net you a rate of about £100 ($190) for a room with a double bed and a sofa bed, with the possibility of a free upgrade to an executive room with complimentary chocolates and sparkling water, and bigger bathrooms complete with posh toiletries. The hotel also boasts an indoor pool and whirlpool. Kids eat free in its restaurant.

WHERE TO DINE

One of the most family-friendly restaurants in Whitstable is the **Crab and Winkle** at the harbor (South Quay, The Harbour; © **01227/779377;** www.crab-winkle.co.uk), where you'll be able to linger over a meal—of lobster, local sea bass, or fish pie—because there's so much activity for the kids to watch on the quayside. Staff members are extremely friendly, and there's a full kids' menu. You can get breakfast here till 11:30am. **Pearsons Crab and Oyster House** (Sea Wall, The Horsebridge; © **01227/272005**), which is virtually on the beach and has great views, also welcomes kids, and has a beer garden for fine weather. Alternatively, get takeout from one of the many fish and chip shops and eat on the beach.

Index

See also Accommodations and Restaurant indexes, below.

ACCOMMODATIONS

Flip-flops

Beach towel

Dip in for great gifts...

Available from London's Transport Museum online shop

London's Transport
Museum
Covent Garden Piazza

www.ltmuseum.co.uk